Modern Competitiveness in the
Twenty-First Century

Modern Competitiveness in the Twenty-First Century

Global Experiences

Edited by
Jessica M. Bailey, Claudette Chin-Loy,
Nikolaos Karagiannis, and Zagros Madjd-Sadjadi

LEXINGTON BOOKS

Lanham • Boulder • New York • Toronto • Plymouth, UK

Published by Lexington Books
A wholly owned subsidiary of The Rowman & Littlefield Publishing Group, Inc.
4501 Forbes Boulevard, Suite 200, Lanham, Maryland 20706
http://www.lexingtonbooks.com

Estover Road, Plymouth PL6 7PY, United Kingdom

British Library Cataloguing in Publication Information Available

Library of Congress Cataloging-in-Publication Data

Modern competitiveness in the twenty-first century : global experiences / edited by
Jessica M. Bailey.
    p. cm.
Includes index.
ISBN 978-0-7391-6628-4 (cloth : alk. paper)
1. Competition I. Bailey, Jessica M., 1947-
HB238.M63 2011
338.6'048—dc22

                                                        2011016092

♾™ The paper used in this publication meets the minimum requirements of American
National Standard for Information Sciences—Permanence of Paper for Printed Library
Materials, ANSI/NISO Z39.48-1992.

Printed in the United States of America

Table of Contents

Part I: Economic Development & Competitiveness

Part II: Tertiary Education, Health Insurance, & Competitiveness

Tables

Figures

Foreword

Competitiveness in the world of business is certainly not a new topic. Yet, the tasks of becoming and remaining competitive in today's global economy have taken on new dimensions. Rapidly changing technology has created an environment that may make products and services move quickly through the supply chain. At the same time, competition can move a product from being a "must have" to being obsolete, sometimes in a matter of months. Being an entrepreneur is now considered a profession and today's start-up operations can become the economic engine for an entire region, or for that matter, an entire nation. Yet, as is often the case, the more things change the more they stay the same, and many of the traditional barriers to success remain. Bureaucracy, the lack of qualified workers, political unrest and other such factors continue to create barriers for entrepreneurs in many countries, including the United States.

The days of a purely local or even national economy, however, are behind us. At one time cities competed with each other to attract new businesses to create local jobs. Now countries are offering incentives to attract foreign investments from multinational enterprises. The stakes for garnering new jobs for any location have been getting higher and higher. For example, we have seen U.S. textile and apparel operations receive significant incentives to locate in Central and South America while U.S. states have offered lucrative incentives to land automotive operations that have moved from Germany and the Far East to the United States—all in pursuit of the competitive advantage.

While one might proffer that much of the movement of jobs from any country is truly designed to increase the bottom line, the truth is that businesses must make the effort and take the steps to become and remain competitive. The global marketplace is not a level playing field. That fact places even more pressure for businesses to provide products and services that meet the wants and needs of consumers at appropriate pricing levels.

In addition to the basic tenets of business that impact all economies, the nature of a global marketplace requires a new focus on the socio-cultural aspects of international business development. That factor affects how investments are made, how operations are managed and what products are developed.

As a chief administrator who has also been in the classroom, I understand the need for curriculum reform on American campuses, particularly in American business schools. Not only must we teach our students the basics of a business education, we must provide them with the understanding of what it takes to be competitive, an understanding of how to do business in the ever-changing, technology-driven world. Our business schools must offer students the ability to learn beyond subject matter.

There are no simple answers to the complexities facing all organizations today. Adapting to today's economic environment can sometimes seem a daunting task. Rather than be overwhelmed by the challenges, today's leaders of business, government and education must seize the opportunities that abound to change policies, change models, and even change directions.

This book explores those avenues of change, as well as the relationships among the many factors that can create and support success in a competitive environment. The chapters deal with issues ranging from economic development strategies, and education and health insurance competitiveness to socio-cultural and legal issues, and the effect of information technology developments on managers. The contributors have brought together an expanded body of knowledge, as well as a thought-provoking platform for developing alternatives to improve competitiveness in the twenty-first century. The collective works of these scholars, I am sure, will contribute significantly to the growing body of literature and knowledge about twenty-first century global competitiveness.

Donald J. Reaves, Ph.D.
Chancellor,
Winston-Salem State University

Introduction

SETTING THE THEORETICAL FRAMEWORK

Societies and economies all over the world are grappling with the consequences of globalization and the accompanying changes in the rules of international trade (e.g., loss of preferential markets and erosion of preferences, fragility of interconnected financial markets) that affect the nature of their daily competitive decisions. To fully understand the context within which nations must function in order to be competitive in modern markets requires an accurate image of the meaning and implications of globalization in today's world, as well as an accurate conceptualization of globalization.

Globalization

Globalization describes a process by which regional and national economies, societies, and cultures have become integrated through a globe-spanning network of communication and trade. Globalization broadly refers to the expansion of linkages, the organization of social life on a worldwide scale, and the growth of a broadly defined consciousness, hence to the consolidation of world society. It generally serves to refer to various worldwide epoch-defining changes in the organization of societies, economies and politics. Globalization (and the information technology connectedness revolution), however, challenges some of the basic functions of the nation-state, and limits its policy space and the efficacy and effectiveness of national management instruments.

Although the term globalization is sometimes used to refer specifically to economic globalization (i.e., the integration of national economies into the international economy through trade, foreign direct investment, capital flows, migration, and the spread of technology), globalization is also universally recognized as being driven by a combination of technological, socio-cultural, political, and biological factors that exercise a strong influence on the economy. The globalization process has effects on the environment, on culture, on political systems, on economic development, on prosperity, and on human well-being in societies around the world. This has resulted in increasing global competition for traditional products and contributed to negative social ills such as unemployment, rising criminality, health and educational challenges, and the like. This situation is compounded by rising energy costs, environmental problems, a serious threat from climate change, financial insecurities, threats of terrorism, and rampant civil and ethnic unrest.

One important consequence of globalization is that it exercises strong pressure on prices, margins and wages. Some nations with high domestic standards of living and operating costs find themselves facing a harsh adaptation process, which has led to emphasis on deregulation, privatization, labor flexibility, a higher acceptance of risk, and the responsibility of the individual through a minimalist approach to the welfare system. The result, in some circumstances, is a fostering of entrepreneurship and, in others, a more egalitarian approach to responsibilities and an extensive welfare system. The twenty-first century is witnessing the emergence of a third alternative to competitiveness, one that softens the social consequences of the egalitarian and the increasingly free-wheeling deregulated environment. The third way strikes a balance that seeks to correct the apparent ills of both, maintaining a competitive posture.

The results of these modern-day pressures have changed the pattern of geographic specialization between countries, such that the contemporary era of globalization is characterized by:

- intensified global competition and the emergence of new centers of production;
- an exceptionally innovative technological environment;
- the proliferation, spread, and restructuring of transnational corporations (TNCs);
- a diversified global financial system; and
- important changes in the state's role in domestic and global economic affairs, much of which is directed toward harnessing and protecting individuals and companies from the opportunities/threats inherent in the new world environment.

These changes in globalization inevitably result in increased pressure on nations to raise their levels of competitiveness and pursue different approaches to competitiveness *vis-à-vis* their global rivals.

Understanding National Competition

Competition is a key feature of success in a globalized world. Competition is, by definition, a contest between individuals, groups, nations, animals, etc. for territory, a niche, or a location of resources. It arises whenever two or more parties strive for a goal which cannot be shared. Competition has been studied in disciplinary contexts, including psychology, sociology and anthropology. Social psychologists, for instance, study the nature of competition. They investigate the natural urge of competition and its circumstances. They also study group dynamics to detect how competition emerges and what its effects are. Sociologists, meanwhile, study the effects of competition on society as a whole. Anthropologists study the history and prehistory of competition in various cultures, and investigate how competition manifested itself in various cultural settings in the past, and how competition has developed over time. No matter the context, competition, which can exist on different scales or levels, can have both beneficial and detrimental effects. Many evolutionary biologists view inter-species and intra-species competition as the driving force of adaptation and ultimately of evolution, while some social Darwinists claim that competition also serves as a mechanism for determining the best-suited group, politically, economically and ecologically. On the negative side, competition can drain valuable resources and energy, and can hurt participants involved.

In addition, philosophers and psychologists have identified a trait in most living organisms which can drive the particular organism to compete. This trait, unsurprisingly called competitiveness, is viewed as an innate biological trait which coexists along with the urge for survival. Competitiveness, or the inclination to compete, though, has become synonymous with aggressiveness and ambition in the English language. More advanced civilizations integrate aggressiveness and competitiveness into their interactions as a way to distribute resources and adapt. However, Stephen Jay Gould and others have argued that as one ascends the evolutionary hierarchy, competitiveness (the survival instinct) becomes less innate, and more a learned behavior. The same could be said for cooperation. In humans, at least, both cooperation and competition are considered learned behaviors, because the human species learns to adapt to environmental pressures.

Within a business context, competition is defined as "the effort of two or more parties acting independently to secure the business of a third party by offering the most favorable terms." It was described by Adam Smith in *The Wealth of Nations* (1776) and by later economists as allocating productive resources to their most highly valued uses and encouraging efficiency. Competition, according to the theory, causes nations to develop new products, services and technologies, which would give consumers greater selection and better products at lower prices. Consequently, the term is applied to markets, where it is used to refer to the extent to which the market structure may be regarded as perfectly or imperfectly competitive. The pressures of globalization have led countries down very different paths with regards to modeling their economic growth and competitiveness. For example, business and economic competition in many countries is often limited or restricted. Often, competition is subject to legal restrictions. It may be prohibited, as in the case with a government monopoly or a government-granted monopoly. Tariffs, subsidies or other protectionist measures may also be instituted by government in order to prevent or reduce competition, primarily as a means of protecting indigenous industries. Depending on the respective economic policy, pure competition is, to a greater or lesser extent, regulated and stifled by policy and law.

Conversely, other countries pursue a very different tactic. Competition between countries may be subtle to detect, but is quite evident in the world economy. There is competition to provide the best possible business environment for attracting the direct investments of multinational corporations to their shores.

Such competition is evident by the policies undertaken by these countries to educate the future workforce as part of an overall strategy to attract multinational corporations by assuring the availability of a well-educated labor force. For example, East Asian economies such as Singapore, Japan, India, and South Korea tend to emphasize education by allocating a large portion of the budget to this sector, and by implementing special programs. Education and skills have become assets that can be accumulated like infrastructure and industrial power.

The influence of competition is apparent in many aspects of education today. On a global scale, national education systems, intending to bring out the best in the next generation, encourage competitiveness among institutions and students (e.g., through scholarships). Competition defines a large component of extra curricular activities in which students participate. In North America, such competitions include TVO's broadcast Reach for the Top competition, FIRST Robotics, Duke Annual Robo-Climb Competition (DARC) and the University of Toronto Space Design Contest. In Texas, the University Interscholastic League (UIL) has twenty-two high school-level contests and eighteen elementary and junior high contests in subjects ranging from accounting to science to writing. Critics of competition have maintained that excellence, rather than competition, is a superior motivating factor (Kohn 1986) and that competition may actually have a negative influence on the achievement levels of students. However, competition remains a factor in the development of the abilities and performances of students worldwide.

Why do nations compete? The short answer is to increase their standard of living. Classical economists evaluated the competitiveness amongst nations using statistics on the factors of production: labor, capital, natural resources and land. Ricardo's famous theory on *comparative advantage*, which is still valid today, was indeed an early attempt to understand how nations compete. However, economists later came to realize that factors regarding production alone could not explain everything. For example, historians questioned why China under the Tang dynasty (seventh to tenth century AD), did not have an industrial revolution, when its technological level—which included paper money, oil, and steel—was far more advanced than Britain's was at the end of the eighteenth century. The answer came from scholars such as Marx and Engels who claimed that the socioeconomic environment of a nation is crucial to its economic development. Britain had a dynamic class, the bourgeoisie, eager to succeed and to make money while China, under the Emperor, created a closed society—it was inwardly focused on the search for perfection.

Robert Solow, MIT economist and Nobel Prize winner, studied the growth factors that drove the U.S. economy between 1948 and 1982. His work underlined the fundamental importance of technological innovation and increased know-how in an economy. Michael Porter of Harvard University, in his book *The Competitiveness of Nations*, proposed using a "diamond approach" which illustrates the systemic relationship between factors of competitiveness. Recent scholars emphasize "knowledge" as an increasingly important input factor for competitiveness. Therefore, competitiveness involves different areas interacting with one another; four such broad areas have been emphasized: political and legal, educational, socio-cultural and economic (Farmer and Richman 1965), which were then matched up with such business functions as planning, marketing or production.

In recent years, the concept of competitiveness has emerged as a new paradigm in economic development. Competitiveness captures the awareness of both the limitations and challenges posed by global competition, at a time when effective government action is constrained by budgetary constraints and the private sector faces significant barriers to competing in domestic and international markets. The term is also used to refer in a broader sense to the economic competitiveness of countries, regions or cities.[1] Recently, countries are increasingly looking at their competitiveness on global markets. Ireland (1997), Saudi Arabia (2000), Greece (2003), Croatia (2004), Bahrain (2005), the Philippines (2006), Guyana and the Dominican Republic are just some examples of countries that have advisory bodies or special government agencies that tackle competitiveness issues. Even regions or cities, like Dubai or the Basque Country, are considering the establishment of such bodies.

The institutional model applied in the case of *National Competitiveness Programs* (NCP) varies from country to country; however, there are some common features. The leadership structure of NCPs relies on strong support from the highest level of political authority. High-level support provides credibility with the appropriate actors in the private sector. Usually, the council or governing body will have a designated public sector leader (president, vice-president or minister) and a co-president drawn from the private sector. Notwithstanding the public sector's role in strategy formulation, oversight, and implementation, national competitiveness programs should have strong, dynamic leadership from the private sector at all levels—national, local and firm. From the outset, the program must provide a clear diagnostic of the problems facing the economy and a compelling vision that appeals to a broad set of actors who are willing to seek change and implement an outward-oriented growth strategy. Finally, most programs share a common view on the importance of businesses-winners. Thorough programs that support the association among private business leadership, civil society organizations, government institutions and political leadership can better identify barriers to competitiveness, develop joint decisions on strategic policies and investments, and yield better results in implementation.

National competitiveness is important for any economy that must rely on international trade to balance import of energy and raw materials. Competitiveness is said to be particularly important for small open economies, which rely on trade and typically foreign direct investment to provide the scale necessary for productivity increases to drive increases in living standards. The European Union (EU) has enshrined industrial research and technological development (R&D) in her Treaty in order to become more competitive. In 2009, around €12 billion of the EU budget went on projects to boost Europe's competitiveness. The way for the EU to face competitiveness is to invest in education, research, innovation and technological infrastructures.[2]

The International Economic Development Council (IEDC) in Washington, DC, published the *Innovation Agenda: A Policy Statement on American Compe-*

titiveness. This paper summarizes the ideas expressed at the 2007 IEDC Federal Forum and provides policy recommendations for both economic developers and federal policy makers that aim to ensure America remains globally competitive in light of current domestic and international challenges. International comparisons of national competitiveness are conducted by the World Economic Forum, in its *Global Competitiveness Report*, and the Institute for Management Development, in its *World Competitiveness Yearbook* (WCY). The *World Competitiveness Yearbook* ranks and analyzes the ability of nations to provide an environment in which enterprises can compete. Businesses use it for basic research on location decisions, while governments use it to compare their countries' performance with their competitors. The *World Competitiveness Yearbook* analyzes competitiveness using 286 valuable statistics for forty-nine industrialized and emerging economies. The statistics are grouped into four input factors: economic performance, government efficiency, business efficiency, and infrastructure. These four dimensions shape a country's competitiveness environment, are often the result of tradition, history or value systems, and are so deeply rooted in its "modus operandi" that, in most cases, they are not clearly stated or defined.

Countries manage their environments mainly according to these four fundamental factors. However, it is possible to integrate these dimensions into an overall systemic theory, which also includes such important issues as:

1. Attractiveness vs Aggressiveness
2. Proximity vs Globality
3. Assets vs Processes
4. Individual Risk Taking vs Social Cohesiveness

Understanding Firm Competition

These national strategies, however, have nothing to do with the extent to which individual firms are "competitive." It is a known fact that competition may lead to wasted effort and to increased costs (and prices) in some circumstances. In addition, companies competing for financing in the equity and debt markets are not only competing for customers and expertise but also for investors' attention in order to generate the necessary funds for their operations as corporations. Competitiveness, by extension, is a comparative measure of the ability and performance of a firm, sub-sector or country to sell and supply goods and/or services in a given market, and is widely used in economics and business management. The two academic bodies of thought on the assessment of competitiveness are the *Structure Conduct Performance Paradigm* and the more contemporary *New Empirical Industrial Organization Model*. Predicting changes in the competitiveness of business sectors is becoming an integral and explicit step in public policy-making, even though the usefulness of the concept, particularly in the context of national competitiveness, is vigorously disputed by economists such as Paul Krugman.[3] Within capitalist economic systems, the drive of enterprises is to maintain and improve their own competitiveness. During the twentieth century, well-known economists contributed to a better understanding of competitiveness. Schumpeter emphasized the key role that entrepreneurship has played, serving as an engine for development. More recently, Peter Drucker applied the same theory to management.

Some scholars claim that nations themselves do not compete; rather, their enterprises do. There is no doubt that competitive enterprises are the main engines of a country's competitiveness. Enterprises now benefit from enormous choices in selecting their business locations. This is a consequence of nations feeling compelled to compete to attract or retain enterprises. Over the past thirty years, the economic responsibilities of governments have increased so much that it is simply impossible to ignore the state's influence on modern firms' competitiveness. A significant part of the competitive advantage of certain nations today stems from government intervention for the benefit of selected firms.

Country competitiveness and openness to global business activity are linked to a country's standard of living, which is delivered via the firms of the business sectors in any capitalist system. Competitiveness cannot only focus on the ability to show aggressiveness on world markets through exports and foreign direct investments. It is also the ability to develop attractiveness for wealth creation activities along with a fair distribution of economic gains, which should occur simultaneously. More importantly, competitiveness thrives on a balance of the economic imperatives with the social characteristics of a firm's employees that result from history, value systems and tradition. A good example of this from the early 1900s was the German philosopher Max Weber, who studied the relationship between culture and economic development in his book *The Protestant Ethic, Protestantism and the Spirit of Capitalism*. It is striking to compare the value systems in East Asia today with those of the United States and Europe in the nineteenth century. The current East Asian value system is based on the Confucian principles of hard work, loyalty, discipline, saving and education. These closely resemble the Protestant work ethic that dominated Europe and the United States in the nineteenth century and was at the root of the Great Industrial Revolution.

The most convincing support for the argument that there is a similarity between competition among nations and competition among firms is apparent in the areas of education and know-how. In a modern economy, firms do not rely only on products and services; they also compete with brains. Likewise, the ability of a nation to develop an excellent education system and to improve knowledge in the labor force through training is vital to competitiveness. Knowledge is perhaps the most critical competitiveness factor for both the firm and the nation. As countries move up the economic scale, the more they thrive on knowledge to ensure their prosperity and to compete in world markets. Firms, too, seek efficiency in their labor force which can only be maximized through improved education and training. How knowledge is acquired and managed is each individual nation's responsibility. Indeed, nations do compete in the educational arena because it bears a direct relationship to the ability of individual firms to compete. The International Association for the Evaluation of Educational Achievement in Washington, DC, makes an annual assessment of the educational performance of nations around the world. In recent years, the results highlight the formidable efforts that East Asian nations have made to improve education. In addition to being competitive in the short-term because of cheap labor, they aim to develop their competitiveness level so that it is based in the long-run on an educated workforce.

Influence of Technology

During the past two decades, the technological revolution—computers, telecommunications and internet—has had a profound impact on the competitiveness of nations. Today, infrastructure cannot be considered only in the traditional terms of roads, trains, harbor facilities and even airports. Technological infrastructure is becoming a key asset for the future competitiveness of a nation. The availability of cheap and efficient telecommunication systems, connections to the internet, and development of mobile telephony, traditional or linked to the internet, are just a few of the new technological priorities that nations desire to possess in order to bolster their competitiveness. Some countries such as South Africa, Mexico, and Poland are leapfrogging some technological infrastructure, by focusing on mobile rather than fixed phones. Governments, however, face the phenomenon that internet companies can bypass their social legislation, which was demonstrated recently by a series of public versus private faceoffs.[4]

Technology also impacts education. Many countries, such as the USA, Britain or France have an objective to connect the entire school system to the internet. Sweden and Finland are very advanced in providing distance learning through telecommunication or the internet. The new technological requirements of enterprises have forced countries to give a priority to technology. Attracting research centers, and developing cooperation between local universities and enterprises, is becoming just as important for the competitiveness of a country as attracting FDI. The internet allows companies to develop e-commerce, e-procurements, auctions, and e-marketplaces across borders. This pushes countries to develop an advanced technological infrastructure, notwithstanding a shortage of IT skills which remains endemic in many countries. Therefore, the priority of a competitive nation is to develop the people who will operate the new technological infrastructure and strive to be on the leading edge of future developments. Ireland has heavily invested in this field to provide local and foreign enterprises with a young and qualified labor force that has IT skills. This is one of the reasons why the country is so attractive to foreign investment.

Empirical observation confirms that resources (capital, labor, technology) and talent tend to concentrate geographically (Easterly and Levine 2002). This result reflects the fact that firms are embedded in inter-firm relationships with networks of suppliers, buyers and even competitors that help them to gain competitive advantages in the sale of their products and services. While arms-length market relationships do provide these benefits, at times there are externalities that arise from linkages among firms in a geographic area or in a specific industry (textiles, leather goods, silicon chips) that cannot be captured or fostered by markets alone. Advanced technological capabilities can overcome this problem. The process of "clusterization," the creation of "value chains" or "industrial districts" are models that highlight the advantages of networks. Computerized networking has become a realistic alternative to geographic concentration.

THE STRUCTURE OF THE BOOK

The book is composed of five parts (Parts I, II, III, IV and V) or sixteen chapters, which link competitiveness with economic development, tertiary education, health insurance, socio-cultural and legal issues, and analyze important aspects of competitiveness in the context of the Caribbean region and of selected countries (i.e., Greece, Czech Republic, The Bahamas and Vietnam).

Part I links competitiveness with economic development issues, and comprises chapters 1, 2 and 3. In the opening chapter of Part I, Pagiavlas and Madjd-Sadjadi present economic development and entrepreneurial approaches that may operate as substitutes or complements in setting regional economic development strategies. They begin by reviewing various approaches to economic development with their corresponding perceived benefits and costs, then move on to examining the benefits and costs of industrial targeting via entrepreneurial strategies, and conclude with a discussion of why both approaches are not only complementary, but actually necessary, for competitive reasons.

In chapter 2, Obayuwana, Stewart and Testas argue that several less-developed and developing countries have created unique opportunities for overseas investments and successfully influenced the location decision of multinational enterprises, which are the architects of foreign direct investment (FDI). Their conclusions raise doubts on the strategies that are currently pursued by many developing countries to attract FDIs in their effort to boost growth, endogenous competency and competitiveness.

In chapter 3, Karagiannis, Madjd-Sadjadi and Stitts summarize past development efforts in the Caribbean. The main task of the chapter is to chart a Caribbean Developmental State framework: an institutional system which appears to have been used with enormous success in East Asia but has been neglected in the region. In the final part of the chapter, the authors identify key strategic requirements and offer alternative policy recommendations, which the Developmental State approach implies and suggests.

Part II links competitiveness with tertiary education and health insurance issues, and contains chapters 4, 5 and 6. In chapter 4, Bailey and Sadri argue that the business school curriculum, as taught in most schools in the United States, has remained essentially unchanged for decades. According to the authors now is an appropriate time for a *rifacimento*, a radical refashioning, similar to a recasting or new modeling. Bailey and Sadri propose a curriculum which is designed to address the criticisms of business education and places emphasis on such important issues as holistic learning and ethics while increasing the competitiveness of business school graduates.

In chapter 5, Herring, Higgins and Dengler contend that there is a significant need for faculty to be more productive in all the roles of their profession. The authors examine all areas of faculty personal productivity, and emphasize that it applies to teaching, research, and service, as well as other roles and tasks. Among the productivity factors particularly examined are clutter control, time management, focus, organizing, and management of email. Recommendations for further research are made. According to the authors, improvements in any of these productivity factors combined are expected to boost the competitiveness of tertiary education institutions.

In chapter 6, Richardson analyzes the Massachusetts mandatory health insurance program which has been closely monitored as a harbinger of future outcomes for a nationwide move in this direction. To date, according to the author, the results have been mixed as mandatory health care reforms have resulted in fewer uninsured but have also created incentives for costs to rise even faster. Finally, Richardson argues that, in the long term, health care reforms will need a combination of market incentives and government standards to enhance efficiency while at the same time assuring that "bad risks," such as unemployed people with pre-existing conditions, receive proper medical care.

Part III links competitiveness with socio-cultural and legal concerns, and includes chapters 7, 8, 9 and 10. Chapter 7 by Mohammed and Gibbs assesses the competitiveness deficiency in the Caribbean and examines impediments and challenges to building dynamic, competitive sectors in the region. The authors then move on to exploring issues such as traditional perceptions and practices of doing business by the private and public sectors as well as a business culture that focuses on securing domestic market share. These practices may become even more entrenched as the economic slowdown intensifies and domestic players seek to erect protectionist barriers. Effective utilization of the important issues of capacity, in terms of legislation, and expertise to monitor and enforce can provide policy guidance on a way forward.

In chapter 8, Mujtaba and Cavico attempt to show that Machiavellian thinking still exists in the minds of adult students as well as in the workforce. The authors also attempt to apply to real-life, modern day, business dilemmas to the teachings of one of history's great philosophers, Niccolo Machiavelli, as described in his seminal Renaissance work, *The Prince*. According to Mujtaba and Cavico entrepreneurs, executives, managers and leaders who wish to maximize their positions, secure power, and attain success and prosperity, should be roused by, learn from, and perhaps be beguiled by, the frankness, directness, and evident practical applicability of Machiavelli's provocative thoughts and precepts to the twenty-first century business world. The authors conclude that managers and leaders should proceed cautiously as they adopt the philosophies written for the sixteenth century mindset and environment while applying them in the twenty-first century business world.

Chapter 9 by Mujtaba and McFarlane examines how information technology (IT) developments have affected the role of managers, both positively and negatively, with the four fundamental functions of management theory as bases for analysis. The functions of planning, organizing, controlling and leading are used as the major IT elements under which all managers carry out their roles to be both effective and efficient. The authors further examine information technology developments and their effect on the roles of managers from a Mintzbergian viewpoint.

Chapter 10 by Katsivela examines the recent repeal of the liner conferences' antitrust immunity at the European Union (EU) level, and briefly presents the United States (U.S.) laws and policies preceding and following the EU reform. According to the author, time may be needed to effectively wean liner conferences away from carrier collective rating but principles of worldwide uniformity should, in the end, be the primary concern of U.S. legislators.

Part IV deals with Caribbean competitiveness aspects, and contains chapters 11, 12 and 13. In chapter 11, Freckleton examines the constraints on export competitiveness in CARICOM, and assesses the prospects for enhancing competitiveness. The chapter provides an overview of CARICOM's export performance over the past two decades followed by an analysis of the constraints on export competitiveness in the region. Finally, the author suggests private-public partnerships, foreign direct investments and access to external financing as essential policy measures to improving the Caribbean export competitiveness.

Chapter 12 by Alleyne provides an overview of the private sector in the Caribbean and examines the policy environment that fosters its development. The chapter also examines the prospects for developing competitive firms and activities given that Caribbean firms face many challenges, and offers policy recommendations aimed at boosting the competitive dynamics of the region's businesses.

In chapter 13, Clayton, Karagiannis and Bailey analyze the Caribbean tourism industry according to its principal characteristics and set the sector in the context of endogenous development, taking into account issues like local participation, business development, environmental concerns, greater regional cooperation, more emphasis on thorough planning, and the creation of a more diversified product. The combination of these factors would largely define a new policy framework of an alternative tourism model for Caribbean territories. According to the authors, the primary goal of such an exercise must be to implement strategies and policies that would seek to retain more of the industry's earnings in the local economy.

Part V analyzes national competitiveness aspects in the context of selected countries, and includes chapters 14, 15 and 16. Chapter 14 by Bitzenis, Marangos, Vlachos, Astroulakis, Meramveliotakis and Tsitouras seeks to determine competitiveness, entrepreneurship, and the quality of the business environment in Greece based on the analysis of the motives and barriers of inward FDIs in the country for the period 1995-2003. The results from this analysis reveal that the main motives for FDI in Greece were the prospects for market growth, political stability, economic stability, social stability, the size of the Greek market, and the 2004 Olympic Games. The primary barriers to entrepreneurship in the Greek market mentioned by multinational enterprises were bureaucracy, followed by the taxation system, corruption, and the labor market. A thorough understanding of these motives and barriers would help the formulation of the appropriate policy response aimed at further stimulating FDIs in Greece.

In Chapter 15, Sen asserts that commentaries by Porter (2008) and Pincus (2009) both have missed key aspects of Vietnam's competitiveness whose recent erosion is due to political economic malaise of Vietnamese capitalist development that is crony, state-run and debt-financed. According to Sen, human resource development appears thwarted by old socio-political feuds. Further, compared with the size of the aggregate economy, the author claims that Vietnam's FDI inflows and workers' remittances are large enough to make the policy recommendation of currency depreciation costly and ineffective.

In the last chapter of the book, Pesakovic and Saunders offer an exploratory study (a contribution in the area of comparative studies) by comparing two countries: one small transition economy, Czech Republic, and one small-island country, The Bahamas. The authors investigate FDI in the banking industry, and the outcomes on the local economy. According to Pesakovic and Saunders, although the foreign ownership in the banking sector is dominant in the case of The Bahamas and the Czech Republic, it is evident that there are differences in the outcomes of FDIs. The authors also suggest that more research in this area needs to be conducted.

Overall, the contributions to this edited book not only expand and update the body of knowledge, including contemporary material in addition to old views and thought but, more importantly, provide a rich menu for alternative policies related to various aspects of competitiveness at the turn of the century.

This publication could not have been possible without the input of many persons. Special thanks go to the contributors for their willingness to participate and respond to our suggestions. We are greatly indebted to Lenore Lautigar and the staff of Lexington Books (Rowman & Littlefield Publishing Group) who have provided excellent support throughout the period it took to prepare this edited book, and Charles Parrott for his valuable technical assistance. We would also like to thank the editors of the journals *Cato* and *Tourism and Hospitality: Planning and Development* for kindly permitting the publication of slightly revised versions of the articles "Mandatory Health Insurance: Lessons from Massachusetts" and "Sustainable Tourism in the Caribbean: Alternative Policy Considerations" which appear in this book as chapters 6 and 13 respectively. Last, but not least, we would like to thank our families for their continuous encouragement and support, and our students. We owe them more than we can recount.

J. M. Bailey, C. Chin-Loy, N. Karagiannis & Z. Madjd-Sadjadi
Winston-Salem, North Carolina and Ft Lauderdale, Florida
November 2010

NOTES

1. The OECD, since its creation, has fostered the development of free movement of capital, goods and services, at first among industrialized nations, and then worldwide. Free trade areas such as NAFTA and regional integration organizations such as the European Union have reinforced this trend. Finally, the fall of the Berlin Wall and the technological revolution of the 1990s have accelerated the development of a world that is fundamentally open and transparent.

2. The "official" definition of the OECD of a nation's competitiveness is "the degree to which a country can, under free and fair market conditions, produce goods and services which meet the test of international markets, while simultaneously maintaining and expanding the real incomes of its people over the long term."

3. Krugman (1994) argues that "As a practical matter, however, the doctrine of *competitiveness* is flatly wrong. The world's leading nations are not, to any important degree, in economic competition with each other." As Krugman notes, national economic welfare is determined primarily by productivity in both traded and non-traded sectors of the economy.

4. Privacy is another concern for most governments. Protecting the privacy of citizens (who can develop, use, and transfer data banks with personal information on individuals) is a concern and is also a source of contention between the United States and Europe today. In addition, technology is a non-negligible risk to a nation: hackers have proven that they can penetrate many tightly secured systems, even in defense. Destroying the technological infrastructure of a country can be as damaging for its security as a traditional military attack. Threats, blackmail or plain actions using the latest technologies are becoming a reality for both companies and governments.

PART I

Economic Development & Competitiveness

Chapter 1
Regional Development Options and Strategies: Industrial Targeting and Entrepreneurship

Zagros Madjd-Sadjadi & Notis Pagiavlas

INTRODUCTION & THEORY

In this chapter, we discuss economic development and entrepreneurial approaches that may operate as substitutes or complements in setting regional economic development strategies. We begin by discussing various approaches to economic development with their corresponding perceived benefits and costs. We then move on to discussing the benefits and costs of industrial targeting via entrepreneurial strategies. We conclude with a discussion of why both approaches are not only complementary, but actually necessary, for competitive reasons.

State and regional economic development incentives for businesses have two interrelated dimensions. The first one is the broad or narrow focus on particular targeted industrial groups (industrial targeting), and the second is an emphasis of targeted efforts on either exogenous or endogenous firms. A simple schematic below represents the four potential combinations of these dimensions. The top row denotes development plans that do not employ industrial targeting. The bottom row is for strategies that are targeting specific industries, in an attempt to alter or extend the comparative advantage of a region. Strategies devoid of this industrial targeting rely on more broad-based approaches that emphasize costs, or the resources of existing firms in the region. The left column is reserved for approaches that attempt to attract outside (i.e., non-endogenous) firms to come to the region. This can occur either by targeting specific industries or by emphasizing low costs in the region. The right column deals with expansion plans for firms that are already in the area, either in specific industries or across the business spectrum (Figure 1.1).

FIGURE 1.1
Regional Development Options

		Endogeneity	
Industrial targeting		**No**	**Yes**
	No	Low-cost leader	Market-based competitive advantage
	Yes	Comparative advantage alteration	Comparative advantage extension

Based on this model, development strategies may be cross-classified as four types: 1. low-cost leader strategy; 2. comparative advantage alteration; 3. market-based competitive advantage; and 4. comparative advantage extension. The low-cost leader strategy often does not target individual industries, but instead relies on simply keeping entry costs (especially taxes) low. Comparative advantage alteration may also be termed "industrial sector targeting," often a top-down approach to economic development. This combination represents the most traditional approach to economic development, associated explicitly with relocation incentives. The market-based competitive advantage approach is sometimes referred to as "new wave" economic development (Bartik 1991) and typically directs its efforts at small, local companies with entrepreneurial tendencies.

The comparative advantage extension represents an attempt to meld traditional sector targeting with entrepreneurial development policies.

A brief discussion of comparative and competitive advantage is critical to clarify the options above. If a region had a comparative advantage of any type, it would be able to produce a good or service at a lower opportunity cost than comparable regions. This does not necessarily mean that it provides a context for lower costs on an absolute basis, but rather that the good or service affords the best possible use of the resources in that region when compared with others. The practical view for this option is that although it may be possible to do all things, it is almost never desirable to do so. A simple example may serve to illustrate this: when production managers come through the ranks, they are often among the best qualified at the technical aspects of their jobs. This also allows them to spot errors in the production process faster than other individuals. The people who replace them on the production line often cannot perform the original job as well. However, the company is better off having the manager in place since the expertise in identifying errors in the production process is more important than the actual production process itself, thus, a better use of resources.

Economic theory for centuries suggests that regions trade on the basis of comparative advantage, which is not based on individual products, but rather a universal capability that often translates to market advantage(s). These in turn may be manifested as lower costs, but also may be found in terms of an ability to adapt to changes in the marketplace, to develop innovative products in niche markets, and to specialize in products where one's region can exploit economies of scale and scope. These advantages, more dynamic in nature, can lead to long-term sustainable success in market areas in ways that comparative advantage, a more static concept, cannot (Porter 1990; 2008).

If the various approaches to economic policies were complementary, localities could find success in comparative advantage extension. If they were substitutes, an area would be better off with one of the other three strategies.

LOW-COST LEADER STRATEGY

The low-cost leader strategy is the most common approach for governments to design and manage economic incentives. They try to keep taxes low and, to attract prospects, they aggressively promote this fact. The bundle of economic incentives allows the market to dictate the most optimum industrial structure. The theoretical foundations guiding this approach assume perfect competition and perfect information. In actuality, the world is characterized by neither of these conditions. As it is neither a regulatory state nor a developmental state, the low-cost leader cannot react quickly to changes in economic conditions and thus could find itself with a comparative advantage in something that it did not desire. While this served the needs of a pre-industrial society and, even to a limited extent, a society that was moving from agrarian to industrial in the 1800s, the growth of cities and the advancement of government into many other areas has tended to render this strategy less effective in the long run.

This does not imply that one cannot carry out a low-cost leader strategy in the modern world. However, many jurisdictions couple the low-cost strategy with a designated economic development agency in attracting large industrial firms to relocate or establish branch plants in its jurisdiction. This is done through a variety of marketing, financial, and nonfinancial incentives. There are often goals of job creation and an expectation that the funds will "pay for themselves" in some fashion or another. Development occurs via favorable rezoning efforts, industrial revenue bonds, tax abatements, tax increment financing, loan programs, infrastructural improvements, and even eminent domain. Such a strategy can lead to uneven, or even counterproductive, development since activities are not coordinated with an overall master plan. Still, it is important to examine each of the elements to this strategy since they are used in conjunction with other strategies.

Marketing programs to attract businesses typically emphasize the aspects that might attract a firm to an area, often focusing on educational institutions and achievements, or the low cost of living in an area. They include targeting advertising to the decision-makers in large companies and may include trips to corporate offices by both economic development and elected officials. Once a company is attracted, tailored infrastructure improvements and expedited permitting processes (including key zoning hearings) reduce start up costs and facilitate operations.

None of the above activities is particularly controversial, especially if the costs were paid by the firm through recovery fees for expedited or tailored procedures. However, two types of incentive mechanisms have been taken to task in recent years. Eminent domain, made infamous in the Kelo v. City of New London, 545 US 469 (2005) Supreme Court case, is particularly egregious according to opponents of this type of economic development strategy when it is used to benefit private businesses in the interest of increasing tax revenues at the expense of existing landowners. The Supreme Court ruled that such a taking was legal under the theory that public use and public purpose amounted to one and the same under the U.S. Constitution's Fifth Amendment, as expanded by the Fourteenth Amendment's Due Process Clause to the states and, by extension, localities, which are creatures of the states. Yet, there was a vigorous and spirited dissent in the 5-4 vote and, as a result of public uproar, thirty-seven states passed new limitations that either severely or completely restrict the use of eminent domain to benefit private interests (Lopez, Jewel, and Campbell 2009), bringing the total number of states that have placed such limitations to forty-three (Root 2009).

Another type of incentive is financial in nature in the form of industrial revenue bonds, tax abatements, tax increment financing, loan programs, or below-market price land sales. While these measures often have specific goals tied to them, it is not at all clear whether, in the absence of such incentives, a similar result would not have occurred at a lower total cost. Surveys to confirm the effectiveness of these incentives may include an element of self-selection bias. Furthermore, it is difficult to separate out the impact of financial incentives from the relative attractiveness of the area in other respects using such means.

Case study approaches (such as Bartik et al. 1987) attempt to control for these effects by including transportation and wage information, in addition to taxes, in examining possible locations that an actual firm has considered. However, this introduces additional problems because such decisions may also hinge on qualitative factors that cannot be easily quantified.

Industrial revenue bonds as well as direct government loan programs provide below-market rate financing for firms by giving them access to municipal funds or the municipal bond market. This results in significant savings when compared to other financing methods. Since the money is paid back by the firm, it appears on the surface not to cost anything to the municipality. However, there always is a chance of default and the local government must put forward its own credit in order for these to materialize. This can limit the ability of governments to procure bonds for alternative purposes. While revenue bonds are usually considered among the safest investments because they are tied to a revenue stream, they are not without cost, for this exact reason. Still, this represents probably the most acceptable direct government financial incentive that can be provided from the perspective of the whole community.

Tax increment financing districts similarly attempt to have economic development "pay for itself." Since such projects tend to raise property taxes, it is generally argued that the increase in the property tax will pay for the development in question. This, however, is not without its problems. First of all, this general argument can be applied to any new or improved development, since all will raise revenue whether the financing is needed from government or not. To use an analogy, college pays for itself because one increases one's income over time and thus people can pay back governments for college with higher salaries. However, some people would go to university regardless of whether they were given a subsidy or not. In such cases, one cannot use traditional cost-benefit analysis without taking into consideration the counterfactual: while the costs are well-known and specified, the benefits are somewhat hidden when some of the people going to public universities would have gone to private universities in the absence of the public option. In addition, there is the problem of separating out the returns to education from the returns to experience, as well as accounting for the increase in income accruing to those who are not entering college from the resulting labor market segmentation. Therefore, in some cases, the benefits are greater than they appear when one examines only those going to college, whereas in other cases the benefits are lower.

The same is true for tax increment financing districts. When property values increase, some of the benefits are seen not just in the project at hand but in all projects surrounding it. Property values are not isolated but tend to rise and fall with properties that are in close proximity and of similar character. That is evident in the fallout from the recent housing market implosion as falling demand has hurt not only those who are falling behind on their payments, but also many innocent bystanders. As foreclosures rise, property values fall not only for the foreclosed property but also for all of the properties in the area, creating a vortex that limits the ability of other individuals to relocate and refinance. It can cause a plunge in local government property tax revenues, especially in those areas where property tax rates are limited by law and when assessments and re-valuations are carried out during the downturn. At the same time, increases in property values due to infrastructure improvements will usually have the opposite effect but when property tax rates are limited by law, these gains will not be immediately captured by the local government.

Tax abatements or credits are another type of financial incentive. They are often tied to job targets at relatively high unemployment regions. As Bartik (1991) notes, transferring jobs from places where labor supply is generally tight to areas where unemployment is high can be welfare-improving not only for the particular locations that receive such jobs, but for the country as a whole. However, this presupposes that the labor market has rigidities that do not allow the wage rate to fall in the high-unemployment regions. Indeed, such incentives may function as a mere workfare program in states where high-employment areas are implicitly subsidizing those in high-unemployment areas to get jobs. The net impact of a program that has as an outcome job creation implicitly lowers the marginal cost of labor. On the face of it, since such programs reduce the public burden of such individuals, is this not to be commended? On the other hand, such programs place a premium on "place" prosperity rather than "people" prosperity and suggest that rather than having individuals move to where the jobs are, the jobs should move to where the people are, even if the market forces would suggest such moves are uneconomical, a stance that is contrary to conventional economic wisdom (Courchene 1986; 1992).

Yet, since large firms would typically act as monopsonists or oligopsonists in the local labor market, such subsidies are, in fact, reasonable from standard economic theory. A monopsony or oligopsony in the labor market acts similarly to a monopolist or oligopolist in the product market, but in the opposite direction. Whereas having some degree of monopoly power raises prices to the consumer, it lowers wages to the laborer in the case of labor market monopsony. Thus, just as economic theory would suggest a case for reducing the price of the product to the consumer in a monopoly market, it would also suggest that one should raise the wage to labor in a monopsony market. This is accomplished by providing subsidies to the hiring firm since it offsets the cost of raising wages. This is especially true in the manufacturing sector where most tax abatements are found, since such companies employ skilled labor that is not as easily substitutable. However, these raised wages have to come from somewhere, typically as taxes on other businesses and/or individuals in the area. Thus, it can turn into a situation where one is paying oneself one's raise. It is only because people think at the margin that this can effectively alter human behavior.

Below-market price land sales are probably among the most controversial since they result in a direct loss on the land in questions relative to the ability to sell and since they do not alter the marginal cost of production, their employment impact will be muted when compared to other methods. Still, these subsidies can create problems since the cost of them are passed on to other firms or individuals in the region. Normally, the goal is not merely to have jobs but to raise living standards. It also can encourage firms to reduce capital spending since labor costs are lowered in the process. Such a strategy will provide jobs but also lower overall economic growth and may diminish the ability of the region to get ahead in the competitive marketplace.

MARKET-BASED COMPETITIVE ADVANTAGE

The second type of economic development incentive combination is the one that promotes a market-based competitive advantage. This can transform the role of government as service provider and represents, to a lesser degree, a quasi-entre-preneurial approach. Government financing, either in the form of direct loans and equity positions, or in terms of indirect support for private initiatives through backing programs, is one major financial avenue under this method. There is a concentration on local and small businesses and, as such, government leverages its fiscal position to help a wide variety of participants through every-thing from training programs for entrepreneurs, small business incubators, community college and university courses and programs that assist in workforce and entrepreneurial skills development, and research and high technology co-operatives between industry, government, and academia, both public and private.

One drawback of this approach is that, in the absence of industrial targeting, there is no opportunity to take advantage of agglomeration economies and knowledge spillover. Agglomeration economies are those benefits that accrue to firms due to industrial concentration. As industrial presence throughout a supply chain expands in a local economy, transportation costs are lowered. A larger industrial base also encourages the development of business service industries, which can create similar benefits to what a large corporation finds in economies of scale, since smaller firms now can hire out key functions such as accounting, information technology, payroll processing, and marketing to firms that spe-cialize in these areas. While large corporations tend to internalize these func-tions to reduce costs even further, smaller firms often find that the large fixed costs associated with such endeavors make it more feasible and profitable to purchase these services from outside sources (Coase 1937).

Knowledge spillover is another noticeable benefit that extends from indus-trial targeting. Knowledge is not created in a vacuum and the ability to interact with other individuals in the same industry produces many benefits, not only for the individuals concerned but also for the companies involved. It is rare for a major high-technology presence to present itself outside of the traditional knowledge gateways, such as Triangle Research Park in North Carolina, Route 128 in and around Boston, and Silicon Valley in the San Francisco Bay Area. Firms engaged in financial services find benefits from headquartering in areas where other such firms are located, such as in San Francisco, New York, and Chicago. They often find a ready supply of labor that has the skill sets necessary to complete the tasks at hand: one is much more likely to find a banker with experience in handling foreign transactions in New York City than in a remote Midwestern location.

Business parks and incubators are often developed with this in mind but their success may be due more to the diversity of ventures that spring within them rather than devotion to just one industry. Indeed, more than 50 percent of all business incubators are "mixed use" in that they house clients from multiple industries (Knopp 2007). While individual companies may exhibit economies of scale (in that they become more efficient as they become larger since at least some areas of a firm need not increase in size in line with the firm as it expands) and economies of scope (in that as a firm grows it can often develop related products at a lower cost of development), the business incubator allows firms to share ideas and business services to allow them to grow and develop as compliments.

Romer (1986), Henderson (1986), and Arthur (1990) suggest that industrial concentration creates significant positive externalities that allow co-locating firms in the same industry to raise productivity. Porter (1990) argues that local competition in an industry will increase innovation since the competitive process drives firms to innovate. On the other hand, Jacobs (1969) argues that most of the benefit from knowledge spillover occurs between industries, rather than within them. This latter approach is also seen in universities, which often find that there are important benefits from interdisciplinary approaches since, for example, there is much that economics can learn from biology and vice versa. Indeed, the industrial targeting approach may not be as beneficial as once thought since in a thirty-year study of large firms in 170 cities, Glaeser et al. (1992: 1151) found that "cross fertilization of ideas across industries speeds up economic growth."

COMPARATIVE ADVANTAGE ALTERATION

Many jurisdictions are engaged in industrial targeting, which seeks to alter the comparative advantage of an area by inducing "high-value-added" firms to locate in the area. Industrial targeting when carried out effectively can lead to reductions in cost that accrue to all members of the industry merely because of a large-scale industrial presence. Silicon Valley and Route 128 in Boston are high-tech corridors that are examples of this. Google could not have started in a remote area and expected to find enough skilled engineers to hire. Similarly, the intellectual capital of the San Francisco Bay Area's universities has contributed greatly to the area's success. Hollywood does not host its film production in Michigan, while automobile manufacturing is not found to a significant degree in Southern California. In these cases, there is not a sufficient pool of actors and artists in Michigan or automotive engineers in Southern California. It is the unique pool of talent that allows newer firms to thrive and survive. Similarly, the area around High Point, North Carolina has been long a hub of furniture manufacturing in the United States. Those areas that establish a comparative advantage in this manner tend to keep it over a long period of time and thus it is something to be desired. However, what happens when the comparative advantage begins to erode (as in the case of domestic or foreign competition)? How does one transition effectively to a new comparative advantage? Industrial targeting attempts to answer these questions by creating new comparative advantages or (to a lesser extent) building on existing ones.

Most industrial targeting strategies attempt to bring large-scale employers to an area to create a critical mass of employment in an industry. Thus, a well-placed employer can act as an engine for growth. Still, the process is very challenging as other regions are engaged in a similar process. Industrial targeting is often guided by expert advice of consultants from outside the area. Prestigious firms provide reports that develop an overall strategy that more often than not looks suspiciously similar to other ones the consultant may have produced in the past. Ironically, the only reliable way for an area to succeed is to develop its own niche that leverages its unique comparative and competitive advantages. This does not mean that industrial targeting cannot succeed, only that it must consider the local conditions and resources first and then devise strategies that parlay the unique assets of a region into a master plan that allows the area to move *with* market forces rather than *against*, or *despite* them.

Another issue with industrial targeting is that it can engender a competitive pressure to escalate benefits in other jurisdictions and therefore starve a government of tax revenue (San Francisco Office of Economic Analysis 2006). This potential problem can be illustrated with a case in North Carolina and the film industry. The state began with a 15 percent refundable tax credit (maximum of $7.5 million) that essentially lowered all production expenditures in the state on even moderate scale (more than $250,000) productions. It also lowered the effective sales tax to 1 percent on goods and services procured. This meant that not only will a film production company receive $150,000 for every $1 million spent in the state, but it will have to pay only a 1 percent sales tax whereas other businesses must pay the current state sales tax of 7.75 percent. Film crews can also receive a rebate on their accommodation spending when they stay in the state for more than ninety days, and they can use state property without paying any fees. Even with all of these benefits already in place, on January 1, 2010, the tax credit rate increased to 25 percent, while maintaining the same $7.5 million maximum (North Carolina Film Office 2009). This effectively increased subsidies to smaller productions.

Such tax credit, while plausible in its intent, may be perceived as a massive subsidy that provides no sustainable economic benefit. There is no evidence that elimination of the subsidy would eliminate the film industry but, if the industry needed to be subsidized on such a massive scale, perhaps elimination of the film industry would be in the best interests of the state. After all, while North Carolina film production totaled $235 million in 2004 (San Francisco Office of Economic Analysis 2006), it had fallen to $91 million by 2008, even with the 15 percent tax credit in place (North Carolina Film Office 2009). A 25 percent tax credit (assuming that all film production was under the $30 million production cap and a return to the film production total that existed in 2004) would mean at a minimum there will be an increase in government costs of $59 million with virtually no increase in tax revenue. Given that Gross State Product in North Carolina is roughly $340 billion, and the state budget is about $20 billion, the state only receives less than 5.9 percent of Gross State Product (Office of the

Governor 2009). Thus, film production would have to have an economic multiplier of more than four just to break even, assuming that taxes were not raised on anyone else and that film production would entirely disappear in the absence of the incentives. This is an economic multiplier that has not been found for any industry in any country in any year in the past. In such cases, "winning" the battle for jobs can mean losing tax competitiveness in all other industries. Since state budgets must be balanced, these funds had to be made up by raising taxes on everyone else, thus reducing economic activity by the corresponding multiplier for those industries.

COMPARATIVE ADVANTAGE EXTENSION

The fourth type of economic development approach is comparative advantage extension, which is little practiced in the United States. It coordinates an overall approach by targeting sectors of the economy through government dirigisme with a developmental state approach that is focused on entrepreneurial activity. One characteristic of this approach is that both positive and negative approaches may be utilized, recognizing that taxes and subsidies are two sides of the same coin and the combination of both can effectively push development further than either alone. Indeed, when taxes work at cross purposes with subsidies, the combination is an ineffective and ineffectual policy, which is lethal to business expansion (Karagiannis & Madjd-Sadjadi 2007). Most importantly, the key arguments against subsidies cannot be made when unwanted sectors are taxed. Taxes raise government revenues and allow for the provision of more services and evidence suggests that good schools and infrastructure trump low taxes in the minds of many business leaders. A meta-analysis by Bartik (1991) of forty-two studies confirms what is often suspected: enhancements to public services are conducive, while welfare programs are inimical, to local economic growth.

In the end, this type of economic development may have the most to offer. It is difficult to alter one's comparative advantage and one is always at risk of having other competitors spend valuable resources to try to stymie one's efforts. Since governments have limited funds available to them, going after a new comparative advantage can prove difficult, especially if one is utilizing the subsidy approach. Attempting to bring in firms from other areas can be equally problematic, not only for cost reasons but because those costs tend to be borne by firms already in the area. Furthermore, local firms tend to have a greater affinity for a region and are more likely to stay put than fleet-footed firms focusing on finding financial incentives.

However, what happens when one does not have the comparative advantage fitting the realities of the twenty-first century? Strategies can be employed to abolish one's current comparative advantage through tax and regulatory disincentives such as is currently occurring in North Carolina with the tobacco industry. However, the temptation to replace a current comparative advantage with one that is not based on homegrown talent must be seriously challenged. Many other regions are similarly situated and are competing for the same firms. A region that concentrates on developing its industrial clusters by bringing in branch plants from the outside is more likely stifle entrepreneurial drive, since costs will be raised for the smallest and most nimble businesses in the region to compensate for the bundle of incentives provided to bigger and more established outfits. In addition, such an approach often backfires as any firm that moves primarily on the basis of financial incentives may be equally certain to be on the lookout for such payouts from other regions. Instead, relying on the entrepreneurial spirit will usually lead to superior outcomes in the long run. After all, it is often better to be the innovator than merely the assembler of technology. This practice is manifested more clearly in third world countries, who often insist on technological transfer agreements and partnering with local suppliers as part of the grand bargain of inviting large firms into their areas. This allows such firms to engage in "learning-by-doing" (Arrow 1962) and thus act as a springboard for the development of nascent indigenous industries.

ENTREPRENEURSHIP AS ECONOMIC DEVELOPMENT

One of the most critical questions facing national and regional economic policy is, "How does entrepreneurship contribute to long term economic growth?" A plausible answer would be that since entrepreneurs create new businesses, by logical extension they create new jobs, challenge existing competitors, improve market offerings, and contribute to positive changes in economic and societal terms. In a global context, countries with relatively high levels of entrepreneurship would enjoy stable and prosperous economic growth rates and wealth creation (Wong et al. 2005). However, an equally plausible answer leading to probably very different policy decisions might be that high levels of entrepreneurship indicate too few traditional wage-earning job opportunities that "force" citizens to pursue their own ventures. In this case, entrepreneurship directly correlates with slow economic growth and weaker economic development (Bosma et al. 2005).

While appearing contradictory in essence, these contextual motivations for entrepreneurship are end points of the spectrum that trigger entrepreneurial creation. Based on a series of studies and reports by the Global Entrepreneurship Monitor (GEM) (Reynolds et al. 2005), there are fundamentally two types of basic motivations to start up a new venture: necessity and opportunity recognition. Necessity entrepreneurship refers to the case of having no other viable choice to be meaningfully employed, while opportunity entrepreneurship often connotes optimization of choice options to start a new enterprise based on the perception that a market gap exists. Necessity entrepreneurship often is uncorrelated to economic development, while opportunity entrepreneurship has a significant positive effect. Subsequently, a standard index of the ratio of opportunity-to-necessity entrepreneurship could be a useful tool in designing economic development strategies and public investment policy (Naudé 2008). Strategies that target specific industries while encouraging entrepreneurial effort can help to enhance this ratio and thus make for a dynamic and prosperous society.

Before one discusses the benefits and costs of utilizing entrepreneurship as an economic development strategy or alternative, it's critical to clarify the core elements of entrepreneurship reflected in its myriad definitions.

Definitions of Entrepreneurship

Traditionally, the term entrepreneurship from its French language roots reflects two interrelated meanings: first, the creation of a new venture and the continual interest in new approaches and methods, and second, the ownership and management of a business for either profit, or not-for-profit. The first one does not necessarily imply ownership as much as a propensity that could successfully be harnessed even within existing enterprises—the notion of "intrapreneurship" (Antoncic and Hisrich 2001). In this sense, the entrepreneur "is someone who specializes in making judgmental decisions about the coordination of scarce resources" (Casson 2003). In his classic book *Wealth of Nations*, Adam Smith referred to the "enterpriser" as an individual who undertakes the formation of an organization for commercial purposes. He reacts to economic change, thereby becoming the economic agent who transforms demand into supply.

Schumpeter (1952: 72) recognized the entrepreneur as the prime mover in economic development, playing a major and critical role in the innovation process. He wrote "the function of an entrepreneur is to reform or revolutionize the pattern of production by exploiting an invention or, more generally, an untried technological method for producing a new commodity or producing an old one in a new way, opening up a new source of supply of materials or a new outlet for products by organizing a new industry." Entrepreneurship accordingly consists of "new" activities that are not typically performed in the context of business routines. According to Ronstadt (1984: 28), "entrepreneurship is the dynamic process of creating incremental wealth. This wealth is created by individuals who assume the major risks in terms of equity, time, and/or career commitment of providing value for some product or service. The product or service itself may or may not be new or unique but value must somehow be infused by the entrepreneur by securing and allocating the necessary skills and resources."

Consequently, entrepreneurial activity can be defined as the activity that involves the discovery, evaluation, and exploitation of opportunities within the framework of an individual-opportunity nexus (Shane 2003). An operational definition of entrepreneurship reflecting "firm formation rate," could be defined as the process whereby an individual or group of individuals, acting independently of any association with an existing organization, creates a new organization (Sharma and Chrisman 1999).

Entrepreneurial Approaches and Outcomes

Voslee (1994: 2) suggests that there is no clear understanding of how to generate entrepreneurship and sustainable economic development. He argues that governmental intervention hinders more than facilitates development "unless they are market friendly." Gries and Naudé (2008) provide the following propositions that summarize the empirical literature: 1. growth in a regional economy is driven by an expansion in the number of start-up firms that supply intermediate goods and services; 2. improvements in human capital will enhance the rate of start-ups; 3. improvements in the relative rates of return to entrepreneurs and business conditions will raise start-up rates; 4. an increase in regional financial concentration will reduce the start-up rate in a region; and 5. increased agglomeration/urbanization in a region has an a priori ambiguous effect on start-up rates.

Audretsch et al. (2007: 1) describe a "scholarly disconnection" stating that "macroeconomics has largely not considered the role that entrepreneurship plays in economic growth and employment" and "management—the academic discipline most squarely focused on entrepreneurship—has typically not considered the implications for the broader economic context." Therefore, despite progress over the years, entrepreneurship within the context of economic development remains a relatively under-researched phenomenon. Lingelbach et al. (2005) pointed out that entrepreneurship in developing countries is the least studied economic and social phenomenon in the world.

In a global context, using data from thirty-seven countries surveyed by the GEM in 2002, Wong et al. (2005) find that only high-potential entrepreneurial activity is positively associated with economic growth in their sample. In the United States, entrepreneurs of necessity often represent disadvantaged populations that see themselves as people with special needs that can only be met by outsiders. They become more consumers of services than producers. They focus wonderful talents of creativity on outwitting the system, or bypassing it entirely. Their socio-economic circumstances and backgrounds prevent them from optimizing resource utilization within a system that views solid credit worthiness and business experience as fundamental cornerstones of new venture creation and support. Hesitant to directly support partially qualified residents, most state or regional resources are diverted to service providers, a practice that often leads to inflexible bureaucratic structures that result in the opposite of the intended effect. In that sense, a prevailing view that outside experts can provide real help often leads to projects that do not precisely reflect local conditions, as stated in the economic development section above. As a result, critical relationships with local residents are weakened within the community, including those between neighbors. An emphasis instead is placed on the advice of expert consultants, social workers, quasi-governmental entities (like the Chambers of Commerce), and reluctant funders. However, historic evidence suggests that meaningful development is achieved when local communities are committed to investing directly in aspiring entrepreneurial projects. Interestingly, numerous studies have found that children whose parents were entrepreneurs are more likely to become entrepreneurs themselves (Davidsson and Honig 2003).

A very interesting challenge facing even the most intelligently designed regional programs is lack of consensus of what constitutes "success." Typical metrics to assess and evaluate progress include new venture creation and start ups, growth rates within a particular timeframe, "sales" by entrepreneurs, retention of

regionally graduated students, number of employees of entrepreneurial companies, number of minority-owned firms, venture creation by women, patents,
technology licensing arrangements, funding availability, and many others. Yet,
despite the particular definition of success, the importance of entrepreneurship is
clearly evident from the fact that small businesses employ more than 50 percent
of the workforce and create over 65 percent of all new jobs. While the probabil-
ity of failure in typical conditions in year one of a new venture is 80 percent,
properly supported ventures can increase success rates to 70 percent by year
three. Home grown businesses actually have even better results as they tend to
stay afloat at about an 85 percent rate during the fifth year of operations. Interestingly, despite strong evidence that most high technology firms do not grow as
fast or as high as expected (a contributing factor to the Internet market "burst"
that occurred during the early twenty-first century), public policy decisions and
subsequent investments are based on the assumption of "rapid growth" that perhaps unconsciously ignore the more pragmatic approach of slower growth strategies (Slatter 1992). The critical interdependency of high-tech new firms on the
systemic infrastructure and the broader system (Carlsson and Jacobsson 1994)
suggests that a strategy of attracting individual firms may not yield the long term
benefits envisioned by public investment policies.

When measuring outcomes, one should distinguish between different types
of entrepreneurial ventures: the lifestyle or "Mom and Pop" types create wealth
for the owner(s), and offer limited employment and community wealth generation opportunities. The more stable, moderate growth ventures create wealth for
owners and a relatively larger number of employees. The "Gazelles," those defined with accelerated growth rates of at least 20 percent for five consecutive
years typically create wealth for owners, investors, and employees, offering
higher wages and significant employment and community wealth generation
opportunities.

Highfield and Smiley (1987) empirically analyzed the determinants of start-
ups in the USA over the period 1948 to 1984, using rates of incorporation as an
indicator of start-ups. They found that five factors were significant in affecting
start-up rates: real GNP growth, expenditure on equipment (investment), the
unemployment rate, real interest rates, and inflation. Reynolds (1993), and
Reynolds and Storey (1993) identified six broad determinants of entrepreneurial
start-ups in a region: demand (measured by the size of the population and size of
the economy), unemployment, urbanization (agglomeration), personal household wealth, specialization (industry-level differentiation), and government
spending on infrastructure, education, and health.

SUMMARY & CONCLUSIONS

We find that entrepreneurship is an important part of any business strategy and
when it coincides with industrial targeting, this approach can extend a region's
natural comparative advantage. In fact, even when a region lacks a well-defined
comparative advantage, targeting indigenous industrial development is a supe-

rior strategy to that of encouraging the establishment of branch plants from the outside. Since these plants are established by extensive use of public financial resources, local governments should insist that branch plants establish connections with locally owned and operated suppliers to experience benefits from knowledge spillovers. This can lead to spurring entrepreneurial growth in other sectors of the economy. Actually on a practical level, a key qualitative criterion for selecting a relocation area over others is what is often termed "overall quality of life." Within this concept, a key determinant to attract highly qualified managers is the variety of career prospects of spouses and immediate family members. One could argue that the active promotion of entrepreneurial ventures enhances the likelihood of relocation, especially in the cases that a "lifestyle" venture (a flower shop, a restaurant, a retailing store) is appropriate for family members that desire such activities.

In addition, it is beneficial not to place one's proverbial eggs all in one basket when it comes to industrial clusters. Growth is enhanced when a broad spectrum of industries is actively engaged to create new industries or spur revolutionary innovation within an existing industry. Innovation often provides temporary monopoly control for a region (McDaniel 2002) that is difficult for others to match and can lead to long-lasting structural changes in the national economy as resources gravitate to a region that has such innovations. Local governments are key stakeholders in encouraging opportunity entrepreneurship among the area's population. This is especially true in areas where "necessity" entrepreneurship has taken hold. Rather than seeing business formation as an urgent societal need, a viable goal is to create the environment that cultivates hope and optimism. This is enhanced in part by industrial parks and incubators, which encourage entrepreneurs to build connections with similarly situated individuals and thus are more likely to produce entrepreneurial "Gazelles" as opposed to only lifestyle-based ventures.

To achieve meaningful economic and by extension social development, the need for a closely knit community is apparent to most regional efforts. This fact is further reinforced by continuing budget constraints that include state and federal sources. It appears increasingly unlikely that significant resources will be available from outside a community. A key strategy therefore is to "connect" all pieces of a complex community puzzle with the intent to leverage limited resources with active collaborations that harness diverse talents and creative energies.

A coordinated new strategy must recognize that entrepreneurship is a critical component of a regional economic development program. New venture formation is unquestionably one of the most important economic and social activities for a region, especially as it positively affects innovation that cuts across industries and clusters. Cross-fertilization of innovative approaches and ideas augments the pool of existing or future entrepreneurs, including social or non-profit ventures. Active networks and capital availability are the most critical factors for a vibrant entrepreneurial region. Networks of key infrastructural partners—including institutions of higher education—facilitate exchange of ideas, keep abreast of developments in a particular field, and introduce residents to potential partners that provide knowledge and critical services.

Porter (1995) suggests that a more effective means to promote economic growth is to develop the necessary environmental infrastructure that facilitates market forces themselves to pursue profitable enterprises. A proper strategy includes a persistent public awareness campaign of the importance of entrepreneurship, a broad spectrum of educational systems including "coaching," and financing options to accommodate varying degrees of risk and credit histories. Often underemphasized elements include zoning rules for smaller home-based business, permission of mixed use development, land use designations that support target industries, high speed telecom options, and commercial space or shovel-ready land within or outside designated parks.

In conclusion, the complex nature of entrepreneurship tends to produce a very diverse spectrum of entities that hardly fit into a neat framework or typology with a clearly defined strategy. It's best described by Wennekers and Thurik (1999: 50) as follows: "At the aggregate level of industries, regions and national economies, the many individual entrepreneurial actions compose a mosaic of new experiments. In evolutionary terms this can be called variety. A process of competition between these various ideas and initiatives takes place continuously, leading to the selection of the most viable firms and industries."

REFERENCES

Antoncic, B. and R. D. Hisrich. "Intrapreneurship: Construct Refinement and Cross-Cultural Validation." *Journal of Business Venturing* 16, no. 5 (2001): 495-527.
Arrow, K. "The Economic Implications of Learning by Doing." *Review of Economic Studies* 29, no. 3 (1962): 155-73.
Arthur, W. B. "'Silicon Valley' Locational Clusters: When Do Increasing Returns Imply Monopoly." *Mathematical Social Sciences* 19, no. 3 (1990): 235-51.
Audretsch, D. B., Grilo, I., and A. R. Thurik. *Handbook of Research on Entrepreneurship Policy*. Cheltenham: Edward Elgar, 2007.
Bartik, T. J., Becker, C., Lake, S., and J. Bush. "Saturn and State Economic Development." *Forum for Applied Research and Public Policy* (Spring 1987): 29-41.
Bartik, T. J. *Who Benefits From State and Local Economic Development Policies?* Kalamazoo, MI: W. E. Upjohn Institute for Employment Research, 1991.
Bosma, N., de Wit, G., and M. Carree. "Modelling Entrepreneurship: Unifying the Equilibrium and Entry-Exit Approach." *Small Business Economics* 25, no. 1 (2005): 35-48.
Carlsson, B. and S. Jacobsson. "Technological Systems and Economic Policy: The Diffusion of Factory Automation in Sweden." *Research Policy* 23, no. 3 (1994): 235-48.
Casson, M. "Entrepreneurship, Business Culture and the Theory of the Firm." In *Handbook of Entrepreneurship Research*, edited by Z. Acs and D. Audretsch, 225-45. Dordrecht, The Netherlands: Kluwer Academic Publishers, 2003.
Coase, R. "The Theory of the Firm." *Economica* 4, no. 16 (1937): 386-405.
Courchene, T. J. "Avenues of Adjustment: The Transfer System and Regional Disparities." In *The Canadian Economy: A Regional Perspective*, edited by D. J. Savoie, 25-62. Toronto: Menthuen, 1986.
———. *Rearrangements: The Courchene Papers*. Oakville, ON: Mosaic Press, 1992.

Davidsson, P. and B. Honig. "The Role of Social and Human Capital Among Nascent Entrepreneurs." *Journal of Business Venturing* 18, no. 3 (2003): 301-31.
Glaeser, E. L., Kallal, H. D., Scheinkman, J. A., and A. Shleifer. "Growth in Cities." *The Journal of Political Economy* 100, no. 6 (1992): 1126-52.
Gries, T. and W. A. Naudé. "Entrepreneurship and Regional Economic Growth." WIDER Research Paper RP 2008/70, United Nations University, Helsinki, Finland, 2008.
Henderson, J. V. "Efficiency of Resource Usage and City Size." *Journal of Urban Economics* 19, no. 1 (1986): 47-70.
Highfield, R. and R. Smiley. "New Business Starts and Economic Activity: An Empirical Investigation." *International Journal of Industrial Organization* 5 (1987): 51-66.
Jacobs, J. *The Economy of Cities*. New York: Vintage, 1969.
Karagiannis, N. and Z. Madjd-Sadjadi. *Modern State Intervention in the Era of Globalisation*. Cheltenham: Edward Elgar Publishing, 2007.
Kelo v. City of New London, 545 U.S. 469, 2005.
Knopp, L. *2006 State of the Business Incubation Industry*. Athens, OH: National Business Incubation Association, 2007.
Lingelbach, D., de la Vina, L., and P. Asel. "What's Distinctive about Growth-Oriented Entrepreneurship in Developing Countries?" *Center for Global Entrepreneurship Working Paper* 1, UTSA College of Business, San Antonio, TX, 2005.
Lopez, E., Jewell, R. T., and N. Campbell. "Pass a Law, Any Law, Fast! State Legislative Responses to the Kelo Backlash." *Review of Law and Economics* 5, no. 1 (2009): 1-5.
McDaniel, B. A. *Entrepreneurship and Innovation: An Economic Approach*. Armonk, NY: M. E. Sharpe, 2002.
Naudé, W. A. "Entrepreneurship in Economic Development." *WIDER Discussion Paper* 2008/20, United Nations University, Helsinki, Finland, 2008.
North Carolina Film Office. "25% Film Incentive." 2009. www.ncfilm.com/incentives-benefits/25-tax-credit.html (accessed September 6, 2009).
Office of the Governor. "The North Carolina State Budget Summary of Recommendations 2009-2011." Raleigh, NC: Office of State Budget and Management, 2009.
Porter, M. *On Competition*. Cambridge, MA: Harvard University Press, 2008.
————. "The Competitive Advantage of the Inner City." *HBR*, May-June 1995: 55-71.
————. *The Competitive Advantage of Nations*. New York: Free Press, 1990.
Reynolds, P. D. "The Role of Entrepreneurship in Economic Systems: Developed Market and Post-Socialist Economies." Paper presented at the Second Freiberg Symposium on Economics, Freiberg, Germany, September 9-11, 1993.
Reynolds, P. D. and D. J. Storey. "Local and Regional Characteristics Affecting Small Business Formation: A Cross-National Comparison." Paris: OECD, 1993.
Reynolds, P. D., Bosma, N. S., Autio, E., Hunt, S., De Bono, N., Servais, I., Lopez-Garcia, P., and N. Chin. "Global Entrepreneurship Monitor: Data Collection Design and Implementation 1998-2003." *Small Business Economics* 25, no. 3 (2005): 205-31.
Romer, P. M. "Increasing Returns and Long-Run Growth." *Journal of Political Economy* 94, no. 5 (1986): 1002-37.
Ronstadt, R. *Entrepreneurship*. Dover, MA: Lord Publishing Co., 1984.
Root, D. W. "As Naked an Abuse of Government Power As Could Be Imagined." *Reasononline*. June 25, 2009. http://www.reason.com/news/show/134366.html (accessed September 6, 2009).
San Francisco Office of Economic Analysis. "Economic Impact Report of the Proposed Film Rebate Program." *File no.* 060065, March 24, 2006. San Francisco, CA: City and County of San Francisco Office of the Controller, 2006.
Schumpeter, J. *Can Capitalism Survive?* New York: Harper & Row, 1952.

Shane, S. A. *A General Theory of Entrepreneurship: The Individual-Opportunity Nexus.* Cheltenham: Edward Elgar (New Horizons in Entrepreneurship), 2003.

Sharma, P. and J. J. Chrisman. "Toward a Reconciliation of the Definitional Issues in the Field of Corporate Entrepreneurship." *Entrepreneurship Theory and Practice* 23, no. 3 (1999): 11-27.

Slatter, S. *Gambling on Growth: How to Manage the Small High-tech Firm.* Chichester: John Wiley & Sons, 1992.

Voslee, W. B, ed. *Entrepreneurship and Economic Growth.* Pretoria, South Africa: HSRC Publisher, 1994.

Wennekers, S. and R. Thurik. "Linking Entrepreneurship and Economic Growth." *Small Business Economics* 13, no. 1 (1999): 27-55.

Wong, P. K., Ho, Y. P., and E. Autio. "Entrepreneurship, Innovation and Economic Growth: Evidence from GEM Data." *Small Business Economics* 24, no. 3 (2005): 335-50.

Chapter 2
Foreign Direct Investments, Endogenous Competency, and Competitiveness: Elements from Global Experiences

Nicholas Obayuwana, David Stewart & Abdelaziz Testas

INTRODUCTION & THEORETICAL ISSUES

Direct investments by multinational enterprises in less developed countries (LDCs), historically, have always resulted in fraught relationship between multinational enterprises (MNEs) and the host governments. This history is replete with occasions of exploitation by the multinational corporations, countered by episodes of expropriation by the host governments. However, multinationals are less likely today than in the 1970s to be branded "agents of imperialism," while their assets are at less risk of outright confiscation by the host countries. Nonetheless, issues of common concern and disagreement between them are still common.

In recent times, the old notion of the "empires of profit" typically assigned to multinationals exclusively from rich first-world countries has been undergoing some surprising metamorphoses. Companies from India, Brazil, Malaysia, and South Africa as well as China are among the so-called third-world countries that have joined the investment fray around the world.

The *Global Development Finance*, an annual World Bank report released on April 16, 2004, indicates that their reach is spreading. The Bank, for example, reports that multinationals from developing countries made $16 billion of foreign direct investment (FDI) in 2002, and $40 billion in 2004, out of which more than a third of the FDI was invested among their peer countries. Most governments of LDCs are now keen to attract FDI.

In the last two decades, developing countries have taken unprecedented steps to privatize and allow the foreign ownership of their normally public-owned service and production sectors. As a result, they have created unique opportunities for overseas investments and successfully influenced the location decision of multinational enterprises, which are the architects of foreign direct investment. According to UNCTAD (2003), the flow of FDI in the service sectors of less developed countries has surpassed all other FDI flows in these countries.

One of the objectives behind the liberalization of policies toward inward MNEs' investment by these countries is aimed at attracting foreign private capital investment to their economies. The idea is based on the assumption that the growth in FDI augments economic growth by bringing in additional capital stock to the developing countries. Many of these countries have taken faith in the virtue of this assumption to attract the much needed capital investment, and therefore embarked on a fresh restructuring of their economies in order to create an enabling environment for the MNEs' investments.

By the same token, MNEs have their own interest in the newly privatized service sectors as they hunt for overseas investments. First of all, developing countries have served as lucrative markets for multinational service providers. Second, the resolve of national governments to sustain market-facilitating policies, particularly by implementing steadfast procedures, has not only reduced the uncertainty of investing in LDCs, but has also helped to increase their active participation. Third, many services are difficult to trade. Hence, it is desirable for foreign firms to be based inside LDCs to serve the local markets. Fourth, the opening up of local public-owned service sectors for non-resident private investment fits with their overall strategy which is aimed at optimizing markets, costs, and competitions in a globally liberalized trade and investment environment. Thus, the pursuit of a free market system by LDCs can attract increased FDI in the newly privatized service sectors.

But there are productive motives too. Some companies become multinationals to escape the confines of their home market. For example, Pepkor, South Africa's biggest retailer, has expanded into Zambia and Mozambique. The phenomenon generally known as "horizontal" FDI, allows firms to hop over the trade barriers that still divide many poor countries from each other. The most devastating impact of this arrangement is that, the foreign entrants, relatively better organized, financially endowed, and sometimes enjoying more concessions derived from corrupt practices, often can and do displace their local rivals.

Other foreign investors are interested in a host country's workers, not its consumers. This "vertical" FDI allows firms to locate different stages of their production wherever they are best suited: marketing where consumers are close at hand; research and development where workers are smart; and assembly where they are cheap. Just as China's low-wage workers attract a multitude of multinationals from the rich world, China's own multinationals are eager to take advantage of ever cheaper labor elsewhere. Hence, they are investing in bicycle production in Ghana, and video players in South-East Asia.

But the growth of FDI alone is not the necessary and sufficient condition to ensure the inflow of foreign stock of capital to LDCs. Even if one accepts that the growth of FDI flows may lead to the influx of foreign capital in LDCs, there is no theoretical or empirical basis to guarantee that it would do so. This is because the reasons for FDI and the international movement of capital are not identical. They are motivated by distinct and independent factors. The cause for FDI is generally explained by the expected return on MNEs' firm-specific stock of knowledge-based assets that are not available to indigenous firms. That is why MNEs could compete with indigenous firms that are more familiar with the local environment. Therefore, it is the desire by the MNEs to raise their total profits that prompts FDI, rather than the expected return on capital.[1]

In contrast, the flow of international capital movement is determined by a present value maximization motive of MNEs that operate in less than perfect international capital markets. When these firms undertake financial investments in foreign countries, they are confronted with different new risks, which are different from what they face in their own countries. As a result, whether or not they transfer their own capital to the host countries depends on the constraints that these new risks would have on maximizing their future wealth. Even when the MNEs face higher net interest payments due to the lower capital-labor ratio of developing countries, these firms tend to curtail the flow of capital to these countries to avoid risky economic or political environments.[2] This is a particular reason why MNEs finance their investment from the local borrowing even if the cost of capital is higher than their home countries. Hence, the MNEs' decision to transfer their own capital to LDCs in order to finance their investments rests on more complex considerations of the effects of new risks.[3]

It is also important to realize that the financial behavior of MNEs in advanced countries sharply contrasts with their behavior in LDCs. In advanced countries, comparable economic and political systems and market structures present unique financial opportunities for foreign investors. Consequently, MNEs usually transmit capital and technology between advanced countries. In contrast, stark differences between the advanced home countries of MNEs and host LDCs are major sources of barriers to the influx of MNEs' capital.[4]

Several differences exist between the MNEs' home countries and the LDCs which explain why these firms choose to finance their FDI from funds generated in the local capital market rather than exporting their own capital. First, they seize on the opportunity of existing market credit imperfections, fashioned by host governments' courtship of foreign investment, often borrowing money at interest rates lower than those available for the indigenous firms. Second, they may face political risks such as political instability or political corruption which may discourage the transmission of foreign capital to LDCs since they affect the level of expected return and the variance of earnings. Third, MNEs tend to avoid risks associated with "economic vulnerabilities" such as severe droughts and floods which are causes for economic growth retardation. Fourth, they may respond to the risk of exposure to exchange rate fluctuations.[5]

In practice, MNEs have two choices of financing their FDI in developing host countries: they can bring their capital along with their technology to these countries, or they can secure much of the capital they need inside the host countries. In the former case, developing countries benefit from the more advanced technology and from the inflow of capital. When the new capital is used to generate the production of additional goods and services, their investment is growth-enhancing and hence the growth-FDI connection is established. The notion of the benefits of FDI to developing countries generally assumes this characteristic. In the latter case, however, whether their investment supports economic growth or inflicts economic harm depends on many other factors, including the type of technology that is transmitted and on the type of capital market that exists in the host countries.[6]

This chapter also unveils some theoretical rationales developed by economists, for predicting the success or failure of FDIs in LDCs. These propositions, though based on studies carried out in Middle Eastern countries, are presumed to be applicable to all less developed countries because of their common traits of underdevelopment.

THE ROLE OF FDI IN THE ARAB WORLD

Foreign direct investment has traditionally been considered a beneficial and important method for developing countries to increase capital. While it is true that FDI can have the effect of bringing permanent, stable capital investment into a developing country, there are also many potential risks which may outweigh the potential benefits. There is now a sufficient amount of data that economists can use to analyze the results of FDI in developing regions over the past thirty years. The results show that FDI brings positive capital growth to some countries, while negative growth to some others, for example some Arab countries.[7]

In order for a developing country to benefit from FDI, it must have the ability to absorb the capital investment. Four factors to consider are: the technology gap, education level of the workforce, financial sector development, and the quality of institutional development.[8] Each of these factors has been used to compile an analysis of the potential outcomes of FDI in Arab countries.

To start with, one needs to indicate that the flow of FDI in Arab countries is low. In the period 1996-2009, the flow of FDI of sixteen Arab countries combined (Saudi Arabia, United Arab Emirates, Egypt, Lebanon, Qatar, Morocco, Sudan, Jordan, Algeria, Tunisia, Libya, Bahrain, Oman, Syria, Kuwait, and Yemen) represented only about 3 percent of the world's total and 10 percent of that of the developing world (Tables 2.1 and 2.2 below). Table 2.1 shows that the flow of FDI in Arab countries has surpassed that of Sub-Saharan Africa, a region that is also known to have attracted low levels of FDI. For the period 1996-2009, the flow of FDI in the Arab World reached about US$450 bn compared with about US$295 bn for Sub-Saharan Africa. This improvement in the position of the Arab World, however, is only a recent phenomenon that first took shape in 2004. Therefore, for example, in 1997, the flow of FDI in Sub-Saharan Africa reached about US$8.5 bn compared with only about US$6 bn for the Arab World. In 2001, the figures were, respectively, about US$15 bn compared with US$9 bn, while for 2002, these were roughly US$13 bn compared with US$8.5 bn.

TABLE 2.1
Flow of FDI in Arab Countries, Developing Economies, Sub-Saharan Africa, and the World, 1996-2009

Region	FDI Flow (US$ mn)
Total Arab Countries (*)	451,200
Developing Economies	4,317,453
Sub-Saharan Africa	295,786
World	14,253,120

(*) Sixteen Arab countries mentioned in text above.
Source: UNCTAD, Foreign Direct Investment database, 2010. http://stats.unctad.org/fdi (accessed September 25, 2010).

TABLE 2.2
Flow of FDI to Individual Arab Economies, 1996-2009

Country/Total	US$ mn	%
Saudi Arabia	129,922	29
United Arab Emirates	71,652	16
Egypt	51,654	11
Lebanon	31,947	7
Qatar	27,742	6
Morocco	20,940	5
Sudan	19,296	4
Jordan	17,116	4
Algeria	15,674	3
Tunisia	15,215	3
Libyan Arab Jamahiriya	14,742	3
Bahrain	12,824	3
Oman	11,650	3
Syrian Arab Republic	6,874	2
Yemen	3,087	1
Kuwait	865	0
Total Arab Countries	**451,200**	**100**

Source: UNCTAD, Foreign Direct Investment database, 2010. http://stats.unctad.org/fdi (accessed September 25, 2010).

Table 2.2 above shows that Arab countries have had mixed results in terms of attracting FDI. Oil-rich Saudi Arabia has had the largest percentage share of the total flow of FDI in the Arab World (about 30 percent) followed by the UAE (15 percent). Syria, Yemen, and Kuwait are ranked last with less than 3 percent contribution to the total.

FDI started to assume relative importance in the Arab World only recently as shown in Figure 2.1 below. It reached its peak in 2008 then started to decline in the subsequent year. In recent years, Arab countries started to have more liberalized trade policies, economic reformist governments, and are now more agreeable to privatization. As a result, the flow of FDI increased. There is also the tendency that the more diversified a country's economy, the larger its capability to attract FDI, as has been observed in the case of Jordan, Tunisia, and Morocco. On the other hand, the large public sectors and closed markets of some Arab countries still deter FDI. In addition, privatization has not gone far enough as economic liberalization is seen to carry high political risks.

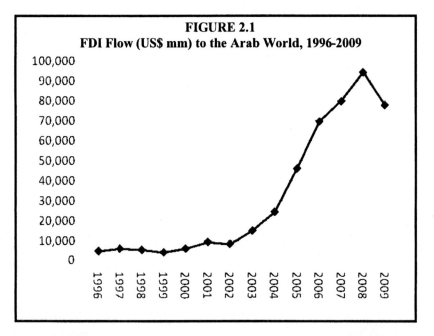

FIGURE 2.1
FDI Flow (US$ mm) to the Arab World, 1996-2009

Source: UNCTAD, Foreign Direct Investment database, 2010. http://stats.unctad.org/fdi (accessed September 25, 2010).

In order to assess the likelihood of successful FDI in the Arab region, one must consider the four previously mentioned factors—technology gap, education level of the workforce, financial sector development, and the quality of institutional development. The study conducted by the Graduate Institute of International Studies in Geneva, Switzerland, looked at how well the Arab region performs against these four factors.

First, it was decided that the Arab region should be examined under two sub-categories: low-income and not-so-low income. The low-income countries are predominantly those without large oil revenues. The research revealed that the wealthier countries have better *technological infrastructure* that would more easily allow foreign investors to develop in the country. It was determined that each of the countries in the region with significant oil revenue would benefit from FDI based on technological infrastructure. However, of the remaining countries, only Lebanon and Tunisia were found to have sufficient technology to benefit from FDI.[9]

The second factor used to determine potential for benefit from FDI is *institutional development,* specifically in terms of business regulation, property rights, and corruption index. The collected data revealed that only four of the thirty-two Arab countries score high enough on the corruption index, and eleven of the thirty-two on the property rights index to realize any benefit from FDI.[10] It should be noted that these two factors are difficult to test empirically and may vary over time. However, in regard to business regulation, every Arab country scored well enough to benefit from FDI with the exception of Libya, Iraq, and Syria.[11]

Testas[12] has studied the role of the above two factors, i.e., technology and institutional development (in addition to macroeconomic environment) with regard to growth competitiveness. This was done by operationalizing a model developed by Jeffrey Sachs and John McArthur[13] and applying a statistical cluster procedure to data for over 100 countries. The cluster procedure sorts cases into groups or clusters so that the degree of association is strong between members of the same cluster and weak between members of different clusters. Each cluster describes the class to which its members belong.

The model identified five optimal clusters, with one in the middle indicating that the member country has average indicators of technological achievement, institutional development, and macroeconomic stability. Among the four Arab countries included in the study, Tunisia and Jordan were identified with a cluster higher than the average, Morocco was associated with the average cluster, while Algeria had membership in a below-average cluster. The author then explained Algeria's poor competitive performance by digging into the work of fourteenth-century scholar Ibn Khaldun[14] who identified three important factors for weak economic performance—high levels of economic and political repression, and weak productive forces.

It is difficult to find scientific data related to education in Arab countries. Researchers measure the education of an Arab country using the average years of education of males above twenty-five years of age. The more educated a country's population, the more likely it is to benefit from FDI. The Arab countries scored well in this category.[15] The majority of Arabs exceeded the calculated threshold and the average Arab score was above the average developing country's score. It must be noted that official education records are ambiguous and the quality of the reported education cannot be verified. Some researchers speculate that education in some Arab countries might be heavily religious and not necessarily translatable into capital development.

Finally, research indicates that a well developed financial sector is vital to benefitting from FDI. There are two ways to assess the financial sectors of Arab countries: stock market capitalization as a percentage of GDP, and the capital investment from a bank-based system. When the region is analyzed using the stock market capitalization approach only Jordan scores high enough to benefit from FDI.[16] However, most Arab countries are highly bank-based and have small, if any, stock markets. Therefore, when the region is analyzed based on the bank-based investment portfolio, virtually every Arab country exceeds the required 12 percent of GDP investment, except Yemen and Sudan.[17] The results indicate that each country must be analyzed individually to determine the development of its financial sector, with the exception of Jordan which appears to have an established, functional market-based financial sector.

The decision to invest government money into financial and tax incentives for FDI is complicated and should be made using criteria such as the ones described here. Countries that are not developed to the point that they can absorb the capital investments may see only slight benefits or even negative returns. These countries should focus on developing their internal capacities, such as human capital, the financial sector, and technological infrastructure to a modern standard, and fine tuning their macroeconomic policies before attempting to lure FDI. FDI incentives can be a drain on a country's economy if it is not successful. Therefore, the country must be able to withstand the effects of failed investments.

FDI LOCATION DETERMINANTS

Critics of FDI argue that investment is concentrated unfairly in a couple of particular areas of the world. Peter Nunnenkamp examines the motive that corporations have to invest in certain regions in his research article "Foreign Direct Investment in Developing Countries: What Policymakers Should Not Do and What Economists Don't Know." What he discovered is that there are three primary determinants that drive what locations receive FDI.

Overall policy framework is an important determinant for FDI. It is important for the country to have a sustained level of stability both politically and economically.[18] In addition, the country should have a positive attitude toward privatized industries. This is evident when one considers the regions that receive the greatest share of FDI, Southeast Asia and Eastern Europe. These countries have open market systems and are favorable to privatization. In contrast, Western Asian and African nations continue to operate in closed markets and oppose privatization. These closed systems are highly averse to FDI.[19]

In addition, economic factors are critical factors to be considered when researching FDI. First, resource-seeking FDI has traditionally been an attractive source to companies. However, the percentage of resource-seeking FDI has recently been decreasing due to countries' ability to excavate their resources. As countries develop, their capabilities increase, therefore less investment is required in order to utilize their natural resources.

Recently, an important economic factor has been a country's business facilitation. This refers mainly to a country's willingness to offer financial and tax incentives to a multinational corporation to lure FDI.[20] The danger is that small countries that have less resources will be at a disadvantage compared to countries capable of offering large incentives. Another danger is the possibility of bidding wars that may force countries to offer incentives so great that it actually leads to a negative return on their economy.[21] The effect can be draining to public finances.

Third, market-seeking FDI has been necessary in order for corporations to expand into global markets. However, the recent liberalization of trade policy has made exporting easier; therefore reducing the need for direct investment.[22]

The most important recent phenomenon in market-seeking FDI has been the impact of regional integration. The European Union (EU) and NAFTA are examples of how small countries are increasing their market size in order to spur economic growth.[23]

North African (Maghreb) Arab countries have used the European Union as an example of how regional integration can improve the chances of FDI in an area by increasing the market size and output capacity. In 1989, five countries—Algeria, Libya, Mauritania, Morocco and Tunisia—founded the Arab Maghreb Union (AMU). One reason for creating the AMU was to facilitate trade among its members, but the benefits are expected to be modest due to a number of constraining factors.[24] For example, the AMU was estimated to increase Algeria's production by less than 0.5 percent[25] and its total imports by less than 1 percent.[26] In terms of welfare effects, the impact is as small as 0.002 percent.[27] Compared with such integration schemes as ASEAN, the results were also modest.[28]

A more important objective for the creation of the AMU is likely to provide a framework for coordinating policies to access export markets in the EU and attracting investment from EU's member countries to speed up economic growth. Thus, in 1995, AMU countries signed a free trade agreement with the EU. Testas[29] has studied the potential effects of AMU-EU partnership agreements using a dynamic model of trade and found significant effects on Algeria's long term GDP growth rate. The predicted increase is a factor of seven stemming from both increased competition and enlarged markets. Applying an import demand model to annual data on Maghreb imports, the same author[30] quantifies significant amounts of trade expansion or 40 percent of AMU's combined total imports.

In conclusion, research indicates that the most effective steps a country can take to attract FDI are to open their financial markets and develop a policy that allows privatization. Countries that are having difficulty luring FDI should focus on creating a stable financial sector and political system to display stability to multinational corporations. Finally, the European Union and NAFTA should be used as an example of how regional integration can improve the chances of FDI in an area by increasing the market size and output capacity.

EFFECTS OF MNEs' INVESTMENT ON THE HOST COUNTRY

One way of assessing the contributions of MNEs to the host country's economy is to focus on the dynamic relationship between their investment and the macro-economic variables of the labor-surplus and capital-poor host country. It is worthy of note that the most potent attribute of the stock of knowledge-based assets is their ability to attract the local labor and capital to the foreign sector from the national sector. At the initial relative price, they initiate a shift of local capital from the national sector to the foreign sector by raising its marginal product in the service industries. At the same time, labor also moves away from the national sector to the foreign sector due to the change in the capital-labor ratio. So, the foreign sector expands just as the national sector shrinks. Given that the foreign sector is relatively more capital-intensive and the national sector relatively more labor-intensive, the expansion of the foreign sector together with the contraction of the national sector tends to reduce employment opportunities in the capital-poor and labor-surplus host country. This inevitably causes the total real national income to decline. The decline in the national income would create excess demand for the non-traded good and disturb the initial equilibrium.

The aforementioned phenomenon is caused by three characteristics of MNEs' behavior in the host country. First, the emergence of these firms is not accompanied by net capital inflow, which leaves the total capital stock of the host country unchanged. Therefore, the capital-intensive MNEs share with the labor-intensive indigenous firms inelastically supplied local capital to produce at the initial equilibrium relative price. The shift of local capital from the national sector to the foreign sector contributes to a decline in employment and lowers the national income.

Second, the MNEs use their more advanced technology to monopolize the foreign sector. Without the monopoly distortion, the resulting market clearing relative price tends to reverse the allocation of labor and capital between the two sectors through its distributional impact at the new equilibrium point.

However, by impeding the allocative efficiency of the relative price, the monopoly power of MNEs hinders local resources from adjusting to factor re-wards, and from being optimally allocated. Third, these firms use their sector-specific stock of knowledge-based assets not only to attract the local resources, but also to retain them in the foreign sector. These assets continue to raise the marginal productivity of capital and labor from the national sector, as long as their operations last, continuously attracting additional capital and labor from the national sector, irrespective of the relative price. Thus, the operation of the global firms tends to adversely affect employment by expanding the capital-intensive foreign sector while inducing the contraction of labor-intensive national sector.[31]

Against the above negative effects of FDIs, there are also benefits, and whether the net effect would be positive or negative would depend on the special characteristics of the country analyzed. On the positive side, investment liberalization increases the level of capital formation by reducing the cost as well as the risk, thus raising the return to capital. Furthermore, the rate of technological progress within the country increases so that, even if input growth remains unchanged, output nevertheless will grow more rapidly.

Testas[32] has analyzed the above effects in terms of Tunisia's FDI liberalization experiments. The author finds that the Tunisian economy reaped significant gains both in terms of increases in the volume of investment and economic activity. It is estimated that almost 30 percent of gross domestic investment was, on average, higher than otherwise would have been if there was no FDI. As a result, the country's GDP increased. The same author[33] has used an empirical growth model to test for the hypothesis that FDI is crucial to the long-term economic prosperity of the AMU as a whole. The findings were such that FDI promotes economic growth and even political stability in such countries as Algeria where a slowdown in economic activities had generated political unrest.

Finally, AMU governments seem to have realized the growing importance of such potential effects in recent years and have done relatively better in attracting more of FDI flows to the region. As can be seen in Figure 2.2 below (based on UNCTAD's recent FDI database), there has been a significant jump in this flow since 2004 even though there was a decline in 2009.

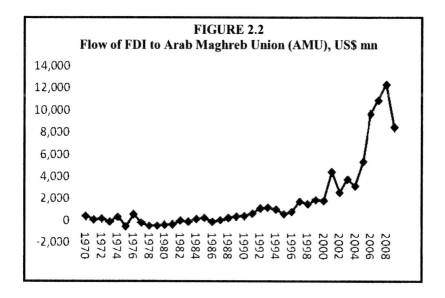

FIGURE 2.2
Flow of FDI to Arab Maghreb Union (AMU), US$ mn

CONCLUSION

Our conclusions raise some doubts about the strategies that are currently pursued by many LDCs to attract the FDI to their economies. First, these countries may attract FDI to the normally public-owned-service sectors, such as in the utilities and telecommunications, simply by liberalizing and privatizing these industries. These measures, however, could be counterproductive because of the overall implications of the monopoly power of foreign investing firms. The effects of monopoly power of the global firms are to worsen unemployment conditions and reduce the real national income of the host countries.

Second, it may be a self-defeating proposition to favor an FDI that characterizes technology over capital investment as such investment leads to the shift of inelastically supplied local capital from the labor-intensive national sector to the capital-intensive foreign sector. The shift of the local capital between the two sectors should be of concern to LDCs. It is not only the major source for the diminution of indigenous firms, but also a key factor for the rise of unemployment in the labor-surplus host country. Sure, the MNEs can bring with them the more advanced technologies, but they only hire a fraction of workers that are released by the indigenous firms because of factor-intensity differential.

The constructive measure to avoid such harmful national interests should be to exhort that the mix of FDI be capital investment. Needless to say, this may be a difficult requirement to satisfy on the part of global firms, given the current scramble for FDI by the host of governments of developing countries.

In practice, however, the impact depends on the country analyzed. Some Arab countries, namely members of the Arab Maghreb Union of North Africa, are expected to reap long term benefits due to their association agreements with the European Union.

NOTES

1. V. N. Balasubramanyam, M. Salisu, and D. Sapsford, "Foreign Direct Investment and Growth in EP and IS Countries," *The Economic Journal* 106, no. 434 (January 1996): 92.

2. Global Reach, *The Power of the International Corporations* (New York: Simon and Schuster, 1974).

3. Robert J. Barro, *Economic Growth* (New York: McGraw-Hill, 1995).

4. Raveendra N. Batra, "A General Equilibrium Model of Multinational Corporations in Developing Economies," *Oxford Economic Papers* 38, no. 2 (July 1986): 342.

5. Raveendra N. Batra, "Multinational Firms and the Theory of International Trade and Investment," *American Economic Review* 70 (June 1980): 278-90.

6. J. Bhagwati, "Domestic Distortions, Tariffs, and the Theory of Optimum Subsidy," *Journal of Political Economy* 71, no. 2 (1963): 44-50.

7. Signe Krogstrup and Linda Matar, "Foreign Direct Investment, Absorptive Capacity and Growth in the Arab World," *HEI Working Paper No. 02/2005*, Geneva: Graduate Institute of International Studies.

8. *Ibid.*

9. *Ibid.*

10. *Ibid.*

11. *Ibid.*

12. Abdelaziz Testas, "Assessing Algeria's Growth Competitiveness: Results from a Cluster Model," *The Journal of North African Studies* 11, no. 3 (September 2006): 263-74.

13. J. Blanke, F. Paua, and X. Salai-i-Martin, "The Growth Competitiveness Index: Analyzing Key Underpinnings of Sustained Economic Growth," in *The Global Competi-*

tiveness Report 2003-2004, ed. M. E. Porter, K. Schwab, X. Salai-i-Martin, and A. Lopez-Carlos (New York: World Economic Forum).

14. Ibn Khaldun, *The Muqaddimah* (Princeton, NJ: Princeton University Press).

15. Krogstrup and Matar, "Foreign Direct Investment."

16. *Ibid.*

17. *Ibid.*

18. Peter Nunnenkamp, "Foreign Direct Investment in Developing Countries: What Policymakers Should Not Do and What Economists Don't Know," *Kiel Discussion Papers* 380 (July 2001).

19. *Ibid.*

20. *Ibid.*

21. *Ibid.*

22. *Ibid.*

23. *Ibid.*

24. Abdelaziz Testas, "Analysis of Factors Constraining Intra-Maghreb Trade," *Journal of Development and Economic Policies* 6, no. 2 (June 2004): 73-92.

25. Abdelaziz Testas, "The Production Impact of Economic Integration," *Development Policy Review* 16, no. 1 (March 1998): 61-72.

26. Abdelaziz Testas, "The Import Price and Volume Effects of Integration among Developing Countries: The Case of the North Africa AMU," *Arab Economic Journal* 9, no. 23 (Spring 2001): 3-16.

27. Abdelaziz Testas, "The Advantages of an Intra-Maghreb Free Trade Area: Quantitative Estimates of the Static and Dynamic Output and Welfare Effects," *The Journal of North African Studies* 7, no. 1 (Spring 2002): 108.

28. Abdelaziz Testas, "The Significance of Trade Integration among Developing Countries: A Comparison between ASEAN and AMU," *Journal of Economic Development* 23, no. 1 (June 1998): 117-30.

29. Abdelaziz Testas, "The Dynamic Impact of Tariff Liberalization between the European and Maghreb Unions: An Empirical Analysis," *The Journal of North African Studies* 4, no. 4 (Winter 1999): 60.

30. Abdelaziz Testas, "The European Union's 'Global Approach' to the Mediterranean Area," *Development Policy Review* 17, no. 1 (March 1999): 25-41.

31. Nunnenkamp, "Foreign Direct Investment in Developing Countries."

32. Abdelaziz Testas, "The Contribution of EU Investment to Tunisia's Economic Development," *The Journal of North African Studies* 5, no. 2 (Summer 2000): 9-24.

33. Abdelaziz Testas, "Foreign Direct Investment, Capital Accumulation and Economic Growth in the Maghreb: Empirical Findings and Implications for Regional Integration and Political Stability," *The Journal of North African Studies* 8, no. 2 (Summer 2003): 75-91.

Chapter 3
Development Policy, Endogenous Competency, and Competitiveness in the Caribbean: The Challenge of the Developmental State Approach

*Nikolaos Karagiannis, Zagros Madjd-Sadjadi &
Doria Stitts*

ABSTRACT

This chapter seeks to provide a Caribbean Developmental State framework. It is recognized that the public sectors of many countries have undergone changes since the 1980s, as governments try to respond to the challenges of the new millennium. Recent years have seen wider-ranging reforms than any other period of the twentieth century, although both the pace and extent of these reforms are greater in some countries than in others.

Thus, states require an alternative. They need to have strong policy instruments which will enable them to plan and finance their strategic goals such as job creation, higher mass living standards, R&D, industrial competency, environmental protection, etc. This retooling of state policy-making requires a re-thinking of the form of government intervention and, especially, an emphasis on its "modern" developmental role. This is a crucial challenge today facing countries in general, and Caribbean islands in particular.

The argument of this chapter is as follows. The first part summarizes past development efforts in the Caribbean. The second main section seeks to chart a "Caribbean" Developmental State framework: an institutional system which appears to have been used with enormous success in East Asia but, unfortunately, has been neglected in the region. The final main part of the chapter identifies key strategic requirements and offers alternative policy recommendations, which the Developmental State approach implies and suggests.

INTRODUCTION

The political economy of development in the Caribbean is characterized by trade relations that take place in a highly monopolized global market; policy issues which serve the interests of transnational corporations and are influenced by multilateral agencies; a lack of focus and clear policies; and, "pork barrel" policies and interference by the political directorates. Foreign capital controls the islands' productive structures—and particularly the most dynamic sectors of their economies—repatriates a high volume of profits, and benefits very narrow sectors and activities. Technological-industrial dependence has been consolidated, and export production is determined by demand from the main hegemonic centers. Foreign financing has become necessary in two forms: to cover the existing deficits, and to "finance" development by means of loans. Caribbean nations encounter unyielding domestic obstacles to their self-determined self-sustained growth, which leads to the accumulation of deficits.

Against this general background, the tourism industry is being seen not just as an economic activity capable of creating income and jobs for the islands' inhabitants and earning important foreign exchange, but as one of the most promising sectors for their future economic growth. However, tourism has further subjected Caribbean nations to outside dependence. The result of this dependence makes Caribbean economies vulnerable and more susceptible to external shocks, as well as more dependent on foreign exchange (Higgins 1994: 5).

PAST CARIBBEAN DEVELOPMENT EFFORTS

This section discerns four broad phases in Caribbean development since the end of World War II (the 1950s up to the mid-1960s; the late 1960s and the 1970s; the 1980s; and the 1990s and beyond). The first phase, the 1950s and 1960s, was characterized by the advocacy of the modernizing potential of industrialization and economic diversification as a means of overcoming the traditional Caribbean problem of dependence on agriculture, and created expectations that other economic benefits would also follow. In some countries, the emergence of modern export industries in the mineral sector was a strong sign of this development thrust.

The theoretical insights underpinning this strategy were provided by W. Arthur Lewis who saw industrialization as an essential part of a program for agricultural progress by providing new jobs.[1] From this point of departure, Lewis sought to set out a policy of industrialization for the Caribbean designed to overcome the dual problems of markets and resources: the region was short of capital, industrial power was expensive and the available raw material base limited, but wage rates were low by the standards of the developed world. Many favorable industries were based not on the use of local raw materials but on the processing of imported inputs. Yet, the small size of individual domestic markets necessitated the establishment of a regional customs union as an essential prelude to any vigorous policy of industrialization (Payne and Sutton 2001: 3).

For Lewis, industrialization was like a "snowball": once started, it would move of its own momentum and get bigger and bigger as it went along. But regional import substitution would account for only a small part of the industrial output necessary to generate full employment; export-oriented industrialization was the main requirement. To attract foreign manufacturers (and therefore get the snowball rolling), Lewis recommended the implementation of a package of investment incentives modeled upon the Puerto Rican experience. Eventually, the inflow of foreign investment would produce sufficient profits, generate sufficient local savings, and transmit sufficient skills to local people to set in motion self-sustaining growth (Payne and Sutton 2001: 4).

Lewis' prescription for industrialization had an immediate impact on newly emerging Commonwealth Caribbean nations. Indeed, foreign capital responded to the entreaties of the region's governments and flowed into the area in substantial amounts, bringing in its wake several manufacturing industries. By 1967, manufacturing contributed 15 percent of the GDP in Jamaica and 16 percent in Trinidad, while the figures for Guyana and Barbados were 13 percent and 9 percent respectively.[2] However, the industries established were only "final-touch" firms, were based on the assembly of imported inputs, had relatively little value added, and generally failed to penetrate export markets. Furthermore, the industries that were set up produced few jobs, had often limited commitment to local development, and were finding it profitable to move their operations to other locales offering new or better packages of inducements and conditions.

The other new industry into which the Caribbean moved in a major way in the 1950s and 1960s was tourism. In some islands, tourism was heralded as the "road to prosperity" even though this sector was vulnerable to vagaries of world markets and the international political economy. As the industry was geared to the affluent North American (and, to a lesser degree, European) societies, it was able to compete only by maintaining high standards of accommodation and hospitality. This required reliance on foreign capital and imports, especially of food, brought about inflated import bills and profit repatriation. To a considerable extent, therefore, tourism became an "enclave" within the Caribbean economy having few linkages with, and contributing little to, the development of other sectors.

Overall, as the Commonwealth Caribbean Regional Secretariat admitted in 1972:[3]

[The post-war era of growth represented] a continuation of the centuries-old pattern of West Indian economy—growth without development; growth accompanied by imbalances and distortions; growth generated from outside rather than within; growth without the fullest possible use of West Indian manpower, entrepreneurial, capital and natural resources; growth resting on a foreign rather than indigenous technological base; and growth accompanied by imported consumption patterns.

As these weaknesses of the modernization view were being exposed and debated by the region's governments and advisers, radical scholars emphasized the dependence of the Caribbean economy on hegemonic centers for: markets and supplies, transfers of income and capital, banking and financial services, business and technical skills, and even for ideas about themselves.[4] While part of broader international currents of radical analysis, Caribbean dependency thought had its own special characteristics, associated with the theory of plantation economy and society.

During the second phase, in the late 1960s and early 1970s, these insights grew into a whole school of thought characterized by the "theory of plantation economy." The bulk of the explanation had come from systematic examination of the instruments that control the Caribbean economies, which brought about a lack of capacity to manipulate the operative elements of the economic system,[5] and several "underdevelopment biases" of plantation agriculture.[6] These various arguments collectively constituted a powerful critique of the condition of economic dependency within the Commonwealth Caribbean, undermining to a very considerable degree the intellectual credibility of the conventional modernization strategy hitherto pursued by Caribbean governments.

Indeed, the vivid excoriation of this strategy as "industrialization by invitation" is a memorable rejection of Lewis' policy prescription. Yet, in the 1970s, Caribbean countries faced severe economic difficulties. Consequently, the validity of the orthodox model of development came increasingly under question in political discussions and, in a number of countries, the state was pushed into a position of greater involvement in the management of the economy. However, even if "the historical options of Caribbean economies are limited either to a 'non-capitalist' path of development for transforming the productive forces and liberating the political and social order, or to the continuation of the neo-colonial mode,"[7] no strong model of development and no thorough strategies were offered. This serious shortcoming became the beginning of a vacuum in the Caribbean development debate. Besides, the collapse of the Grenadian revolution almost brought to an end the second phase in Caribbean development.

In the 1980s (the third broad phase in Caribbean development), as far as the region was concerned, the United States managed to reshape the agenda of politics and political economy to the point where it was able to lay down the parameters of what could be done and even what could be articulated. In accordance with the broad tenets of neoliberalism, its main goal in respect of economic development was to create in the region a growing number of market-based economies capable of competing successfully in international export markets. Besides, the neoliberal policy package was enforced by the International Monetary Fund and the World Bank under the "structural adjustment" prescription. This policy prescription was premised upon squeezing the state, increasing profit margins, weakening trade unions, eliminating inflation through the adoption of monetarist macroeconomic management, and boosting local growth by means of supply-side policies.

The international recession of 1980-82 severely reduced demand for a number of the region's main exports—particularly bauxite, petroleum products, and sugar—and lowered the number of tourists visiting Caribbean islands. This recession created, in effect, three crises in one in nearly all Caribbean economies: balance of payments constraints, fiscal imbalances, and a national debt crisis. Desperate for financial support, Commonwealth Caribbean nations turned to the IMF and other multilateral financial institutions. As a result, their governments were forced to follow the neoliberal prescription during the 1980s. The favored measures were always the same: liberalization of foreign exchange and import controls, devaluation of the currency, and the deflation of domestic demand. After following this prescription, the economy in question would be ready to return to the international marketplace able to achieve higher levels of exports and economic growth.

What is striking about the Caribbean's embrace of neoliberalism in the 1980s is that the intellectual driving force behind the region's development strategy came from outside the region. Nonetheless, the social costs of such neoliberal policies, measured in terms of unemployment, inflation, and sharply declining living standards, were immense. Besides, at the end of the 1980s, Caribbean economies still faced fundamental structural problems associated with the character of their production base as well as with the distribution of their economic assets. Critical analyses of the economic and social impact of structural adjustment did appear and had their impact, especially in drawing attention to the peculiarly harsh costs imposed by such programs (Polanyi-Levitt 1991—among others). Yet, neoliberal prescriptions did not succeed in charting any sort of realistic alternative course of action for Caribbean governments in the critical arenas of economic management and national development.

The last phase, the 1990s and beyond, was characterized by what might be called the consolidation of the neoliberal revolution, tempered only by the realization that more attention had to be paid to human resource development if the new technological imperatives of a globalizing economy were not to pass the region by. Development was seen as a market-driven private sector-led process. The role of the state should be to meet the demands for "good governance" imposed by the international financial institutions, and thereby fashioned to serve efficiently the logic of deregulated competitive markets and integrated global production, led and directed by transnational corporations. The orthodoxy was best expressed by the prime minister of Barbados Owen Arthur in 1996:[8]

> Generally, the strategy has to accept the reality of the globalization of economic forces rather than hanker after a less complicated but impoverished past. The strategy must also recognize that the Caribbean countries, singly and as a group, must make the transition from the old age of preferences to the new age of reciprocity in its international economic relationships. In so doing, it must be designed to minimize the costs and dislocations associated with the transition, and to put in place mechanisms that can allow the region to exploit the market opportunities which are being created by the international liberalization of trade and the formation of mega trade blocs.

CHARTING THE CARIBBEAN DEVELOPMENTAL STATE FRAMEWORK

The Present Context

Recently, there has been much talk of the poor endogenous competency of Caribbean islands, although an increasing number of commentators now seem to be becoming increasingly nervous about this, with the trade account of the balance of payments of Caribbean economies in substantial deficit—due to the low levels of exports and high levels of imports—and the slowdown in economic activity causing concern.[9] Indeed, economic activity in the region has slowed down considerably in the last two decades and growth has been uneven and relatively weak, even though the slowdown in economic activity has not been uniform across all the Caribbean countries. The central element of these discussions to which people refer (particularly in Jamaica) is the continuous increase in the total national debt,[10] and the questions that arise are, what are the sources of this economic performance, and can it be sustained under existing policies?

In the Caribbean, it can be argued that monetary and fiscal policies during the last years attempt to provide an environment conducive to attracting foreign investments while holding down real wages, and supporting the growth of a dual economy. We cannot expect a better performance in the near future under present policies because the real base of economic dynamism has been neglected; indeed that very neglect will undoubtedly hold back the growth of Caribbean economies. It is clear that, in today's circumstances, neoliberal policies cause substantial balance of payments, and other economic and social problems. The fundamentals of Caribbean economies are not right, and their much vaunted "Western-style" modernization and laissez-faire antidote are increasingly seen to be an illusion.

In most of the Caribbean islands, the primary sector is struggling to maintain output and, at the same time, in common with worldwide trends, is tending to become less labor-intensive (even though agriculture's contribution to employment is significant in a number of Caribbean economies). In fact, there has been a significant decline in the proportionate importance of local primary production during the past two decades (IICA 1998: Tables 1 and 18; UNCTAD 2000 and 2003). The declining share (%) of primary production in GDP for most Caribbean economies may reflect the reduced dependence on agriculture. However, most countries in the region are net food importers, and only a few Caribbean countries have achieved some success in transforming their economy from a primary production to a service and/or industry-led economy (IICA 1998: chapter 4).

The ups and downs in the performance of both the agricultural and agro-industrial sectors in the 1990s and the period 2000-9 were due, in large measure, to the problems experienced in the main export sectors and the general stagnation in the other economic sub-sectors among and within Caribbean countries. For those local economies reporting favorable, albeit low average growth rates, this may be attributed to improved production techniques in the major export sectors and relatively good performance in domestic food production (IICA 1998: Table 18 and Annex: Statistical Tables; CARICOM 2000; ECLAC various years).[11]

Besides, according to available data and statistical information (CARICOM 2000; ECLAC various years; UNCTAD various years), the manufacturing sector within the Caribbean has had very mixed fortunes during the 1970s, 1980s, 1990s, and 2000-9 period. Many of the manufacturing units in the region are little more than *enclave* operations of larger extra-regional firms. As such, they tend to transfer only limited skills to the region and are always vulnerable to recession. Subsidiary manufacturing units are always easier to close down than those closer to the home base of the company concerned, and history has shown that the Caribbean is vulnerable to just this sort of action. What's more, there is a widening gap between these firms, mainly transnationals that typically reside in the Caribbean islands, which are integrating at a faster pace with the global economy, and other firms in the slower integrating Caribbean countries.

In the past, the agricultural and industrial sectors were seen as not providing sufficient employment opportunities. This is in part a reflection of the general unattractiveness of agricultural problem islands to industrial investment due to factors such as a lack of skills, an underdeveloped infrastructure, etc. Resources in Caribbean economies have been underutilized, and the growth of resources has been slow, or very slow. The situation is exacerbated by a range of constraining factors which may be summarized as follows (IICA 1998: 25-7):[12]

1. Inappropriate policy environment;
2. Weak institutional framework; and,
3. Declining productivity and competitiveness.

On the other hand, estimates show that tourism is the only sector of regional GDP that has consistently increased its share of total income since the 1980s. Indeed, allowing for some fluctuations, the tourism industry has been the only major sector that has grown steadily in importance during the last twenty-five years or so in the Caribbean region (CTO various years; PIOJ various years).[13] In addition, the sector has given Caribbean countries employment to a sizable proportion of their population.

However, tourism has further subjected Caribbean economies to outside dependence, making them highly vulnerable. The result of this dependence makes the Caribbean more susceptible to external shocks and more dependent on foreign exchange. This dependence exacerbates the region's instability in employment and national income levels (Higgins 1994: 5). Besides, the growth of tourism (and other related services) has had negligible effects on the development of manufacturing industry. Indeed, the benefits from tourism growth have been inadequately exploited because of insufficient linkages with commodity production sectors, and failure to upgrade complementary and related service industries like information services, communication, and banking. As a consequence, there are few linkages between the local sectors of Caribbean economies as well as a serious lack of diversification in production.

Adopting the Strategic Approach

An important point which should be made concerns the relationship between Caribbean governments and local communities within the context of the kind of problems confronting their societies, as well as the goals governments have embraced from the standpoint of endogenous development. Attention will have to be drawn to the part played by tourism in the region, as the lack of overall integrated policies has limited its contribution to Caribbean countries' socio-economic development.

In order to maximize the benefits from tourism, the sector must provide an effective stimulus for local agriculture and agro-industrial production. The fact that decisions relating to a particular sector (e.g., tourism industry) tend to have broader implications for the national economy as a whole requires a clear examination of the interacting influences between the promising activities from the point of view of endogenous competency, and those that may provide short-term benefits but offer little hope as a secure basis for future national well-being.

In formulating policies for economic restructuring and diversification, it is essential, therefore, to recognize the critical elements of the system in terms of deriving a long-term strategy. Simultaneously, it is necessary to juxtapose certain facts relating to the structure of Caribbean economies in order to provide what might be called "an integrated development perspective of the system," and to show the relative position of endogenous strategic components. Failure to do so can easily lead not only to short-run, highly partial considerations, and short-term measures dictated by pressing problems (e.g., national debt, stagflation) but also to the adoption of an ad hoc approach to development which may be in basic conflict with the goal of a stronger economic fabric (Ramsaran 1983: 378; Karagiannis 2002).

Prospects for future growth in the region have been frustrated and lowered significantly due to foreign exploitation and underutilization of existing resources, and the severe economic difficulties Caribbean countries have repeatedly faced. The underutilization of part of their productive capacity is proof of this considerable growth potential. As Caribbean economies operate at well below their level of physical and human capacity, policies to increase aggregate demand can yield substantial economic gains.

Thus, a first requirement of a thorough development strategy is that the expansion of tourism represents a net addition to the effective use of resources and, therefore, to the overall growth of the system. Tourism growth and, thus, overall economic growth will be led by the growth of demand for the local tourism product (i.e., higher occupancy rates), which would translate into higher profits and savings. On the other hand, aggregate demand must be sufficient enough to stimulate production up to the adequate rate of capacity utilization. However, growth of local production must go hand in hand with special consideration of the countries' external trade. In connection with this, the competitiveness of Caribbean economies must come to the fore (Lopez 1998: 6).

In order to expand industrial production and employment, firms must have the financial means to invest in the necessary machinery, capital equipment, critical kinds of science and technology initiatives, and skills training and up-grading, and short-run bottlenecks preventing a fuller utilization of capacities have to be taken care of. Likewise, the renewal of tourism requires investment in tourism plants, facilities, and supporting infrastructure. These bottlenecks may include a lack of the necessary resources and skills, difficulties in obtaining finance, and a lack of business confidence.

Hence, a second requirement of a Developmental State strategy is that selective economic policies should provide the resources and stimuli to carry out the investments in both working and fixed capital, infrastructure, and the *accelerators* of development necessary to raise output and to improve the production and commercial conditions of firms and hotels at national and local levels (Cowling 1990: 24; Lopez 1998: 11-12). Active fiscal policy ought to carry out the investments necessary to improve the supply conditions of businesses and to support the other expenditures associated with the selective policy. Monetary policy ought to ensure that sufficient financial resources are channeled to firms and to intermediary agencies at reasonable interest rates. Besides, it should be considered that the increase in output would translate into higher profits and savings (Lopez 1998: 12).

However, bottlenecks at the firm (hotel) or macro level often hamper a more efficient capacity utilization. These bottlenecks must be seriously considered, would require addressing a number of issues simultaneously, and accordingly a medium and long-term development strategy should have as a basic requirement a close link with a deliberate industrial strategy. Such a directed state action should: 1. consolidate and improve existing production lines; 2. select and give priority to investments in new and technically promising activities; and, 3. adjust quickly in anticipation of, and in response to, global changes in demand and technological innovation (Lopez 1998: 12-13; Bernal 2000: 107). The criteria are obviously dynamic and forward-looking.

Indeed, industrial targeting should single out areas of emphasis in selected fields, and should be directed toward strengthening Caribbean countries' industrial core and upgrading international competitiveness. It should be concentrated on a few focal areas having favorable prospects for development, and be selectively designed so as to support a small group of key dynamic firms managed by modern entrepreneurs. Even a small group of key propulsive industries can be instrumental in emphasizing the accelerators of competency and growth, exert pressure to adapt on other supply firms, and introduce modern concepts of policy making and labor relations. The various spheres of policy (e.g., industrial policy, regional policy) should be directed toward consolidating these focal areas, correcting the imbalances which emerge in the wake of restructuring and repositioning, reconciling contradictory elements therein, and smoothing the path for industrial growth.

What has been asserted should not be taken to imply a rejection of the problems that could arise with the proposed development strategy. But to face them, a sound economic approach ought to complement short-run measures with thorough plans for the future, which include long-term industrial or structural change strategies aimed at diversifying local production, strengthening technological capabilities, and promoting innovation. Greater levels of production, employment, and profits that would be achieved in the short term owing to the fuller use of available resources, would actually spur a transition to more structurally efficient economies. Part of this increased production and income in Caribbean territories would go to higher spending on the modern factors of competency and lead to faster development of skills of the labor force. Not only higher profits would allow additional investment spending but also a greater proportion of income growth will be channeled toward investment. Hence, in the future, it would be relatively easier to incorporate more modern technology and increase productivity, while at the same time raising accumulation rates (Lopez 1998: 18-19).[14]

Obviously, for purposes of designing endogenous competency strategies to achieve the development of productive forces and the transformation and diversification of Caribbean economies, technically proficient strategic planning is absolutely necessary—indeed, it is inevitable—and should be directed toward the creation of new conditions and processes to be effectively and directly determined by the planning authorities. Strategic planning is a pragmatic attempt to increase the countries' long-run capacity to transform themselves by building up the infrastructure and the requisite skills. It is this national strategic planning that can give Caribbean nations their internal autonomy, and determine their capacity for self-determined self-sustained growth and development. In the development of these strategies, local communities generate not only the capacity to spread the use of modern knowledge and industrial techniques into all elements of the economic transformation so as to spur local industrial activities, but they also create a dynamic basis for engagement in the international economy through higher levels of exports (Thomas 1974: 58-60).

Moreover, contrary to the "current orthodoxy,"[15] it appears important to emphasize that it would not suffice to establish technologically modern export sectors.[16] Export-oriented production may benefit very narrow sectors and generate limited resources. In fact, Caribbean countries' exports have not usually developed on initial platforms of production for local needs and internal requirements. Instead, local production should be oriented toward satisfying local demand in the first instance with export specialization occurring as an extension of this. The aim should be to bring about a general improvement in the competency and efficiency of Caribbean economies, in the level of technological infrastructure they rely on, and in the quality of workmanship and service, so that more and more activities may become increasingly competitive.

Modern production techniques, precisely because of their flexibility, make it possible to manufacture in small series on a viable basis. Targeting and flexibility are possible, especially if they can draw on modern industrial planning. Assuming predominance of clear focal areas and initiatives carried out by both competent and effective policy makers and dynamic local businesses, demand for imported capital and goods could decline and exports of local products expand.

Given the recovery of production of local industries and the improvement of their competitiveness, a large part of the additional goods produced will be devoted to exports. Consequently, Caribbean nations would make a greater and better use of their productive resources and capacity, while at the same time easing the constraints on their balance of payments.

In addition, as indigenous technology is the basis for an organic integration of domestic production and demand structures (i.e., human capital formation coupled with consistent technical progress), investment priorities and the choice of technique are determined by the strategies of transformation and diversification, and by the product choices to which these strategies give rise. The overall purpose is to increase the capacity of Caribbean nations to respond at the level of the government, firms, and the population as a whole.

In order to assure realization of these development goals, economically active states must play a significant role. Likewise, well-educated, well-trained, and efficient technocratic planners play key roles. The government provides the "national purpose" framework, while the technocrats supply planning and overview. This "national purpose" proves possible to bring together social and political forces in the interests of socially defined agendas. In addition, the growth-oriented transformation must lead in a corporatist direction and strategic partnership between a developmental state, forward-looking businesses, and various social segments. A broad-based consensus is also required and could afford scope for national strategic planning. Besides, if such thorough alternative strategies are to solve such problems, they presuppose participation. Indeed, participation is a vital element ensuring that sufficient motivation, creativity, and human effort are forthcoming to guarantee that such technically proficient strategies can be successfully carried out in the Caribbean.

This is a more feasible and realistic suggestion in light of the fact that these strata and decision makers which serve the powerful interests of the hegemonic centers and the dominant transnational corporations are those which tend to reject the concept of local development in the region, and seek to maintain the economic and political order of dependent productive structures by siding with backward-looking segments, officials, and policy makers; by engaging in modern experiments with neoliberalism; and also as a result of deteriorating terms of trade, and the astonishing technological developments taking place in the leading industrial economies. However, only under such national strategic planning systems and well-conceived and vigorously executed development plans will trade serve a different function, because Caribbean economies themselves will be reoriented to serve different purposes.

Lastly, any economy is underpinned and imbued by social values, codes of behavior, and ethics, which are in turn reflected in the structure and functioning of government sector institutions and private sector firms. As political will may not be clearly agglomerated and administrative capacity is inadequate in Caribbean states, governments have not been successful in indicating a clear course for the public sector to adopt. Yet, the adjustment of their social and political conditions to their urgent social and developmental needs cannot be avoided. If Caribbean countries are to develop growth-oriented, learning-based productive activities, therefore, it would be necessary to adopt a number of measures to remodel their key social, economic, and institutional factors that will be required to provide the necessary underpinning (Clayton 2001: 15). More importantly, these thorough development strategies assume a much better state action, and would require efficient and competent administrative personnel. But so does any strategy capable of overcoming barriers and laying down the basis of endogenous competency and growth in any developing economy.

Devising the necessary action to stimulate tourism growth and industrial regeneration, while raising the quantity and quality of productive investment necessary to allow the fullest and most efficient utilization of existing resources, seems to be a more sensible way to confront the future. Such an approach seems, certainly, a better option for the endogenous development and competency of Caribbean economies, than a frantic search for accelerated, "Western-style" modernization—a "vision" that decision and policy makers in the region aspire to. The alternative and more realistic development paradigm would require the pursuit of Developmental State strategies and policies. This is what Caribbean economies need (Lopez 1998: 19).

ALTERNATIVE DEVELOPMENT POLICY RECOMMENDATIONS

Industrial strategies have not been seen to be pivotal in Caribbean economies; thus, they have not been developed in a systematic or coherent fashion as a centerpiece of their governments' approach to economic policy making. State interventions have usually been seen as *reactions* to pressing problems, and the policies which flow from these interventions appear to be consonant with the *market failure* analysis. Therefore, the general concept of a developmental role for the state is rather alien to the general economic and political culture in the region (Karagiannis [2002: 54-55] provides a clear distinction between the "mainstream market failure view" and the "strategic Developmental State argument").

Further, fiscal budgets in the Caribbean *via* the political process often reflect the view of the political parties in power, and the class and interest group biases are usually maintained. Thus, although this deliberate policy is used, in fact the politicization of the budgetary process in Caribbean states highlights programs and policies which are akin to what is called "pork barrel policies." This process has a great deal of importance in shaping the fiscal policies of Caribbean governments (Jones-Hendrickson 1985: 83-4).

While the state has survived as a democratic institution (largely so), it lost a great deal of its effectiveness as a development tool because it was transformed into a mechanism for winning elections and meeting populist demands. Because of the "winner takes all syndrome" in Caribbean nations, the state became an instrument of disintegration rather than an institution around which society could cohere to deal with the development challenge. In a small society, the state is a large institution as an employer and dispenser of resources—hence the intense desire by various groups, not just special interests, to capture it.

During the last two decades or so, neoliberal policies have been the central routes to modern economic solutions in the region. But there are serious doubts about whether these economic policies have been translated into significant social and economic development, endogenous competency, and industrial competitiveness. While appropriate macroeconomic policies can contribute much toward enhancing the performance of local economies, nevertheless such policies only deal with the "symptoms" of deeper structural problems. For this reason, the construction of a production-based approach to economic development and a much sharper focus on strategic industrial policy are seen to be necessary to resolve these deeper problems, and would offer concrete alternative solutions to Caribbean economies. Some alternative policy recommendations for the Caribbean development discourse in general, and tourism industry in particular, are outlined below.

Macroeconomic Steering

Given the importance of macroeconomic steering, there are a number of measures that the government could take in an effort to facilitate conscious development efforts. An appropriate macroeconomic policy should pay particular attention to:

1. a faster, non-inflationary growth of domestic demand;
2. the efficiency and effectiveness of government spending and taxation (which should be maximized);
3. sound government finances/investments;
4. the management of the national debt, which should be designed in the context of the long-term strategy for overall development;
5. competitiveness (the role of imports/exports and the growth of exports);
6. the relationship between the financial sector and the productive sector; and,
7. the social and political environment (or sociopolitical characteristics).

A proactive fiscal policy action would: 1. attempt to reduce non-essential over-consumption; 2. emphasize a prudent government expenditure management and planning (i.e., long-term planned investments in human capital formation, skills, technological capacity, technical change, R&D, innovation, and information); and, 3. consider alternative sources of government revenue.

By curtailing over-consumption, the amounts of local savings available for investment purposes could be markedly increased. In addition, various national savings plans and savings vehicles can increase the levels and shares of Caribbean economies' savings. The savings thus enforced could be channeled by the government into productive prioritized investments. Furthermore, higher levels of output and income ensuing from a higher degree of capacity utilization and a better utilization of equipment can be the source of higher levels of savings required to match higher levels of investment (which will bring about further increase in output and income levels and so on).[17]

Monetary policy, on the other hand, ought to: 1. ensure that the overall development effort is not to be thwarted by endemic short-termism, speculative ventures, and "capital flight" (that can actually starve the real economy of in-

vestment capital); 2. provide a stable financial framework for the successful implementation of government policy; and, 3. ensure that sufficient financial resources are channeled to dynamic industries and to intermediary agencies at
reasonable interest rates. This will require significant state intervention in the
capital market by means of both direct control measures and interest rate policies. In particular, Caribbean governments will have to issue direct instructions
to the banks, close off the options available for rent seeking and capital flight,
and guide prioritized investments by selective credit policies.

As financial institutions have a critically important role in this growth
process, it is particularly important that they are well-managed, have a clear set
of strategic goals, and promote longer time horizons. In this regard, the government must take steps to ensure that the financial services sector is properly
supervised (Clayton 2001: 16). Together, appropriate monetary and exchange
rate policies to facilitate productive initiatives, and higher levels of national
savings to finance higher levels of investment, are essential.

Investments on the Accelerators

Recent developments in the financial markets have significantly encouraged
endemic short-termism and various speculative ventures. These developments,
in conjunction with weak or absent state supervision, can foster a dysfunctional
business culture and a "casino economy" mindset, in which insider trading, conflicts of interest, and more direct forms of corruption can increasingly become
common (Clayton 2001: 16).

Further, some support the view that the hotel sector's high operating costs
in Caribbean islands is a serious barrier which may discourage productive investments. The only logical alternative, then, is to consider the capacity-creating
aspect of government expenditure, and Caribbean states should rely heavily on
higher levels of public investment. Indeed, planned investments on knowledge,
training, technological innovation, and research, will boost the endogenous competency of local economies toward higher rates of economic growth and "high
wages high productivity." The key issue here is that investment responsibilities
should be closely tailored to the needs of the private sector (again, private investment in plant, facilities, supporting infrastructure, etc. is highly desirable
and essential).

Investments in education, health, and nutrition of the poor, in particular, not
only meet real, basic needs of a wide spectrum of the Caribbean population and
increase their welfare directly, but also enhance their capacities for productive
labor. Indeed, such investments and/or higher wages can affect the productivity
of the poor, thereby enabling them to earn higher incomes, which in turn would
permit them to purchase the bundle of goods and services they need with their
own earnings (necessary to open up their access to opportunities for a full life).
But, on the other hand, social programs are likely to have limited impact on the
countries' economic growth and competitiveness unless the overall development

strategies also contain explicit consideration of growth-generating policies and competency-inducing plans.

Strategic Planning

The growth in dominance, the global perspective, and ambitions of the major financial and industrial corporations may cut across the interests of any particular nation. The fundamental issue relates to the asymmetry of power between these large corporations and local communities. This power can be used to secure their own objectives, often at the expense of communities (Cowling 1990: 12). The ultimate consequence of transnationalism is to tear loose the productive capacities of the region. This is an important issue in the Caribbean case. Besides, the direction in which Caribbean tourism is pointed at present seems to be somewhat random, depending on the current state of the global market rather than based on long-term development plans. Thus, we have a basis for recommending a framework of, and establishing a role for, strategic planning in Caribbean nations.

The second and related reason for requiring strategic planning is the systematic short-termism of the market system, given that financial institutions usually adopt a short-term perspective with regard to investment, and impose this perspective on firms (industries, hotels, resorts, etc.), especially the small ones. Consequently, new or small establishments may be severely constrained in their investment ambitions by the short-term perspective of the financial institutions, since it is these firms (and hotels) which will find difficulties to fund their own growth.

This sort of financial environment is hardly conducive to the rational planning of the long-term future of the industrial base. Short-term decision making is crowding out long-term issues, and leaving businesses weaker in the long term. Hence, within Caribbean economies, we need to establish institutional structures to plan for the future. Just as there are systemic arguments for relying on the creative dynamics of the market forces to play a centrally important role in Caribbean economies, there are parallel arguments for imposing on these market forces coherent strategies, within which they are allowed to operate (Cowling 1990: 11-12, 13-14).

For local production to achieve its full potential, it is imperative that the state should stay focused and draw up thorough strategies for implementation. Initially it is important to divide consideration of the key issues related to the structure of Caribbean industries into three sections: 1. issues influenced by government policy and general policy issues; 2. issues influenced by specific industries or sectors; and, 3. market-driven issues. On this account, we limit strategic intervention to those parts of Caribbean economies where government intervention is going to have its most significant potential impact on their overall dynamism and intensive economic growth. Indeed, strategic industrial policy targets and centers around strategic sectors, which can be expected to fuel future economic growth. By recognizing differentiation of sectors and industries, policy can address the problems that are rooted in the development of these sectors and industries, and thus become effective.[18,19]

In some sectors, the region already has a strong basis on which to build (e.g., tourism, agro-processing, food production, etc.). These sectors require significant investment spending, rejuvenation, and repositioning, and have to address a number of serious economic, social, and environmental issues simultaneously; but all of these problems are, in principle, solvable. Provided that the immediate problems are solved, the targeted sectors are clearly capable of considerable further expansion. In fact, the mutually beneficial relationship between tourism and agro-industry can provide the foundation which alternative endogenous development strategies can build on. When the priorities are right, scarce resources will increasingly be allocated efficiently, productivity and profitability will increase, and the propulsive and dynamic sectors will become increasingly attractive to the private sector.

In addition, the growth process is expected to lead to a widening of the local markets,[20] which in turn will require and/or bring about better transportation and communications systems. Consequently, after resources have been developed and/or put to use, changes in technology will broaden the Caribbean production base, will provide sufficient stimulus to the mobilization of resources of all kinds and/or the inducement to invest, will bring about a net addition to the effective use of resources and, therefore, to the overall growth of the region.

The proposed approach takes into account the inter-relations among a number of "stylized facts" such as local resources, capital, social structure, the level of technology and skills, scale, and transformation.[21] Such a pragmatic approach can successfully contribute to long-term supply-side initiatives aimed at creating or promoting particular sectors and prioritized activities, and create external economies and economies of scale, conditions, and opportunities conducive to faster growth of existing and incoming enterprises (a "big push"). Economies of scale and learning will bring about multiple effects on, and changes in, the structure of local economies. The object, of course, would be to increase value-added to the sectors and strengthen intersectoral linkages (e.g., tourism and commodity production sectors), which would then be capable of spilling their expansionary forces into other sectors and activities: the support and development of indigenous resources, firms, and industries; the maximum utilization of investment (mainly in R&D and skills); the removal of bottlenecks on the demand side which are imposed by the narrow size of the local markets and their poor manufacturing base; an improvement in the range of services likely to be available to people and to industry (e.g., transportation, information); the exploitation of external economies; the application of productivity-enhancing production methods and techniques so as to raise efficiency and competitiveness; the restructuring, transformation, and diversification of Caribbean economic activity; and, the capacity to correct the Caribbean tendency toward external disequilibrium and high dependency on foreign economic activity, and withstand the effects of future structural changes and cyclical downswings.

Production and Operations Quality

In this technological age, a quality emphasis should encompass the entire organization of local production, from suppliers to customers, including: equipment layout; purchasing and installation of proper machinery and equipment; layout strategy (e.g., capacity needs, inventory requirements, etc.); facility location and expansion; supporting facilities and utilities; products technology training; maintenance training; sanitary arrangements and utility specifications; refrigeration specifications; implementation of quality control programs; and just-in-time decisions and scheduling.

For both local firms and national economies to compete effectively in the global economy, products and services must meet global quality and price expectations. As the Caribbean area faces crucial challenges, especially in light of strong international competition, it is essential to ensure that quality standards and value for money are improved. Inferior products will harm Caribbean firms' revenues and profitability, and will further deteriorate the balance of payments of Caribbean economies (Heizer and Render 1996: 79-80).

As firms in the Caribbean begin to produce quality products and services, it is extremely important for the economy to support the effective and efficient distribution of these products. The role of intermediaries and partners along the distribution channel must be managed and monitored in order to ensure that products and services are coordinated, delivered, and processed in the most optimal manner. While the location of the Caribbean basin provides an excellent opportunity for product transport, the Caribbean is also part of a disperse market with varying levels of trade. Thus, challenges related to the variability in freight rates, the number and size of carriers, the transit time and distance related to the various routes, and port infrastructure must be addressed in order to avoid any detrimental effects on the supply-chain management strategies of the economy (Wilmsmeier and Hoffmann 2008). Besides, as manufacturing firms globalize their operations, concepts such as green manufacturing, product life-cycle management, and the use of information technology need to be addressed in order to meet profitability and sales objectives (Chowdary 2005).

Understanding the cultures of the various economies involved while delivering superior customer service must also be taken into consideration within the strategic framework. As brands become global, generating loyal customers and retaining those customers is a key factor in sustaining growth and profitability objectives. As the market becomes more competitive and saturated with a variety of brands, it will be important to develop a relationship with consumers through an in-depth understanding of their buying habits, frequency of purchases, transactional modes, and perceptions of quality and price. Utilizing interactive media such as email, the internet, and other direct marketing techniques can allow the consumer to be directly involved in the relationship, and provides a mechanism for the firm to stay abreast of the changing social and economic trends of its markets (Hlavinka and Gomez 2007).

Politico-Institutional Changes

In this chapter, it is argued that industrial/sectoral strategies and policies should be concerned with the long-term aim of altering both the direction and pace of domestic development. However, it is unlikely that significant state intervention would be warranted given the inadequate capacity and competence of government institutions—the institutional impediments to the countries' economic development. For this important reason, the pursuit of interventionist strategies as well as successful and effective policy reforms (a set of wide-ranging changes) would require the politico-institutional structures and means to formulate, implement, and enforce developmental policies and production-oriented selective interventions in certain key sectors of Caribbean economies.

First, determined developmental elites, who surround themselves with skilled development planners and technocrats, are absolutely necessary in order to devise and implement effective national strategies. Besides, it is essential for Caribbean governments to reduce "pork barrel" intervention and patronage so as to insulate decision makers and technocrats from the excessive influence of powerful interests and societal pressure. These executive "new look" elites would possess accurate intelligence, inventiveness, commitment, effectiveness, and active, strategic, and sophisticated responsiveness to a changing economic reality (Evans 1992: 148).

Potentially weak central cores or state governments may be captured by powerful interests, and can hardly implement institutional structures that decisively promote structural changes and economic reforms. Besides, changes in the structure of class relations during the last decades induced erosion of political institutions in the Caribbean. In contrast, the Developmental States are distinguished by "strong" politico-institutional structures.[22] Building strong technostructures and embedding them into networks of cooperative and consultative relations with targeted dynamic industries and other social segments is both feasible and operational in Caribbean territories.[23]

Moreover, competitive wages for well-educated, well-trained technocrats can attract more talented individuals and increase capacity, integrity, and professionalism. Indeed, the executive technostructure must be in a position to recruit from among the best and the brightest people of outstanding talent based on meritocratic criteria. Once the central bureaucracy acquires a reputation for attracting the most competent and talented, the system can develop a momentum of its own. It continues to attract such people (even at lower salaries than the private sector) because selection is based on meritocracy. Its personnel can be motivated by the belief that what they are doing promotes the national development and welfare. This sense of "national mission" can motivate the executive technostructure to stay focused and use its powers in line with "national purpose" goals. The more the state intends to intervene and to play a leading role, the more important are the staffing, motivation, authority, professionalism, and responsibilities of the central core. On the other hand, external pressure on appointments and patronage should be eliminated (Wade 1990: 371).

Secondly, the involvement of business elites and social segments in public policy making through institutionalized channels represents an adequate means to establish a state-business-society interface by which the mutual exchange of information can be encouraged, risk sharing facilitated, bureaucratic autonomy and flexibility enhanced, and a consensual process of policy formulation realized. This combination of social connectedness and bureaucratic autonomy (which Evans [1995] calls "embedded autonomy") may represent the institutional basis for effective and accountable state involvement in Caribbean economies, while being independent of societal pressures (Ahrens 1997: 125).[24]

Thirdly, in order to make state activities more effective, both effective procedures and increased participation are of vital importance. Indeed, the new institutional structures must allow for participation at all levels. Furthermore, loose and transparent links between the strategic planning agencies and Ministries and Government Departments involved in the industrial strategies and investment planning (such as Education and Training), and sectoral agencies and local authorities/boards would decentralize much of the work of the executive elites.[25]

To be successful our planning must be democratic, and our institutional structures must allow for participation at all levels. Indeed, participation by the "social partners" can improve the organization of production and help restrain the power of interest groups which have access to government decision making (Cowling 1990: 28).

Fourthly, preconditions for the practicability and success of these radical policies and alternative strategies in the Caribbean may include: the governments' credible commitment to production-oriented strategies (which include agriculture, industry, and the entire services sector); an improved quality of state action; the replacement of the short-term perspective of the Treasury and the financial institutions with one much more favorable to productive investment and industry; recognition of the importance of state capabilities, capacities, efficiency, and effectiveness; accountability, autonomy, professionalism, and manageability of the executive developmental elites; mechanisms of consensual conflict resolution as well as political and social stability through transparent and efficient procedures; the organizational design of, and the incentives within, the public sector and the institutional environment: incentives to pursue collective ends while restraining arbitrary action, favoritism, and corruption (Ahrens 1997: 116).

Lastly, particularly in the course of a fundamental redirection of the existing pattern of development, as in the case of Caribbean economies, simply matching such a radical policy framework to existing political institutions will be counterproductive. Effective governance is a dynamic process that requires continually "fine-tuning and adjusting institutions and policy solutions to changing technological, social, political, and economic environments" (Ahrens 1997: 119). To the extent that a chosen path falls short in this respect, this will need changes and adjustments in certain policy areas. However, it is difficult to retain a disposition against change in a world where basic conditions are subject to constant mutation. Without such commitments, capacity, competence, accountability, professionalism, seriousness, and effectiveness, such policy will founder on short-term expedients, the inefficiency and ineffectiveness of the civil service, the power of the transnationals and other foreign interests, or the mindset of the people.

Other Important Issues

In addition, the "new" tourism has already begun taking on a different shape—responding to, and internalizing a number of signals (social, cultural, technological, ecological, economic, and institutional) that emanate from the global environment. Flexible specialization, as a core element of the "new tourism best practice," is driven by new information technologies as well as new managerial and organizational principles of creativity, scope economies, product differentiation, and niche markets (Poon 1993: 274).

Therefore, much more attention has to be placed on these important issues, as the new tourism is a highly complex and volatile industry. Likewise, as new tourism depends upon environmental quality, the issue of environmental protection has to be accorded a greater priority by policy makers in order to cope with a product that has already begun to deteriorate. In fact, although the Caribbean environment is the islands' basic tourism resource, there appears to be a huge gap between this recognition and putting effective controls in place. Hence, a much closer link is required between tourism policy and environmental control and preservation.

Furthermore, good air access to Caribbean territories from all the main generating markets is of outmost importance. As the Caribbean is highly dependent and vulnerable to changes in the structure of air services, the region is facing the prospect of becoming a "service taker" in its main market regions.

Yet, the growing influence of the major Computer Reservation Systems (CRS) in the USA, Canada, and Europe is a further source of concern to the Caribbean. The only solution for the region's carriers may be to form cooperative alliances in the key areas of marketing and scheduling with some of the major carriers in order to avoid being entirely left out (as cost-effective and efficient marketing and distribution are crucial to the success of tourism promotion).

Indeed, the building of strategic alliances and partnerships within and outside of the tourism industry is expected to enhance the competitiveness of the sector (Poon 1993: 273). This action can:

- assist toward establishing a Caribbean-wide air transport policy and promote regional cooperation in air services including marketing agreements;
- improve airport infrastructure;
- monitor Computer Reservation Systems (CRS) developments closely and ensure that the region in general is not disadvantaged in this area;
- strengthen the capital and management bases of the airlines;
- monitor and forecast air transport developments to the extent that these developments affect the Caribbean.

With cooperative arrangements and regional approaches to tourism, Caribbean nations can share the huge expenses of building marketing intelligence systems, information technology networks, and the promotion and public relations campaigns. Likewise, to develop any viable food production program, a joint CARICOM approach should be undertaken. Most individual Caribbean islands cannot grow most of the basic foodstuffs, but collectively this goal could be achieved in order to meet the demands of the region. It is indeed these cooperative arrangements and united effort that can considerably increase the strength of the bargaining power of the entire region (Poon 1993: 276).[26]

CONCLUSIONS

The current economic difficulties, and fiscal pressures in particular, are making Caribbean governments more prepared to tackle difficult institutional issues than would be the case in more normal times. At the same time, the current conditions in world economy may increase the potential advantages of pursuing governed-market policies in Caribbean territories.

It is argued here that in a world of imperfect competition, and inadequate access to modern knowledge and know-how to use it, there are sound analytical grounds for following Developmental State policies and adopting a production, capital accumulation, and innovation-oriented approach in Caribbean nations. In such a world, the optimal degree of openness or the optimal degree of competition for Caribbean economies may not be maximum openness and close integration with the world economy. In fact, the neoclassical/neoliberal assertions do not correspond to the real world (e.g., "level-playing field"); consequently, suggestions and solutions which emanate from these paradigms may be inappropriate.

It would generally be wrong to consider that the NICs' economic policy-making could, or indeed should, be transplanted to Caribbean economies which are characterized by different historical and cultural circumstances, and different socio-political characteristics. What is important to learn from the East Asian success story, however, is the approach to the problem (i.e., the "strategic approach"). To begin to be successful will require a high quality of state intervention, and a certain degree of commitment by Caribbean governments to domestic development.

Recent calls for globalization, further liberalization and deregulation, minimalist state and "good" governance seem to entirely miss the point: in today's circumstances, Caribbean societies will not be able to build their own capabilities or make speedy transitions from poverty without activist states which approximate the model of a Developmental State (ideally but not necessarily the "western democratic type"). Without such states, the human cost of the "New Liberal Order" may be immense in the Caribbean. In short, contrary to the current orthodoxy, development requires thorough strategic action, and this is most likely achieved from Developmental State policies.

NOTES

1. A. Lewis, "The Industrialization of the British West Indies" (1950): 7.
2. Commonwealth Caribbean Regional Secretariat, *CARIFTA and the New Caribbean* (1971), 10.
3. Commonwealth Caribbean Regional Secretariat, *From CARIFTA to Caribbean Community* (1972), 17.
4. A. McIntyre, "Some Issues of Trade Policy in the West Indies" (1971): 165.
5. H. Brewster, "Economic Dependence: A Quantitative Interpretation" (1973): 90.
6. G. Beckford, *Persistent Poverty: Underdevelopment in Plantation Economies of the Third World* (1972), 183-214.
7. C. Y. Thomas, *Dependence and Transformation: The Economics of the Transition to Socialism* (1974), 116-7. See also: C. Y. Thomas, "The 'non-Capitalist Path' as Theory and Practice of Decolonization and Socialist Transformation" (1978): 10-36; and R. Gonsalves, *The Non-Capitalist Path of Development: Africa and the Caribbean* (1981).
8. O. Arthur, "The New Realities of Caribbean International Economic Relations" (1996): 47-8.
9. See CARICOM, *Caribbean Trade and Investment Report 2000* (2000); Economic Commission for Latin America and the Caribbean (ECLAC), *Selected Statistical Indicators of Caribbean Countries*, various years; UNCTAD, *Handbook of Statistics*, various years.
10. Planning Institute of Jamaica (PIOJ), *Economic and Social Survey Jamaica*, various years.
11. See IICA, *Performance and Prospects for Caribbean Agriculture* (June 1998).
12. See IICA, *Performance and Prospects for Caribbean Agriculture* (June 1998).
13. See Caribbean Tourism Organization (CTO), *Statistical Tables*, various years; PIOJ, *Economic and Social Survey Jamaica*, "Sectoral Performance: Tourism," various years.
14. Both analysis and development suggestions are based on the views of Kalecki (1971) and Kaldor (1978).
15. Neoliberal globalization or the "New Liberal Order" in its ideological usage is the label employed for the post-Cold War, United States-led project of the 1990s to organize the world according to the principles of neoliberal economics (privatization, financial deregulation, trade and exchange rate liberalization, fiscal and monetary orthodoxy, labor market reform, and social welfare reform, as the "new orthodoxy" with presumed universal applicability).
16. See, for example, A. Clayton, "Developing a Bio-Industry Cluster in Jamaica: A Step Towards Building a Skill-based Economy" (2001).
17. Again, both analysis and development recommendations are based on the views of Kalecki (1971) and Kaldor (1978).
18. It is argued here that, even under the current conditions of globalization and the pressures from international organizations such as WTO and IMF, governments still have room for Developmental State policies. In a rather similar vein, Chang claims that

> [I]ntelligent governments should try ... to use TNCs in a strategic way in order to acquire necessary capital, technology, marketing networks, and so on. What exactly the "strategic way" means will depend on various factors, such as the country's relative bargaining position, the technological nature of the industry, the role of the particular industry concerned in the bigger scheme of industrial development, and so on.... (Chang 1998: 111)

An intelligent government pursuing a strategic industrial policy will not have a "uniform" policy towards TNCs across industries, as many neoliberal economists recommend. Each industry serves different functions in the greater scheme of industrial development, and it would be foolish to have either uniformly restrictive or uniformly liberal policies towards TNCs across different industries. This also means that the same industry may, and indeed should, become more or less open to FDI over time, depending on the changes in the various internal and external conditions that affect it. (Chang 1998: 111-12)

19. Research suggests that nations which do best in the global arena are those which manage change and use their institutional arrangements to protect their national economies from international vagaries and disorder (Tyson 1992; Chang 1994; Singh 1995 and 1998; Boyer and Drache 1996; Karagiannis 2002;—among others).

20. Moreover, stopover visitors expand the domestic markets. Indeed, the growth of demand for an authentic Caribbean flavor (tourist consumption *plus* food and beverage souvenirs) provides the opportunities for the growth of supply of local specialties by local producers.

21. The proposed framework would also incorporate the informal economy.

22. "Strong" in the sense that the government is able to credibly commit itself to "national purpose" policy making; serious and capable of signaling its commitment to sustainable economic development.

23. This approach allows "considerable autonomy in determining the mode of operation, and adjusting it as experience accumulates." The main objective is "a dynamic economy rather than sticking to a set of rigid rules imposed by a central bureaucracy." (Cowling 1990: 25)

24. "Embeddedness" does not mean cozy relations between the state and individual private firms, but a strategic government-business interface that is distinguished by transparent consultation, cooperation, and coordination mechanisms. (Ahrens 1997: 126)

25. In fact,

[I]nstitutions can formalize the commitment to such [development strategies], and their structure, procedures, and personnel can act to ensure that such commitments cannot easily be reversed, but they are simply ratifying [plans] already established. The history of planning shows how fragile was the commitment, despite the creation of many new institutions [in Caribbean territories], and [the lack of teeth of these institutions was quite obvious.] With clear goals, and a determination to pursue them, institutions with teeth should be forthcoming. (Cowling 1990: 23)

26. The past history of intra-regional cooperation is not such as to raise hopes very high.

REFERENCES

Ahrens, J. "Prospects of Institutional and Policy Reform in India: Toward a Model of the Developmental State?" *Asian Development Review* 15, no. 1 (1997): 111-46.
Baker, D., Epstein, G., and R. Pollin, eds. *Globalization and Progressive Economic Policy*. Cambridge: Cambridge University Press, 1998.
Beckford, G. *Persistent Poverty: Underdevelopment in Plantation Economies of the Third World*. Oxford: Oxford University Press, 1972.
——— . *Caribbean Economy: Dependence and Backwardness*. Kingston: ISER, 1975.
Benn, D. and K. Hall, eds. *Globalization: A Calculus of Inequality*. Kingston: Ian Randle Publishers, 2000.

Bernal, R. L. "Globalization and Small Developing Countries: The Imperative for Repositioning." In *Globalization: A Calculus of Inequality*, edited by D. Benn and K. Hall, 88-127. Kingston: Ian Randle Publishers, 2000.

Boyer, R. and D. Drache, eds. *States Against Markets: The Limits of Globalization.* London: Routledge, 1996.

Brewster, H. "Economic Dependence: A Quantitative Interpretation," *Social and Economic Studies* 22 (1973).

Caribbean Tourism Organization (CTO). *Statistical Tables.* Bridgetown, Barbados: CTO, various years.

Caribbean Community (CARICOM). *Caribbean Trade and Investment Report 2000.* Georgetown, Guyana and Kingston, Jamaica: CARICOM Secretariat and Ian Randle Publishers, 2000.

Chang, H-J. "Globalization, Transnational Corporations, and Economic Development: Can the Developing Countries Pursue Strategic Industrial Policy in a Globalizing World Economy?" In *Globalization and Progressive Economic Policy*, edited by D. Baker, G. Epstein, and R. Pollin, 97-116. Cambridge: Cambridge University Press, 1998.

Chowdary, B. V. "Information Technology in the Caribbean Manufacturing Firms: An Industrial Survey." *Global Journal of Flexible Systems Management* 6, nos. 3 & 4 (2005): 1-10.

Clayton, A. "Developing a Bio-Industry Cluster in Jamaica: A Step Toward Building a Skill-Based Economy." *Social and Economic Studies* 50, no. 2 (2001): 1-37.

Commonwealth Caribbean Regional Secretariat. *CARIFTA and the New Caribbean.* Georgetown, 1971.

————. *From CARIFTA to Caribbean Community.* Georgetown, 1972.

Cowling, K. "The Strategic Approach to Economic and Industrial Policy." In *A New Economic Policy for Britain: Essays on the Development of Industry*, edited by K. Cowling and R. Sugden, 6-34. Manchester: Manchester University Press, 1990.

Cowling, K. and R. Sugden, eds. *A New Economic Policy for Britain: Essays on the Development of Industry.* Manchester: Manchester University Press, 1990.

Evans, P. B. "The State as Problem and Solution: Predation, Embedded Autonomy, and Structural Change." In *The Politics of Economic Adjustment*, edited by S. Haggard and R. R. Kaufman. Princeton: Princeton University Press, 1992.

————. *Embedded Autonomy: States and Industrial Transformation.* Princeton: Princeton University Press, 1995.

Girvan, N. and O. Jefferson, eds. *Readings in the Political Economy of the Caribbean.* Kingston: New World, 1971.

Gonsalves, R. *The Non-capitalist Path of Development: Africa and the Caribbean.* London: Latin American Bureau, 1981.

Heizer, J. and B. Render. *Production and Operations Management*, 4th edition. New Jersey: Prentice Hall, 1996.

Higgins, K. J. *The Bahamian Economy: An Analysis.* Nassau: The Counsellors, 1994.

Hlavinka, K. and L. Gomez. "The Total Package: Loyalty Marketing in the World of Consumer Packaged Goods." *The Journal of Consumer Marketing* 24, no. 1 (2007): 48.

Inter-American Institute for Cooperation on Agriculture. *Performance and Prospects for Caribbean Agriculture.* Port-of-Spain, Trinidad & Tobago: IICA, June 1998.

Johnson, C. "Introduction: The Taiwan Model." In *Contemporary Republic of China: The Taiwan Experience 1950-1980*, edited by J. S. Hsiung. New York: Praeger, 1981.

————. *MITI and the Japanese Miracle.* Stanford, CA: Stanford University Press, 1982.

Jones-Hendrickson, S. B. *Public Finance and Monetary Policy in Open Economies.* Kingston: ISER, 1985.

Kaldor, N. *Further Essays on Economic Theory*, London: Duckworth, 1978.

Kalecki, M. *Selected Essays on the Dynamics of a Capitalist Economy: 1933-1970.* Cambridge: Cambridge University Press, 1971.

Karagiannis, N. "The Development of the Bahamian Economy at the Crossroads." *Social and Economic Studies* 49, no. 4 (2000): 37-64.

——— . *Developmental Policy and the State: The European Union, East Asia, and the Caribbean.* Lanham, MD: Lexington Books, 2002.

Lalta, S. and M. Freckleton, eds. *Caribbean Economic Development: The First Generation.* Kingston, Jamaica: Ian Randle Publishers, 1993.

Leftwich, A. "Bringing Politics Back: Toward a Model of the Developmental State." *The Journal of Development Studies* 31, no. 3 (1995): 400-27.

Lewis, A. W. "The Industrialization of the British West Indies." *Caribbean Economic Review* II (1950): 1-61.

Lopez, J. "Growth Resumption and Long-run Growth in Latin American Economies: A Modest Proposal." *International Papers in Political Economy* 5, no. 1 (1998).

Onis, Z. "The Logic of the Developmental State." *Comparative Politics* 24, no. 1 (1991): 109-26.

Owen, A. "The New Realities of Caribbean International Economic Relations." Lecture in the *Distinguished Lecture Series*, St. Augustine, Trinidad: UWI, 1996.

Payne, A. and P. Sutton. *Charting Caribbean Development.* London: Macmillan Caribbean, 2001.

Planning Institute of Jamaica (PIOJ). *Economic and Social Survey: Jamaica.* Kingston, Jamaica: PIOJ, various years.

Polanyi-Levitt, K. *The Origins and Consequences of Jamaica's Debt Crisis: 1970-1990.* Kingston, Jamaica: Consortium Graduate School of Social Sciences, 1991.

Poon, A. "Caribbean Tourism and the World Economy." In *Caribbean Economic Development: The First Generation*, edited by S. Lalta and M. Freckleton, 262-79. Kingston, Jamaica: Ian Randle Publishers, 1993.

Ramsaran, R. F. *The Monetary and Financial System of The Bahamas: Growth, Structure and Operation.* Kingston, Jamaica: ISER, 1983.

Thomas, C. Y. *Dependence and Transformation: The Economics of the Transition to Socialism.* New York: Monthly Review Press, 1974.

——— . "The Non-capitalist Path as Theory and Practice of Decolonization and Socialist Transformation." *Latin American Perspectives* 5 (1978): 10-36.

United Nations-Commission for Latin America and the Caribbean (UN-ECLAC). *Selected Statistical Indicators of Caribbean Countries.* Port-of-Spain, Trinidad: ECLAC, various years; www.eclacpos.org. *Selected Statistical Indicators Online*, 1991-2001.

United Nations-Conference on Trade and Development (UNCTAD). *Handbook of Statistics.* Geneva: UN, various years.

Wade, R. *Governing the Market: Economic Theory and the Role of Government in East Asian Industrialization.* Princeton, NJ: Princeton University Press, 1990.

Wilmsmeier, G. and J. Hoffmann. "Liner Shipping Connectivity and Port Infrastructure as Determinants of Freight Rates in the Caribbean." *Maritime Economics and Logistics* 10, nos. 1 & 2 (2008): 130-52.

PART II

Tertiary Education, Health Insurance, &
Competitiveness

Chapter 4
Rifacimento of the Business School Curriculum: Increasing Competitiveness in the Twenty-First Century

Jessica M. Bailey & Morteza Sadri

ABSTRACT

The business school curriculum, as taught in most schools in the United States, has remained essentially unchanged for decades. Now is an appropriate time for a *rifacimento,* that is, a radical refashioning, similar to a recasting or new modeling. The term refacimento previously was used in reference to literary works, but is now used to suggest an updating, like a change in purpose to adapt to a change in taste. Such is exactly what is needed for the business curriculum which has been the subject of criticism from many quarters. After reviewing the structure of the typical business curriculum and noting some of its main shortcomings, there is an examination of some common assumptions and the need for looking at the entire business school curriculum differently. A format for a new business school curriculum is proposed which includes more opportunities to develop problem-solving skills, achieve the objectives of general education, develop an appreciation of ethics, integrate knowledge from several disciplines, and increase the overall competitiveness of graduates.

RIFACIMENTO

The Old Oxford English Dictionary defines *rifacimento,* a word of Italian derivation, as "a new-modeling or recasting of a literary work." This new modeling or recasting has been extended beyond the literary arena and been adapted to include other art forms and commercial applications. For example, music is often subjected to a re-creativity which totally refashions the result; this refashioning is often achieved by the application of new technologies, such as computerization. The result is a repurposing that adapts the product, or art form, to a change in tastes.[1]

However, it should be noted that rifacimento implies more than just a slight shift in the brand image or a minor modification of a product or a work simply to be more appealing to an audience. Rifacimento implies a repurposing that is more in-depth and denotes a conversion strategy. It is appropriate when there is a shift in thinking, a radical change in goals, or a fundamental deviation in purpose which makes modification essential and asserts the promise of different, and sometimes higher, levels of achievement. It is a remaking, a restructuring.

Business school education is primed for just such a rifacimento. Criticisms of basic undergraduate business education have come from educators and business analysts alike. Nearly fifty years ago, Calkins noted, in the wake of two major appraisals of business education undertaken by foundations, that the state of business education was weak and in need of modification. Both the Gordon[2] and Pierson[3] studies found that business education at the time lacked clear purpose, a substantive body of fundamental knowledge, intellectual rigor, or adjustment to the needs of students and businesses.[4] Over the last half century, those weaknesses have been addressed, especially among accredited business school programs. However, recent criticisms have touched upon modern problems being faced nationwide.

Today, business school education is criticized as being partly responsible for the financial crisis facing global markets at the end of the first decade of the twenty-first century. As foundational curricula have solidified across disciplines over recent decades, less and less emphasis has been placed on the value and place of ethics in business decision-making. Ethics, having been relegated to secondary status in many schools' curricula or eliminated entirely, have proven to be absent from the decision-making of unscrupulous business professionals.

Another frequently heard criticism is that there is a lack of understanding of the implications of decisions on various parts of the organization, strategy, or overall plans. For example, marketing can develop elaborate strategies which accomplish exactly what is intended, but the marketing decision makers do not understand the cost and implications of those decisions, in either dollar value or long-term impact on the firm. This shortcoming indicates that the disciplines of business are frequently taught and, consequently, learned in silos. Too little attempt is made in the traditional business school curriculum to help students understand the integration and interrelationship of the various disciplines of business.

Last, business education is also accused of failing to develop the soft skills among their students that are so necessary for business success. These are the skills that managers find invaluable to organizational management and market/sales achievement, such as written communication, oral communication, critical thinking, and appreciation of diversity. These skills are typically taught in general education curricula that are required of all students, regardless of major.

However, the business curriculum has been accused of doing a poor job of developing these skills in what are known as the *upper-division courses.*

TWENTIETH CENTURY BUSINESS SCHOOL CURRICULUM

The typical undergraduate business school curriculum, which has been in place for much of the last half century, can be divided into five main parts, similar in structure to the composition of the majority of undergraduate degree programs. Normally, the total curriculum is comprised of general education courses, required courses for all students of the field, required courses of the specialized major, capstone courses, and electives.

General education, which is often referred to as liberal arts education, has its roots in the Renaissance of the fifteenth century and is based on the belief that education in a broad range of subjects is necessary in order for a society to develop active and responsible citizens. Today, the topics included in the general education curricula of various colleges and universities have varied, but the long-standing ideals have not. A college education has come to mean, in part, the acquisition of skills and knowledge to be informed, thoughtful individuals who are equipped to make critical decisions. It also denotes having the ability to enjoy lifelong learning, as well as intellectual and artistic pursuits.[5]

TABLE 4.1
Components of the Business Undergraduate Curriculum

Type of Courses	Required of
General Education	All university students
Business Core	All business school students
Specialized Major	All students in the major
Capstone	All business school students or all students in the major, depending on whether it is a capstone course among the major requirements or a capstone course of the business core
Electives	Not required

The second set of courses in the curriculum is the core courses of the major, often known as the business core. These courses constitute the typical courses that are necessary to expose students to requirements of the field; it provides them with a firm, generalized foundation in business. In most modern business school curricula, this set of business core courses form the foundational knowledge in the various disciplines of business (economics, finance, management, marketing, accounting, organizational behavior, etc.) This is knowledge that is required of any well-read student of business. Of course, the composition of this set of courses may vary from school to school, but the underlying principle remains the same: that there is core business knowledge required of well-educated business school students.

The third set of courses is that which contains specialized courses of the major. These courses, which tend to be courses in one disciplinary area, provide students with a depth of understanding of their chosen fields. Again, the number of courses of this designation varies per school and/or per major, but they provide the depth necessary for a full understanding of any specialized field. For example, the area of marketing would require in-depth coursework in such topics as advertising, communications, consumer behavior, international marketing, pricing, research, retailing, sales, and strategy, just to name a few. These courses are designed to provide a depth of understanding of topics which are sub-sets of the specialized major. After taking these classes, students are well-versed in a variety of aspects of their major fields.

Fourth, there are courses that are uniquely designed to demonstrate the relationships among the various courses that students have taken; they are known as the capstone courses. Capstone courses are meant to enhance understanding by emphasizing the interrelatedness of various subjects. These courses are designed to pull together concepts to which the students have been previously introduced and to encourage synthesis of concepts. There may be capstone courses that relate to the business core courses described earlier, or capstone courses related to the set of specialized courses in any one particular disciplinary major. Because of their unique nature, capstone courses are usually taken at or near the end of the entire curriculum.

The final part of the typical curriculum is elective courses, which are included in order to provide an opportunity for each student to explore areas of interest that are not required. These are courses that are selected by the student because of his/her interest in the subject matter. They are not required courses.

ASSUMPTIONS

The twentieth century model of business school education that was just described and which continues to dominate so many business schools today, rests upon a set of assumptions that many educators are finding faulty. First, the model assumes that the primary objective of the curriculum is to convey information to students. This is in response to the criticisms of a half century ago that business education lacked a clear purpose, a substantive body of fundamental knowledge, and intellectual rigor. It could be argued, however, that the primary objective of the twenty-first century curriculum should be something much simpler and more appropriate for our highly competitive and globalized environment—problem-solving. What business schools need to be focused upon as their primary objective is not just the conveyance of ideas, but the ability to solve problems. Such a focus will better equip graduates to compete against other job candidates, but also to think and act in the best interests of the firm.

Second, the model assumes that students will be exposed to the skills and training for the general education learning goals via the general education courses exclusively; these courses are usually separate and distinct from business courses. Consequently, responsibility for the teaching and assessment of the general education courses rests primarily on the arts and sciences division of the university. This is despite the fact that the learning goals of most general education curricula should be demonstrable throughout a student's matriculation.

Third, the way business school education has been delivered, traditionally, assumes that learning in one course is transferred automatically across the curriculum to other courses. This assumption is contradictory to the fact that much of higher education takes place in silos, due, in part, to the structure of the typical curriculum, which separates disciplinary content into discrete courses and tends to wait until the end of the curriculum to attempt to tie concepts together. The interrelated nature of curricular content needs to be emphasized when the content is initially introduced to students; this is preferable to teaching in highly specialized modules and keeping disciplines separate. A more interdisciplinary approach to the achievement of learning objectives is needed, one that provides the ability to visualize and manage the interconnectedness of various disciplines and make applications across the curriculum.

Fourth, the popular model of business school education assumes that one or two capstone courses toward the end of the curriculum are adequate for tying together all of the necessary information from the business core courses and/or the specialized major courses. The typical Business Policy or Business Strategy course in most undergraduate curricula is designed to integrate the separate functional areas of business expertise. The tools that are routinely utilized in these courses are case analysis, case studies, simulations, team-based activities, and practical experiences that entail working with existing business. These exercises do enable students to apply knowledge from several disciplines, but the balance between breadth and depth of coverage is seldom ideal. In addition, the practice of waiting until the end of the curriculum to introduce the integrative capstone format requires a deviation from the focused approach which concentrates on only one disciplinary topic at a time and some students struggle with this difference.

Last, the way many business schools have delivered their curricula has been based on an assumption of a common ethical standard, shared by all or, at least, the majority of students. This ethical standard was assumed to have a basis in Judeo-Christian, male-dominated values consistent with Western civilizations. Likewise, it was thought to be based upon a value system shared by all or most students. Such is no longer the case as traditional pillars of moral and ethical leadership have deteriorated and value and belief systems have tended to vary more widely over the years.

THE TWENTY-FIRST CENTURY STUDENT

The aforementioned assumptions might have been appropriate for the typical business school student of a half century ago. However, another reason for changing the basic business school curriculum is the changing business school student. The typical twenty-first century student would have been considered atypical in the past. More and more often, the typical college student may be one who delays enrollment after high school graduation, attends college part time, works full time, is financially independent, has children or other dependents, is a single parent, or has a GED.[6] Having taken the non-traditional route to higher education, their lives are fragmented by work and lifestyle responsibilities that demand their attention and time and require prioritization of efforts in ways that are unknown to the typical first-time full-time undergraduates.

In addition, the millennial students, as those of the twenty-first century are called, are known to be high-achieving, intelligent, and optimistic. On most college campuses, however, they are more academically disengaged than past generations of first-time college students. Despite higher grades, they lack connection with the academic material, are less likely to ask questions, and tend not to explore the bounds of inquiry through traditional methodologies. They tend to spend much less time studying than students did in the past.[7] This is due, in part, to the high need for achievement to which they are accustomed and the fact that their parents play such a large role in their lives.

It is not atypical to find college students who do not read books on a regular basis, whether to fulfill academic requirements or for pleasure. They display noticeably shorter attention spans and expect course content to be delivered to them in some format that can be grasped virtually, effortlessly. Being a generation of instant gratification, modern-day students want rapid resolutions, fast cycles of learning, and instantaneous solutions.

Importance of Problem-Solving

What is needed is a new way of thinking about the undergraduate business curriculum, one that views the curriculum holistically, as opposed to a collection of courses to be tied together at the end. Ideally, this new curriculum would not be restricted by discrete course designations and credit/hours, but that is impractical and not likely to be pursued by universities at this time. What is herein proposed is a model for the business school curriculum that addresses the criticisms of the typical curriculum while giving it a more competitive focus. This new modeling of the curriculum will have as its primary focus developing in students the ability to solve problems.

Since business school education over the last half century appears to have addressed the shortcomings noted by the Gordon and Pierson studies, that is, a lack of a substantive body of fundamental knowledge and intellectual rigor, business education should be resigned to and embracing of problem solving as its *raison d'etre* in the twenty-first century. The reason that this is so important is the fact that no business environment is ever totally free of problems. Even successfully functioning organizations are continuously faced with the challenge of improving. As we prepare undergraduates to become professionals, we must be mindful of the fact that businesses and governmental agencies are constantly dealing with problems of some sort, whether they be problems originating in the past, being generated in the present, or anticipated for the future. In all cases, the most important skill with which business schools should be empowering their students is the ability to solve problems. That means that the business school curriculum must be designed to develop the specialized skills that are needed for productive problem-solving.

There are many models that delineate the sets of skills necessary for problem-solving. Those skills are, essentially, those required for analysis, organization, synthesis, planning, implementation, and control. Rudelius described steps in the process of solving problems as defining the problem, enumerating the decision factors, considering relevant information, identifying the best alternative, implementing the chosen alternative, and evaluating the decision.[8]

It is the instilling of these skills throughout the curriculum that will enable students to be able to solve business problems when they engage in their professional careers. Not only do these skills need to be instilled, but students must be given ample opportunity to apply these skills to situations that draw from several disciplines—first, through exposure to simple cross-disciplinary problems and, then, through exposure to more complex problems. In addition, students need to have real experiences in which they can witness the interrelatedness and complexity of the elements of typical problems and can develop an appreciation for the mechanics of utilizing the tools of problem-solving.

The art and skill of problem-solving should permeate the undergraduate business curriculum because that is the essential reason for this type of professional education. For example, beginning at the early stages of matriculation, business school students should be introduced to and practiced in processes for solving problems. This would include being introduced to some of the time tested techniques that are routinely used in order to diagnose problems and determine solutions. These processes and techniques can be reiterated, reinforced, and intensified from semester to semester, in order to ingrain a systematic and proven approach to solving increasingly difficult problems that are likely to be faced by businesses. A list of tools/techniques would include, but is not limited to, a variety of frameworks. Examples of customer-oriented frameworks are the following:

- *Segmentation Strategies*
This framework offers a range of segmentation approaches to understanding and solving market challenges, from mass market strategy to the mass customization strategy.[9]
- *Market-based Assets*
This framework views objects of marketing's actions as assets of the firm. These market-based assets are valuable to the firm as they can be used to create competitive barriers, lower costs, and provide a competitive edge.[10]

- *Value Chain Analysis*

This framework gauges the firm's success based upon how well it is able to market its product after choosing its value, providing the value, and communicating it to the customer.[11]

Examples of integrative frameworks include:

- **SWOT Analysis**: This framework provides an analysis of a firm's internal characteristics (strengths, weaknesses) and the environment's external characteristics (opportunities, threats).[12]
- **Growth-Share Matrix**: This framework provides a system for analyzing strategic business units and categorizing them as cash cows, stars, question marks, or dogs.[13]
- **Three Cs Analysis**: This framework provides maximum opportunity for marketplace advantage by focusing on the company, customer, and competitors.[14]

Examples of competitor frameworks include:

- **Porter's Three Generic Strategies**: This framework is based on three basic competitive positions: cost leadership, focused strategies, and differentiation.[15]
- **Game Theoretic Frameworks**: These frameworks are based on game theory, which is the study of interactions among players where the payoffs depend on choices. The games can be zero-sum, free-wheeling, or rule-based.[16]
- **Resource-based View of Strategy**: Characteristics of the firm's assets play a role in construction of the most effective strategies. Resources that are valuable and superior lay the basis for the firm's competitive advantages.[17]

Examples of financial frameworks would include:[18]

- **Comparison of Variable and Fixed Costs**: Costing and pricing can be strategically determined based on whether costs vary per unit of output or whether they do not fluctuate with output volume.
- **Comparison of Relevant and Sunk Costs**: The difference between expected future costs and past expenditures can enable a firm to accurately price its products and services and evaluate alternatives.
- **Margins**: Of paramount importance to an effective strategy is the difference between the selling price and the cost of the product or service.
- **Break Even Analysis**: By identifying the unit or solar volume at which a firm begins to make a profit, it is possible to asses the risk of an action.
- **Discounted Cash Flow**: By incorporating the theory of the time value of money, a firm can express future cash flows in terms of their present value.

First, students need to be given practice in the crucial initial step in this process, being able to accurately identify the problem. Peter Drucker has maintained that properly identifying the problem is 50 percent of the solution.[19] Too often, there is a tendency to look at symptoms and identify them as the problem;

such as "low market share" or "declining sales." Both of these conditions are not the problem, but merely symptoms of some underlying problem that is causing the low market share or the declining sales. Exercises can be designed that will enable students to think critically and develop hypotheses about the true causes of the symptomatic manifestations that are apparent. These exercises may require the use of deductive logic.

Second, problem solving also involves creativity to develop and justify alternative solutions to be analyzed as possible courses of action. Students should be encouraged to brainstorm to develop lists of possible solutions that might solve problems. The brainstorming may be done individually or in teams.

Modifications to General Education

Involvement of the business school in the teaching of general education courses means that the business school will be engaged in offering courses that involve broad categories of learning that achieve the specific goals that are typically considered to be achievable through general education: written and oral communication, critical thinking, social sciences, ethics, science, mathematics, appreciation of diversity, and a global perspective, just to name a few. There are many business courses that are tailored for inclusion in the general education curriculum, like the following:

- **Business Communication**: This course can enable students to apply oral and written communication principles to current business situations. Exercises may include the development of memoranda, letters, reports, individual and group presentations, online communication, and career interviews. This course can be designed to achieve the goals of written and oral communication, critical thinking, ethics, appreciation of diversity, or the global perspective, while reinforcing problem-solving and logic skills through the use of cases.
- **Introduction to Business**: This course can be designed to introduce the basics of the various disciplinary areas of business. In addition to generating student interest in and enthusiasm for entering the study of business, teaching business terminology, and providing a broad background in business practices, the course can be designed to teach written and oral communication, critical thinking, knowledge of the social sciences, ethics, and the global perspective.
- **Microcomputer Applications**: This course can provide in-depth experience with spreadsheets and database software on microcomputers. A graphical operating environment such as Windows can be used. Students can be required to design and develop projects, which address common business problems. Relevant information systems concepts providing the foundation for advanced study in MIS will be provided. This course can be designed to also achieve the goals of critical thinking and ethics.
- **Principles of Microeconomics**: In this course, a presentation can be made of the fundamental principles and problems of economics, with emphasis on

consumer demand, production costs, and price determination within various market structures. Also, the course can be tailored to teach oral and written communication, critical thinking, knowledge of the social sciences, and ethics.

- **Principles of Macroeconomics**: This course can provide the fundamental principles and problems of economics, with emphasis on income distribution, current domestic and international economic problems, and world economics. Also, the course can be tailored to teach oral and written communication, critical thinking, knowledge of the social sciences, and the global perspective.

- **Legal Environments of Business**: This course can provide a broad analysis of the legal constraints placed on business. Emphasis can be placed on the nature and function of legal regulations; the courts and attendant legal processes, including judicial lawmaking; lawmaking by legislatures; governmental regulation and control of business; and the role and influence of various specific administrative agencies. This course can be structured to include critical thinking, culture and belief, ethics, social sciences, and written and oral communication.

Other courses might be added to the general education curriculum that provide an opportunity to accomplish the goals and objectives while introducing new, more non-traditional courses. Suggested topics are:

- **The History of Women in Business**: This course can present the history of western civilization from the perspective of the role played by women in the functioning of economic systems. It can provide the biography and accomplishments of noted women of the modern age who have impacted the direction of business and its development. The course can teach concepts of critical thinking, social science, history, ethics, and oral and written communication skills.

- **U.S. Business History**: This course can provide an in-depth look at the history of the development of business in the United States, including an examination of major economic cycles, the role of unions, advances in transportation, the impact of the Civil War, and comparison of the industrial versus the agricultural communities. This course can be designed to cover critical thinking, social science, ethics, and oral and written communication skills.

- **Doing Business in …**: This course can be designed to concentrate on specific areas of the world, examining the language, customs, cultural aspects, as well as how business is conducted in that part of the world. These business practices should include greetings, negotiations, gestures, aesthetics, and other protocols that lead to success in business. The course can also cover logic, oral and written communications, social science, history, critical thinking, culture and beliefs, ethics, and the societies of the world.

Quite frankly, business schools are only constrained by a lack of imagination when it comes to the development of topics for general education offerings.

A wide range of truly exciting, and potentially satisfying, courses may be offered as part of the typical general education curriculum which can fulfill the learning objectives as specified by the institution. These courses can assist in developing the soft skills that are so necessary for success in professional careers.

Elimination of Silos

One of the major downsides of the traditional business school curriculum is the tendency to present information in discrete course formats that fails to convey the interrelatedness of disciplinary topics. The real world is an environment in which the business functions of the firm are in operation simultaneously, having a continuous influence on the firm's performance. Students need to be introduced to the content of several business disciplines simultaneously. This can be done effectively by close coordination of assignments and projects for classes that are being taken during any one semester. For example, during a semester, a junior may enroll in three courses (Introduction to Marketing, Organizational Behavior, and Introduction to Finance). All three courses can be coordinated by assigning problems that cross the three disciplinary areas and solve problems in all three areas. A common project might be assigned that incorporates aspects of the three disciplinary areas.

Quite simply, the gap between courses needs to be bridged. Concepts of marketing need to be interwoven with aspects of finance and problems need to be presented to students in a fashion that emphasizes the dynamic and interrelated nature of the real world. One of the most efficient means of doing this is by team teaching. Instructors teaching in any semester can lecture in other classes being taught during the same semester and present information on the interrelatedness of disciplines and the need to think across disciplines in order to understand and solve the problems that are likely to arise.

Inclusion of More Capstone Courses

Many experts agree that one or two capstone courses are not usually adequate for a typical undergraduate business curriculum. When you imagine all of the possible interactions that can be anticipated in a normally functioning business, there are a myriad of interactions that transpire, creating problems that need solving. Students need to be introduced to the concept of problem solving early on and, then, gradually be required to solve typical problems of increasing difficulty that demonstrate disciplinary interplay. If three courses are taken by a student in any semester, a capstone course should be required during that same semester which pulls together aspects of the three courses and allows the student to practice and develop mastery of solving problems across disciplines.

Thus, a student taking the same three courses mentioned earlier would enroll in a capstone course during that same semester. This would allow the inclusion of three or four capstone courses throughout the curriculum. The positive result will be exposing the students to a wide variety of problematic situations and the development of increasingly sophisticated skills in problem-solving, including those with complex ethical dimensions.

The Need for Ethics Training

Another prominent part of the successful business school curriculum must be ethics training. The traditional curriculum is likely to contain one or two courses in ethics/legal environments of business, but many academicians agree that such coverage of this important topic is inadequate. It is thought that ethics should permeate the thinking and decision-making at all levels and for all aspects of businesses because ethics define the underlying principles and values of the organization. In addition to mapping the level of corporate responsibility expressed by any firm, ethics identify the highly individualized personal belief systems held by individuals in the organization. It is upon these systems that decisions are made on behalf of the firm. As traditional societal institutions weaken, the need for such training in the academic arena increases. Students need ethics training in order to build a strong personal belief system and to understand the legal implications of decisions.

Closely aligned with this highly specialized training is the opportunity to provide service to the communities in which students are located. Service is ethics in action and should be incorporated into the curriculum. Opportunities of increasing commitment can be disbursed across the curriculum, enabling students to learn the importance of social responsibility within the framework of the successful capitalist system.

SAMPLE CURRICULUM

What follows is a sample curriculum for the BS degree in Business Administration with a major in marketing. It is designed to transmit the knowledge of general education, the business core, and the courses of the specialized major from a problem-solving perspective, with emphasis on ethics. It provides more opportunities for integration of concepts by the addition of business courses into the general education curriculum and the introduction of more capstone experiences. Also, it develops problem-solving skills that are woven throughout the curriculum and tested through gradually more challenging capstone experiences with intense ethical dimensions. Thus, undergraduates would be acquiring and applying the skills that are likely to make them valuable to their employers. This approach to the curriculum also considers the characteristic challenges of the modern student because of its emphasis on application which allows for the active learning that the twenty-first century student finds engaging.

TABLE 4.2
Courses for the Bachelor of Science Degree in Business Administration Marketing Major, Freshman Year

FALL SEMESTER	CREDIT
General Education Course #1	3
General Education Course #2	3
General Education Course #3	3
General Education Course #4	4
Business Core Course #1 (Microcomputer Applications)	3
TOTAL	16

SPRING SEMESTER	CREDIT
General Education Course #5	3
General Education Course #6	3
General Education Course #7	3
General Education Course #8	1
General Education Course #9	2
Business Core Course #2 (Business Communications)	3
TOTAL	15

The general education courses to be taken during the freshman year are intended to be the normal variety of courses taught in a typical curriculum (English, mathematics, science, art, music, physical education, social science, etc.). The two business courses would cover concepts of general education mentioned earlier. In both instances, problem-solving and ethics would be emphasized.

TABLE 4.3
Courses for the Bachelor of Science Degree in Business Administration Marketing Major, Sophomore Year

FALL SEMESTER	CREDIT
Business Core Course #3 (Principles of Financial Accounting)	3
General Education Course #10 (Principles of Microeconomics)	3
Business Core Course #4 (Business Law)	3
General Education Course #10	3
Capstone Course #1	3
TOTAL	15

SPRING SEMESTER	CREDIT
Business Course #6 (Principles of Managerial Accounting)	3
Business Course #7 (Principles of Macroeconomics)	3
Business Course #8 (Business & Economics Statistics)	3
General Education Course #11	3
Capstone Course #2	3
TOTAL	15

Bailey & Sadri

During the sophomore year, there is an opportunity to introduce one or two capstone courses into the curriculum. In addition to instructors for the three business courses team teaching and/or guest lecturing in each others' classes, the capstone course can focus on problem solving at a very elementary level that would introduce useful skill sets and allow students to experiment with simple problem-solving exercises designed to apply principles from the three business courses being taken. Some of these business courses can also be designed to effectively accomplish the student learning goals of the general education curriculum.

TABLE 4.4
Courses for the Bachelor of Science Degree in Business Administration Marketing Major, Junior Year

FALL SEMESTER	CREDIT
Business Core Course #9 (Principles of Management)	3
Business Core Course #10 (Principles of Marketing)	3
Business Core Course #11 (Principles of Financial Manag/nt)	3
Business Core Course #12 (Quantitative Methods)	3
Elective Course #1	3
TOTAL	15

SPRING SEMESTER	CREDIT
Business Core Course #13 (Organizational Behavior)	3
Business Core Course #14 (Production & Operations Manag/nt)	3
Business Major Course #1 (Consumer Behavior)	3
Business Major Course #2 (Marketing Communications)	3
Capstone Course #3	3
TOTAL	15

The courses of the junior year represent ideal courses through which problem-solving skills can be developed and concepts can be integrated. There can be one additional capstone course taught at this level.

TABLE 4.5
Courses for the Bachelor of Science Degree in Business Administration Marketing Major, Senior Year

FALL SEMESTER	CREDIT
Business Major Course #3 (Principles of Retailing)	3
Business Major Course #4 (Salesmanship)	3
Business Major Course #5 (Marketing Strategy)	3
General Education Course #12	3
Practicum	3
TOTAL	15

TABLE 4.5 Continued

SPRING SEMESTER	CREDIT
Business Major Course #6 (Marketing Research)	3
Business Major Course #7 (International Marketing)	3
Elective #2	3
Elective #3	3
Capstone Course #4	3
TOTAL	15

The courses taking during the senior year provide an ideal opportunity to integrate concepts of the major, as well as concepts from the overall curriculum. The capstone course would offer the most challenging coursework of the program.

CHALLENGES

As business schools begin to consider refashioning their curricula for the twenty-first century, certain implications need to be examined. These may have an impact on the success of the rifacimento.

First, business schools need to be aware of the impact of such a remodeling on other academic units on campuses. Traditionally, decisions about the general education curriculum are made at the university level, involving the faculty and administrative units that teach the courses. Any changes in the overall general education curriculum must secure approvals at the university level. Thus, the inclusion of business school classes into the general education curriculum may meet resistance if the assumption is made that the inclusion of these courses necessarily denotes exclusion of others. This is true within disciplines where the teaching of these general education or "service" courses has become the primary teaching responsibility of the faculty of these departments. For example, on some campuses, the number of English majors has dwindled over the decades, yet the demand for professors of English has not because these professors are primarily engaged in teaching general education courses in English, to be taken by all students on campus. These service courses represent the bulk of the teaching of many English departments and are, thus, adamantly protected from elimination/replacement. The introduction of more business courses into the general education curriculum can be more easily accomplished when the university's offerings are more cafeteria-style, i.e., designed to allow students to choose from a wide variety of courses rather than a limited set of prescribed courses.

Second, the existence of silos in the teaching of business is not likely to disappear. The reality is that members of the faculty have their highly specialized areas of expertise and are hired to teach within their fields. Because of this, business schools must coordinate to serve the needs of cohorts of students. Team-teaching, common projects, guest lecturing, and overall cooperation and interdisciplinary thinking are required in order to help students visualize the interrelatedness of the business disciplines. Faculty dedicated to the concept of cross-disciplinary learning will be able to introduce concepts in various classes with the view in mind of tying seemingly disparate aspects together.

Third, there is, again, a need for coordination in order the accomplish the goal of introducing the students to increasingly more complex and difficult capstone experiences so that they can, over time, build a sophisticated level of problem-solving skill. These capstone courses can begin early in the overall curriculum, but are best positioned to begin during the sophomore year.

Last, the emphasis on ethics becomes more complex as societies become more diversified and less dominated by religion. Withering ethical standards inevitably lead to acceptance of a wider variety of points of view and opinions. Ethics training has, of necessity, matured with the changes in popular mores over the last half century. Incorporating valid ethical training into the curriculum is becoming more challenging than ever.

CONCLUSION

This proposed curriculum is designed to address the criticisms of business education while increasing the competitiveness of business school graduates. This new perspective on the curriculum will enable twenty-first century students to be better equipped for their professions because it will emphasize problem-solving. The ability to solve problems is paramount to any successful business.

Also, the importance of ethics should not be minimized. The values and beliefs that underlie strong ethical systems should be the guiding force behind the corporate cultures that undergird the capitalist system.

This approach to the curriculum can also enable students to envision the disciplinary areas of business in a more holistic manner. By introducing concepts across disciplines and developing the skills needed to solve problems across disciplines, students will realize the interrelatedness of these concepts and be prepared for the real world.

NOTES

1. William Safire, "On Language: Rifacimento," *New York Times*, February 15, 2009.

2. Robert A. Gordon and James E. Harwell, *Higher Education for Business* (New York: Columbia University Press, 1959).

3. Frank C. Pierson et al., *The Education of American Businessmen* (New York: McGraw-Hill, 1959).

4. Robert D. Calkins, "The Problems of Business Education," *The Journal of Business* 34, no. 1 (January 1961): 1-9.

5. http://www.ucol.uncc.edu/gened/

6. http://www.nasfaa.org/publications/2007/cntg091207.html

7. http://www.studentprograms.vt.edu/publications/millennials.php

8. Roger Kerin and Robert Peterson, *Strategic Marketing Problems: Cases and Comments*, 10th edition (Upper Saddle River, NJ: Pearson-Prentice Hall, 2004), 51.

9. Roger J. Best, *Market-Based Management*, 2nd edition (Upper Saddle River, NJ: Prentice Hall, 2000), 118-23.

10. Rajendra K. Srivastava, Tasadduq A. Shervani and Liam Fahey, "Market-Based Assets and Shareholder Value: A Framework for Analysis," *Journal of Marketing* 62 (January 1998): 2-18.

11. John A. Czepiel, *Competitive Marketing Strategy* (Englewood Cliffs, NJ: Prentice Hall, 1992), 38-44.

12. Malcolm McDonald and Adrian Payne, *Marketing Planning for Services* (Oxford: Butterworth-Heinemann, 1996), 77-117.

13. Steven P. Schnaars, *Marketing Strategy: Customers & Competition*, 2nd edition (New York: Free Press, 1998), 49-59.

14. Subhash C. Jain, *Marketing: Planning & Strategy*, 6th edition (Cincinnati, OH: South-Western College Publishing, 2000), 23-27.

15. Roger A. Kerin, Vijay Mahajan and P. Rajan Varadarajan, *Contemporary Perspectives on Strategic Market Planning* (Boston: Allyn and Bacon, 1990), 303-9.

16. Pankaj Ghemawat, *Strategy and the Business Landscape* (Reading, MA: Addison-Wesley, 1999), 60-70.

17. Jay Barney, "Firm Resources and Sustained Competitive Advantage," *Journal of Management* 17, no. 1 (1991): 99-120.

18. Roger Kerin and Robert Peterson, *Strategic Marketing Problems: Cases and Comments*, 10th edition (Upper Saddle River, NJ: Pearson-Prentice Hall, 2004), 33-46.

19. *Ibid.*, 51.

REFERENCES

Barney, Jay, "Firm Resources and Sustained Competitive Advantage." *Journal of Management* 17, no. 1 (1991): 99-120.

Best, Roger J., *Market-Based Management*, 2nd edition. Upper Saddle River, NJ: Prentice Hall, 2000.

Calkins, Robert D. "The Problems of Business Education." *The Journal of Business* 34, no. 1 (January 1961): 1-9.

Czepiel, John A. *Competitive Marketing Strategy*. Englewood Cliffs, NJ: Prentice Hall, 1992.

Ghemawat, Pankaj. *Strategy and the Business Landscape*. Reading, MA: Addison-Wesley, 1999.

Gordon, Robert A. and James E. Harwell. *Higher Education for Business*. New York: Columbia University Press, 1959.

http://www.nasfaa.org/publications/2007/cntg091207.html

http://www.studentprograms.vt.edu/publications/millennials.php

http://www.ucol.uncc.edu/gened/

Jain, Subhash C. *Marketing: Planning and Strategy*, 6th edition. Cincinnati, OH: South-Western College Publishing, 2000.

Kerin, Roger and Robert Peterson. *Strategic Marketing Problems: Cases and Comments*, 10th edition. Upper Saddle River, NJ: Pearson-Prentice Hall, 2004.

Kerin, Roger A., Mahajan, Vijay and P. Rajan Varadarajan. *Contemporary Perspectives on Strategic Market Planning*. Boston, MA: Allyn and Bacon, 1990.

McDonald, Malcolm and Adrian Payne. *Marketing Planning for Services*. Oxford: Butterworth-Heinemann, 1996.

Pierson, Frank C., et al. *The Education of American Businessmen.* New York: McGraw-Hill, 1959.
Safire, William. "On Language: Rifacimento," *New York Times,* February 15, 2009.
Schnaars, Steven P. *Marketing Strategy: Customers and Competition,* 2nd edition. New York: Free Press, 1998.
Srivastava, Rajendra K., Shervani, Tasadduq A. and Liam Fahey. "Market-Based Assets and Shareholder Value: A Framework for Analysis." *Journal of Marketing* 62 (January 1998): 2-18.

Chapter 5
Faculty Personal Productivity and Tertiary Education Competitiveness: A Preliminary Examination of Key Factors

Robert A. Herring III, M. Eileen Higgins & Robert Dengler

ABSTRACT

The term "faculty productivity" is often used in academic circles. In many cases, it is a synonym for productivity in the areas of *research* and *publishing*. However, the authors contend that there is a significant need for faculty to be more productive in *all* the roles of their profession. The authors examine all areas of faculty personal productivity, and emphasize that it applies to teaching, research, and service, as well as other roles and tasks. Among the productivity factors particularly examined are clutter control, time management, focus, organizing, and management of email. Recommendations for further research are made. Improvements in any of these productivity factors combined are expected to boost the competitiveness of tertiary education institutions (mainly universities), which is going to be the ultimate and important task of this chapter.

NEED FOR THE STUDY

The following is an excerpt from a book review of Torkel Klingberg's *The Overflowing Brain* (Chabris 2008), which appeared recently in the *Wall Street Journal*:

Take a look at your computer screen and the surface of your desk: A lot is going on. Right now, I count 10 running programs with 13 windows on my iMac, plus seven notes or documents on my computer desk and innumerable paper piles, folders and books on my "main" desk, which serves primarily as overflow space. My 13 computer windows include four for my Internet browser, itself showing tabs for 15 separate Web pages. The tasks in progress, in addition to writing this review (what was that deadline again?), include monitoring three email accounts, keeping up with my Facebook friends, figuring out how to wire money into one of my bank accounts, digging into several scientific articles about genes, checking the weather in the city I will be visiting next week and reading various blogs, some of which are actually work-related. And this is at home. At the office, my efforts to juggle these tasks would be further burdened by meetings to attend, conference calls to join, classes to teach and co-workers to see. And there is still the telephone call or two—on one of my three phone lines (home, office, mobile).

This review brings forth the utter complexity of the work of a modern-day professional or knowledge worker. Given the nature of the topic, this chapter will pose more questions than it will answer. Thus, we postulate that there is a very real need for this research and that it could result in enabling professors to be more productive and competitive. Obviously, the effective use of time is an important factor in the successful career of a professor (Plater 1995).

BACKGROUND

The term "faculty productivity" is often used in academic circles. However, in most cases, it is essentially a synonym for productivity in the areas of *research* and *publishing*. Although related, that is *not* the way in which the authors of this chapter are using the term.

We are interested in *all areas* of individual faculty personal productivity (FPP) for faculty members (hereinafter referred to as "professor" or "professors" for better flow in writing) in colleges and universities. For successful academic careers, it is important that college and university professors be productive in *all* of the many roles of their profession. We, in academia, are all familiar with the "big three" roles of teaching, research, and service. Productivity is important in each of these. But what about all of the big and little administrative—and too often *clerical-level*—details with which professors too often have to contend? We propose that *productivity in all of these areas* is equally important. More importantly, the links between faculty personal productivity and tertiary education competitiveness have to be examined in this fierce global environment.

Academic productivity is a matter of significant concern to many stake-holders in the arena of higher education. Indeed, pressure to increase academic productivity comes from stakeholders such as state legislatures, college and university administrators, boards of regents, other governmental agencies, etc. (Middaugh 2001; Shellenbarger 2009). Control of higher education costs has been of significant concern, which has been exacerbated by the fiscal crises of many state budgets during the current economic downturn. Colleges and universities are expected to "do more with less," as budgets and positions have been cut and teaching loads of faculty have been increased. The fact that there are increasing demands for faculty productivity, especially in the areas of research and publishing, make this research important (Middaugh 2001). Faculty members' career success may be attributed to the number and quality of their journal publications (Bowling and Burns 2010).

Colleges and universities function in an increasingly competitive environment. The competitiveness of a particular institution can logically be considered to be closely related to the productivity of its faculty. This competitive environment has become global. Thus, one can purport a link between the productivity of a nation's colleges and universities, and the competitiveness of the nation in the global marketplace.

The output of colleges and universities has been shown to have a significant economic impact on states. For example, "… the total direct economic impact of University of North Carolina campuses resulting from the productive value of its graduates, spending by its out-of-state students, and federal and privately funded research by its faculty is $8.7 billion *annually* and $10.4 billion if secondary spending impacts are included" (Walden 2009). Determining how to maximize such outcomes is of critical importance to society (UNC Tomorrow 2007). Pressure for excellence and continuous improvement in teaching and research also comes from accrediting bodies such as AACSB-International.

Walden (2009: 3) notes that

> [I]t is difficult to quantify all the benefits of the teaching, research, and service efforts of the University of North Carolina System campuses. For example, the enhanced appreciation a student receives for the great works of literature from a college course, the added knowledge gained about the lifespan of primitive life from research on coastal estuaries, or the enjoyment attained by attendees at university-sponsored cultural and sporting events are all difficult—indeed impossible—to measure in monetary terms.

But before we continue the analysis on faculty productivity, we also need to define "knowledge workers" and discuss productivity factors of knowledge workers. All these related issues are analyzed in the following sections.

KNOWLEDGE WORKERS AND PRODUCTIVITY

Knowledge workers are individuals who are valued for their ability to act and communicate with knowledge within a specific subject area. Davenport (2005: 10) defined knowledge workers as those who "have high degrees of expertise, education, or experience, and the primary purpose of their jobs involves the creation, distribution, and application of knowledge." They can often advance the overall understanding of that subject through focused analysis, design, and/or development. Knowledge workers use research skills to define problems and to identify alternatives. Fueled by their expertise and insight, they work to solve those problems, in an effort to influence decisions, priorities, and strategies.

The productivity of knowledge workers has been classified in numerous ways (Mercer Consulting 2007). Kelley and Caplan (1993) in a study at Bell Labs specified a number of factors that were consistently found in high-performing knowledge workers. Davenport (2005: 172) notes that "Another reason why there is so little knowledge about what impacts knowledge performance is that managers now recognize that the complexity of the work requires a multifaceted approach, which makes individual changes almost impossible to evaluate."

Macan (1994) conducted a study of the time management practices of managers. However, Macan was unable to find a correlation between time management practices and job performance, although there was a significant correlation with job satisfaction.

To some degree, the issue of the productivity of "knowledge workers" and "professionals" (acknowledging that these are very broad terms) could be generalized to faculty productivity. However, the authors postulate that there are some unique differences:

1. Professors typically have at least the following three primary roles:
    a.   teacher
    b.   researcher/writer
    c.   service provider
    In most cases the subject matter of research and subsequent academic publications such as conference proceedings papers, journal articles, and books or book chapters is largely or wholly at the discretion of the faculty member. This stands in contrast to the situation at other organizations in which research is conducted—where the research is likely dictated by organizational needs, particularly in a private sector company.
2. The degree of autonomy of the professor is greater than that of almost any other occupation. Although this quality of academic life is highly prized, it does have its downsides. It becomes critical for professors to learn how to set goals and priorities and to manage and schedule their own time. It seems reasonable that the failure to do so is a primary cause of some professors failing to achieve tenure.
3. The three roles stated above often come into conflict with one another. The time horizons for each are often very different. Consider the "Time Management Matrix" (Covey, Merrill, A. and Merrill, Rebecca R. 1994: 37). This is a 2x2 matrix of Urgent—not Urgent, by Important—not Important. Many of the tasks of the teacher and service role are urgent; tomorrow's lesson plan must be developed, and the report due for tomorrow's committee meeting must be finished. However, a journal manuscript may be of prime importance in a professor's life; but it is often not urgent in that it can often be put off another day. Days turn into months, months turn into years; lack of publication due to such postponement can derail a professor's career.

DEFINING FACULTY PRODUCTIVITY

Academic productivity has been defined in various ways. Anecdotally, the most common usage of the term is to refer to the output of refereed journal articles, or somewhat more generally to research and publishing (Khojasteh and Herring 2006). Middaugh (2001) in his book on faculty productivity has a chapter on "defining faculty productivity," yet he never specifically defines it in the chapter! The National Study of Instructional Costs and Productivity (NSICP), which was begun in 1992, developed five measures of productivity and cost ratios. These metrics involve measures such as student credit hours taught per FTE, faculty and instructional cost per student, etc. (Middaugh 2001: 93). For the outcomes of research, NSICP listed variables such as refereed publications, various types of books, editorial positions held, and externally funded grants received (Middaugh 2001: 81). Many other such variables for teaching and research outcomes are given. Fairweather (2002) defines productivity in terms of individual faculty member outputs, including measures of both teaching and research output.

However, the authors of this chapter are primarily interested in *the behavioral variables* which lead to such outcomes. For example, what are the variables that contribute to the faculty of one university being more productive than those of other universities? Or, within the same college or university, why is a professor X perhaps two to three times or more productive as a professor Y, even if both have similar backgrounds, educational levels, etc.? The authors postulate that the productivity of an individual faculty member is determined by, among other things, a variety of *behavioral actions*. We refer to these actions as Faculty Personal Productivity, or FPP.

If one does look at research and publishing output as a primary goal, the more efficient one is in the other roles, the more time will be available for research and publishing. Not too infrequently one hears recommendations made to increase research productivity by such means as favorable teaching schedules, allocating large blocks of time, sequestering oneself away from interruptions, etc. (Arnold 2008; Perlmutter 2008). However, the authors have been able to find only anecdotal evidence of the effectiveness of such practices on faculty personal productivity.

This is but one example of the factors that we are interested in researching. We are equally interested in how to increase productivity in such areas as class preparation, grading papers, and the many other activities associated with the teaching role. Service too is of consideration; there is the question of how can one obtain committee assignments that are most congruent with one's talents and interests, and also are the *most congruent* with the days and times that the professor is in the office. Are there ways to delegate some administrative and clerical tasks to graduate or undergraduate assistants, or to perhaps better coordinate such activities with secretaries and office assistants?

Alternatively, how can professors find ways and time to do all of those tasks that *used to be done* by secretaries and office assistants in earlier years? For example, one of the authors of this chapter teaches almost exclusively at a satellite campus where there is *no* clerical or secretarial support. Only occasionally are graduate assistants available to assist one or two professors at the satellite campus. Time-consuming, yet not counted in productivity calculations, are those tasks done by professors who do not have clerical support such as *all* typing; photocopying; mailing; phone calls; meeting arranging, note-taking, typing, and distributing meeting minutes; ordering review copies of books and all other items that have to be ordered; typing and copying syllabi and handouts for classes; creating Power Point slides for classes, presentations, conferences, etc. There are even those on some campuses who complain that they, too, have very little clerical support for even the most basic things such as photocopying handouts and other class materials and find themselves spending a significant portion of their days on nonacademic-specific tasks.

Various "administrivia" tasks, although they may be necessary to the effective functioning of a department, school, or university, are *interrupters* that can impede focusing on the main tasks. Multitasking is often recommended for today's professionals with busy schedules. However, there is evidence that multitasking, while it may seem that one is getting more done, may actually be *inhibiting* overall efficiency and effectiveness (Morgenstern 2004).

Regardless of certain academic challenges, results-based institutions should emphasize their competitive strengths in rigorously specified niche academic areas. There are many self-help books available devoted to increasing personal productivity by one means or another, of which the listings in the bibliography are merely a sample. It is not our attempt to duplicate such efforts. Perhaps, ultimately, comprehensive recommendations can be made that are specifically aimed at the duties of a professor.

LITERATURE INADEQUACY

Despite examination of a number of databases with varying key words, we have been able thus far to find only a handful of references which could be considered scholarly research, even peripherally related to the topic (Shevat 1987; Milem, Berger and Dey 2000; Terpstra and Honoree 2009).

Despite the plethora of time management books written for the general public, the authors found only a handful of academically-oriented articles and newsletters on the topic of time management (e.g., McGee 2006), and a lack of links to university competiveness is quite obvious. This chapter seeks also to fill this gap. As stated previously, there are recent references on productivity measures for colleges and universities. However, there is little or no explanation of the *individual behaviors* which enable faculty members to become more productive.

A PROPOSED LIST OF FACTORS OF FACULTY PERSONAL PRODUCTIVITY

From common experience, and a review of self-help books, there are a number of factors that are surmised to have an impact on the productivity (or lack thereof) of faculty members. Furthermore, most if not all of the factors are interrelated. A few significant ones are the following:

Clutter Control

The cluttered professor's office, with books and papers scattered all over, including on the floor, is a stereotype. However, the stereotype certainly has some truth to it. Although the resident of such an office may say "I know it looks messy, but I know where everything is," it is doubtful that such is the case in many situations. The authors have personally struggled with clutter control, and, in fact, still struggle with this and many of the other factors.

Time Management

Perhaps more books have been written about time management than any of the other factors (e.g., Smith 1992). Why does professor X get so much more done in a typical day than professor Y? Certainly, a knowledge and practice of time management principles *within the context of the faculty role* is a major factor. Mitchell (2007: 240) aptly states:

> I have found personally that two general principles have emerged with respect to time. First, to do good research takes blocks of time. You cannot spend 15 minutes here and 20 minutes there and expect to get anything done. Thinking, reading, and writing demand hours of uninterrupted work. Second, teaching and service work, which are filled with deadlines NOW, will overwhelm discretionary time allocated for research. One needs to guide time and distribute it wisely.

Focus

The ability to focus on important tasks and see them through to completion is paramount to a successful career. There may well be other factors that in turn affect focus, such as "flow," defined by Czikszentmihalyi (1990: xi) as "the positive aspects of human experience—joy, creativity, the process of total involvement with life." How can faculty members get into a state of *flow* more often and tap the inner wellspring of creativity?

Organizing

Collections of books, articles, and other publications—whether in paper or electronic form—are both a blessing and a curse for many faculty. Research/writing and course management alone require files of some manner. What things should be saved, and in what format, and where? Certainly the lack of an ability to effectively organize and file often leads to problems with clutter.

Management of E-Mail and Contact Management

This one deserves a category all by itself. Many professors see e-mail management as one of their major challenges. There are some books and articles that have been written about coping with this modern-day problem ("Herding cats and barrels of monkeys"; Morgenstern 2004).

Other Factors

Additionally, the support of college and university administration, at all levels, can play a significant role in encouraging, or hindering, FPP.

Finally, the role of the "inner self" is relevant to FPP. For example, Allen (2001) states "Getting things done is about the agreements we make with ourselves and how well we're going to honor them. We spend so much time worrying about the agreements we make with others, but it begins with making and keeping agreements with ourselves, eliminating the negativity that happens when we don't."

Certainly, most of us know that to make headway in our lives and with our ideas we have to take time for reflection. But in the sticky area of productivity, when all we want to do is step on the gas and go full-tilt ahead, who has time for reflection? Not making (or taking) time for this essential element of creativity is bound to eventually increase stress and wheel-spinning, both counter-productive to productivity. How can professors make more time for quality, uninterrupted reflection?

We have been looking at individual factors. But it is the individual behaviors which, in the aggregate, determine how productive a professor will be; the productivity—*a measure of competitiveness*—of a college or university is comprised of the aggregate productivity of its faculty.

CONCLUDING POINTS

First of all, what are the relevant research questions for this topic? A few preliminary ones can be stated:
- What elements of FPP do professors consider to be relevant to being successful? Being successful can also include accomplishing necessary

tasks in a shorter rather than a longer period of time, in order to allocate time to other activities (family, leisure, community, etc.) of a well-rounded professor's life.

- Are some techniques more effective than others in addressing the factors?
- Is there an interest among professors in enhancing their FPP?
- Are there best practices that can be identified?

In addition to elaborating on initial work on faculty productivity by Dengler and Herring (2008), the chapter seeks to accomplish the following:

- To generate research in the subject.
- On an ongoing process, to identify and provide access to self-help resources and best practices to assist academics with personal productivity.
- To design and conduct a web-based survey of Decision Sciences Institute and Academy of Management members.
- To encourage interested persons to develop collateral paper presentations for future conferences.

An ultimate goal, after significant research has been conducted and findings generated, is to be able to provide tools for professors to maximize their FPP. The authors invite comments and suggestions from readers in furtherance of this stream of inquiry. Thus, FPP is deemed crucial in the universities' efforts to be more successful and competitive.

REFERENCES

Allen, D. *Getting Things Done: The Art of Stress-Free Productivity.* New York: Viking Penguin, 2001.

Arnold, D. "Publishing Tips for Business Faculty," *Southeast Decision Sciences Institute Proceedings* (CD-ROM), 2008.

Aslett, D. *How to Have a 48-Hour Day.* Pocatello, ID: Marsh Creek Press, 1996.

——— . *The Office Clutter Cure.* Pocatello, ID: Marsh Creek Press, 2008.

——— . *Clutter's Last Stand.* Cincinnati, OH: Writer's Digest Books, 2008.

Bowling, N. and G. Burns. "Scholarly Productivity of Academic SIOP Members: What Is Typical and What Is Outstanding?" *The Industrial Organizational Psychologist* 47, no. 4 (2010): 11-18.

Bruch, H. and G. Sumantra. *A Bias for Action.* Harvard, MA: Harvard Business School Press, 2004.

Center for Excellence in Teaching, Boston University. "Time Management for Faculty." http://www.bu.edu/cet/develop/time.html

Chabris, C. F. "You Have Too Much Mail: The Overflowing Brain," *Wall Street Journal,* December 15, 2008, 17(A).

Conlon, M. "Smashing the Clock." *Business Week* no. 4013 (December 11, 2006): 60-68.

Covey, S. R. "The Seven Habits of Highly Effective People." Discussion notes prepared by Joseph M. Mellichamp. http://www.leaderu.com/cl-institute/habits/habtoc.html

Covey, S. R., Merrill, A. R. and R. R. Merrill. *First Things First.* New York: Simon & Schuster, 1994.

Czikszentmihalyi, M. *Flow: The Psychology of Optimal Experience.* Harper Perennial, 1990.

Davenport, T. H. *Thinking for a Living: How to Get Better Performance and Results from Knowledge Workers.* Boston, MA: Harvard Business School Press, 2005.

Dengler, R. & R. Herring. "Interactive Workshop on Academic Personal Productivity." Paper presented at the Decision Sciences Institute Annual Meeting, Session QP-21, November 2008.

Fairweather, J. S. "The Mythologies of Faculty Productivity: Implications for Institutional Policy and Decision Making." *The Journal of Higher Education* 73, no. 1 (Jan-Feb 2002): 26-48. Special Issue on *The Faculty in the New Millennium*, published by Ohio State University Press.

Green, S. D. "Green Productivity Solutions." http://www.sgps.biz/page2.html

"Herding Cats and Barrels of Monkeys: Time Management for Faculty." http://cuttingedge-ucation.wetpaint.com/page/Time+Management+for+Faculty?t=anon

Hummel, C. E. *Tyranny of the Urgent.* Downers Grove, IL: Intervarsity Press, 1994.

Ibekwe, L. A. *Using Total Quality Management to Achieve Academic Program Effectiveness: An Evaluation of Administrator and Faculty Perceptions in Business Schools at Historically Black Colleges and Universities.* Ph.D. Dissertation, 2007.

Johnson, S. *Who Moved My Cheese?* New York: G. P. Putnam's Sons, 1998.

Kayser, T. A. *Mining Group Gold: How to Cash in on the Collaborative Brain Power of A Group.* New York: McGraw-Hill, 1995.

Kelley, R. E. and J. Caplan. "How Bell Labs Create Star Performers." *Harvard Business Review* 71, no. 4 (July-August 1993).

Kelley, R. E. *How To Be A Star at Work: Nine Breakthrough Strategies You Need to Succeed.* New York: Times Books (Random House), 1998.

Macan, T. H. "Time Management: Test of a Process Model." *Journal of Applied Psychology* 79, no. 3 (1994).

Mandel, M. "The Real Reasons You're Working So Hard . . . and What You Can Do About It." *Business Week* (October 3, 2005): 60-67.

McClain, L. T. "Lessons in Time Management." *The Chronicle of Higher Education,* December 16, 2003. http://chronicle.com/jobs/news/2003/12/2003121601c.htm

McGee, J. A. "Reading List for Aspiring Knowledge Workers." *Future Tense,* February 27, 2006. http://futuretense.corante.com/archives/2006/02/27/a_reading_list_for_aspiring_knowledge_workers.php

Mercer Consulting. *Knowledge Worker Productivity Measurement Examples: Survey of Research,* 2007.

Middaugh, M. F. *Understanding Faculty Productivity.* San Francisco: Jossey-Bass, 2001.

Milem, J. F., Berger, J. B. and E. L. Dey. "Faculty Time Allocation: A Study of Change Over Twenty Years." *Journal of Higher Education* 71, no. 4 (2000): 454-75.

Mitchell, T. "The Academic Life: Realistic Changes Needed for Business School Students and Faculty." *Academic of Management Learning and Education* 6, no. 2 (2007): 236-51.

Morgenstern, J. *Never Check E-mail in the Morning: And Other Unexpected Strategies for Making Your Work Life Work.* New York: Fireside, 2004.

Palmer, P. J. *The Courage to Teach: Exploring the Inner Landscape of a Teacher's Life.* New York: Jossey-Bass, 1998.

Perlmutter, D. D. "Do You Really Not Have the Time?" *The Chronicle of Higher Education,* August 22, 2008. http://chronicle.com/jobs/news/2008/08/2008082201c.htm

Plater, W. M. "Future Work: Faculty Time in the 21st Century." *Change* 27, no. 3 (1995): 22-33.

Ridenour, F. *The Traveler's Guide to Life at Warp Speed: 30 Short Readings to Help You Slow Down and Catch up with God.* Ventura, CA: Regal Books, 1990.

Shevat, R. S. *An Examination of the Consonance between Faculty Work Preferences and Administrative Expectation, and the Perceived Need for the Reorganization of Work for Purposes of Faculty Satisfaction and Institutional Efficiency in One College.* Ph.D. Dissertation, 1987.

Smith, K. *It's About Time.* Wheaton, IL: Crossway Books, 1992.

Terpstra, D. E. and A. L. Honoree. "The Effects of Different Teaching, Research, and Service Emphases on Individual and Organizational Outcomes in Higher Education Institutions." *Journal of Education for Business* 84, no. 3 (2009): 169-77.

University of North Carolina, *UNC Tomorrow 2007.*

Walden, M. L. "Economic Benefits in North Carolina of UNC Campuses," January 2009. http://www.northcarolina.edu/nctomorrow/UNC_Economic_Impact_-_Walden.pdf

Chapter 6
Mandatory Health Insurance: Lessons from Massachusetts[1]

Craig J. Richardson

What lessons can be learned from the successes as well as pitfalls of mandatory health insurance? Now that the Obama administration has enacted far-reaching health care reforms that increase the role of government, the case of Massachusetts is worth serious study. Massachusetts' three year experiment with mandatory health insurance (known as *Chapter 58 legislation*) has been judged by some health economists to be a qualified success, since it reached a primary goal of lowering the number of uninsured in the state (Gruber 2009; Long 2008). On the other hand, Tanner (2008: 5) argues that previously uninsured citizens signed up for health insurance because it was free or heavily subsidized, not because of the mandate itself. Official state statistics claim the number of uninsured in the state dropped from 11 percent in 2005 to less than 3 percent in 2009 (www.MAHealthConnector.org 2009). Tanner (2009) disputes this number and suggests the number is closer to 5 percent, using Urban Institute and Census surveys as evidence. What supporters and foes of mandatory health insurance both seem to agree upon is that the number of uninsured has fallen in the state since Chapter 58, and yet there remain between 150,000 and 200,000 uninsured citizens.

Unlike a market-based solution, which would shrink the role of government while enhancing individual choices, Massachusetts state government mandates that individuals purchase health insurance using the "carrot and stick" approach. First, it created the Commonwealth Care Program in 2006, which allows lower income state citizens to obtain health insurance subsidies, and second, it fines individuals (up to $912 per year in 2009) and qualifying firms ($295 per employee) if the individual is not insured.

There are reasons to be concerned about the rapidly growing expense of this program, which even advocates such as Gruber (2009) admit were put aside in the quest for universal coverage. The costs have risen from $133 million in 2007, to an estimated $800 million by the end of 2009, as seen in Table 6.1, Row a. As is also seen in Table 6.1, Row b, this has been only partially offset by the $275 million drop in state expenditures for the uncompensated care pool, which Massachusetts pays to hospitals if individuals do not have health insurance. Note that since expenditures on uncompensated care only dropped by 34 percent, this suggests that a substantial number of citizens are still uninsured, or are continuing to seek treatment through the emergency room rather than a primary care physician. Meanwhile, rows d and e represent changes in costs for state provided medical insurance for the poor, or MassHealth, as the state phased out its old Medicaid program. Lastly, Table 6.1, Row g, shows the increased payments to hospitals for indigent individuals who previously did not qualify for any government health programs.

TABLE 6.1
Massachusetts Health Care Reform Spending, FY06-FY09 ($ million)

State Program	Actual FY06	Actual FY07	Actual FY08	Estimated FY09	Change FY06-FY09
a) Commonwealth Care	0	133	628	800	800
b) Uncompensated Care for Hospitals	656	665	416	406	-250
c) Subtotal (a+b)	**656**	**798**	**1,044**	**1,206**	**550**
d) MassHealth Coverage Rate Expansion	0	224	355	452	452
e) Supplemental Payments to Medicaid MCOs (Federal Share)	385	0	0	0	-385
f) Subtotal (d+e)	**385**	**224**	**355**	**452**	**67**
g) Supplemental Payments to Safety Net Hospitals	0	287	287	200	200
h) Grand Total (c+f+g)	**1,041**	**1,309**	**1,686**	**1,858**	**817**
State Share of Expenditures (50%)	521	655	843	929	409
Annual Increase		134	189	86	
Average Increase (FY06-09)					102
Annual Change (%)		25.7	28.8	10.2	78.5

Source: Raymond 2009: 6 (Table 2), which relied on data from Massachusetts state government. Further analysis by author.

The rapid growth in expenditures is not altogether surprising as Massachusetts only pays 50 cents for every $1 it spends on expanding its health care initiative. The Federal government pays the other half in matching funds. From 2006 to 2009, Massachusetts' health care initiative (which includes supplemental payments to Medicaid and hospitals for unfunded care) increased from $1.04 billion to $1.86 billion, an increase of 78 percent, as seen in Table 6.1. Even if the Federal government continues to pay half of the increase in these expenses, the growth rate in the state's spending on its health care initiative still averaged almost 26 percent from 2006-2009. The state now spends 33 percent more per person on health care than the national average, while in 1980 it was 23 percent more (Sack 2009). In total, annual state expenditures on the state's health care initiative are projected to be $409 million higher in 2010 than in 2006 (after receiving an additional $409 million in Federal reimbursements), which is an average increase of $102 million per year, as seen in Table 6.1. However, Federal reimbursements are not guaranteed, and must be negotiated by the state (Dembner 2008). This puts Massachusetts in a particularly vulnerable position if there are future Federal budget cuts, since their health care expenses could potentially rise even more quickly.

A $409 million increase in state expenditures ordinarily might not cause much alarm during the budgetary process, since this was just a 2% increase in its $20 billion state budget, and a recent report by the non-partisan Massachusetts Taxpayers Foundation (MTF) even states that the cost increase has been "marginal" (Raymond 2009. 7). The same report shows little concern about the underlying rapid rate of growth, since newly revised projections for 2010 show that enrollment and expenditures will plateau. However, these projections need to be taken with great caution, as past projections have been wide of the mark, as noted by MTF's most recent report (Raymond 2009). In any case, in the current fiscal crisis that Massachusetts and the nation faces, these higher health care costs take on greater significance. In 2009, the state collected $2 billion less tax revenue than in 2008, a drop of 10 percent. With only $500-$800 million left in its "rainy day fund," the state is rapidly burning through its reserves (Massachusetts Taxpayers Foundation 2009.) Thus, greater access to health care, a primary goal of the program, has been achieved, but the large increase in costs has put increased pressure on an already strapped state government.

As this chapter will explore, there is another, more hidden aspect of the Commonwealth Care program that may drive future costs far higher than originally projected. Embedded within the heavily subsidized program are several perverse incentives affecting firms and individuals. First, the program unintentionally gives incentives for smaller firms to discontinue health insurance so that their employees can sign up for cheaper state-subsidized care. Second, it gives incentives for employed individuals to earn less in order to qualify for higher benefits. Because subsidies immediately fall off as one crosses defined income brackets, instead of being slowly withdrawn, there are sudden and large implicit marginal tax rates that can exceed 100 percent in some cases. Enrollment in Commonwealth Care is expected to have "moderate" growth in 2010 according to state government projections, primarily due to the economic downturn (Governor's Budget FY2009-2010). What remains to be seen is if this enrollment will accelerate as more individuals and firms make choices that allow them to qualify for subsidized care, as they see the rewards for doing so.

The outline of the rest of this chapter is as follows. First, it seeks to explain the mechanics of mandatory health insurance as it was enacted in Massachusetts, and the special difficulties of making health insurance a mandated purchase. Second, it explores in further detail the perverse incentives detailed above, with particular detail paid to the problems caused by the staggered health insurance subsidies for consumers. Finally, the chapter examines some alternatives to Massachusetts' current system that would somewhat ameliorate the perverse incentives embodied in the current system, as well as contain the state's growing medical costs.

BACKGROUND

In 2005, nearly a half million people in the state of Massachusetts—over 11 percent of the population—were without health insurance. As a result, Massachusetts' uninsured often sought primary medical care in emergency rooms, which is a highly inefficient and costly delivery mechanism for non-emergency care. Indeed, one in five U.S. adults (21 percent) reported they went to the emergency room for a condition that could have been treated by a regular doctor. In comparison, only 6 percent of patients in Germany report such unnecessary emergency room use (The Commonwealth Fund 2008). In addition, in Massachusetts as well as the rest of the country, persons without health insurance may have no money to pay their bills after hospital stays. This creates a need for hospitals to seek additional revenue to cover these losses. Hospitals typically cover these losses by charging insurance companies higher rates, resulting in higher insurance premiums for the insured population. However, 85 percent of uncompensated care is reimbursed by government, with over two-thirds borne at the Federal level (Hadley and Holahan 2004). Uninsured individuals typically receive less care in a given year, wait longer to get treated, and have higher mortality rates (ibid).

In 2006 the state, led by then-governor Mitt Romney, led a drive to address the problem of its medically uninsured population. The legislature then passed a bill (known as Chapter 58) that created and enforced a mandatory health insurance program, the first of its kind in the country. The idea of the experiment was threefold. First, it sought to create better access for all state residents by making health insurance not only more available but more affordable. It does this through subsidizing the cost of private insurance to those who meet the affordability requirements, but do not qualify for Medicaid. The goal is to shrink the number of people seeking primary medical care in the emergency rooms, and improve overall health outcomes of the state's formerly uninsured citizens. Second, it aims to create more efficiency in the system by acting as a buying representative on the behalf of thousands of small employers and individuals. This allows it to negotiate better rates with a number of private insurers, through economies of scale. Third, it seeks to sharply increase the level of responsibility of Massachusetts' citizens, by mandating that all people have health insurance coverage, and requiring larger employers to play a role as well. Jonathan Gruber (2008), a health economist at MIT, was one of the primary architects of the plan, and argued that mandatory health insurance was a more cost-effective method than the government providing universal coverage.

MASSACHUSETTS RESIDENTS' NEW HEALTH CARE CHOICES

Mandating health insurance presents a dilemma that is vastly different from mandating, say, that an automobile owner pays for annual registration fees. With an automobile owner, the state can take a person's license away, denying him or her the right to drive. The general public will find no problem with this tactic. However, if a person shows up to a hospital with a life-threatening condition and no health insurance or ability to pay, a hospital will not turn away the patient. This is not only Federal law, it is also difficult to imagine doctors turning away these patients, or the general public agreeing to this type of policy. Thus, the state has far less leverage in enforcing and/or mandating payments in the area of health care. Unlike any other good, consumers of health care goods have in many instances an "effective demand" without having any money. This wrinkle presents particular challenges for policymakers, regardless of ideological stripe, in crafting an improved health care system for the United States.

The Chapter 58 legislation attempts to broach this problem, by offering Massachusetts residents three health broad insurance outcomes, depending upon their income level and employment status. Put simply, health insurance is either "free," paid for at the market rate, or state-subsidized (see Tables 6.2 and 6.3).

For those whose income falls below the Federal Poverty Level (FPL), Mass-Health provides "free" insurance (Table 6.2 provides the official FPL thresholds for individuals and families in 2008). This is a Massachusetts health care program which is reimbursed through Medicaid, the Federal aid program. Mass-Health is also under financial pressure due to the sharp level of reimbursements it is requesting from Medicaid in recent years, but is not directly affected by the new mandatory health insurance program.

If residents' incomes are 300 percent or more above the Federal Poverty Level they will not qualify for any state aid, but may choose to elect to buy health insurance through Massachusetts' Commonwealth Choice program, or purchase directly in the private market through employee-based plans. The advantage of the Commonwealth Choice Program is that allows the state to serve as a bargaining agent on an individual's behalf, which is particularly helpful if she or he is self-employed. The state negotiates for more inexpensive group rates, and gives individuals without health insurance a choice of policies from which to choose, at varying prices and amenities. Indeed, health premiums rose only 5 percent between 2007 and 2008 through the use of this program, indicating its relative success (www.MAHealthConnector.org 2009).

TABLE 6.2

Massachusetts: An Example of State Subsidized Health Insurance
by Federal Poverty Guidelines, 2008

	Single Person		Family	
Poverty Level (FPL, %)	Income ($)	Yearly Cost ($)	Income ($)	Yearly Cost ($)
0-150	0-15,600	0	0-31,800	0
150.1-200	15,601-20,800	468	31,801-42,400	936
200.1-250	20,801-26,000	2,160	42,401-53,000	4,320
250.1-300	26,001-31,200	2,633	53,001-63,600	5,266

Source: Massachusetts State Government Health Connector. These are rates quoted for individuals and families living in central Massachusetts in 2008, from the insurance company BMC Healthnet. Similar rates applied from other insurance carriers.

TABLE 6.3
Mandated Health Insurance: Three Possibilities for Individuals

MassHealth	Commonwealth Care	Private Market/Commonwealth Connector
Income < 100% FPL	Income is between 100-300% FPL	> 300% FPL or
	Employers don't provide health insurance AND firm size < 12	Work for firms with > or = to 12 workers
"Free"	Subsidized by government	Market rate

Note: FPL refers to the Federal Poverty Level, which is indicated on Table 6.2.

It is the middle range, for the individuals and families between 100-300 percent of the FPL thresholds that is deserving of more attention, since this range provides very generous health insurance subsidies to qualifying individuals who sign up for Commonwealth Care. These subsidies do two things. First, they strongly discourage individuals from earning more (thus losing the benefits) and second, they encourage other individuals to earn less, so they too can qualify for Commonwealth Care. Over certain ranges, the subsidies are curtailed abruptly with a small earnings increase (and vice versa), leading to extraordinarily high implicit marginal tax rates, as will be discussed shortly.

Who exactly is eligible? Commonwealth Care is designed to assist adults who are not offered employer-sponsored insurance, do not qualify for Medicare, Medicaid or certain other special insurance programs, and who earn no more than 300 percent of the FPL. In 2008, 300 percent of FPL was $31,200 for an individual and $63,600 for a family of four. In addition, if an adult worked in a firm with eleven or more employees, the firm is expected to contribute a set amount toward the health insurance costs, and the individual is not eligible for

Commonwealth Care. It is the hidden "devil in the details" that has created unintentional perverse incentives for both employers and employees. The state government is struggling to combat these incentives on the employer side, but has no plans to change them on the individual side. We now examine each group in turn.

PERVERSE INCENTIVES FOR EMPLOYERS

Massachusetts' legislation was designed to lessen the financial blow of mandatory health insurance to individuals by requiring all employers with eleven or more employees to make health insurance available for individual purchase, through Section 125 cafeteria plans. (Firms below this size are exempt from these requirements.) There are now three requirements for qualifying employers. First, they are now required to satisfy certain requirements to avoid a "fair share assessment" which is a financial penalty from the state. Primarily, employers can avoid the assessment if they have at least 25 percent of their full-time employees (35 hours per week) enrolled in the company-offered health insurance plan. If the employer does not meet this benchmark they can still avoid the assessment by paying at least 33 percent of the premiums due on the full-time employees who are enrolled in the company-offered plan. Failing to meet at least one of these tests can result in an annual "fair share assessment" of $295 per employee per year, which is pro-rated for part-time employees. In addition, the firms must offer the same coverage to all employees. Third, employers must disclose how they are meeting these guidelines to the state government. The law was popular with many employees, as 166,000 signed up for health coverage since the law was enacted (Draper et al. 2008).

Yet there have been unintended consequences. Nationwide trends have led to employer health care premiums growing an average of 73 percent between 2000-2005, according to a Kaiser Family Foundation survey (2006), and as a result, employers have been forced in many cases to lower wage increases or health benefits (Sood et al. 2007). With Massachusetts now offering heavily subsidized health insurance to workers making between 100 to 300 percent of the Federal Poverty Level, there are obvious incentives for those firms paying in that range to consider dropping health insurance benefits and offer higher wages instead, in what is called "crowding out." Employers can then promote that employees sign up for state subsidized care. A study by Long and Masi (2008) finds little evidence of crowding out, but other evidence by Draper et al. (2008) suggests otherwise, at least for small business owners. Small group enrollment in private health insurance declined by 15,000 in 2007 (even as overall enrollment increased in Commonwealth Care), and a recent survey showed that some small businesses are feeling the pinch from rising health care costs and expect to be "less committed" to offering health care coverage as the costs continue to rise. The same survey showed growing frustration from businesses about the increasing responsibilities that firms are expected to provide. In particular, starting January 1, 2009, firms have had to offer health care plans which included prescription drug coverage. They also are required to provide the state quarterly information on their employees' health care program, versus annual reports when the law was passed (Draper et al. 2008).

Other perverse incentives have also arisen. For a firm that has eleven workers, it might be financially advantageous for the manager to fire one employee in order to take advantage of the Commonwealth Care Program, and not pay any fair share assessments as well as eliminate all health insurance responsibilities. Likewise, other small firms might hesitate to hire more than ten workers who were getting subsidized health care, because now they would be obligated to provide it, or suffer the financial consequences. Thus, there are significant incentives that push small firms toward shrinking rather than growing.

To date, Massachusetts has approximately 44,000 firms, and of those, 19,000 have eleven or more employees, thus subjecting them to the "fair share" assessment. As of March 2008, approximately 650 of the 19,000 did not pay their "fair share" and thus paid a total of $6.6 million in assessments. The employees working in the remaining 25,000 firms with fewer than 11 employees had to obtain health insurance either on their own or through the Connector program (Long and Masi 2008: w291). One would predict that the relative share of firms with less than eleven employees will grow in coming years, given the current incentives to do so. In addition, one would expect more employers to shoulder the fair share assessment rather than the cost of providing health insurance. Raymond (2009: 6) projects that fair share assessments will grow to $12 million in 2009 and $20 million in 2010, presumably as employers find ways to avoid paying for their employees' health insurance.

PERVERSE INCENTIVES FOR INDIVIDUALS

Like any government subsidy program that depends upon income levels, problems arise when the individual begins to earn more income. The subsidy is withdrawn, resulting in an implicit tax rate that may exceed the tax rate for the wealthiest income tax bracket. By way of example, suppose a person earned $20,000 and received a $5,000 government subsidy. Suppose also that for every additional $1,000 a person earned, $200 of the subsidy were removed. In this case, if a person received a raise to $25,000, then the $5,000 raise would mean a $1,000 decrease in the subsidy. Thus, the implicit tax would be 20 percent, on top of existing Federal and State income taxes paid.

This implicit tax, although high, is at least smooth and predictable in this example. Unfortunately, the implicit tax rates of the Commonwealth program have sudden transitions, leading to highly unusual and perverse incentives to earn less, not more, in order to qualify for government subsidies, as seen in Table 6.3. They occur because the jumps in health care costs are immediate, rather than occurring at the margin. Thus, a $1,000 increase in income can throw an individual into a completely new and far more expensive category, resulting in an implicit marginal tax rate that can exceed one hundred percent for small income changes. Richardson (1994) identified similar perverse incentives in the failed 1994 Clinton health care initiative, which sought to mandate that employers provide health care. In this case, small employers hiring one more worker might have suddenly paid thousands more dollars in health care costs for all their workers, as the firm moved to a higher bracket with less generous subsidies, and had to now cover all the workers at a higher rate.

Take for example a couple with two children living in central Massachusetts. Let's also suppose the father works, earning $30,000 a year while the mother stays at home with the children. Assume the family signs up with the health insurance company BMC Healthnet, which offered the following state-subsidized rates below as seen in Table 6.2 in 2008. (This rate structure was typical of other health care providers' premiums, and information on multiple plans was obtained from a health care representative working for the Massachusetts Connector program.) Now at this point the family pays nothing for health insurance, as the family income is less than 150 percent of the Federal Poverty guidelines, as seen in Table 6.2. However, if the family earns another $10,000, then the family loses the free benefit but still qualifies for subsidized health insurance, since now it earns between 150-200 percent of the Federal Poverty guidelines. Since the net cost of health insurance has risen from $0 to $936 per year, the implicit marginal tax rate is 9.4 percent on the $10,000 raise. The changes are also shown in Table 6.2.

However, if the family's income next rises from $40,000 to $50,000—say the stay-at-home spouse gets a part-time job—then the family moves into the next bracket, which is 200-250 percent of Federal Poverty guidelines. Now, the health care premium increases from $936 to $4,320, a difference of $3,384, and a whopping 33.8 percent implicit tax rate. It's even worse for another family that earns $40,000, and gets a raise to $45,000. This creates a nearly 68 percent implicit tax rate on the raise. For a family close to the far edge of the FPL bracket, making say $42,000 and earning a small raise to $43,000, they will now see net losses. Their net income at $42,000 after paying for $936 in health insurance costs would be $41,064, while at $43,000 they would pay $4,320 for health insurance, and thus earn $39,680. The implicit marginal tax rate on $1,000 worth of extra income is now 338 percent. The perverse incentives built into this system are doubtless causing many families as well as individuals to think carefully about accepting pay raises. In some cases, it will benefit them to work less in order to qualify for cheaper health insurance from the state. These dynamics were ignored in the original cost projections for the state, and will probably drive enrollment to higher levels than have been originally predicted, as people who currently obtain health insurance through the marketplace switch to state-subsidized insurance plans.

For now, Massachusetts appears wedded to the idea of mandatory health insurance, so there is a strong case for ironing out the perverse incentives. One step in the right direction would be to have health insurance subsidies to individuals decline at a constant percentage rate rather than having sudden transitions as illustrated in this chapter. As stated earlier, this percentage rate can be seen as a constant implicit tax rate. In one scenario, the subsidies could begin declining after earnings increased past the 100 percent of FPL level, until one reached the market price for health insurance.

The big question is: what should that percentage rate be? Lower percentage rates improve work incentives but will cost the state more money to implement, and vice versa. If we use an 8 percent rate as an example, then $80 of every $1,000 a person earned above the FPL would be applied toward paying for private health insurance. If the market price of health insurance was $500 per month, or $6,000 per year, then a person would receive subsidies until he or she earned $75,000 over the FPL, or about $85,000. Although the implicit tax rate is fairly low, one can see that this would be a very expensive program to subsidize, as most individuals would qualify. The double-edged sword here is that as one improves work incentives by lowering the percentage rate paid to health insurance, it costs the state more money. This means the state must raise taxes somewhere else to pay for it, again potentially destroying work incentives. In any case, a smooth transition schedule of some sort is still preferred to the one in place today, as it will lessen crowding out behavior by firms and keep work incentives oriented in the right direction.

With regard to firms, the current rules in place have created an environment where firms will find it increasingly expensive to operate. If Massachusetts relieved firms of the responsibility to provide health insurance (and the Federal government simultaneously eliminated the tax benefits) individuals would begin to shop for health insurance in much the same way as they do for car, flood, and fire insurance. Free market forces would put downward pressure on health insurance premiums, as individuals would be better able to signal which types of benefits they were willing to pay for. It would also eliminate the perverse incentives that currently exist in Massachusetts' business environment toward hiring.

CONCLUSION

The success or failure of the Massachusetts mandatory health insurance program has been closely monitored as a harbinger of future outcomes for a nationwide move in this direction. To date, the results have been mixed, as has been demonstrated in this chapter. Mandatory health care reforms have resulted in fewer uninsured but have not contained soaring costs in the health care system. Instead, the reforms have created incentives for costs to rise even faster. Here is a summary of some of the reasons.

1. Massachusetts' expenditures on its health care initiative have been discounted by 50 percent, thanks to matching funds from the Federal government, which has encouraged a rapid increase in state expenditures.
2. Growing burdens on businesses have meant that an increasing number are choosing to steer their employees into the state-subsidized system rather than provide health insurance themselves. In addition, some will hesitate to expand beyond ten employees when faced with the cost of providing health insurance or state penalties.

3. Consumers of health insurance over certain income ranges have strong incentives to earn less money in order to qualify for more generous subsidies.

Mandatory health insurance improves access, but the nut has not yet been cracked to solve the second and now more pressing problem of efficiency and cost containment. An argument for making health insurance mandatory is that individuals get access to much medical care anyway, regardless of whether they can afford it, by simply showing up at the emergency room or not paying their medical bills. But the case of Massachusetts also offers cautionary lessons for the United States as the Obama administration seeks wide-ranging health care reforms that move more in the direction of mandatory health insurance. In the long term, health care reforms will need a combination of market incentives and government standards to enhance efficiency while at the same time assuring that "bad risks," such as unemployed people with pre-existing conditions, receive proper medical care.

NOTE

1. This paper was first published in the *Cato Journal*, Vol. 29, no. 2 (Spring/Summer 2009). The author thanks Michael Cannon for many helpful comments. He also thanks the American Institute for Economic Research in Great Barrington, MA, for supporting this research through a 2008 Research Fellowship.

REFERENCES

Cannon, M. "A Fork in the Road: Obama, McCain and Health Care." *Cato Institute Briefing Paper* (July 28, 2008).

Dembner, A. "Subsidized Care Plan's Cost to Double." *Boston Globe* (February 3, 2008). http://www.boston.com/news/health/articles/2008/02/03/subsidized_care_plans_cost _to_double/?page=1

Draper, D., et al. "Massachusetts Health Reform: High Costs and Expanding Expecta- tions May Weaken Employer Support." *Issue Brief No.* 124, Center for Studying Health System Change, October 2008. www.hschange.org/CONTENT/1021/#ib2

Gruber, J. "Response: In Massachusetts, We Got Reform Right." *The New Republic* (March 22, 2009). http://blogs.tnr.com/tnr/blogs/the_treatment/archive/2009/03/22/ response-in-massachusetts-we-got-reform-right.aspx

———. "Covering the Uninsured in the United States." *Journal of Economic Literature* 46, no. 3 (2008): 571-606.

Governor's Budget FY 2010. "Health Care Reform," Massachusetts, 2009. See also: http://www.mass.gov/bb/h1/fy10h1/exec10/hbudbrief20.htm

Hadley, J. and J. Holahan. "The Cost of Care for the Uninsured: What Do We Spend, Who Pays, and What Would Full Coverage Add to Medical Spending?" Kaiser Commission on Medicaid and the Uninsured, 2004. http://www.kff.org/uninsured/ upload/The-Cost-of-Care-for-the-Uninsured-What-Do-We-Spend-Who-Pays-and- What-Would-Full-Coverage-Add-to-Medical-Spending.pdf

Kaiser Family Foundation. 2005 Kaiser/HRET Employer Health Benefit Survey, 2006.

Long, S. and P. Masi. "How Have Employers Responded to Health Reform in Massachusetts? Employees' Views at the End of One Year." *Health Affairs* 27, no. 6 (2008): w576-583.

Massachusetts Taxpayers Foundation. (2009). "MTF Forecast: Revenues Collapse in Fiscal 2009 and 2010," May 5, 2009.

————. "State Faces Large Deficits in both Fiscal 2008 and 2009: Threatens Massive Depletion of Reserves." *Massachusetts Taxpayers Foundation Bulletin*, May 13, 2008.

Massachusetts Health Connector. "Facts and Figures," April 2009. See various figures at: http://www.mahealthconnector.org/portal/binary/com.epicentric.contentmanagement .servlet.ContentDeliveryServlet/About%2520Us/News%2520and%2520Updates/Cu rrent/Week%2520Beginning%2520March%25209%252C%25202008/Facts%2520a nd%2520Figures%25203%252008.doc

Richardson, C. R. "Clinton Plan's Perverse Incentives." *Wall Street Journal* (March 15, 1994, A20).

Sack, K. "Massachusetts Faces Costs of Big Health Care Plan." *The New York Times* (March 15, 2009). http://www.nytimes.com/2009/03/16/health/policy/16mass.html? ref=weekinreview

Sood, N., Ghosh, A., and J. Escarse. "The Effect of Health Care Cost Growth on the US Economy." U.S. Department of Health and Human Services: Office of the Assistant Secretary for Planning and Evaluation (ASPE), September 2007. http://aspe.hhs.gov/ health/reports/08/healthcarecost/report.html

The Commonwealth Fund. "Why Not the Best? Results from the National Scorecard on US Health System Performance," July 17, 2008. http://www.Commonwealthfund. org/Content/Publications/Fund-Reports/2008/Jul/Why-Not-the-Best--Results-from- the-National-Scorecard-on-U-S--Health-System-Performance--2008.aspx

PART III

Socio-cultural and Legal Issues & Competitiveness

Chapter 7
New Approaches to Competitiveness Building in the Caribbean: Challenges of Creating a Pervasive Competition Culture

Debbie A. Mohammed & David Gibbs

INTRODUCTION

The issue of competitiveness continues to be a major challenge for Caribbean Community (CARICOM)[1] countries as they transition into new exportable goods and services without the support of preferential markets and pricing arrangements. The reality of operating in an environment of reciprocal trade has clearly revealed just how difficult it is for these microstates to effectively defend their home markets, while simultaneously attempting to penetrate international markets. A large part of this disconnect could be attributed to *smallness*, since domestic markets tend to be very small and sectors are often heavily segmented, populated by a few firms. In this type of scenario, domestic firms often focus primarily on securing and maintaining local market share. To the extent that competition is deemed important, this is manifested mainly in terms of marketing strategies that target domestic, possibly regional consumers while regulations governing competition tend to be viewed with some indifference by both the public and private sectors.

This chapter contends that competition and competition policy are integral elements for building competitiveness within CARICOM and that developing a competition culture is a necessary first step toward sustainable competitiveness in the region. Indeed, fostering competitiveness through dynamic competition and effective competition policies is even more imperative for the region as the fallout from the global economic crisis translates into negative economic growth for these countries, increased joblessness, declining export prices and revenue shortfalls, which have already forced the Organization of Caribbean States (OECS)[2] to seek International Monetary Fund (IMF) assistance.[3]

Revitalizing economic activity to boost consumer spending, increase exports and attract and keep investments must be urgent policy considerations for the region. One such way will be to build competitiveness in specific niche areas, understanding clearly that competitiveness takes on new meaning as governments and firms the world over employ innovative policies and strategies to stimulate their economies. The benefits of predictability, stability, and commitment to dynamic competition make competition policy a necessary requirement for competitiveness. Creating a culture that embraces and promotes competition is therefore critical to provide the impetus for enacting competition policies and adherence to these. Assuming the relevant government stimulus policies are in place, the objective of this chapter is to examine what are the impediments to building dynamic, competitive sectors in the region and to provide policy guidance on a way forward.

Section one provides a realistic context for assessing the competitiveness deficiency in the region. It highlights the current economic crisis confronting CARICOM economies and the need for a new approach to competitiveness and competitiveness building. Section two discusses the concepts of competition and competition policy, and explores how these impact competitiveness. It also looks at the state of competition in the region and how competition policy is utilized. In section three, the challenges to creating a culture of competition are addressed. Issues such as traditional perceptions and practices of doing business by the private and public sectors, as well as a business culture that focuses on securing domestic market share are explored. These practices, one may argue, may become even more entrenched as the economic slowdown intensifies and domestic players seek to erect protectionist barriers. The issue of capacity, in terms of legislation, and expertise to monitor and enforce these is also discussed. Section four concludes with policy recommendations aimed at building and sustaining a culture of competition for competitiveness in the region.

CARICOM'S CURRENT ECONOMIC POSITION AND COMPETITIVENESS IMPLICATIONS

The World Bank's 2009 review[4] of the effects of the global financial crisis warned that Latin America and the Caribbean are among the regions that would experience "a dismal financial climate" and result in negative growth in 2009. These pronouncements confirmed what officials at the Caribbean Development Bank (CDB) and Finance Ministries across the region were forced to accept, that while the intensity of economic slowdowns would vary from country to country, generally, the economic outlook for all CARICOM member countries was grim.

The negative impacts of the global financial contagion on domestic economies were certainly not unexpected given the interconnectedness of financial and investment markets. For CARICOM countries though, it was clear that an external shock of such magnitude would have profound consequences for economic survival and development goals, given their peculiar vulnerabilities and economic structures. Notwithstanding almost six years of improved current account positions, declines in public external debt relative to output, increases in international reserves and financial sector reforms which strengthened Latin America and the Caribbean's ability to withstand the global crisis, the World Bank (2009: 118)[5] notes that increased risk aversion and falling external demand compounded by declines in commodity prices and remittances, precipitated sharp declines in growth in "virtually all countries in the region."

For the small economies of CARICOM those very consequences arising from the financial crisis spell serious economic fallout for much of the region. CARICOM countries are some of the smallest and most vulnerable in the world, which severely inhibits their ability to respond quickly or effectively to external shocks. The issue of size also becomes important since the narrow range of available resources in essence determines economic activity. As such, CARI-COM states characteristically concentrate on production for export of a few commodities, which "creates excessive dependence on international trade and increases (their) vulnerability to external shocks" (Mohammed 2008: 3). In the wake of the global financial crisis, falling commodity prices served to depress the terms of trade of several commodity exporters including Antigua, Belize, Guyana and Jamaica; while the Latin America/Caribbean region as a whole experienced reduced incomes of approximately 2.2 percent of gross domestic product (GDP) (*Global Development Finance* 2009: 118).

This scenario, combined with the fact that inflows of external capital declined significantly in 2008, and trade in both goods and services plummeted for Latin America and the Caribbean as a whole (*Global Development Finance* 2009: 118), reinforces the extreme vulnerability of CARICOM states which, because of their small domestic markets and investment base, rely heavily on inflows of external capital to stimulate or expand economic activity. While many governments globally have been able to institute financial stimulus measures to revitalize major sectors of their economies, this is simply not a realistic option for most CARICOM states. Ability to attract and to keep investment inflows at a sustainable level is therefore critical not just for economic recovery, but for developing new, competitive products and services with export potential.

What is also worrisome is that even those CARICOM states that have shifted to service exports, away from uncompetitive commodity trade that relied heavily on preferential markets and pricing arrangements, have not been spared the effects of the global financial crisis. Indeed, the World Bank (*Global Development Finance* 2009: 123) expects "the number of tourists and tourism revenues to be affected" which is expected to undermine private consumption and affect government revenues "substantially."

Already five OECS member countries,[6] whose economies depend on tourism or offshore financial services, have sought IMF assistance to meet revenue and other shortfalls that have intensified in the first quarter of 2009. According to the Eastern Caribbean Central Bank (ECCB), the OECS region has experienced a 3.9 percent decline in GDP over the comparative period in 2008, with tourism, construction, manufacturing and retail trade all negatively affected. Inflows of FDI and remittances contracted, business confidence fell, and unemployment levels increased. It was against this background that OECS countries sought IMF financing (*Business Guardian*, July 21, 2009). Barbados' tourism industry is among the hardest hit by the economic slump, with long stay arrivals falling by 8 percent between January and May. Unemployment rose by 10 percent and economic activity contracted by 3 percent during the first half of 2009, a first since 2002 (*Gleaner*, July 29, 2009).

Declining remittances, occasioned by massive job losses in the major developed economies, have also severely impacted private consumption and investment within the region. Remittance inflows into Jamaica for the first quarter of 2009 declined by 15 percent to US$ 414.6 million when compared to the same period last year; while transfers to Guyana for 2009 were projected to decline by 20.9 percent as a consequence of the global financial crisis (*Stabroek News*, May 31, 2009).

It is not surprising that CARICOM countries are experiencing severe economic shortfalls as a result of contracting GDP, rising unemployment and declining exports. International borrowing and attracting foreign capital also seem unlikely since Standard & Poor's 2009 ratings predictions for the Caribbean are quite dismal. Jamaica has been downgraded from negative in 2008, while Barbados' ratings have been revised from stable in 2008 to negative in 2009. Trinidad & Tobago's ratings have been placed on Credit Watch with negative implications (*CanaNews*, May 30, 2009). Even in Trinidad & Tobago, with almost one decade of robust growth, debate is now raging as to whether the economy's contraction in the fourth quarter of 2008 by 1.1 percent, followed by contraction of 3.3 percent in the first quarter of 2009 signifies it is in recession (Douglas-Newsday, August 10, 2009).

Grenada's Finance Minister, Nizam Burke lamented, "many of our economies are contracting, people are losing their jobs and poverty is on the rise." He noted that the region's plans to significantly reduce poverty by 2015 were now in "serious jeopardy" since low tourist arrivals, less remittances and stagnating revenues were now forcing governments "to expand safety nets to cushion the effects of this crisis on the poor and the most vulnerable" (*CanaNews*, May 30, 2009). Yet, he noted that this crisis provided a "wonderful window of opportunity" for the region. He alluded to the need for creativity from the region, to address this dire situation. Similarly, the European Union's International Development Minister, Mike Foster noted that recovery for the Caribbean must be focused on helping governments and the private sector to " unleash potential for innovation to compete more strongly in new markets" (*CanaNews*, May 30, 2009).

The problem of export competitiveness has long bedeviled the region. In an era when preferential arrangements buoyed the region's commodity exports, the issue of enhancing competitiveness was little more than an abstract concept. Even attempts at diversification through manufacturing or service sectors have not fully appreciated nor incorporated the role of competition and competition policies as important bases for growing domestically and subsequently, internationally competitive firms.

This chapter contends that new approaches are needed to stimulate the business sectors of the region. Regional governments simply do not have the financial resources to keep businesses afloat and it is evident that inflows of private capital are dwindling as investors remain risk averse, and poor international ratings make the region a less than attractive investment.

Key to instilling confidence in both local and foreign investors will be government's policies that facilitate and promote competition as well as the attitude of the private sector in embracing the philosophy of competition. In essence, the culture of doing business in this region must move beyond simply "turning a quick profit" to one that ensures players in various segments of economic activity can all benefit from dynamic competition fuelled by innovative firm strategies and supported by targeted government policies that encourage new sector development, promote stability and predictability in economic endeavors, and suitably reward creativity and risk taking. This may be a daunting task for regional policy makers given the current state of competition within CARICOM.

COMPETITION POLICY, COMPETITIVENESS AND CARICOM ECONOMIES

It is widely recognized that Caribbean economies have certain debilitating structural features, which compromise their ability to develop a competition culture that could give rise to more competitive economies. These features include: scarcity of players, presence of government monopolies, private sector collusion which inhibits the entrance of new players and national and regional protectionist trade policy frameworks.

A major consequence of these structural peculiarities is that the interests of the consumers are undermined by an absence of diversity of goods and services. Orthodox theory holds that competition law, as part of a menu of policies, can address some of these deficiencies leading to enhanced competition and a consequential culture of competitiveness with the consumer being the ultimate beneficiary.

By competition law we mainly refer to the antitrust laws and, in general terms, to the competition authorities and courts responsible for applying it. The logic behind competition law is to improve the functioning of the market. Competition law may help to achieve this by functioning as a market-opening device, or at least prohibiting market restriction by incumbent companies thus enhancing access to potential players. It also prohibits the unfair use of market dominance by incumbent players. The intended outcome is the optimization of resource allocation and productive efficiencies, thus providing consumers with a better quality, more diverse range of goods and services often at lower costs and on better terms. At the macro level, the country may benefit too by developing competitive advantage and comparative advantage in specific sectors, leading to improved foreign exchange earnings, more employment, a better platform for sustainable development, and an improved quality of life for its citizens.[7]

Competition policy relates to government's policies, which are "directly aimed at promoting competition among producers, at least to a significant extent." Thus, competition policy encompasses competition law as well as foreign direct investment policy, privatization and deregulation, trade policy, foreign exchange policy and other policies that liberalize markets and promote competition.[8]

Competition law, by contrast, deals primarily with the conduct of firms and seeks to constrain the strategies available to firms as they engage in competitive rivalry.[9] Competition law normally includes prohibition of anticompetitive agreements, abuse of a dominant market position and merger control regulations to prevent excessive concentration that could lead to abuse of a dominant position. Competition law, therefore, is a subset of competition policy, being one of the instruments through which governments protect and promote competition in the market. It is also referred to as anti-trust or anti-monopoly law and is designed to prevent anti-competitive business practices by firms and unnecessary government intervention in the market place.[10] Whereas competition policy impacts upon border barriers and increases market access to foreign goods and services, competition law protects the process of competition within the border. Like intellectual property law, competition law is restricted in its application to the national jurisdiction. Only after a foreign firm gains access to the market bypassing border barriers can it benefit from, or be disciplined by, competition law.

Tonoyan (2002: 4) agrees that the principle objective of competition law should be to promote and encourage competition as a vehicle to promote economic efficiency and maximize consumer welfare. It should also promote freedom of choice, prevention of abuse of economic power and lessening the effects of government's intervention in the market. The typical conduct provisions in competition law are horizontal agreements and vertical constraints. The former refers to implicit to explicit agreements between firms operating with identical or similar products in the same market. The latter, according to Tonoyan (2002: 8-9) refers to agreements between firms operating at different stages in the production or marketing chain. The typical structural provisions in competition law relate to mergers, acquisitions and joint ventures.

To analyze whether competitive forces are at play, the focus is on the *relevant* product market. Competition rules do not focus on local *production*, but rather on the *provision* of the product from both local industry and foreign sources. Hence, if firms face competitive pressure, they would be forced to produce at the lowest possible cost and sell at the lowest possible price to consumers or be pushed out of that particular market sector in search of some other more profitable venture. In the process, they will make use of resources in the most efficient way, and will innovate in order to have a competitive edge over rivals.

It is recognized that there are winners and losers in competition regimes. Stewart (2004: 25-26) notes "conventional wisdom holds that the social impact should not be addressed within competition law, but rather, other government policies should address its fallout by providing welfare, re-tooling of labor, and incentives for re-allocation of resources." Dhanjee (2003: 4)[11] outlines two main types of efficiencies promoted by competition: *static efficiency* (optimum utilization of existing resources at least cost) and *dynamic efficiency* (optimal introduction of new products, more efficient production processes and superior organizational structures over time). Competition's cost savings are passed on to all consumers—the general public's purchasing at the retail sector, business users of intermediate inputs, as well as governments undertaking public procurement. Utton (2006: 7) identifies three issues: collusion, horizontal and vertical exclusion and mergers, which form the core concerns of most competition policy regimes. As such, competition law will usually be applied to deal with these matters.

The *Jamaican Green Paper* on the proposal for a Competition Act[12] identified two main objectives: 1. to provide for competition and rivalry in the markets and to secure economic efficiency in trade and commerce, and 2. to promote consumer welfare and protect consumer interests. It is suggested that these two objectives converge into a singular theme: to promote a market-driven economy in which competitors have, relative to each other, a fair opportunity to engage therein, to the benefit of the consumer.

State of Competition Culture in the Caribbean

It is arguable that in the Caribbean competition is still viewed with a level of skepticism, if not antagonism. These small economies may at best seek ingenious ways to either adapt competition law to their own peculiar circumstances, or at worst argue for domestic government anti-competitive policies ranging from subsidies, government procurement policies, import regulations, tariffs and widely advertised buy domestic campaigns to exclude foreign firms.

In the Americas in 2006, there were fourteen countries with competition laws and competition authorities. In CARICOM, only Jamaica and Barbados have implemented competition law. In addition, CARICOM only recently established a regional competition policy authority located in Surinam, and even this is still in a state of suspension. It is clear that many CARICOM states have not seen national competition law as a priority. In the wider Caribbean (including Latin America), Costa Rica has perhaps the richest experience with competition policy.

Thus, there still remains a level of ambivalence by CARICOM states about the usefulness of including competition law as part of their general neo-liberal, pro-free trade reforms. Some admit to the need for competition law, but fear that poorly drafted competition legislation—especially in an environment of incompetent, unsophisticated and underdeveloped governmental, legal and regulatory institutions and expertise—could do more harm than good. Robinson (2008: 10) warns anti-merger provisions could potentially inhibit corporate flexibility and restrict the rewards that firms should normally derive from the functioning of the market. Since developing countries are often inclined to preserve as many protectionist barriers as possible to safeguard their economies, competition law is sometimes regarded as another step on the continuum of liberalization and may leave developing countries feeling more vulnerable to external forces.

The Caribbean has made some modest attempts in the last few years to implement a regional competition policy. An essential part of the provisions developed to create the CARICOM Single Market and Economy (CSME)[13] is a regional competition regime,[14] which now constitutes protocol nine of the revised *Treaty of Chaguaramas*. Its intended purpose is to prevent the private sector from reversing the benefits to be derived from the removal of governmental barriers to the free flow of goods and services among member states. This is deemed critical since CARICOM's small, open economies appear to be susceptible to anticompetitive conduct, which could negatively impact the objectives of a CSME predicated on the creation of a single regional economic space. The advent of the CSME has arguably hastened the imperative for competition law at both the national and regional levels. Apart from the efficiency and consumer welfare goals indicated above, competition law/policy is also aimed at market integration in a regional context.[15] In addition, the logic behind the CSME is to provide space for regional enterprises to hone their skills and become more competitive before taking on the extra-regional market.

There is the perception that throughout the region, certain segments of business activity and certain ethnic groups, because of their dominance of particular segments, tend to engage in collusions controlling particular sectors of commercial activity. These include textiles, haberdasheries, hardware supplies, automotive parts and accessories, supermarkets and restaurants and commercial banking where allegations of interest rate setting, price fixing and inter-locking directorates are common. In Trinidad and Barbados, for example, it is not uncommon to find streets lined with homogenous stores usually connected by family ties and serviced by family-connected supplier and distribution networks. Under such circumstances, competition law plays an important role in combating these anti-competition tendencies. However, one may argue that such communities have themselves broken the dominant colonial stranglehold on economic activity and to that extent have added a dimension of competition to a formerly "closed" retail sector. The commercial banking sector in the Caribbean, with its uniform fees and interest rates, does not suggest the existence of a competitive culture. The absence of widespread outcry from citizens suggests that there is, at best, ambivalence to the absence of a competitive culture.

There is also the sense that competition law and competition policy are still little known, almost esoteric concepts in the minds of many business persons, who view it as the preserve of the officials of the competition authority. This can perhaps be gleaned from the observation that competition law is a little discussed source of conversation in their public utterances. It remains to be seen how and to what extent, the current global economic crisis causes a reassessment of competition policy, especially given the move by governments around the world to intervene in the economy by (in effect) nationalizing some banks.

CHALLENGES OF CREATING A COMPETITION CULTURE IN CARICOM COUNTRIES

We have already noted that in a competitive market there are no restrictions to the entry or exit of players in and from the market. Neither are there restrictions imposed on the determination of volumes and prices. Proponents of such market arrangements argue that these promote high quality and reasonably priced goods. Our contention however is that the existence of such a market requires more than the enactment of a body of laws and institutional arrangements such as competition policy, but must be imbedded within a wider competition culture if it is to be sustainable.

By competition culture we refer to a situation where a society holds a general consensus that competition is the laudable, effective and preferable way of organizing economic activity. Jenny (2007: 6) states that competition culture is fundamentally related to the attitudes of consumers and producers. As such it is an ethical notion and speaks to the core values held by a group of persons.

There is a growing body of literature, which attempts to trace and explain the emergence of a competition culture in countries and regions as diverse as India, Canada, the Caribbean and South Africa. Competition is the driving force behind market economies and as countries embrace market fundamentalism, competitive practices emerge. Widespread attitudes among consumers of easy surrender and producers who resign themselves to complacency with the status quo are reflective of a weak competition culture.

Few would take umbrage with our statement that a competition culture requires more than simply legislating and enforcing competition law. Our second and related point that organizing an economy based on notions of competing players will only be sustainable if there is a wider culture of competition, speaks to the notion of adding legitimacy to a mode of economic relationships.

The challenge for many developing and emerging economies is how to move from competition policy as a strictly legislative undertaking to competition culture as a legitimizing and self-sustaining environment. We have already noted that the goal of competition policy is to promote fairness and efficiency, leading to consumer well being. Wang (2004: 2) however contends that different countries—developed, developing and transitional—have different histories and distinct national circumstances and thus different problems to solve and obstacles to surmount when adopting competition policies or developing competition culture.

Thus, even though competition law/policy may be transplanted from country to country through government policy, the values and concepts inherent in the law do not as easily take root. Wang (2004: 3) provides a number of recommendations on how to build a culture of competition in transitional countries. These include stimulating the reform of monopoly industries, reducing government's functions to curtail its intervention in the market and enhancing the study and research into competition policy. Mauris (2002: 1) also credits advocacy as a key means of inculcating a competition culture in the United States in the post-World War II period.

Wang (2004: 4) further notes that it requires the collaboration of key stake-holders: industry, government, consumers, agencies, enterprises and scholars, in order to create an environment of free and fair competitions in which a competition policy can operate. Without this, the attainment of economic development culminating in enhanced social welfare is derailed.

Based on the preceding discussion, current norms and attitudes surrounding the conduct of business in the Caribbean may shed some light on the competitiveness dilemma that confronts the region today. Enhancing competitiveness in existing products and services and building new competitive sectors are un-doubtedly major priorities for every CARICOM government. Yet, only two countries, Jamaica and Barbados, have established Fair Trading Commissions that are operational. Trinidad and Tobago continues to review legislation for the establishment of a Fair Trading Commission, but after more than five years of "review" the general sentiment is that there is little "official" commitment to providing the legislative environment that will facilitate free and fair competition. This is interesting since Trinidad and Tobago is considered to be the in-dustrial giant of the region. While some may point to the establishment of the CARICOM Competition Commission—the regional body that will oversee mat-ters of competition and consumer gains in the region—it must be noted that the Commission, created to support the broad objectives of the CSME, is still not fully operational. Further, many suggest that CARICOM's lack of haste to have a functioning Commission is more reflective of extra-regional pressures (arising from recently negotiated trade agreements) rather than a true regional commitment to create a more predictable business environment.

The Caribbean presents a number of challenges, which inhibits the easy emergence of a competition culture. Clearly there are historical reasons stem-ming from the existence of plantation economies, which explain why the region's economies have been dominated by monopolies and oligarchies. In countries like Barbados and Jamaica, colonialism meant that mainstream economic activity was reserved for one, minority, segment of the population which itself inhibits, rather than encourages, robust competition. Furthermore, such activity developed largely along family lines making business collusion, rather than competition, an attractive policy. Nepotism easily emerged as one of the defining features of commercial life. Also, the merchant class, which controlled the commanding heights of Caribbean economies, often dominated political life in the various legislatures and assemblies. In this scenario, it would have been unreasonable to expect the business elite to develop an economic model that did not cater to their own self-interests and feather their own nest.

In this context of social exclusion and marginalization of large segments of Caribbean populations, the eventual emergence of post-independence Caribbean governments saw welfarism, and social and economic protection for small, newly emerging entrepreneurs as a key imperative. Furthermore, these small economies with narrow production bases, high dependence on exports, lack of export diversity (both products and markets) and absence of economies of scale were thought to be extremely vulnerable to cheaper extra-regional imports. The terms of trade also saw regional economies competing on highly disadvantageous terms. Import substitution and protectionism rather than competition and an outward-export strategy commended itself as the favored policy.

Given these prevailing regional and international circumstances, a range of anti-competitive practices such as business collusion and government involvement in the economy, seem to be the preferred and more attractive option for organizing economic life. More significantly, this situation made it easy for an anti-competition culture to emerge. Today, this culture of anti-competitive practices is well entrenched, permeating all segments of the economy, involving private and public sector players. Indeed, the mantra throughout the Caribbean is that the "official" ways of doing business through formal channels tend to be inefficient in terms of both time and money.

In some countries, a few powerful firms dominate certain segments, appearing to have differentiated products when in fact it is the same company using different brand names, as the bottled water, juices and snacks industries in Trinidad reveal. In the case of the bottled water industry, two major bottled water producers now dominate the market, having bought out less competitive firms. However, they continue to sell these products using various brands and bottling addresses. The implications for product pricing and availability are quite startling. Price fixing is also prevalent in a range of industries throughout the region. Many businesses argue that market size and structure does not easily accommodate many players in any one industry and so they see buy outs, market dominance and ability to set prices as simply effective strategies to be utilized by businesses in small economies. Indeed, some maintain that their practices are not "anti-competitive" but rather incentives to offset inefficiencies of market segmentation, government bureaucracies and lack of effective legislative and business structures that impede entrepreneurship in small economies.

This anti-competitive behavior is not limited to entrepreneurs, as governments too, tend to engage in such behaviors, particularly in the areas of public procurement and award of state contracts. Some may argue that it is simply a case of ensuring expediency in state-financed projects, of ensuring cost efficiencies or simply getting the job done correctly, on time and on budget, which is in the taxpayers' interest. Consumers too, tend to be ambivalent or unaware of how to effect changes to this system of business, which gives some legitimacy to the continuation of such practices.

It is evident that such practices are untenable at a time when the region needs to attract investors and develop new areas for exports. Understanding the role that competition can play in sector and country competitiveness and the benefits to both policy makers and local entrepreneurs will be essential for inculcating a new culture based on competitive practices.

The development of such a competition culture assumes new urgency given the current global financial crisis. There are two contending approaches which are vying for public acclamation. Caribbean countries can use this period of turmoil as an opportunity to revisit, contest and perhaps discard old orthodoxies, especially those which were widely held to be complicit in the development of the crisis.

Singh (2009: 1) states, "The current crisis has more than anything in recent memory forced policy makers to revisit old orthodoxies and perhaps in many places to reopen ideological debates and issues that some may regard as long settled and long closed." Singh, Minister of Finance of Guyana, also referred to the re-opened debates on the efficiency of markets, the occurrence of market failure, the provision of public goods including global public goods such as financial stability, and the role of the state especially in ensuring sound regulation in the interest of stable markets. He noted:

> Some would even argue that excessive competition or overly aggressive and unregulated competitive behavior was actually an important contributory factor in the genesis of the United States sub-prime mortgage market crisis that was to lead to the subsequent global financial meltdown and the onset of global recessionary conditions.

The alternative is to stick with the familiar by allowing economic players the safety and comfort of a protectionist model. This latter approach is an attractive option given the political reality that any change may result in some fallout such as business collapses, job losses and threats to entrenched interests and incumbent businesses. In the short term, at least, this is a politically safe, if not economically sustainable approach.

Morris (2009: 198) states that a real danger is that in a fully liberalized economy, manufacturing industries, including those for the home market may disappear even if one is able to control dumping and subsidized imports. Thus, along with competition policy, the challenge for the Caribbean has to be an improvement of productivity, and the production of high quality goods and services. A competition culture, in which excellence is rewarded and sloppiness is punished, can provide the incentive for workers to adopt this new approach. Such a culture is likely to breed innovation, creativity and excellence.

Singh (2009: 2-3) concedes that establishing a culture of competition is a challenging undertaking in the Caribbean region due, among other factors, to smallness. He further notes:

> The question of promoting competition in small markets is by no means an easy one to answer. In other words, the potential for natural monopolies to arise is considerably greater in smaller markets than in larger markets. Indeed, because of the obvious barriers to entry that exist in small markets such as ours, the potential for dominant market positions to develop and in turn potentially to be abused is considerably greater than elsewhere.

BUILDING AND SUSTAINING A CULTURE OF COMPETITION IN CARICOM

In light of the foregoing, this chapter argues that building and sustaining competitiveness in existing or new product areas requires that the region's business and government sector understand the significance of competition and work toward building a culture based on dynamic competition. As the preceding section illustrates, this will be a daunting task for many of these small states, particularly since the practice of anti-competitive behavior is so entrenched, and provides acceptable benefits to entrepreneurs.

This is one of the key areas in which the CARICOM Competition Commission can facilitate competitiveness in the region. Given that most of CARICOM's member states have extremely limited financial resources to expend on educating their publics on the issues surrounding competition policy, coupled with the reality of very limited expertise in the areas of competitiveness, competition law and competition policy, the Regional Competition Commission will be expected to play a major role in educating the region's public and private sectors, as well as consumers and other stakeholders. Additionally, it is envisaged that the Regional Commission, through institutional arrangements with well-established competition authorities globally, can provide the technical training, attachments and internships that will go a long way toward building a cadre of regional personnel trained in such specializations.

The regional Competition Commission will also be expected to provide the technical and legal expertise to assist national jurisdictions in setting up local competition authorities. Under the CSME and the recently concluded CARIFORUM-EU Economic Partnership Agreement (EPA), competitiveness is viewed as the vehicle through which CARICOM states can become more integrated into the global economy. As such, the development of, and adherence to competition policies throughout the region is regarded as critical to attracting investment inflows, developing a range of new sectors, and expanding existing sectors.

While the regional and local competition authorities have a major role to play in changing the existing business culture within CARICOM, obviously the private sector, both the established businesses and the micro-entrepreneurs, will have to re-assess their business practices. Since manufacturing sectors in many of these countries tend to be unable to compete even in the domestic market with products imported from extra-regional producers, the implications of increased domestic competition under the EPA, or the potential for CARICOM's extra-regional competitiveness are alarming.

The region's private sectors must now decide whether they are capable of successfully defending their home markets, and identify strategies that will ensure that consumers remain loyal to their brands. Issues of product pricing, product choices and quality undoubtedly factor into such strategies, and must be guided by dynamic competition aided by competition policies. Once domestic businesses are able to capture market share and hone their competitive strategies locally, this gives them the confidence to look outward to the international market. Evidence of profit making, both actual and potential, will be the critical motivating factor in getting the region's private sectors to embrace a culture that is based foremost on competition.

Owing to the small size of domestic businesses and segments, commercial organizations such as the Chambers of Commerce, Retailers Associations, Manufacturers Associations and Small Business Associations, must be on board to endorse and encourage competition while emphasizing the value of partnerships and clustering for the purposes of sharing information on new product trends and external competitors, as well as developments in product research and technologically innovations.

Regional governments too, must show that they are committed not just to the *idea* of competition but also to actually creating an environment within which competition legislation is operational, as are rewards and penalties. A key dimension to the creation of this competition culture will be consumer education. Programs targeting various levels of the education system, primary to tertiary, will be important for instilling the benefits of competition to consumers. Additionally, public awareness programs that specifically address how anti-competitive practices disadvantage consumers, coupled with governments' active support for competition, can go a long way to change the mindset of consumers and businesses competition in the region.

Additionally, Caribbean governments must embark on a new educational thrust designed specifically for the secondary and tertiary levels that encourages entrepreneurship, and stimulates and rewards creativity as well as the application of novel approaches to modify products and processes. This will necessitate a shift in the focus of many curricula, such that education is not seen as solely an academic exercise, but rather that education institutions are key inputs into the economic functions of the wider society.

CONCLUSION

What is needed at this juncture is the development of a cadre of Caribbean nationals who have a natural orientation to investing in commercial enterprises as well as the requisite intellectual capability that places innovation, invention and risk taking at the forefront of business decisions. This attitude shift must be significantly different from what currently results from seeing business as a less preferred option to the "acceptable" professions of law, medicine or formal business studies. We envisage here the entry of a growing number of young, bright, globally conscious Caribbean nationals starting businesses in a range of traditional and new sectors. But this will require a conscious, deliberate and structured effort by both government and private sectors to develop a new generation empowered with a comfort level, savvy, and a sound grounding in the fundamentals of starting and operating enterprises. Such individuals would not be unduly deterred or antagonistic toward competition, but rather would see it as a legitimate approach to enhancing economic rewards. It is imperative that there be consensus among political parties in the region on the efficacy of competition and competitiveness, not only to provide incentives to attract new players into new industries, but also to reward and encourage existing players to enhance products and expand markets. This approach will also help to ensure continuity in pro-competition public policy when a new political administration assumes the reins of government.

NOTES

1. CARICOM consists of fifteen nations: Antigua and Barbuda, Bahamas, Barbados, Belize, Dominica, Grenada, Guyana, Haiti, Jamaica, Montserrat, St Lucia, St Kitts and Nevis, St Vincent and the Grenadines, Suriname, Trinidad and Tobago.

2. The OECS sub-grouping of CARICOM consists of nine member countries: Anguilla, Antigua and Barbuda, British Virgin Islands, Dominica, Grenada, Montserrat, St Lucia, St Kitts and Nevis, and St Vincent and the Grenadines.

3. See: "CARICOM Economies Turn to IMF for Help," *Trinidad Guardian*, July 21, 2009.   http://guardian.co.tt/business/business/2009/07/21/caribbean-economies-turn-imf-help

4. World Bank, *Global Development Finance 2009: Charting a Global Recovery.* http://web.worldbank.org/WBSITE/EXTERNAL/EXTDEC/EXTDECPROSPECTS/EXT GDF/EXTGDF2009/0,,contentMDK:22218327~enableDHL:True~menuPK:5924248~pa gePK:64168445~piPK:64168309~theSitePK:5924232,00.html

5. World Bank, *Global Development Finance 2009* (Appendix: Regional Outlook). http://siteresources.worldbank.org/INTGDF2009/Resources/gdf_Annexure_105-150_web.pdf

6. Grenada, St Lucia, Dominica, St Vincent and the Grenadines, and St Kitts and Nevis.

7. Delroy Beckford, "Exploring the Interface between Trade Policy and Competition Law," Fair Trading Commission (Jamaica), Vol. XIII (December 2008): 17.

8. Vautier Kerrin, Lloyd Peter and Tsai Ing-Wen, *Competition Policy, Developing Countries and the WTO* (Cambridge, UK: Cambridge University Press, 2003), 228.

9. Audretsch et al. 2001: 14.

10. Tonoyan Artashes, "Do We Need A Competition Law and Policy and What it Should Be," September 2002, 4.

11. Rajan Dhanjee, "The Tailoring of Competition Policies to Caribbean Circumstances—Some Suggestions," Center For Regulation and Competition, University of Manchester, U.K. (2003), 4-5.

12. Stacey-Ann Robinson, "The Fair Competition Act: Answering the Jurisdiction Question," Fair Trading Commission (Jamaica), Vol. XIII (December 2008): 12.

13. Caribbean Single Market and Economy (CSME) was first agreed upon in 1989 and formally established in 2005. It's aimed at the establishment of a single economic space—seamless and borderless—to allow for the free movement of capital, labor, goods, services, the right of establishment of businesses and the harmonization of macroeconomic policy among the members of CARICOM. The Prime Minister of Barbados has a lead role in the establishment of the CSME. While the single market component has been formally established, the single economy component is scheduled to be established in 2015.

14. See: www.caricom.org/competition/policy

15. Dhanjee 2003: 4.

Chapter 8

Machiavellian Thinking in the United States and Jamaica Impacting Management, Entrepreneurship, and Leadership Practices

Bahaudin G. Mujtaba & Frank J. Cavico

ABSTRACT

The Prince was written by Machiavelli in the sixteenth century, and the author used Caesare Borgia, a local dictator, as his model prince. Instructions were provided on how a prince should rule, whose advice the ruler should rely on, and how one should conduct oneself to gain the most from one's leadership. This type of leadership is still present around the globe in today's environment. As such, this chapter is an essay on Machiavelli and the influence of this thinking around the globe as demonstrated by the small study presented. The study used the Mach V Attitude Inventory scale to explore the question: To what extent do new masters of business administration students who are working adults attending their initial courses, agree (high Machs) or disagree (low Machs) with Machiavelli's ideas? To what extent do students (tomorrow's leaders), in the United States of America and in Jamaica, who are working adults attending their initial courses, agree or disagree with Machiavelli's ideas? The study further compared the scores of both groups to see if culture is a factor on Machiavellian attitude.

The findings also indicate that 35 percent of the USA students (compared to 34.24 percent of Jamaican students) were high Machs while a majority in both groups had scores indicating they were low Machs. The findings show that there is a statistically significant difference between high Mach and low Mach respondents in both countries. As such, Machiavellian thinking still exists in today's

Jamaican and American organizations. The results showed no significant differences between the scores of Jamaicans and Americans. As such, culture did not seem to be a differentiating factor in the scores of respondents in this study. However, the findings did show that Machiavellian thinking still exists in today's organizations. This fact would seem to be significant given the attention that researchers and writers have given to the styles of leadership needed for effective organizations. Accordingly, the practical application of Machiavellian principles relating to management, leadership, and entrepreneurship in the twenty-first century organization is presented.

MACHIAVELLIAN PRINCIPLES AND THINKING

The term "Machiavellian" is often used to mean "of, like, or befitting Machiavelli," "being or acting in accordance with the principles of government analyzed in Machiavelli's *The Prince,* in which political expediency is placed above morality and the use of craft and deceit to maintain the authority and carry out the policies of a ruler is described," "characterized by subtle or unscrupulous cunning, deception, expediency, or dishonesty: *He resorted to Machiavellian tactics in order to get ahead,*" or a follower of the principles analyzed or described in *The Prince*, especially with regard to techniques and strategies of political manipulation. So, a "Machiavellian" is perceived to be someone who uses manipulative strategies and tactics to benefit himself or herself.

Shameful! Dreadful! Contemptible! Detestable! Immoral! Amoral! Evil! These sample assertions have been the sort of denunciations cast at Niccolo Machiavelli (1467-1527), the Italian philosopher and Florentine public servant, in direct response to his political treatise, *The Prince*, a "little" book on political theory and the practical applications thereof. Pursuant to this "immoral" interpretation, Machiavelli rightly is condemned as a "bad" and dangerous "Machiavellian." This negative view, perhaps the prevailing "popular" one of Machiavelli, has engendered the most consternation and vociferous protest against "Machiavellianism."

In reading *The Prince*, it's very easy to see the context upon which it was written, during early 1600s. Given this reference, the mindset of the sixteenth century, and the politics of the time from the city state rule in Italy, one should proceed cautiously with his/her application. Many individuals agree with Machiavelli despite the fact that his writings may have been shocking and controversial, but perhaps because he dared to put into words the actions of men for his time period. Perhaps, many parallels can be made between today's business leaders and Machiavelli's Prince since, supposedly, among many others, even President Bill Clinton has made references which had their base in Machiavelli's writings. However, perhaps the modern business person has missed a point that Machiavelli stated, and that is that leaders reflect on their actions: "Nevertheless, you should be careful how you assess the situation and should think twice before you act. Do not be afraid of your shadow. Employ policies that are moderated by prudence and sympathy. Avoid excessive self-confidence which leads to care-lessness and avoid excessive timidity, which will make you insupportable." Some individuals claim that modern business has adopted only the parts of Ma-chiavellian theory which suit its purpose, and as such, businesses have missed the big picture. One must keep in mind the context of Machiavelli's writings and the society in which it was written for in the sixteen century. Some of what he said about men's loyalties are still true, but the present society is much different than Florence in 1600. Perhaps, just as Sun Tzu's *The Art of War*, which is still being taught, since there are valuable principles to be learned, Machiavellian concepts should be taught as well but they must be considered in the context in which they were written, and one must be very careful to "translate" their message to today's society. Machiavelli did say that a prince is often forced to know how to act like a "beast" but he must learn from the fox and the lion to be effective. He also said, "A prudent ruler cannot, and must not, honor his word when it places him at a disadvantage and when the reasons for which he made his promise no longer exist." His writings still impress people four centuries after they were written, and parallels can be made between his thoughts and today's business leaders.

METHODOLOGY AND RESEARCH RESULTS

The study of effective styles of leadership has received much more attention than ever before over the past few years, and continues to grow as more and more senior executives of large corporations are making the "evening news" for wrong-doing. Over the years, research on Machiavellianism has examined the actions of leaders, and the results have been controversial and interesting simul-taneously. For the purpose of this study, masters of business administration stu-dents attending a weekend program in the United States and Jamaica were sur-veyed to determine the extent to which they practiced Machiavellianism. The students were 95 percent working professionals, and some had their own busi-nesses. Thus, a large number of them have been exposed to "high Mach" and "low Mach" behavior. They have had an opportunity to make an informed choice about managerial and leadership behaviors.

Over eighty working adult students attending class for their first or second semester in the masters program at a non-traditional format during weekends were given the survey in their Twenty-First Century Management Practices course during the discussion on leadership theories, or the surveys were admi-nistered to them in their Ethics course. The return rate was 52 percent with five incomplete forms leaving thirty-seven usable surveys for the study. The Mach V Attitude Inventory Instrument was used to determine the extent to which they agreed with Machiavellian concepts. The survey includes twenty groups of statements with each group consisting of three different responses. The partici-pants were to choose the statement that they considered most true based on their experience and personal preferences. Of the remaining two questions, they were asked to identify the statement that they considered most false. The third statement, which is considered to be average, was left unmarked. The following is a sample question demonstrating what is to be completed by each person completing the survey where "*Most True* = +" and "*Most False* = -." So, the most true statement gets a "+" sign and the most false statement gets a "-" sign and they are asked to leave the last of the three statements unmarked.

_____ A. It is easy to persuade people but hard to keep them persuaded.
_+_ B. Theories that run counter to common sense are a waste of time.
_-_ C. It is only common sense to go along with what other people are doing and not be too different.

In this example, statement B would be the one this person believe in *most strongly* and statements A and C would be ones that are *not* as characteristic of this person's opinions. Of these two, statement C would be the one this person believe in *least strongly* and the one that is *least* characteristic of his/her beliefs. Once the scores for all surveys were completed, total scores were determined by the number of high-Mach responses and low-Mach responses. The possible range for the scores is between 40 and 160 as per design of the instrument. Higher scores indicate a high Mach and lower scores indicate a low Mach. The neutral point is 100 for the survey. From the thirty-seven respondents, eleven (or 30 percent) scored at the neutral point with scores of 100 on the Mach V Attitude Inventory Instrument.

Descriptive statistics was performed to identify those students who were high Machs and those who were low Machs. Although not necessary, a *t*-test was conducted to determine whether there was a significant difference in the mean scores of the high Machs and the low Machs. As expected, there was a significant difference.

Thirteen or 35 percent of the respondents scored above the neutral point on the Machiavellianism scale, suggesting that they are high Machs. Twenty-four respondents or 65 percent scored at or below the neutral point. The mean score for the high Machs was 110 and for the low Machs 91 (not including those with the neutral score). From the thirty-seven respondents, eleven scored at the neutral point with scores of exactly 100 on the Mach V Attitude Inventory Instrument. As such, their scores were not counted with low Machs. Therefore, the final numbers for comparison are thirteen low Machs and thirteen high Machs which would obviously show a significant difference. Twenty-four American respondents (65 percent) and twenty-one (60 percent) Jamaican scored below the neutral point suggesting that they are low Machs. Four Jamaican students scored 100, which were not calculated in this part of the study. The American mean score for the high Machs was 110 and for the low Machs 91. The Jamaican mean score for the high Machs was 108, and for the low Machs 94. The result of the *t*-test for the American students (*t*= -8.5764, p= .000) suggested that there are statistically significant differences in the mean scores. Similarly, the result of the *t*-test for the Jamaican students (*t*= -8.2068, p= .000), showed that there are statistically significant differences in the mean scores. Both Jamaican and American student scores tend to show the presence of high Mach management style. Perhaps both cultures continue to reward and reinforce high Mach behavior because it is more efficacious than low Mach behavior. These results support previous research conducted by Preziosi and Gooden in 2003 with working MBA students attending their last course in the program. Preziosi and Gooden found that 41.4 percent of respondents scored above the neutral point (100) on the Machiavellianism scale, suggesting that they were high Machs, and 58.6 percent scored below the neutral point suggesting that they were low Machs.

Overall, power still seems to be driving the corporate executive, manager, and entrepreneur because power is not only a "good" end but also a "good" means. If one acquires, uses, and wields power correctly, one will be rewarded with success, wealth, fame, and ultimately glory, and thus attain the eminence of *The Prince.* According to Preziosi and Gooden (2003), the principles and practices of inclusion (empowerment, participation, etc.) continue to be the focus of many theorists and researchers. Many are of the opinion that most successful organizations require leadership and management built around this philosophy (Cavico and Mujtaba 2011). They continue to suggest that less effective organizations, at least over the short term, tend to be exclusionary. Exclusion is more in line with Machiavellian behaviors than inclusion. So, why do over one-third of the research study participants end up with high Mach scores? Why do such a high percentage place a high value on authoritarianism? Is this what they see constantly in their organizational environments? This is a question, as well as a statement, of the need for continued research that will address the impact of inclusionary versus exclusionary behaviors in building a successful enterprise. Perhaps, the educational institutions teaching management leadership skills, while emphasizing knowledge, skills, and techniques, may also be de-emphasizing the prospective manager's faith and trust in others which is further reinforced by visual pictures of senior organizational leaders being taken to jail for wrongdoing. Perhaps, these high Mach scores are a reference to the authoritarian style of some professors who are classroom teachers in the colleges. Also, the current work environment may be dominated by many high Mach managers who will do whatever it takes, including immoral means, to achieve the stated numerical objectives of the organization.

One conclusion with regard to the culture factor is that this study demonstrated no significant differences between the scores of Jamaican and American students included in this sample. As such, the Jamaican and American cultures did not seem to be a differentiating factor in the scores of these two groups. Perhaps, the Jamaican and the American cultures encourage similar thinking and attitudes with regard to management styles and strategies used in the corporate environment to get ahead and secure resources for one's personal or professional objectives. A quick review and examination of the results showed that a larger percentage of males (approximately 54 percent) tend to be high Machs compared to only 28 percent of females who scored high in this study. Although some females did score high, they did not score high at the same rate as the males included in this study. Future research can further look into gender to see if it is a factor in the attitudes of employees and managers with regard to Machiavellian thinking.

Regardless of gender or culture, successful managers tend to create an inclusionary work environment where there is empowerment and participation of employees in the overall decision making process. One can further state that successful organizations require management practices built around this inclusionary philosophy. On the other hand, less effective organizations, at least over the short term, tend to be exclusionary, which are more in line with Machiavellian behaviors than inclusion.

The next section is devoted to the business application of Machiavellian principles exemplified by *The Prince*. The business application, interpretations, and extrapolations are somewhat subjective since they are based on the personal thoughts and experiences of the authors and not necessarily any scientific studies.

MACHIAVELLIANISM AND BUSINESS

Managers' "Power" Strategies and Tactics

Although the entrepreneur, CEO, or other top executive typically is thought of as The Prince of the business realm, many managers also are "princes" in their own domains. There they rule, develop their knowledge and skills, and display their ambition; and, moreover, where some very ambitious ones may be plotting to overthrow their Prince. The major difference between the person at the apex of the organization and those just beneath him or her is the extent of the realm, and perhaps, also, the degree of ambition as well as the level of success in satisfying it. In many cases, the head of the organization simply is the most ambitious and successful of its management leaders and aspiring Princes. Regardless of the domain, for a Machiavellian-based manager, power is the key—the acquisition, retention, and exercise of power; and thus the astute manager will be concerned above all else with acquiring power in his or her sphere as well as commanding greater influence within the organization. Promotion to greater spheres naturally leads to greater power in decision making and ruling over subordinates.

In the pursuit of corporate power, the Machiavellian manager must be keenly aware that conduct within the firm readily can become truly "Machiavellian." Abusive tactics, such as deception, manipulation, and exploitation can be employed to advance selfish individual interests at the expense of others and the company. These tactics can harm seriously those who themselves possess little knowledge, expertise, or power. A "Machiavellian" manager, for example, may attempt to sabotage the careers of his or her co-workers by making anonymous false charges on the corporation's ethics "hot-line." He or she may seek to acquire control of scarce resources needed by others; or may engage in the withholding or distorting of information, or may attempt to overwhelm a party with information. The "Machiavellian" manager may feign power, expertise, friendship, concern, favor, or respect; and thereby manipulate others to show deference, loyalty, indebtedness, and trust; and persuade them to perform actions that they would not ordinarily do. He or she can exploit particular personal vulnerabilities, such as vanity, gullibility, sense of responsibility, or generosity, so as to unknowingly place a person in a position of dependency and servility. The "Machiavellian" manager, of course, will associate with the influential "power-brokers," and seek to ingratiate himself or herself with them, and thereby build an image and develop a base of support to advance ideas and ambitions. Yet, if his or her policies are failing, the "Machiavellian" manager will attempt to undo, obliterate, or minimize any association with nonsuccess. If one challenges the "Machiavellian" manager, he or she will attack them, blame them for any failures, and denigrate any rival accomplishments as unimportant, self-serving, poorly timed, or just lucky. One always must remember, as Machiavelli stressed, that appearances are essential; and thus the "Machiavellian" manager always must seem to be important, intelligent, confident, honest, moral, sensitive, personable, and popular.

A manager in a position of power thus must take care to fortify his or her corporate domain in order to withstand the assailing forces of any corporate "invaders," from either outside or inside the firm. In Machiavelli's time, the Prince secured his principality with brick, stone, and mortar in the form of high and strong city walls, and manned these positions with his loyal subjects. How does a modern-day "Machiavellian" manager secure his or her position? Principally, by acquiring, shrewdly using, and perhaps concealing information. That is, the manager will use, release, or conceal information only if it is advantageous for him or her to do so. Thus, any time an information type decision is made, it must serve, at the very least, as another brick or stone in the rising wall around the manager's domain. Information that is essential for controlling a process, or critical to extricate the organization or an ally from a difficult situation, are examples of "solidifying" protective information.

Another excellent example of a manager fortifying his or her position can be seen in the manager's treatment of his or her subordinates. Subordinates generally should not be viewed as a threat, even especially talented ones. A wise and prudent manager always will seek out, and intelligently utilize, capable individuals in an effort to better serve the firm, as well as to inure to the benefit of the manager. An empowerment style of management, therefore, is not in disharmony with Machiavellian-based business values. Empowerment should produce more trust, initiative, and innovation among one's subordinates. Employees who are permitted to be self-supervised, and are allowed to work freely (within established guidelines, of course) to achieve identified and agreed-upon goals will feel trusted and respected as colleagues and partners; and thereby should have their potential unleashed to achieve mutually beneficial results. Values, such as communication, team-building, participation, delegation, and self-management are fundamental to successful performance; and these values do not contravene

Machiavelli's counsels. At work, therefore, it will be very important for a manager to create a team of very qualified individuals, as well as an appropriate system of communication between and among them. Properly flowing communication will promote understanding, and increase knowledge. Enhanced communication clearly is conducive to achieving the "good" of profits and power.

Individuals, moreover, must be selected, and given their "team" assignments based on their strengths of course, and their weaknesses too. Such assignments should be made with a motive to providing individuals an opportunity to excel, to develop additional skills, and acquire useful knowledge. The Machiavellian manager should strive to establish a mutually beneficial career-learning and career-advancing environment; and such an environment will inure to the benefit of the manager as well as his or her subordinates. The manager's subordinate employees very well could be equated to Machiavelli's "native troops," that is, those with a sense of loyalty and dedication to the Prince. Such "troops" more easily can be managed and directed by the manager. They also will work more diligently and loyally for the manager than Machiavelli's "auxiliary" or "mixed" troops, perhaps today's part-time employees, independent contractors, and consultants. All of the latter work primarily because they are getting paid; and once the money runs out, so does their loyalty, which probably is leaning to some other personal objective anyway.

Certainly, the team-work, empowerment, and open communication style of management does entail some risks, for example, unpredictability of behavior, difficulty in supervision and control, and especially the risk of creating competitive power centers. The careful "Machiavellian" manager, therefore, clearly and explicitly must indicate definite goals, establish available resources, identify degrees of authority, lines of accountability, channels of communication, and agree upon specific consequences. These managerial guidelines and channels, however, should not be so rigid or fixed to deter new ideas, suggestions, recommendations, and sources of information. Managers will need this information to understand their markets, people—employees, subordinates, and superiors, and especially their competition—internally as well as externally. Gaining a clear understanding of the power structure of the firm, and the factors that affect it, are crucial to the attainment of the manager's ultimate goals of position, power, and profits.

When a manager's methods have been proven successful, Machiavelli, of course, would counsel their continuation, but Machiavelli also advises, definitely and forcefully, to adopt new methods when a manager is confronted with conditions of change. Recognizing the need, and possessing the courage and capability to change, emerge as difficult challenges for a manager, yet indispensable to a manager's success.

Machiavelli also argues for an aggressive approach to detecting and solving problems. He thereby counsels to address problematic issues at an early, and presumably more tractable, stage, rather than temporizing until they fester into bigger dilemmas. Machiavelli, in fact, notes that problems which are difficult to perceive are frequently the simplest to cure, but those that become obvious often are the most complex to solve. Preparation and vigilance thus are important values for the manager. Machiavelli emphasizes that without opportunity, one's talents will be wasted; but without capability, an opportunity will be wasted and squandered. The astute CEO and entrepreneur, therefore, should recognize, advance, and support knowledgeable, skillful, and perceptive managers, and reward their valuable contributions. In particular, those managers who take the initiative and increase the wealth of the firm and its owners and "stakeholders" should be encouraged and honored by the firm's principals.

Interestingly, in reading *The Prince*, one almost can presume that Machiavelli had foreknowledge of management's (at least U.S. business management's) obsession with the immediate "bottom-line" focus on short-term profits, instead of concentrating on the long-term financial growth and health of the firm. Machiavelli, in fact, warned that people of little prudence will perform an action for immediate gain, without comprehending the harm this action will cause in the future. One problem that arises from *The Prince* is Machiavelli's advice to the Prince to rule through fear. This counsel, at first glance, might cause perplexity for the modern day "team-oriented" business manager. Yet when Machiavelli talks about "fear," he does not necessarily mean fear that produces immobilizing insecurity, for example, the fear of a cowered underling of arbitrary punishment by "the boss." That degree of intimidating fear would hinder open, honest, and essential communication, and clearly would be counter-productive. "Fear," rather, should be the fear of not meeting clear, specific, and reachable objectives, or the fear of doing expressly forbidden actions.

A manager following a Machiavellian-based management philosophy and style must be aware of certain significant "moral" practices—"moral" in the "pure" Machiavellian sense that they will result in power for the manager. A manager must know the people to whom he or she reports. Understanding them and being sensitive to their needs and concerns are key ingredients to success. A manager, therefore, may need to solicit, cautiously of course, advice on the more subtle aspects of the "office politics" of his or her firm. Making friends with the "power-brokers" in the firm naturally will be most helpful. Similarly, it will be essential for the manager to know well his or her own employees and staff. Treat them well, reward those who perform ably; and tactfully transfer or dismiss nonproductive individuals. Maintain open, but not unlicensed, communication with one's staff, as well as one's superiors, other personnel, and clients. Remain accessible too; and keep key personnel properly informed and interested in plans being formulated and projects undertaken. Demonstrate competence, Machiavelli would counsel. Initiate programs and execute them well; and keep one's critical managerial role clearly visible and prominent. Build on programs that are already established and functioning well. Share credit with one's "team" members for the successes, but, once again, make sure that one's managerial role is perceived as an indispensable element to the process. Anticipate problems, and work to solve them early, quickly, and ordinarily "behind the scenes." Yet, cultivate a reputation for helping others solve problems. Be disposed to offer one's time and advice when requested, but be realistic too. Avoid being negative and confrontational, but be prepared to vigorously defend the quality of one's work, effort, or role, if questioned. Definitely do not "burn any bridges," and do not make any unnecessary enemies. Always seek to bring about those policies and programs that increase long-term organizational power and profits, particularly so when the manager's own recognition, reward, power, and prestige are enhanced within the organization.

What will the personal life of such a Machiavellian manager look like? What characteristics would he or she display? Typically, such a person would be extremely work-oriented, and dominated by a passion to achieve and excel. He or she will work very hard at work—on the job, at home, on "vacation"—all in a focused, sustained effort to achieve success and recognition. The Machiavellian manager constantly will be studying, reviewing, learning, consulting—all with the objective of meeting certain goals. Of course, one problem with such a manager is that the truly personal dimension to one's life, that is, one's family life, may suffer, but that is a "price" to be paid for pursuing influence and power, and attaining success, fame, and riches, ultimately on a "princely" scale.

Entrepreneurs—Machiavelli's Business "Founders"

In the modern world, founding a political principality, let alone conquering a kingdom, is a problematic undertaking, but Machiavelli's philosophy also has real meaning for modern day business entrepreneurs. Entrepreneurship and corporate "empire-building" are excellent business opportunities for a person with "princely" ambitions. Machiavelli's "lessons" for the aspiring entrepreneur are evident: be a "tough," smart, single-minded, dedicated, visionary leader; work persistently and diligently; bend and break the "rules" if absolutely necessary; do not be overly concerned with traditional notions of value, ethics, and morality; achieve success and attain the ultimate goals of wealth, fame, and glory.

Entrepreneurs are a singular class of managers as well as leaders. An entrepreneur in the business realm, as Machiavelli's aspiring Prince in the political realm, must be a farsighted, highly motivated, creative, energetic, persistent, and proficient person; and a fearless one too, who is willing to take chances and to accept the risks inherent in venturing into a new business endeavor. Entrepreneurs, in fact, frequently are the creators and disseminators of new technologies or unique methodologies that change the way business and society operate.

In *The Prince*, Machiavelli discusses at length and attempts to solve the problems confronting an aspiring "founder." This examination, although in a political context, does make Machiavelli's work relevant to an enterprising individual in the business sector. The entrepreneur can start a business; the Prince could found a principality; an entrepreneur can conquer markets; and the Prince could subjugate cities.

Accordingly, many practical examples cited by Machiavelli for establishing a political entity can be translated into modern business terms. His commentary on the manipulation of people, and the orientation and tactics utilized by manipulators, certainly are subjects that the aspiring entrepreneur might be motivated to study.

Entrepreneurs definitely manifest a commensurate fundamental need for "princely" achievement and renown as well as a desire for power. They are, and they seem to know they are, grades "above" the ordinary person. To be successful, they must maintain dominion over and manage their followers, yet also inspire and lead them to attain the entrepreneur's aims. Structure, organization, and processes naturally are necessary ingredients to administration, command, and control; but the entrepreneur, like the Prince, must possess the capacity and courage to confront competitive challenges, change tactical directions and strategic objectives, as well as have the ability to make swift expeditious decisions. As Machiavelli emphasized, a "founder" succeeds by adapting one's way of proceeding to the nature of the times, and, conversely, does not succeed by rigidly adhering to a method that is out of harmony with the times. Today's founder, the business entrepreneur, whose "political" arena is the "marketplace" (at least initially!), would be wise to heed Machiavelli's advice.

Entrepreneurs need, and resourcefully strive for, the power essential to accomplish their goals. Machiavelli, however, recognized that "founders" often can become enthralled with, and corrupted by, their own power; and perhaps thereby distance themselves from the "real" issues, their true confidants, and loyal followers, or even worse, degenerate into abusive autocrats. Machiavelli, therefore, counsels that a "founder" not only select certain sagacious and sensible people as advisors, of course making them dependent upon and obligated to the "founder," but also allow them the openness to provide honest opinions, and reward them for so doing. Such trusted counselors will aid the entrepreneur's deliberations, and also, vitally, will serve to keep the entrepreneur centered on the legitimate needs, ends, and means of the enterprise, rather than on any potentially ruinous personal cravings for strict control and absolute dominance.

Entrepreneurs, finally, must attract and select faithful and competent people whose vision, attitudes, attributes, and work ethic are compatible with the entrepreneur's. Such congruity will help to build a cohesive, unified, and energized work force, which surely is indispensable to the enterprise's ultimate success. The entrepreneur must recognize their capability and loyalty, reward them accordingly, and as a result keep them faithful and motivated. In the long run, followers and employees need to "buy into" the entrepreneur's personal vision, as well as ambition, and truly must want to build a great enterprise together with the entrepreneur.

Surely there are messages for entrepreneurs to be found in Machiavelli's work. Entrepreneurs will be aided in establishing great enterprises, achieving huge financial gains, and acquiring lasting fame, by adopting some of the strategies and tactics spelled out or suggested in *The Prince*. Yet, the astute entrepreneur must consider carefully the ramifications to the more "Machiavellian" aspects of Machiavelli's methods. The risk and severity of legal punishment, the negative reaction from society as well as a company's constituent groups, and the existence of potentially like-minded competitors, all serve to bound the entrepreneur, even a "princely" one, to "mainstream" as opposed to more "Machiavellian" methods. Machiavelli's Prince was in essence a "law unto himself," but the modern entrepreneur confronts an extensive, pervasive, and powerful legal system, which makes it very difficult for an individual, even a shrewd and ambitious entrepreneur, to consistently and persistently utilize immoral means which the law also proscribes as illegal. Yes, it is quite possible to achieve power, riches, and fame by employing the full range of Machiavelli's tactics and weapons, but it is also very unlikely for the entrepreneur to maintain this level of ascendancy and success.

Certainly not all of Machiavelli's theories and counsels are appropriate for modern day entrepreneurs, but some do merit very close attention by the aspiring entrepreneur. For the entrepreneur, these recommendations include the importance of strong visionary leadership, the value of participative, empowered, and loyal management, the advantages of a cohesive and committed work force. Vitally, the entrepreneur needs to possess the intelligence of mind, strength of character, and boldness of heart to change course in whatever direction the winds of prosperity and the variations of affairs demand for the attainment of the objective of success.

One of the most critical elements in building a successful enterprise is the strength of its leadership. As an entrepreneur strives to secure power and become an effective leader, he or she must obtain the loyal support of others and convert them into dedicated followers. To accomplish this object, the entrepreneur must convince others that his or her vision is worth following; and that he or she has the talent and the will to realize the vision. To emphasize these "good" values of strength and talent, Machiavelli would contend that the entrepreneur, to be a leader, must publicize significant aspects of his or her business career, or important aspects of one's work, which the entrepreneur has executed in an outstanding manner. The entrepreneur, moreover, must demonstrate that he or she can anticipate problems, resolve difficult dilemmas, and remove or circumvent impending "roadblocks." As for any other less auspicious or successful aspects of one's work and career, Machiavelli would counsel that one maintain the outward appearances of power, control, success, and, of course, morality.

Machiavelli, as well as the leadership of his day, strongly emphasized the value of loyalty, and concomitantly possessed very little tolerance for disloyalty. Thus, in today's business world, any perceived disloyalty typically is dealt with promptly, and harshly too, for example, by the loss of a raise or promotion or even the loss of one's position. "Whistle-blowing," moreover, easily could be construed as a "mark" of disloyalty. Yet, "whistle-blowing" by employees or followers, solicited by, and properly channeled to, the entrepreneur, executive, or manager is permissible. A wise person, and aspiring Prince, in order to attain and maintain power, needs to secure information and gain knowledge. He or she as well needs to seek the advice of competent and trustworthy counselors. Unsolicited or improperly given information or suggestions, however, ordinarily should not be tolerated as it undercuts the entrepreneur's status and power.

Machiavellian-Based Business Leadership

A Machiavellian leader, whether acting in the capacity of a business manager, executive, or entrepreneur, strives to attain power, riches, rank, fame, and above all, personal eminence and grandeur. In order to achieve these lofty and exalted goals, the Machiavellian leader first must be cognizant of the true nature of people. Most people are, stressed Machiavelli, ignorant, unmindful, and stupid, self-interested, selfish, and petty, suspicious and envious, ungrateful, disagreeable, and malcontented, readily deceived and misled. They merely are satisfied by, and even impressed with, superficial appearances and outward show, rather than substance and reality; and they are too weak, fearful, and stupid to be either completely good or bad, though venal and easily corruptible and readily prone to evil. If anarchy is to be avoided, and order and progress to be secured, the majority obviously cannot rule; but rather the people need a strong leader to discipline and control them and to convince, persuade, manipulate, command, or frighten them into acting prudently and properly for their own common good.

In order to be a successful leader of the people, and to gain one's own position, wealth, and glory, the Machiavellian leader must be well aware that leadership definitely does not consist of adhering to any objective, universal, veritable, or ethical code, law, or principles of leadership. True leadership, rather, is a relative, situational, contingent, suitable, adaptive, and amoral conception; that is, the leader must do, and has the right to do, depending on the circumstances, whatever the leader deems necessary, fit, and efficacious to get the people to perform correctly, to maintain the leader, and advance the leader's objectives, and achieve the leader's greatness. The leader, moreover, must do whatever it takes to fulfill these purposes, repudiating any notion of "higher law," as well as ignoring any questions as to the conventional rightness or wrongness of the means utilized. Leadership, therefore, is simply a matter of expediency, which Machiavelli extols as the only one true and inviolable principle of leadership.

In purely private matters, for example, dealings with family and friends, the conventional virtues, values, and moral standards can be sustained; but when one enters the domain of public affairs and concerns, one must leave behind any notions of conventional morality, goodness, or rightfulness, because such "good" thoughts and precepts are irrelevant, and perhaps even "bad," for the ambitious leader, who instead must take on a morally neutral approach.

The overriding issue for the leader, therefore, plainly is not whether a particular action is consistently good, right, or moral, or bad, wrong, and immoral; rather, the superseding principle is whether the circumstances require the use of a specific, expedient, efficacious means. Any traditional "badness" of the proposed method must be weighed carefully against the anticipated, desirable, good consequences of achieving the objective. It is thus quite possible that a customarily "bad" means will be outweighed by the prospects of securing a sufficiently good end, as defined and calculated by the leader, of course. Immorality and vice, as well as morality and virtue, all have their uses; and the sharp leader cleverly can alternate between good and bad. Such actions as fraud, deceit, dissimulation, manipulation, cunning, intrigue, stratagem, disrespect, and abuse are not necessarily "bad"; rather, they are merely instruments to be utilized if the situation demands their use; and they actually may rise to the level of laudable "virtuous" actions, depending on the good ends they further. If the situation requires, for example, that the leader's followers be lied to, misused, or even betrayed, and these "bad" actions are indispensable to the leader's success, then so be it! Machiavelli counseled, for example, that a reputation for morality is a very important ingredient to the leader's formula for mastery; and if it is necessary for the leader to deceive the people as to the leader's true character, such deception not only is permissible, but good too! The goodness or badness of any action just depends on the particular circumstances and consequences involved; traditional moral norms are irrelevant; and actions become disassociated not only from moral standards but also from the actors performing them. The leader thereby is licensed completely to perform actions that do not conform to the exemplar of the classic virtuous ruler; and the leader also is enjoined not to render conventionally "good" deeds if to do so would thwart the leader's good purposes. "Good" and "bad" are merely seemingly good or bad; and the leader is not bad by using an expedient "bad," that is, an actually good, effective means.

Intelligence, reason, and judgment accordingly emerge as truly virtuous qualities for the successful leader. Realizing that traditionally "good" acts may serve neither the public nor the "princely" good, the astute, calculating, and perceptive leader cautiously will alternate between good and bad, virtue and vice, and moral and immoral. The leader may have to utilize a means, traditionally classified as "bad," which due to its efficaciousness in a particular situation now may be deemed a "good" action. In certain circumstances, for example, it may be counterproductive and "bad" to be kind and compassionate, and instead "good" to be severe and cruel. If innocent people have to be dishonored, betrayed, or abandoned for a greater good, so be it. Yet, Machiavelli warns that the leader must be very careful, circumspect, and proportionate in employing conventionally "bad" means. Do not indulge or tolerate disproportionate or pointless badness, admonishes Machiavelli, or else one will become subject to hatred and contempt and one's purposes ultimately will be frustrated. "Bad" means are temporary, necessary expedients which must be used in appropriate, direct, and expeditious ways, and always to accomplish great goals, of course. The leader, moreover, who is obliged to apply "bad" methods, naturally should attempt to appear as conventionally "good"; and otherwise actually may be quite conventionally good, but always ready and willing to change to the contrary if circumstances dictate.

Carefully alternating between good and bad and eschewing extremes, however, do not mean that the leader should give way to feeble half-measures, weak compromises, and generous concessions. Irresolution, vacillation, and continuously choosing the "safe" middle course must be rejected. Such signs of weakness and indecision surely will undermine the leader's power. The leader, instead, may have to opt for the bold course of action; and execute it well. Such a Machiavellian leader hence will be able to successfully effectuate change. Whether by reason and common sense, persuasion and manipulation, or command and coercion, the Machiavellian leader must act, act decisively, and act well.

A fundamental question concerning a "Machiavellian" approach to leadership is whether Machiavelli really is teaching evil. Machiavelli, in fact, at times does abjure traditional moral virtue and goodness, and instead seems to sanction the "Machiavellian" virtues of egoism, ambition, expedience, and the shrewd use of good and bad. Yet, for the leader to attain and maintain power and authority, and ultimately to achieve great glory, must not the leader also consider the needs and aspirations of the leader's followers, the community, as well as society as a whole? That is, must not the leader's personal ambitions and "princely" goals be advanced and achieved fully in the context of benefiting the public; and, therefore, does not the common good become the ultimate, almost utilitarian, criterion for even the "Machiavellian" leader?

Perhaps, the arrival of a crisis allows a leader to act in an absolutely "Machiavellian" manner. A leader confronting an emergency may be impelled to take swift, decisive, strong, even draconian, measures to save the organization; and in such a situation the leader must do quickly whatever is necessary to ensure survival, without the consultation, participation, or approval of followers or managers, even though the leader's determination directly affects them. The leader must be allowed to act, moreover, without the "niceties" of ethical evaluation or moral justification. Yet, if there is a true crisis, and the leader has forged bonds of trust with his or her followers, then one's followers should be willing to rely on the leader's judgment, and accept, and perhaps welcome, the leader's prompt, unilateral, forceful exercise of power.

In the short term, however, it may be expedient for a leader to be "Machiavellian"; but is it efficacious in the long term for a leader to be "Machiavellian" in the sense of being deceptive and manipulative and disrespectful and abusive? Dissimulation cannot be concealed forever; and eventually one will run out of people to mistreat; and thus this exercise of "raw power," and coercive, intimidating leadership, ultimately will fail as it cannot sustain itself indefinitely. People simply neither will follow nor labor for individuals they mistrust or detest; and thus such a "Machiavellian" immoral or amoral "boss" will confront insuperable impediments in attempting to motivate, direct, or sustain such activity.

A leader, therefore, must be very careful in asserting Machiavelli's rationales as the pretense for expedient, short-term, or crisis-caused authoritarian conduct. Once one acknowledges that "Machiavellian" behavior is at any time or period acceptable, one risks falling into the trap of portraying present circumstances as fittingly critical, problematical, exceptional, or tactical for swift, arbitrary, "tough," "Machiavellian" handling; and one thereby steadily sanctions autocratic conduct. Moreover, regardless of the unsettled, troublesome, or exiguous nature of a situation, is it ever morally permissible or appropriate for a leader to act in such a despotic and tyrannical manner?

It is never ethically permissible nor appropriate, one can strongly argue, to mistreat, disrespect, betray, deceive, manipulate, or exploit people. It is always immoral to behave in such a wrongful manner and to contravene fundamental natural rights; and no crisis, real or perceived, no short term advantage, can ever justify such misconduct. True leadership, as well as successful long-term leadership, are said to be built on certain, fundamental, inviolable ethical principles, such as integrity, honesty, trust, and respect, which are constant, permanent, non-contingent, and categorical norms. Effective leadership, of course, will require at times course "corrections" and changes in strategy and tactics; but true leadership also will demand steadfast adherence to ethical principles and moral rules.

A person who is ethically deficient may lack a necessary predicate for successful, long-term leadership; and when such a person confronts a crisis or is tempted by short term advantage, or for that matter, simply faces the unavoidable problems of authority and administration, he or she may act in such an immoral way so as to destroy any leadership effectiveness. A leader who is demanding, and even exacting, very well can be acceptable and even necessary; but one who is abusive and coercive is never acceptable; and in the long term such leaders will be failures. Trying to lead by fear, suspicion, and manipulation hinders genuine communication and interaction, breeds apathy and mistrust, suppresses motivation, undermines commitment and loyalty, prevents empowerment, and eventually engenders serious problems and wrong decisions.

If leading by fear, manipulation, and paternalism is neither morally acceptable nor practically efficacious, are there feasible leadership techniques for the results-oriented individual? Truly effectual, successful, and long-term leadership always comes down to certain essential attributes—morality, honesty, and integrity. Treating one's followers and one's employees with dignity and respect, trusting and empowering them, as opposed to coercing and controlling them, will create not heedless, mindless, enervated automatons, but knowledgeable, energetic, and motivated associates who wholeheartedly believe in the leader and who are enthusiastically committed to achieving the leader's vision. Such leadership is principle-centered, values-based, and vision-inspired; and the only type of leadership capable of producing and sustaining transformational and beneficial change.

Challenges and Problems with Machiavellian Values

The value of power is the key value—instrumental and intrinsic—emphasized by Machiavelli. Yet, the serious risk of so underscoring the value of power is that power will become an end in itself. This object of power, however, may be unattainable. Acquiring, possessing, and maintaining power over others may require one to strive continually to increase the power that one possesses. The power that one does have, therefore, may not be able to be used to achieve any constructive, let alone notable, purpose; rather, power is merely the means to obtain more power, which is the vehicle to secure even further power, and so on indefinitely. The obvious negative result is an incessant, repetitive, "naked," power struggle, with an endless deferring of goals. The Machiavellian liberation from traditional values and moral restraints, and the granting of moral legitimacy to self-interest and "bad" conduct, may make some people more energetic and creative, but a concomitant decline in moral standards might engender increasing malaise, suspicion, distrust, perfidy, social disunity, and perhaps anarchy.

Machiavelli counsels that a person acting in a public affairs capacity ought to be able to do whatever he or she desires, so long as the action is for the community as a whole, and not merely for that person's own, sole, personal satisfaction and aggrandizement. Yet how realistic is such a scenario? Machiavelli himself saw the problem with his own advice. He notes how difficult it is to find a good person willing to employ bad means, even though the ultimate goal is greater good; and he also observes how infrequently a bad person, after having acquired power, is willing to use it for good ends. If a person cannot succeed by moral means, perhaps it is preferable that he or she not succeed at all, because if successful, the objective would no longer be the same cause for which the person initially sought to attain power.

Perhaps Machiavelli is too much the realist, and gives too much attention to material and "scientific" elements. His "crime" may not be one of immorality or amorality, but rather an underestimation of the moral factor in public (including business) affairs. One must consider, moreover, the long term consequences of utilizing "Machiavellian" tactics on oneself, others, and one's organization. Prolonged use of such tactics could engender debilitating outcomes. One who exercises power in such a manner, and aggressively seeks to secure and use even more power, may find that he or she is corrupted thereby. The use of power can establish a regimen not only of control over less powerful individuals, but also their abusive and undignified treatment. Those controlled and so treated may feel like failures, and perhaps may regress to a depressed and apathetic state, or even may feel frustrated and become aggressive and hostile. In the business context, capable employees might leave the corporation, or their performance could deteriorate, in response to a manager using demeaning and unscrupulous tactics. An organization might become plagued by ruthless competition, antagonistic rivalries, and actual conflict. A society's economic and social health, as well as the livelihoods of many individuals, are too dependent on business to regard business as some type of "pure" "Machiavellian" "power-game."

Admittedly, building a power-base is important in establishing or conducting a business, but gaining power as one's ultimate goal is not a license for adopting an inverted value system or practicing a spurious or specious code of ethics. There neither is a separate set of moral standards for business, nor for an executive, manager, or entrepreneur acting in a corporate or entrepreneurial capacity. One is not relieved of moral responsibility by acting "merely" in a public affairs or business capacity. One cannot hide behind and attempt to operate under a separate, unique, and dual system of ethics and values applicable only to business and public affairs. There is, and should be, one system of values and ethics, one set of moral rules, and one ethical code that applies to everyone alike, including businesspeople. Otherwise, a pernicious potential consequence of the duality mode of thinking is the acceptance or acquiescence by some in the political and business communities that the "public" system or code can be, is, and should be, morally "inferior" to the private code.

In many ways, moreover, society today, and especially its "background" institutions of law and morality, have improved since Machiavelli's time. Consequently, a ruthless, determined, and ethically publicly empowered individual would find it considerably more difficult to utilize consistently and extensively Machiavelli's more "Machiavellian" precepts in a modern business setting. In addition, enhanced awareness and scrutiny, the greater availability of information, as well as increased competition, render it practically impossible for anyone to act successfully in the "marketplace" in such a "Machiavellian" manner on a large scale and for a lengthy period of time. In particular, the relative level of knowledge and access to information enjoyed by people today, as compared to the citizens of Machiavelli's Italian city-states, should act to expose and to deter any persistent "Machiavellian" behavior.

An entrepreneur, executive, or manager cannot expect, unlike the Prince, to have his or her every wish carried out with the force of law, deceiving and manipulating some, and compelling, coercing, and punishing others. The Prince no longer is the only reigning ruling power, with no other "higher" authority to obey. Machiavelli's Prince may have had the license to commit expedient wrongful acts, but today the government and legal system, as well as society as a whole, will constrain the scope of activities of even the most ambitious and relentless aspiring Prince. The dispersion of power throughout the system, politically, legally, and economically, and the existence of competition and public pressure, serve as serious obstacles to a modern day entrepreneur who tries to emulate Machiavelli's Prince.

A modern day entrepreneur, for example, can be prosecuted criminally pursuant to anti-trust law for committing monopolizing practices in an attempt to "corner the market" or to maintain a monopolistic "principality." An advertiser who lies, or even misleads, can be fined heavily for its deceptions and forced to cease these practices. A wide array of powerful government regulatory agencies has been established for the express purposes of overseeing business, investigating possible wrongdoing, preventing these abuses from happening, and punishing their occurrence, criminally as well as civilly.

A government system and structure based on the law, rather than the dictates of an arbitrary decision maker, should minimize considerably the risk that a completely unscrupulous and aggressively ambitious person will "make it to the top" of the business world; and even if so, that he or she will stay there. The legal system will help to protect society from such people and the "Machiavellian" "shortcuts" they might employ to achieve success; and "shortcuts," one should note, pointed out plainly in *The Prince*, and thus conceivably warned about therein by Machiavelli! The law now proscribes most of these "shortcuts," and punishment is a real contingency; and thus all actors and participants in business endeavors and dealings should be cognizant of the legal limitations and consequences to their actions. Unlike Machiavelli's Italian city-states, business corporations today are not powers in, of, and amongst themselves; rather, there are "higher" powers to answer to.

There also are serious problems with Machiavelli's conception of human nature. Machiavelli claimed that most people are selfish, gullible, treacherous, and above all, stupid. Granted, the world is filled with ethical "traps" as well as ruthless people; and one surely would be wise to exercise caution with regard to both. Yet, so long as there are choices to be made in life, and the freedom to make them, the frailty of human nature, combined with the randomness of life, will lead some to choose, perhaps even grasp at, the "wrong" option. The traits of lying, cheating, and stealing, for example, are said to be an inherent part of human nature. Yet, most people are not so depraved; there also exists some degree of control over one's "baser" nature. The majority of people generally follow the conventional moral path, though people, as fallible human beings, sometimes stray.

Society, today, and its supportive institutions, such as family, church, and school, strive to teach people "right from wrong." Ethical principles and moral standards certainly are not overlooked, let alone traduced. Societal norms, and people as well, obviously have changed from Machiavelli's more aristocratic and brutal time of the few lordly princes, their regal principalities, and their many "inferior" subjects. Immoral individuals and organizations, therefore, cannot so easily fool, seduce, or overawe the "public," because people have become more knowledgeable, intelligent, ethical, and emboldened. Aspiring "Machiavellian" Princes fail to comprehend that many sensible, capable people, and equally ambitious ones too, not only possess the ability and strength equal to or greater than the Prince's own, but also have chosen to behave in a manner consistent with moral norms; and they very well will use their power to defend themselves and society from others who would use their skills and "smarts" in harmful ways.

No modern business person, whether entrepreneur, executive, or manager, realistically can expect to subscribe to and practice all the objectives and tactics discussed in *The Prince*, at least not without encountering justifiable personal and public outrage as well as societal sanction. Despite what has been documented in history, a "Machiavellian" person or business today would not be able to sustain itself for long.

One major factor militating against "Machiavellianism" is that entrepreneurs, executives, and managers are dependent upon people, especially employees in a business context. These employees very well could possess different virtues and morals than the Prince. There actually may be a few people who are consciously and morally aware of what transpires in the business; and who courageously will object to, refuse to participate in, and even "blow the whistle" on perceived wrongdoing. People who do possess the awareness of ethics and the concomitant desire to act morally, may feel that they may have an obligation to incorporate ethical analysis into their daily lives and to choose accordingly. They also may feel that it is incumbent upon them to use this "virtuous" knowledge to encourage, and even insist on, moral behavior in the business world and in all human activity. There is one more possibility for the downfall of the "Machiavellian" prince, and one that Machiavelli surely would recognize and appreciate; and that simply is "bad luck." Someone, such as a government or media representative, randomly may choose to look into the Prince's dealings, and thereby find illegal and immoral activities, or perhaps a random event may expose "Machiavellian" activities to scrutiny. Nonetheless, Machiavelli does seem convinced that satisfying one's self-interest, accumulating power, and achieving lasting personal success and fame, through expedient means if necessary, are the paramount justifiable goals in life. Still, the true "Machiavellian" entrepreneur or manager, in order to achieve these complimentary goals of maximizing organizational and individual power, must be astutely aware of the needs, and be prepared to satisfy the legitimate claims, of the enterprises' "stakeholders." Doing the best possible job to provide real value to all constituents, on a long-term, sustaining basis, will best ensure the Machiavellian manager's survival, success, and "princely" rewards.

One cannot truly attain lasting success and distinction by following a narrow, self-serving, and egotistical "Machiavellian" philosophy. Founding and managing a successful enterprise certainly are measures of accomplishment; but does not real success and renown include the values of morality and social responsibility? Creating a morally abiding and socially responsive enterprise, as well as an economically productive one of course, are the veritable "tests" of enduring "princely" eminence. Achieving power and profits, and then utilizing these resources efficaciously in a constituent-based manner, will ensure that the business person will be respected and admired for his or her "princely" achievements, rather than merely being held in awe due to his or her power, wealth, and individualistic feats.

The acquisition of power and the assumption of a business role afford the executive, manager, or entrepreneur the opportunity to change others' lives on a large scale. Since power, pursuant to Machiavelli's scheme, possesses instrumental as well as intrinsic value, the business person can use power for good ends, such as creating and distributing wealth. One also can establish one's authority in moral matters, develop Codes of Ethics, and prescribe and administer standards of right and wrong in a business setting. Business affairs, especially in the modern corporate context, entail enlarged responsibility, accountability, and gravity in the use of power. The likelihood of significant "real-world" consequences, therefore, compels the Machiavellian executive, manager, and entrepreneur to formulate carefully and seriously, calculate cleverly and accurately, justify sensibly and shrewdly, and implement prudently and carefully business policies.

REFLECTIONS, IMPLICATIONS, AND SUMMARY

Machiavelli is regarded as the well-known exponent of "public" morality, power objectives, and "Machiavellian" tactics. Machiavelli's name also is used popularly to symbolize a sinister "real-world" "moral jungle" view. Machiavelli does expose the supposed distinction many people assert between traditional values, morality, and ethics and the "true" business ethics of immorality or amorality. Comprehending this contradiction, and resolving it are not merely abstract theoretical challenges, but very concrete and practical ones too. It is much too simplistic, however, to use Machiavelli as the synonym for wicked realism. Machiavelli does recognize traditional moral values and standards; he does not deny the intrinsic value of conventional moral rules and values. Yet, he also recognizes, and wants his readers to understand, that the real world of "values" is not a homogeneous one. There is not just one world of values, which alone exists in reality. Discerning this reality does not mean that the Machiavellian solution is simply a matter of recommending "Machiavellian" tactics. Machiavelli, rather, is urging people to confront the real world, know what "real-world" tactics they and others are using, and realize that some of these tactics are in fact "bad." Yet, even Machiavelli never regards "badness" as a tactic to be used continually and regularly; but rather only as a temporary, expedient, necessary means to attain, secure and maintain power even more firmly. In the "real" world, Machiavelli believes, it will be impossible to act always in compliance with traditional moral standards and values, at all times, in all places, and in all situations. Such consistent compliance may be contrary to human nature, and hardly a new discovery. Machiavelli's point, however, is that the contravention of traditional morality, although in a conventional ethical sense adjudged as "bad," can act as a "good" means in certain concrete, actual circumstances in order to effectuate a greater good.

Machiavelli clearly recognizes, and wants his readers to be keenly aware, that certain means, although deemed to be necessary, are in fact bad and immoral. The moral character of the means thus remains unchanged, even though they are used for an overall greater good. One not only must be cognizant of the fact that a bad means is a bad means, but also that the bad means must only be employed in the most delimited manner. Then, as soon as the greater good end is achieved, one can dispose of the bad means. One, moreover, must be true and honest to oneself and others; admit that one does not always have "clean hands" by having used such means; and one ought to confront directly and accept forthrightly that reality.

So, are there any redeeming qualities to Machiavelli's message for the modern day executive, manager, or entrepreneur? As a political philosophy as well as a collection of practical political techniques, certain of the more "Machiavellian" aspects may be condemned as morally deplorable; and very few contemporary political or business people would countenance following strictly and completely all of Machiavelli's counsels. Yet, one should not disregard summarily *The Prince* as lacking worth or merit, and certainly not view it as not having applicability to modern day business management and entrepreneurship. Much can be learned from Machiavelli's theories, principles, and methods. The wise, decent, yet practical, person, who wishes to be a successful business entrepreneur, executive, or manager, but who may be compelled to function in an environment where not everyone is acting morally, should use *The Prince* as a defense mechanism (which actually could be the manner which Machiavelli intended!). Therefore, *The Prince* could be construed as a means to become aware of, and devise counter-measures to, the potentially abusive, exploitative, manipulative, immoral actions of one's dangerous "Machiavellian" opponents. The wise person neither ignores nor minimizes determined, resourceful, unscrupulous adversaries; but rather seeks to discern their selfish motives and deplorable methods; and learns how to deal with them effectively. Machiavelli's apparent cynicism about human nature and people's capacity for goodness can produce a very pragmatic "worldly" view of public affairs; and one that an astute, enterprising, good person would be hard-pressed to refute, despite the many "good" exceptions to the "bad" general rule. With this recognition of potentially immoral ambitions and actions in others, and perhaps temptingly lurking in oneself too, a well-intended individual can gird himself or herself to resourcefully do battle with the ruthless "enemy" without or within. Moreover, a political entity or politician, who attempts to behave morally in an otherwise immoral society, may suffer adverse consequences at the hands of immoral or amoral adversaries. The business firm and business person, whether entrepreneur, executive, or manager, similarly may be forced to accept some short-term disadvantage or defeat in order to live and stand by ethical principles. The moral business person and firm thus must be patient and steadfast; and allow the proper institutional safeguards and society as a whole to deal with and rectify immoral behavior. Where safeguards do not exist, one can work assiduously to create them; and when society is disinterested or dull, one can agitate to arouse, elevate, and unite individuals.

Overall, there is a great deal of practical, substantive, and good material in Machiavelli's *The Prince*; and one can find many good examples of right conduct which are ethical, admirable, and efficacious. Yet, one must be very careful to ensure that only the positive aspects of Machiavelli's work are emulated, and that the distinctly "Machiavellian" offerings are learned only in a defensive sense. As intelligent, rational, and presumably moral individuals, business entrepreneurs, executives, and managers must possess the capability and character to choose the appropriate parts of Machiavelli's teachings, and to use them sagaciously and ethically to achieve success, both in business and in their personal lives. One can act eruditely, properly, and practically, and pick the right parts of *The Prince*, and use them in a moral manner to attain one's good objectives; or one can act in an ignorant, foolish, and impetuous fashion and condemn the work in its totality as merely an outbreak of virulent ambition and moral depravity. A careful reading of Machiavelli's *The Prince* (and especially in the context of his other more democratic and republican works) will indicate that Machiavelli himself did not necessarily believe that his "Machiavellian" means are always necessary, let alone moral; and that perhaps his true political and ethical beliefs were more moderate and noble. Hopefully, an open-minded and reflective reader of *The Prince* can give some credence to this more positive Machiavellian outlook.

This chapter has attempted to show that Machiavellian thinking still exists in the minds of working adult students as well as in the workforce; and, it further attempted to apply to real-life, modern day, business dilemmas the teachings of one of history's great philosophers, Niccolo Machiavelli, as described in his seminal Renaissance work, *The Prince.* Executives, managers, entrepreneurs, and leaders who wish to maximize their positions, secure power, and attain success and prosperity, should be roused by, learn from, and perhaps be beguiled by, the frankness, directness, and evident practical applicability of Machiavelli's provocative thoughts and precepts to the twenty-first century business world. Managers and leaders should also proceed cautiously as they adopt these philosophies written for the sixteenth century mindset and environment while applying them in the twenty-first century business world.

REFERENCES

Badaracco, J. L. Jr. *Defining Moments: When Managers Must Choose Between Right and Right.* Boston, MA: Harvard Business School Press, 1997.

Beauchamp, T. L. *Philosophical Ethics.* New York: McGraw-Hill Book Co., 1982.

Brinton, C. *A History of Western Morals.* New York: Paragon House, 1990.

Bronowski, J. and B. Mazlish. *The Western Intellectual Tradition.* New York: Harper & Row, 1962.

Cavico, F. J. and B. G. Mujtaba. *Baksheesh or Bribe: Cultural Conventions and Legal Pitfalls.* Davie, FL: ILEAD Academy LLC., 2011.

———. *Business Ethics: The Moral Foundation of Leadership, Management, and Entrepreneurship,* 2nd edition. Boston, MA: Pearson Custom Publications, 2009.

———. *Legal Challenges for the Global Manager and Entrepreneur.* Dubuque, IA: Kendal Hunt Publishing Co., 2008.

———. "Machiavellian Values 'The Prince:' Bullying, Beguiling, Backstabbing, and Bargaining in the Twenty First Century Management." Paper presented at the 12th Annual International Conference on Leadership in the 21st Century: Working, Living, and Surviving Organizational Life, The Association on Employment Practices and Principles (AEPP) Proceedings, Fort Lauderdale, FL, 2004.

Cavalier, R. J., Govinlock, J. and J. P. Sterba, eds. *Ethics in the History of Western Philosophy.* New York: St. Martin's Press, 1989.

Chappell, T. *The Soul of a Business: Managing for Profit and the Common Good.* New York: Bantam Books, 1993.

DeGrazia, S. *Machiavelli in Hell.* Princeton, NJ: Princeton University Press, 1989.

Franken, W. K. *Ethics,* 2nd edition. Englewood Cliffs, NJ: Prentice Hall, 1973.

Garver, E. *Machiavelli and the History of Prudence.* Madison, WI: The University of Wisconsin Press, 1987.

Green, R. M. *The Ethical Manager: A New Method for Business Ethics.* New York: Macmillan Publishing Co., 1993.

Hamlyn, D.W. *A History of Western Philosophy.* London: Penguin Books, 1988.

Hampshire, S. *Morality and Conflict.* Cambridge, MA: Harvard University Press.

Heller, A. *Renaissance Man.* New York: Schocken Books, 1981.

Henderson, V. E. *What's Ethical in Business.* New York: McGraw-Hill, 1992.

Hulliung, M. *Citizen Machiavelli.* Princeton, NJ: Princeton University Press, 1983.

Jackall, R. *Moral Mazes: The World of Corporate Managers.* New York: Oxford University Press, 1988.

Machiavelli, Niccolo. *The Prince* (translated and edited by Robert M. Adams). New York: W.W. Norton Co., 1977.

——— . *The Prince*, 2nd edition (translated and edited by Harvey C. Mansfield). Chicago: The University of Chicago Press, 1998.

MacIntyre, A. *A Short History of Ethics*. New York: Macmillan Publishing Co., 1966.

Mackie, J. L. *Ethics: Inventing Right and Wrong*. New York: Penguin Books, 1990.

Mansfield, H. C. *Machiavelli's Virtue*. Chicago: University of Chicago Press, 1995.

Mattingly, G. "Machiavelli." In *Renaissance Profiles*, edited by J. H. Plumb. New York: Harper & Row, 1965.

Morris, T. *If Aristotle Ran General Motors: The New Soul of Business*. New York: Henry Holt & Co., 1997.

Mujtaba, B. G. *Coaching and Performance Management: Developing and Inspiring Leaders*. Davie, FL: ILEAD Academy Publications, 2008.

——— . *Cross Cultural Management and Negotiation Practices*. Davie, FL: ILEAD Academy Publications, 2007.

——— . "Privatization Trends in the Global Economy and Considerations for Developing Countries: Private Sector Challenges in Afghanistan." In *Global Economy—How It Works: Difference Cases, Different Results*, edited by M. Baliamoune-Lutz, A. Z. Nowak and J. Steagall, 192-211. Warszawa, 2006.

——— . *Business Ethics Survey of Supermarket Managers and Employees*. Doctoral Dissertation, Nova Southeastern University. UMI Dissertation Service—Bell & Howell Co. (UMI no. 9717687), 1997.

Mujtaba, B. G. and T. McCartney. *Managing Workplace Stress and Conflict amid Change*. Coral Springs, FL: Llumina Press, 2007.

Mujtaba, B. G. and D. McFarlane. "Competitive Advantage and Market Organizations in the 21st Century: Market Driving or Market Driven." In *Handbook of Globalization, Governance, and Public Administration*, edited by A. Farazmand and J. Pinkowski, 981-1002. Boca Raton, FL: Taylor & Francis, 2007.

Mujtaba, B. G. and F. Cavico. "Cross-Cultural Comparison of Machiavellian Thinking in the Attitudes of Jamaican and American Students Pursuing a Graduate Degree in Business Administration." *Huizenga School Assessment Journal*, Report no. HS04-19-04 (April 2004).

Nash, L. L. *Good Intentions Aside: A Manager's Guide to Resolving Ethical Problems*. Boston, MA: Harvard Business School Press, 1990.

Norman, R. *The Moral Philosophers: An Introduction to Ethics*. Oxford: Clarendon Press, 1991.

Nuttall, J. *Moral Questions: An Introduction to Ethics*. Cambridge: Polity Press, 1993.

Pohlman, R. and B. G. Mujtaba. "The Impact of Sarbanes Oxley's Act on Human Resources Management." In *The 2007 Pfeiffer Annual: Human Resource Management*, edited by R. C. Preziosi, 179-194. Wiley, 2007.

Preziosi, R. C. and D. Gooden. "Machiavelli Revisited: MBA Students' Perspectives." International Business and Economics Conference Proceedings, Las Vegas, Nevada, October 2003.

Rachels, J. *The Elements of Moral Philosophy*. New York: McGraw-Hill, 1986.

Russell, B. *A History of Western Philosophy*. New York: Simon & Schuster, 1972.

Solomon, R. C. *Ethics and Excellence: Cooperation and Integrity in Business*. New York: Oxford University Press, 1992.

——— . *Ethics: A Short Introduction*. Dubuque, IA: Brown & Benchmark, 1993.

Strauss, L. *Thoughts on Machiavelli*. Chicago: University of Chicago Press, 1958.

Watson, C. E. *Managing with Integrity*. New York: Praeger, 1991.

Chapter 9
Virtual Performance Management and Information Technology in the Twenty-First Century Workplace

Bahaudin G. Mujtaba & Donovan A. McFarlane

ABSTRACT

The impact of information technology (IT) developments on the traditional roles of managers has been great in the twenty-first century's global environment of business. As such, this study provides a historical perspective on the subject of information technology reviewing managerial roles and functions from the Industrial Revolution and Scientific Management era up to the contemporary technological and service-oriented market economies where managers use information technology to survive in the industry and eventually build a competitive advantage in achieving organizational goals. The chapter examines how information technology developments have affected the role of managers both positively and negatively, with the four fundamental functions of management theory as bases for analysis. The functions of planning, organizing, controlling, and leading are used as the major IT elements under which all managers carry out their roles to be both effective and efficient. The authors further examine information technology developments and their effect on the roles of managers from a Mintzbergian viewpoint.

INTRODUCTION

The role of the manager in contemporary organizations has dramatically changed in recent years, and several major factors have been responsible for this shift (Mujtaba and McFarlane 2005). These factors include global competition,

147

advances in new information technologies, and the development of e-commerce (Jones and George 2009). As a result of the changes brought about by the recent developments in information technology, and the globally competitive effects of the marketplace, managerial roles have become very complex. Managers must now effectively blend their styles of management into an integrative approach with adequate IT considerations and strategies to achieve organizational goals. According to Bassellier, Reich and Benbasat (2001), the information technology competence of business managers is an important concept to be considered in accounting for organizational success and performance. Managers need to recognize how IT has changed their traditional roles into acting as global managers while effectively utilizing an integrated approach to leading, planning, controlling, and organizing. Effective utilization of IT can and has greatly enhanced the productivity of those who acquire the requisite knowledge and make use of it in their day-to-day operations toward better performance. Performance management is a process that enables firms to evaluate and continuously improve both individual and corporate performance, against clearly defined, pre-determined objectives, goals, and targets. Performance management has been greatly impacted by IT as one considers non-comparable data, the volatility of the global environment, the effect of distance, and level of subsidiary maturity in developing economies. IT has also impacted performance with regard to a firm's monitoring and control systems both at the local and global levels. As such, it becomes necessary to define the set of IT-related explicit and tacit knowledge that a manager possesses, which enables him or her to exhibit IT leadership in business (Bassellier, Reich and Benbasat 2001: 159).

Managers must recognize that if they are to successfully guide workers to achieve organizational goals, they are to see themselves as IT managers and act the role. This requires having new and innovative technical, conceptual, and human skills to effectively comprehend business within the global environment where networks and virtual opportunities and threats are affecting strategies at all levels (Kaifi and Mujtaba 2010; Mujtaba and Kaifi 2010). Bassellier et al. (2001) refer to the combination of these skills required for effective IT management as Explicit IT Knowledge; a manager's knowledge of technologies, applications, systems development, and management of IT form his or her explicit IT knowledge (Bassellier, Reich and Benbasat 2001: 159). The manager's job in today's organization cannot be completed without the use of important information and communications technology systems and tools, identified by Laudon and Laudon (2004) as supply chain management systems, customer relationship management systems, enterprise systems, and knowledge management systems. Managers must effectively utilize the resources offered by these information and communications technology systems to successfully compete in a new business environment where essentially the concept of management becomes encamped around what is essentially IT management.

HISTORICAL AND CONTEMPORARY PERSPECTIVES: THEORETICAL OVERVIEW

The Industrial Revolution and Scientific Management

Over the decades the science of management has rapidly changed, especially after the second hundred years of the Industrial Revolution (Dilworth 1989: 45). The Industrial Revolution can be thought of as the first significant technological movement to affect the science of management holistically along with the roles of managers. Emerging out of the Industrial Revolution was the Scientific Management Era which led to profound developments in organizations across Europe and the rest of the world. The role of the manager became more complex after the Industrial Revolution and the changes which followed in operations systems and task-orientation led to increased focus on workers, systems thinking, and theory. Thus, other significant management thoughts surfaced along with Scientific Management and led to even more complex roles for managers to perform within organizations.

The Industrial Revolution brought about the need for new management skills as it was characterized by a shift of the production process to large factories. This meant that the role of the manager shifted from a mere supervisory level with majority of time devoted to worker control, to encompassing several duties and responsibilities. This was due to the fact that specialization of labor brought about new requirements for management, since coordination became crucial and much more difficult to achieve (Dilworth 1989: 45). Despite the great impact of the Industrial Revolution on productive processes and society, new management skills did not become immediately recognized and it took much longer than required for managers to deviate from their traditional approach to management. Therefore, other important social and political revolutions did play their parts in bringing about the transitions in management which continued into the present century.

The Information Technology Revolution and Management

The birth of the computer and the Information Technology Revolution was another influential factor impacting the science of management and bringing about changes to the role of managers. According to Jones and George (2009) new information technologies are having profound effects on the way an organization operates. At the level of organizational structure, IT is changing methods of organizing (Mujtaba and McFarlane 2005). This means that the role of managers within organizations has dramatically changed to encompass technology integration along all lines of duties and responsibilities. As such, the concept of "technology" has come to define a functional area of management within organizations. This concept of technology refers to the combination of skills, knowledge, tools, machines, computers, and equipment that are used in design, production, and distribution of goods and services (Jones and George 2003: 290). With this in mind, the role of managers has become very complex as knowledge management becomes the major definitional and descriptive terminology ascribed to what were simply called managerial functions or skills. Knowledge management is the practice of harnessing and exploiting intellectual capital in order to gain competitive advantage and customer commitment through efficiency, innovation, and effective decision making (Yeh 2005).

Managers must manage knowledge in the form of information, communicating across networks and organizational boundaries. As such, knowledge management entails utilization of "a systematic process that helps organizations identify, select, organize, disseminate, and transfer important information and expertise" (Turban and Aronson 2003: 347) internally and externally between cooperative teams, businesses, and enterprise networks in achieving organizational goals. The use of IT for managing organizational knowledge, resources, information systems, and strategic business plans has transformed the role of the manager into a highly technical and conceptual framework, where interaction is virtual in its approach and application. Organizing, planning, controlling, and leading are still the fundamental bases of managerial roles. However, they are carried out through and within different information technology media which today characterize activities, operations, and functions within business organizations. The task is therefore, for managers, to effectively and efficiently utilize information technology in all its forms to plan, organize, lead, and control workers and activities within the organization. The recent developments in information technology have resulted in a need for managers to engage in technology management as a major part of their role of organizing, planning, leading, and controlling. It is through rigorous and sound information technology management that managers are able to achieve organizational goals. Technology management requires managers to share and integrate expertise within and between functions and divisions through real-time interconnected information technology (Jones and George 2009). Knowledge has become the driving force in our economy today (Yeh 2005) and this has increased the role of IT in managerial duties and functions. Yeh (2005) further contends that as a new economy resource of tremendous importance, knowledge powers the ability of professionals to be their best and to deliver value service to customers.

With their changing roles, managers must now become familiar with knowledge management systems in order to effectively carry out their tasks. Allee (1997) agrees, and states that the knowledge management system is the framework of an integration of elements in organizational culture and organizational information technology infrastructure, along with the organization's store of individual and collective experiences, values, learning and insights, etc. It is through IT that managers in the global economy and market of the twenty-first century coordinate these factors, using specific knowledge management activities to guide the organization and its members through strategic planning, organizing, controlling, leading, and integration of knowledge resources in arriving at organizational outcomes (Nonaka and Takeuchi 2001).

Because the manager's roles essentially involve the constant use of IT to plan, control, lead, and organize resources of various kinds from a knowledge-based or information-led orientation, managerial roles are carried out within what Mellander (2001) calls a "learning organization." As such knowledge dissemination and responsiveness (Yeh 2005; Oxbrow 2000; McEvily, Das and McCabe 2000) become essential factors in achieving competitive advantage as managers use IT strategies to organize resources, control processes, plan for change, and lead employees to effectively achieve an organization's goals.

FIGURE 9.1
Effectiveness and Efficiency Variables

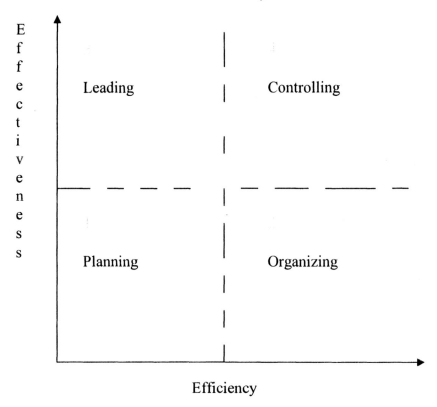

As demonstrated in Figure 9.1, the four functions of management can be seen as the moderating variables of effectiveness and efficiency. The recent information technology developments have called for effective managers with higher technical, conceptual, and human skills across all organizational boundaries (Robbins and Coulter 2003). As such, IT has affected organizational structures, bringing along new kinds of jobs and task reporting relationships among electronically connected people, promoting superior communication and coordination (Jones and George 2009). This has changed the role of managers from simple business managers to information technology managers. Managers must now embrace their informational roles with greater attention as they become monitors, disseminators, and spokespersons for organizational change, problem solving strategies, transition of business processes and activities, along with their responsibilities to effectively communicate business needs to employees (Williams 2000). Managers must now plan, organize, lead, and control across technology systems, managing and dealing with a wide range of problems and people on a regular basis. Often such problems and individuals are remote and managers will find themselves engaged in virtual planning, organizing, leading, and controlling. Therefore, simple management has become virtual and technology management for managers. The role of managers has therefore become more complex, more technological, less time-consuming, and wider in scope. The definition of the managerial role has grown with increasing information technology systems as they affect departmental and organizational boundaries. In essence, managers are now global IT managers.

MANAGERIAL ROLES IN E-COMMERCE, THE NEW ECONOMY, AND THE EMERGING DIGITAL FIRM

The developments in information technology have led to increased activities on the internet, e-commerce, and strategic networking. These have changed the role of managers as their duties and responsibilities include e-commerce, network, database and systems management, while maintaining control over time, people, and other resources. Managers must now engage in a variety of different functions which require greater skills and abilities. Planning, controlling, leading, and organizing functions are carried out through virtual networks linked across organizational and systems boundaries. Today's managers are in fact information technology managers since IT has revolutionized all aspects of business.

Managers must now view management from an information technology perspective as they strive to achieve effectiveness and efficiency through planning, organizing, leading, and controlling organizational resources and market factors to achieve business goals using IT systems and strategies. IT systems and strategies are now at the center of management functions.

Performance management is a function of being both effective and efficient. Therefore, performance management requires both leadership and management skills which include planning, organizing, leading, and controlling (Mujtaba 2007). The relationship between effectiveness, the four traditional functions of management, and efficiency can be graphically visualized as demonstrated in Figure 9.2. Managers coordinate these functions using IT systems and strategies to achieve organizational goals.

FIGURE 9.2
Performance Management Model

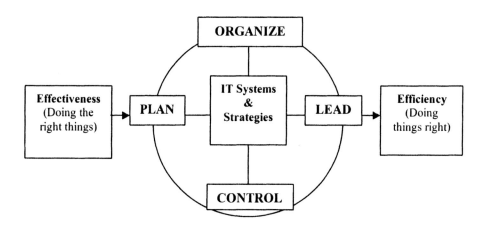

One important development which today characterizes the volatile global business environment in which managers carry out their roles is the emergence of the digital firm under new economy incentives. The concept of a digital firm is uniquely described by Laudon and Laudon (2004) who state that the digital firm is one in which nearly all of an organization's significant business relationships with customers, suppliers, and employees are digitally enabled and mediated. Though the transition to completely digital firms is still in bloom, the implications as to the changing roles of managers in a uniquely modern IT environment are very evident. Today, effective managers are those using information and communications technology systems to plan, control, lead, and organize business processes, activities, and people; essentially these managers become involved in IT resource management, since every resource within a firm becomes an extension of the IT function. The fact is that managers and their subordinates must utilize modern systems in performing their duties.

Managers in today's business world must utilize information technology to level the playing ground or competitive market arena. In making decisions, developing action plans, and resolving organizational conflicts and problems, managers must use IT to coordinate the resources which will result in effectiveness and efficiency at all levels. Laudon and Laudon (2004: 14) believe that "a substantial part of management responsibility is creative work driven by new knowledge and information." As such, they contend that "each level of management has different information needs and information systems requirements."

The managers of today are performing their roles and responsibilities within an environment characterized by unprecedented changes. Therefore, managers must plan, organize, lead, and control change itself along with the transforming roles of resources in business. Change must be strategically planned for and controlled in order to achieve organizational goals. According to Laudon and Laudon (2004: 14), "Information technology is one of many tools managers use to cope with change." Using IT infrastructure, managers in organizations are able to accomplish goals and perform tasks through applying available technology services effectively. IT infrastructure simply describes the physical arrangement of hardware, software, databases, networks, etc. (Turban, McLean and Wetherbe 1996).

E-commerce—"the process of buying and selling goods and services electronically involving transactions using the Internet, networks, and other digital technologies" (Laudon and Laudon 2004: 23-24)—has taken over the way business is conducted in the economies of the twenty-first century. Managers must plan, organize, lead, and control within the context of electronic trade and the structural and business relationships which are derived from it. This entails carrying out managerial duties and responsibilities "using information flows in new and dynamic ways" such as coordinating resources and monitoring their interaction (both information and human resources) to create and deliver value (Laudon and Laudon 2004: 24).

The four functions of planning, controlling, organizing, and leading will always remain the fundamentals upon which managerial roles, duties, and responsibilities are devised. The transitions we have witnessed represent therefore change within perspectives as far as these functions are adapted to encompass and respond to processes such as globalization, industrialization, digitalization, e-commercialization, enterprise and organizational convergence, and transformations concordant with contemporary technological and socioeconomic developments.

STRATEGIC IT FRAMEWORKS AND MANAGERIAL TASKS

The role of managers now involves managing IT systems, as well as managing physical and human resources through the use and application of IT to business situations and problems. Managers must accomplish business goals of profits, productivity, success, and growth through effectively utilizing IT systems. According to Turban, McLean, and Wetherbe (1996), information systems help businesses to increase sales, reduce costs by lowering inventory, increase quality of products, create alliances with suppliers, reduce costs by negotiating high quality at low prices, reduce costs by optimizing the use of shelf space, increase productivity, and concentrate on their core business. Part of the changing role of managers resulting from increased use of IT is to recognize and devise methods to effectively integrate IT into daily business functions and processes. IT must become the tool through which the manager accomplishes tasks as he or she plans, organizes, leads, and controls the various input resources into the value creation process. IT has resulted in the managers' roles and responsibilities being transformed into an all-encompassing systemic approach to achieving organizational goals as she or he now adds systems, networks, databases, procedures, hardware, and software to the traditional management of people resources.

In carrying out managerial roles and responsibilities managers must come to understand the interdependence of IT and other technology systems in accomplishing tasks at all levels of the organization. This involves the development and management of IT frameworks such as the value chain model and competitive forces model. Such a framework describes the structuring of strategic information systems (SIS) which better facilitates understanding and classification of the relationship among strategic management, competitive strategy, and information technology (Turban et al. 1996). With this knowledge managers are able to conceptualize and plan for changes, control internal and external environmental controllable factors impacting business success and performance, lead their companies to the front of the competition, and organize work teams and resources in what are essentially becoming virtual-boundaryless organizations.

Strategic IT frameworks are essential in management decisions and can be effectively used to integrate systems, tasks, and functions to reflect more cohesiveness in organizational task-related performance and output. Using IT as a strategic factor to achieve high productivity is a challenge for managers who are unable to view workers and the entire business system and its processes from a purely technological viewpoint. Managers in today's business world must take advantage of IT as a strategic driver of people, systems, and resources, recognizing that IT is the value driver in the new economy where globalization and the transformation of enterprise are in full swing (Mujtaba and McFarlane 2005).

Planning

Planning is one of the four fundamental areas under which the role of managers can be examined. Planning is the process of defining organizational objectives and then articulating strategies, tactics, and operations necessary to achieving these goals (Holt 1990). Today's managers have a variety of tools and systems which are designed to facilitate effective and efficient planning. The process of planning entails deciding which goals the organization will pursue; deciding what course of action to adopt to attain these goals, and deciding how to allocate organizational resources to attain these goals (Jones and George 2009). The information technology systems managers have available to them today make planning a much easier task than it was for their predecessors. There are systems and processes in place to facilitate decision making at the planning level and these range from decision support systems to computer programming and mathematical and materials requirement planning systems. Managers must therefore be capable of carrying out their planning based on possession of a variety of conceptual and technical skills required to comprehend systems and processes based on input-output criteria. Managers are now able to input data into systems and run configuration processes and tasks to determine decisional outlays. There are such systems as the Material Requirements Planning (MRP) system, which is a computer-based method for managing materials required to carry out a production schedule (Dilworth 1989: 150). The MRP system is also called a rough-cut capacity planning system or resource requirement planning system. It helps a manager to determine how much capacity is available and how this capacity will be allocated for production, and how to develop detailed specific models of what products to produce and when. Through the use of information technology managers are able to develop master schedules, or master production schedules, to facilitate efficient and effective planning. Computer systems are used to develop flow-charts of production and capacity planning processes, graphical load reports, or load profiles. With aggregate planning systems managers are able to reduce the time spent in the planning process, while maximizing the use of resources including time, people, capital equipment, and the resulting operational costs.

Developments in information technology have expanded the role of managers as organization-wide planners engaged in several activities across the board. Managers must now plan activities at interdepartmental levels and this involves cooperative pooling of resources. Communication across departments is facilitated through networking and sharing of information which is vital to achieving production targets and other organizational goals. Developments in information technology such as teleconferencing, email, and video-conferencing have aided the planning process as managers are now able to engage in virtual planning across boundaries. The result of planning is a strategy (Jain 1997; Thompson Jr., Strickland III and Gamble 2005), and the recent developments in information technology have facilitated strategy development, selection, and formulation, as well as implementation. There are now computer simulation programs and games which aid in the planning process. Managers no longer have to depend solely on their natural abilities in planning organizational goals and allocating resources. Integrated software packages and product scheduling systems are available on information networks which provide immediate feedback. One of the important information technology developments includes advanced linear programming systems for aggregate planning (Dilworth 1989: 163). Managers are able to use mathematical formulas and concepts for gauging their decisions and arriving at cost-effective production targets. This results in greater efficiency and achievement of organizational goals. Linear programming, using Linear Decision Rule (LDR) and numerous other methods, has become part of the conceptual skills requirements for today's managers in carrying out their roles in global companies (Dilworth 1989: 164). Therefore, the planning role of managers has become less time consuming, but more complex and sophisticated as a result of the recent developments in information technology. Though managers spend less time planning they have more tasks consideration, are in need of greater technical and conceptual skills, and must be able to view planning from an organizational wide-approach, considering global competition and rapid changes.

Organizing

The organizing role of managers has been greatly affected by the recent information technology developments. Organizing is the management process of determining how best to arrange an organization's resources and activities into a coherent structure (Griffin and Ebert 2004). It is the process which managers use in order to establish structures for the interactive working relationships that allow organizational members to cooperate in achieving business goals. The developments in information technology have greatly facilitated managers' abilities to carry out this role as IT systems now provide several communicative tools for networking. Managers are now able to interact with workers through teleconferencing, videoconferencing, emails, twittering, blogging, instant messengers, and other social media devices which reduce time spent in meetings and face to face communications. Managers are able to organize work teams through virtual commands and instructions given over local and wide area networks. As a result, they are able to organize activities of financing, production, and marketing with greater accuracy. Managers are able to better utilize work space and plant capacity through using systems configurations to determine production outlays and departmental boundaries. Using synergistic systems, managers can now place workers into inter-functional teams based on information retrieved and stored in computer systems. They are better able to set production schedules and organize a time frame around which to plan activities, employee training, and resources allocation.

The recent developments in information technology have resulted in greater task analyzability, which is the degree to which programmed solutions are available to solve the problems encountered by managers in playing their roles (Jones and George 2009). Managers are now able to analyze and develop, as well as select from several solutions in dealing with problems arising in the daily operation of business. There is readily available information for managers to address issues of production, labor, and resources shortage or oversupply. Managers can use statistical and plant layout information to determine how to organize production within their operating departments. Information technology systems and processes allow managers to choose from a variety of technological production methods such as small-batch, mass-production, or continuous process (Jones and George 2009). Managers are therefore less likely to make errors in production, as well as cost mistakes that will affect company profits. Through utilizing technological systems and tools, managers are better able to organize jobs and employees according to task identity, task significance, skill variety, and autonomy, while using systems to record and ascertain feedback.

The organizing role of managers has become easier as a result of available information technology tools which allow for more accurate information and less time spent on classifying and gathering relevant data. Managers are now able to organize work teams through electronic media. Organizing production tasks, department structure, product, and market structure, are now a matter of pushing the right buttons and inputting correct data into electronic database systems designed to configure models based on product or service categories, etc.

Companies in the twenty-first century are concentrating heavily on teamwork to accomplish organizational goals and having the most up-to-date information technology systems will be vital in achieving such objectives. Managers must effectively utilize information technology systems and tools to organize departments according to functions and importance within organizations. Activities and operations relevant to delivering superior value and increasing quality, and overall efficiency and effectiveness in resources allocation, costs, and sound management must be organized around technology information systems which link departments, networks, and businesses. Information technology developments have made the organizing role of managers more coordinated and less time consuming. The developments have produced superior systems and tools which guarantee more accurate use of space and labor within organizations, as well as better use of available time and limited resources.

Controlling

The role of a "controller" is basic to all managers regardless of the type of business or kind of business organization. Managers have a role to evaluate how well the organization and particularly its workers are achieving set goals and objectives, and must take action to maintain or improve performance where necessary (Nickels, McHugh and McHugh 1999). This is what the role of managers as controllers entails. Managers must monitor the performance of individuals, departments, and that of the organization as a whole in order to determine whether or not desired performance standards are being met. This requires great effort on a manager's part and the recent information technology developments have aided managers significantly in this role. Managers now have a variety of IT systems to enable effective control. Control systems have become very prominent in most global organizations. Control systems are formal target-setting, monitoring, evaluation, and feedback systems that provide managers with information about how well the organization's strategy and structure are working (Jones and George 2009).

The recent developments in information technology have brought about effective control systems which alert managers when something is going wrong, giving them time to respond to opportunities and threats within the organizational environment. Managers in the past did not have such systems, and often times were caught unprepared and had to wait until organizational problems arrived to deal with them. Today's managers have at their disposal effective control systems which are characterized by great flexibility to allow them to respond to unexpected events. Such control systems provide managers with accurate information and give them a true picture of organizational performance. Unlike managers of the past who made decisions based on outdated information, today's managers are able to obtain information from computerized information control systems in a timely manner, and therefore are less likely to experience failure (Jones and George 2009; Mujtaba and McFarlane 2005).

According to Laudon and Laudon (2004), new forms of IT have revolutionized control systems by facilitating the flow of accurate and timely information up and down the organizational hierarchy and between functions and divisions. Managers of the past had to depend on time-consuming face to face meetings which produced less accurate results and interpersonal conflicts within the organization. Therefore, the use of computerized control systems has led to greater efficiency in costs and more effective utilization of resources. Managers now spend less personal time controlling systems and people as real time evaluation and monitoring systems are used across organizational departments. Control and information systems have been developed to measure performance at each stage of transforming inputs into finished goods and services (Jones and George 2009). Managers are now able to use feed-forward control to anticipate problems before they arise at the input stage. This includes controlling the quality of the input received from suppliers, as well as labor inputs, time, and other resources inputs which affect the production process. According to Turban, McLean, and Wetherbe (1996), IT can also be used to keep in contact with suppliers and manage their progress.

IT systems also serve well in monitoring and evaluating employees' performance and recording and obtaining information about customers and products. Jones and George (2009) contend that the general development of management information systems provides feed-forward information that provides managers with timely information concerning changes both in the task and general environments of the business. This allows managers to become more effective in their roles as controllers, controlling organizational resources, opportunities, and threats. There are two other forms of control systems which have arisen with the recent developments in information technology. These are concurrent control systems and feedback control systems. A concurrent control system is used at the conversion stage to give managers immediate feedback on how efficiently inputs are being transformed into outputs so that managers can correct problems as they arise (Jones and George 2009). Accordingly, concurrent control through IT alerts managers to the need to react quickly to whatever is the source of the problem, whether it be a defective batch of inputs, machines out of alignment, or workers lacking the skills necessary to perform a task efficiently. This system also enables total quality management throughout production and operation systems. These authors also speak of a feedback control system using IT. This gives managers information about customers' reactions to goods and services so that corrective action can be taken if necessary. This occurs at the output stage and alerts managers about the number of customer returns, while measuring increases or decreases relative to sales of different products, and changes in customer tastes (Jones and George 2009).

Fundamental to the controlling function is the monitoring roles which managers must perform. IT has brought employee monitoring to a new height. Managers are now able to utilize information technology tools and systems to measure employee productivity, obtaining feedback and communicating ideas, resolving conflicts, and ensuring that organizational resources are being effectively and efficiently utilized to achieve targeted objectives. The issue of employee monitoring has over the past years become a topic of high philosophical debate due to the ethical implications and factors which have emerged in the forms and types of monitoring being carried out by managers. As Mujtaba (2003: 23) states, "employee monitoring has emerged as a necessity and yet as a very controversial issue due to the complexity and widespread use of technology."

Many companies have become extremely concerned with the ineffective and inefficient, and mostly, the inappropriate use of networks and business technology resources by employees as a result of the losses in productivity and value which can consequently occur. For example, many businesses over the past years have incurred losses from declines in employee and technology productivity resulting from overuse of network systems for personal or idle uses. Personal use of business information technology systems for pleasure, and non-business related activities have created the need for managers to monitor employees on the job. This monitoring involves the use of IT systems to keep track of employees' progress, their online activities and interactions, work hours, idle time, and productivity levels. Laudon and Laudon (2004) have cited a case in which the personal use of IT systems by employees at Xerox led to the shutting down of the company's email system due to the use of the business' networks to send junk and pornographic materials. With issues such as these, many businesses have started to conduct rigorous IT monitoring, and managers are now faced with a difficult task of violating employees' rights to privacy and work-trust and comfort.

There are also several control processes which are used to measure actual performance using IT systems. Using IT systems managers are able to establish standards of performance, and compare actual performance against chosen standards. Such IT systems allow managers to evaluate results and initiate corrective action. There are also systems for financial measures of performance. Control systems using IT have made it easier for managers to carry out their role as organizational controllers of human resources, tasks, and other resources, while attaining organizational goals in an effective and efficient manner. The availability and variety of control systems striving with information technology developments has given managers cutting edge techniques and tools which have made them more effective managers and reduce the risks of decision making.

Leading

The role of managers as leaders is instrumental to organizational success and performance, especially in the current competitive global economy where gaining a competitive edge means the difference between survival and death. Companies must either strive with or "outdo" their competitors to survive and stay ahead of the game (Johnson and Weinstein 2004). Companies in the global economy require managers who are effective IT leaders. Managers must today have the ability to lead through effective IT management. Using information technology systems managers communicate ideas and articulate clear visions for employees to follow. Managers must use different mediums to communicate organizational goals across the entire company. They must effectively utilize information and technology systems to ensure a progressive organizational culture. Jones and George (2009) suggest that managers best utilize IT to lead by empowering their workforce through the use of powerful new software programs to expand employees' knowledge, tasks, and responsibilities. Another way managers can effectively utilize IT in their role as leaders is to organize self-managed teams or groups of employees, giving them responsibility for supervising their own activities and for monitoring the quality of goods and services they provide (Jones and George 2009; Mujtaba and McFarlane 2005).

Using IT to manage, lead, and direct work teams has great advantages for companies. It helps managers to focus on many critical areas as direct supervision becomes a thing of the past. Self-managed teams, organized by managerial leaders, input results of their activities into computers, and through IT middle managers have direct access to what is occurring. This also decreases the first-line manager's responsibilities and duties, as they are able to share them with workers (Parker 1997). According to Williams (2000), the role of first-line managers in the new IT work context is to act as coaches and mentors rather than to tell employees what to do. Their role is to provide advice and guidance and help teams find new ways to perform their tasks more efficiently.

INFORMATION TECHNOLOGY AND THE MINTZBERGIAN APPROACH TO MANAGERIAL ROLES

According to Henry Mintzberg, the specific tasks that managers need to perform as they plan, organize, lead, and control organizational resources can be effectively reduced to ten roles under three broad categories. These three broad categories include decisional, informational, and interpersonal roles. Some experts believe that IT has significantly changed how contemporary managers approach and play these roles (Williams 2000; Griffin and Ebert 2004).

Decisional roles are related to the various methods that business managers utilize in planning strategy and making use of resources. Under this category the manager has to play the roles of entrepreneur, disturbance handler, resource allocator, and negotiator (Williams 2000). IT helps a manager in the role of entrepreneur by providing more and better information to use in deciding which projects or programs to initiate, and in investing resources to increase organizational performance. In the role of disturbance handler, IT provides managers with real-time information to foresee the unexpected events or crises threatening the organization, and based on this knowledge, they are able to employ quick solutions. In the role as resources allocator, recent developments in information technology have provided managers with human resources software systems. Peoplesoft and SAP give managers easy access to the information they need to decide how to effectively utilize people and other resources to efficiently achieve organizational goals. Managers use IT to perform the negotiator role through electronic commerce and business-to-business networks, linking their organizations to suppliers, distributors, and other managers, as well as customers (Jones and George 2009; Mujtaba and McFarlane 2005).

The informational role of managers includes acting as monitors, disseminators, and spokespersons within the organization or business environment. Managers must use IT systems to obtain and transmit information across organizational boundaries. In performing their basic functional roles, managers use IT systems to monitor the activities of workers and organize and control them on all levels. In the role of disseminators, IT allows managers to quickly and effectively transmit information to all employees and other stakeholders to affect their work attitudes and behaviors (Jones and George 2009). IT has also allowed managers to become more effective spokespersons as they can now reach wider audiences and have more accurate information with which to influence the public and their network businesses.

Interpersonal roles of managers include acting as figurehead, leader, and liaison for the organization. IT can make managers much more visible throughout the organization. In the role of figurehead, IT provides managers with tools such as the Internet to inform employees and other interested parties such as shareholders about the organization's mission and other relevant information. Managers can use the Internet's capability through emails and other electronic communications to act as figureheads and role models for employees. IT allows managers to perform better in their roles as organizational leaders by providing access to better quality information for training, counseling, and motivating employees. In the role of a liaison, IT has made it much easier for today's managers to link and coordinate the activities of people and groups within and outside of the organization (Mujtaba and McFarlane 2005; Jones and George 2009).

CONCLUSION

The role of the manager includes "knowing who knows what, which enables the manager to leverage the knowledge of others" (Bassellier et al. 2003: 159). The effective manager of the twenty-first century therefore possesses tacit IT knowledge, which is "conceptualized as a combination of experience and cognition." The manager's experience, according to Bassellier and his colleagues, relates to personal computing, IT projects, and overall management of IT, while cognition refers to mental models. The mental models which Bassellier et al. (2001) refer to are the manager's process view and his or her vision for the role of IT. Managers in today's competitive business environment must effectively utilize IT to gain competitive edge and increase market share, while delivering a leap in customer service. This requires having great competence in the use and application of IT to address business problems and provide solutions. As such, the outcomes expected from IT-competent business managers are chiefly two behaviors: an increased willingness to form partnerships with IT professionals and an increased propensity to lead and participate in IT projects (Bassellier, Reich and Benbasat 2001: 160).

REFERENCES

Allee, V. "12 Principles of Knowledge Management." *Training and Development* 51, no. 11 (1997).

Bassellier, G., Reich, A. and B. Benbasat. "Information Technology Competence of Business Managers: A Definition and Research Model." *Journal of Management Information Systems* 17, no. 4 (Spring 2001): 159.

Dilworth, J. B. *Production and Operations Management: Manufacturing and Nonmanufacturing*, 4th edition. New York: Random House Business Division, 1989.

Griffin, R. W. and R. J. Ebert. *Business*, 7th edition. Upper Saddle River, NJ: Pearson-Prentice Hall, 2004.

Holt, D. H. *Management: Principles and Practices*, 2nd edition. Upper Saddle River, NJ: Prentice Hall, 1990.

Jain, S. C. *Marketing Planning and Strategy*, 5th edition. Cincinnati, OH: South-Western College Publishing, 1997.

Johnson, W. C. and A. Weinstein. *Superior Customer Value in the New Economy: Concepts and Cases*, 2nd edition. St Lucie, FL: CRC Press, 2004.

Jones, G. R. and J. M. George. *Contemporary Management*, 6th edition. New York: McGraw-Hill, 2009.

———. *Contemporary Management*, 3rd edition. New York: McGraw-Hill/Irwin, 2003.

Kaifi, B. A. and B. G. Mujtaba. "A Study of Management Skills with Indian Respondents: Comparing their Technical, Human and Conceptual Scores Based on Gender." *Journal of Applied Business and Economics* 11, no. 2 (2010): 129-38.

Karimi, J., Somers, T. and Y. Gupta. "Impact of Information Technology Management Practices on Customer Service." *Journal of Management Information Systems* 17, no. 4 (Spring 2001): 125.

Kayworth, T. and D. Leidner. "Leadership Effectiveness in Global Virtual Teams." *Journal of Management Information Systems* 18, no. 3 (Winter 2001/2002): 7.

Laudon, K. C., and Laudon, J. P. *Management Information Systems: Managing the Digital Firm*, 8th edition. Upper Saddle River, NJ: Prentice Hall, 2004.

———. "Monitoring Employees on Networks: Unethical or Good Business?" In *Management Information Systems: Managing the Digital Firm*, 8th edition. Upper Saddle River, NJ: Prentice Hall, 2004.

McEvily, S. K., Das, S. and K. McCabe. "Avoiding Competence Substitute through Knowledge Sharing." *Academy of Management Review* 25, no. 2 (2000): 294-311.

Mellander, K. "Engaging the Human Spirit: A Knowledge Evolution Demands the Right Conditions for Learning." *Journal of Intellectual Capital* 2, no. 2 (2001): 165-71.

Mintzberg, H. *The Nature of Managerial Work*. New York: Harper and Row, 1973.

Mujtaba, B. G. *The Ethics of Management and Leadership in Afghanistan*, 2nd edition. Davie, FL: ILEAD Academy, 2007.

———. "Ethical Implications of Employee Monitoring: What Leaders Should Consider!" *Journal of Applied Management and Entrepreneurship* 8, no. 3 (July/August 2003): 22-47.

Mujtaba, B. G. and B. A. Kaifi. "Management Skills of Afghan Respondents: A Comparison of Technical, Human and Conceptual Differences Based on Gender." *Journal of International Business and Cultural Studies* 4, no. 1 (2010): 1-14.

Mujtaba, B. G. and A. D. McFarlane. "Traditional and Virtual Performance Management Functions in the Age of Information Technology." *The Review of Business Information Systems* 9, no. 3 (2005): 53-64.

Nickels, W. G., McHugh, J. M. and S. M. McHugh. *Understanding Business*, 5th edition. Boston, MA: McGraw-Hill/Irwin, 1999.

Nonaka, I. and H. Takeuchi. *The Knowledge-Creating Company*. Oxford: Oxford University Press, 1995.

Oxbrow, N. "Skills and Competencies to Succeed in a Knowledge Economy." *Information Outlook* 4, no. 10 (2000): 18-23.

Parker, S. R., Wall, T. D. and P. R. Jackson. "That's Not My Job: Developing Flexible Work Operations." *Academy of Management Journal* 40 (1997): 899-929.

Robbins, S. P. and M. Coulter. *Management: 2003 Update*, 7th edition. Upper Saddle River, NJ: Prentice Hall, 2003.

Scott, J. E. "Facilitating Inter-organizational Learning with Information Technology." *Journal of Management Information Systems* 17, no. 2 (Fall 2000): 81.

Thompson, Jr. A., Strickland III, A. J. and J. E. Gamble. *Crafting and Executing Strategy: The Quest for Competitive Advantage, Concepts and Cases*, 14th edition. New York: McGraw-Hill/Irwin, 2005.

Tillquist, J. "Institutional Bridging: How Conceptions of IT-enabled Change Shape the Planning Process." *Journal of Management Information Systems* 17, no. 2 (Fall 2000): 115.

Turban, E. and J. Aronson. *Decision Support Systems and Intelligent Systems*, 6th edition. Upper Saddle River, NJ: Prentice Hall, 2003.

Turban, E., McClean, E. and J. Wetherbe. *Information Technology for Management: Improving Quality and Productivity*. New York: John Wiley & Sons, 1996.

Williams, A. "Arthur Andersen—IT Initiatives Support Shifts in Business Strategy." *Information Week*, September 11, 2000, 14-18.

Williams, C. *Management*. Cincinnati, OH: South-Western College Publishing/Thomson Learning, 2000.

Yeh, Y. M. C. "Knowledge Management Implementation Model in Higher Education Industry: A Case Study in Taiwan." *Proceedings of College Teaching and Learning Conference*, 2005.

Chapter 10
Antitrust Immunity: The Case of Liner Conferences under European Union Law

Marel Katsivela

INTRODUCTION

European shipping is one of the most competitive shipping industries in the world.[1] It represents 42 percent of the world merchant fleet and is present in all segments of the shipping markets.[2] Maritime transport carries 90 percent of European imports and exports and 40 percent of intra-EU[3] trade.[4]

"Liner shipping" is an industry term of art referring to regularly scheduled common carriage of cargo by sea which is the predominant means of ocean transportation.[5] At the EU level, 40 percent of EU's external sea trade, in value terms, is transported by liner carriers.[6] Liner shipping has traditionally been dominated by shipping cartels known as "conferences." A shipping conference is a group of shipping lines that have formed a cartel for the joint setting of rates and service conditions for transporting containerized exports and imports.[7] Uniform tariff setting among conference members is achieved through price-fixing agreements which are agreements among competing ocean carriers to fix or raise rates charged to shippers in order to restrict inter-company competition and earn higher profits.[8]

Competition is an essential part of the *Treaty of Rome* (*EC Treaty*)[9] which constitutes one of the foundation stones of the EU. It encourages innovation and pushes down prices.[10] Antitrust laws regulate or prohibit a variety of practices that restrain trade such as business monopolies, trusts or cartels.[11] Two prohibition rules are set out in the *EC Treaty* regarding antitrust laws. First, agreements between two or more firms which restrict competition are prohibited by Article 81(1) of the *EC Treaty*, subject to some limited exceptions (antitrust immunity) defined by Article 81(3).[12] The most obvious example of illegal conduct infringing *EC Treaty* Article 81(1) is a cartel between competitors (which may involve price-fixing or market sharing).[13] Article 81 of the *EC Treaty*, as applied to liner conferences, will be of interest to our study. Second, firms in a dominant position may not abuse that position (Article 82 of the *EC Treaty*).[14] This is, for example, the case of predatory pricing aiming at eliminating competitors from the market.[15]

The shipping industry has traditionally been shielded, everywhere in the world, from competition law and open competition.[16] Liner conferences have, thus, benefited from an antitrust immunity in most of the world including, until recently, the EU, allowing ocean carriers to enter into agreements that are exempt from antitrust scrutiny.

Like all other transportation sectors, however, shipping has faced increasing efforts to remove its regulatory protections and subject it to open competition.[17] The recent EU reform of antitrust laws did away with the antitrust immunity applicable to liner conferences and their capacity to collectively fix rates. The reform was intended to render the sector more competitive and to set an example to be followed at the international level.

The present chapter will examine the recent repeal of the liner conferences' antitrust immunity at the EU level, and briefly present the United States (U.S.) laws and policies preceding and following the EU reform.

THE DEVELOPMENT OF THE EU COMMON TRANSPORTATION POLICY AND THE LINER CONFERENCES' ANTITRUST IMMUNITY

Article 3, (f) and (g), of the *EC Treaty* provides that: "[t]he activities of the Community shall include: (f) a common policy in the sphere of transport;[18] and (g) a system ensuring that competition in the common market is not distorted." Part III, Title IV (Art. 74-84) of the *EC Treaty* sets out the general objectives of a Common European Transportation Policy and invites the European Council[19] to define this policy so as to ensure competition in the common market. Article 84(1) provides that the transport provisions of the *EC Treaty* apply to inland transport whereas Article 84(2) allows the European Council to regulate in the area of maritime transport: "The [European] Council may, acting by a qualified majority, decide whether, to what extent, and by what procedure, appropriate provisions may be laid down for sea and air transport."[20]

At first, a noted neglect to regulate ocean shipping was observed at the EU level since it took approximately twenty-five years to draft and enforce competition rules applicable to the maritime sector.[21] The delay may be attributed to the fact that until 1973 the European Community was a continental block of countries with about 90 percent of transport carried by road, railway or inland waterways.[22] Since 1973, the accession of seafaring countries has transformed the geography of the EU in a way that, after said year, nearly 90 percent of trade between the Member States was sea borne with almost no competitive land transport alternative.[23] For instance, the accession of Greece—the country with the largest maritime fleet in the world[24]—on January 1, 1981, brought shipping to the center-stage of EU's trade activities.[25] Authors also argue that the slow development of regulation in the area of maritime transport may be attributed to the complex nature of shipping companies' activities and their international and multimodal reach.[26]

The initial noted neglect to regulate ocean shipping at the regional level gave way to four European Regulations in the mid-1980s, which were mostly concerned with developing the sector's competition:[27] unfair pricing practices in maritime transport are concerned of European Regulation 4057/86 (O.J. L378/14 31.12.86); co-ordinated action to safeguard free access to cargo in ocean trades is regulated by European Regulation 4058/86 (O.J. L378/21 31.12.86); freedom to provide international maritime services ("liner" and "tramp" shipping of passengers or goods[28]) is governed by European Regulation 4055/86 (O.J. L378/1 31.12.86). Competition rules and maritime transport, including liner conferences, were subject to European Regulation 4056/86 (O.J. L378/4 31.12.86).

European Regulation 4056/86 constituted the principal measure that laid down the rules for establishing free competition in maritime transport, confirming the principle of the universal application of EU competition rules to this sector (Article 1).[29] It also provided (in its Article 3) that liner conferences' agreements with transport users (such as price-fixing agreements), decisions or concerted practices could be exempted from the prohibitive principle of Article 81(1) (prohibition of horizontal price fixing) of the *EC Treaty* and accorded antitrust immunity under Article 81(3).[30] The exemption was not limited in time.[31] The antitrust immunity laid down by European Regulation 4056/86 only applied to liner conferences and not to tramp vessel operations and cabotage (Article 1).[32]

Article 81(1) of the *EC Treaty* prohibits agreements which affect trade between Member States and which have as their object or effect the prevention, restriction or distortion of competition within the common market. Article 81(1) provides:

> The following shall be prohibited as incompatible with the common market: all agreements between undertakings, decisions by associations of undertakings and concerted practices which may affect trade between Member States and which have as their object or effect the prevention, restriction or distortion of competition within the common market, and in particular those which:
> 1. directly or indirectly fix purchase or selling prices or any other trading conditions;
> 2. limit or control production, markets, technical development, or investment;
> 3. share markets or sources of supply;
> 4. apply dissimilar conditions to equivalent transactions with other trading parties, thereby placing them at a competitive disadvantage;
> 5. make the conclusion of contracts subject to acceptance by the other parties of supplementary obligations which, by their nature or according to commercial usage, have no connection with the subject of such contracts.

Under Article 81(3), a restrictive agreement may be exempted from the prohibition of Article 81(1) if certain conditions apply. Article 81(3) provides:

The provisions of paragraph 1 may, however, be declared inapplicable in the case of:

1. any agreement or category of agreements between undertakings;
2. any decision or category of decisions by associations of undertakings;
3. any concerted practice or category of concerted practices, which contributes to improving the production or distribution of goods or to promoting technical or economic progress, while allowing consumers a fair share of the resulting benefit, and which does not:

    3a. impose on the undertakings concerned restrictions which are not indispensable to the attainment of these objectives;

    3b. afford such undertakings the possibility of eliminating competition in respect of a substantial part of the products in question.

To benefit from the antitrust exemption under Article 81(3) and avoid automatic voidance under Article 81(1), an agreement must cumulatively satisfy four conditions. It must:[33]

1. contribute to improving the production or distribution of goods or to promoting technical or economic progress;
2. allow consumers a fair share of the resulting benefit;
3. not impose on the undertakings concerned restrictions which are not indispensable to the attainment of these objectives; and
4. not afford such undertakings the possibility of eliminating competition in respect of a substantial part of the products in question

The exemption of Article 81(3) can be granted either "individually" by the European Commission upon notification to it of a particular agreement, or by a "group exemption regulation" as it was done with EU regulation 4056/86 for liner conferences.[34] If a liner conference agreement satisfied the conditions laid down in this regulation, it was automatically exempted without need for a prior notification to the Commission.[35]

Shipowners, having traditionally held the upper hand and, therefore, having most to lose from the regulation of liner shipping, have always pressed for minimum government regulation and, therefore, for a group exemption under Article 81(3) regarding their agreements to provide transport services.[36] Until recently, Article 81(3) has created a safe harbor for shipping companies' agreements covered by the European Regulation 4056/86 (such as price-fixing agreements) provided that certain obligations and conditions, which were attached to Article 81(3) by the said Regulation, were respected.[37]

THE REFORM

In 2006, the EU Competitiveness Council[38] decided the repeal of the European Regulation 4056/86 and the abolition of the "block exemption" accorded to liner conferences, with effect from October 18, 2008.[39] This meant that as of October 18, 2008 all EU and non-EU carriers who were taking part in conferences operating on trades to and from the EU had to end their conference activities, such as price-fixing and capacity regulation, on those trades because such activities are no longer permitted.[40] EU competition rules now apply fully to liner conferences on EU trade routes and companies have to assess whether or not their agreements comply with such rules.[41]

The reform eliminated the former notification and exemption system under Article 81 and replaced it by a system of direct application of EU law which can be enforced not only by the Commission but also by the national competition authorities and by national courts.[42] This means that an agreement that fulfills the conditions of Article 81(3) of the *EC Treaty* is legal from the outset and enforceable by national courts.[43] Conversely, a restrictive agreement which does not fulfill the conditions of the exemption rule under Article 81(3) is void and unenforceable from the beginning.[44] Article 81(3) of the *EC Treaty* can be invoked as a defense in all proceedings, including before national courts and national competition authorities without the need for an administrative intervention by the European Commission.[45]

Nothing, however, prevents conferences from taking part in price-fixing agreements on non-EU trade routes after October 18, 2008.[46] To give a concrete example, an EU carrier like Maersk Line, member of the Trans-Atlantic Conference Agreement (TACA), can no longer be involved in price-fixing and capacity regulation on the North Atlantic-EU and EU-North Atlantic trades as of October 18, 2008, but can still do so on the US-Pacific trades.[47]

Cabotage and tramp services may not be equally affected by the repeal of the liner conferences' antitrust immunity because the *EC Treaty* competition rules already applied to them.[48] However, their exclusion from the scope of European Regulation 4056/86 precluded efficient enforcement of EU competition law in these sectors.[49] EU institutions had acknowledged that the lack of effective enforcement powers for cabotage and tramp services was an anomaly from a regulatory point of view.[50] With the repeal of Regulation 4056/86 the enforcement of competition laws for maritime tramp and cabotage services now falls within the EU's competence for competition law[51] and is not carried out only by national competition authorities.

Note should also be made of the fact that the repeal of the antitrust liner conference block exemption does not affect the maritime consortia[52] block exemption under Article 81(3) allowing shipping lines to engage in operational co-operation (vessel-sharing, co-ordination of routes and schedules) but *not* fix prices.[53] These are agreements/arrangements between liner shipping companies aimed primarily at supplying jointly organized services by means of various technical, operational or commercial arrangements.[54] The consortia exemption is of particular significance in terms of volume of trade.[55] In effect, the majority of cargo between the EU and the U.S. is transported by shipping lines in consortia and alliances using individual service contracts instead of conference tariff prices.[56]

With the abolition of European Regulation 4056/86, all shipping services (liner or non-liner) are now subject, in principle, to the same framework of competition rules and where the economic justification for a similar treatment in law exists, that treatment should apply regardless of the legal category to which the service belonged under the old regime.[57]

To help maritime operators understand the implications of this change and how competition law should apply to the sector after the abolition of European Regulation 4056/86, the European Commission adopted, in 2007, Draft Guidelines on the application of Article 81 to maritime transport services.[58] The final Maritime Guidelines were issued on July 1, 2008.[59] These Guidelines set out the principles that EU institutions will follow when defining markets and assessing cooperation agreements in the maritime transport services sectors directly affected by the repeal of European Regulation 4056/86.[60] They cover all maritime sectors, namely cabotage, liner and tramp shipping services, and are intended to help undertakings and associations of undertakings to and/or from a port or ports in the EU to assess whether their agreements are compatible with Article 81 of the *EC Treaty*.[61]

Opponents of the collective ratemaking practices suggest that ocean rates are kept artificially high by conferences allowing, thereby, inefficient carriers to remain in business.[62] Proponents of conference price-fixing agreements state that conferences stabilize rates, control capacity and maintain adequate profit levels for the ocean carrier industry. They argue that the repeal of the antitrust exemption for liner shipping will make it impossible for the industry to arrive at efficient levels of supply and that unbridled competition will lead to destructive competition, instability of prices and undesirable oligopoly.[63] They add that bankruptcies caused by a free market pricing system will lead to major disruptions in the timely movement of international commerce.[64]

On the contrary, the European Commission has concluded that the repeal of the block exemption for liner conferences will bring about substantial benefits to the EU industry and consumers, in particular as regards transport prices, reliability of liner shipping services, competitiveness of the EU liner shipping industry and small EU liner carriers.[65] More specifically, the Commission's main findings of the potential economic impact of repealing the conference block exemption are:[66]

- transport prices for liner shipping services will decline;
- service reliability on deep sea and short sea trades is expected to improve;
- service quality will either be unaffected or will improve;
- either a positive impact or no impact on the competitiveness of EU liner shipping firms;
- no negative impact or even a positive impact on EU ports, employment, trade and/or developing countries; and,
- small liner shipping carriers will not experience particular problems.

The Case of Multimodal Transport

EU institutions recognize the vital importance of multimodal transport at the regional level and favor its development. Although there is no consensus on the definition of intermodal transportation today, "multimodal," "combined," "intermodal" or "door-to-door" transport appear to be synonymous terms involving the shipment of cargo and the movement of people through more than one mode of transportation during a single, seamless journey.[67]

Shipping and multimodal transport are very much interlinked due to the intensification of trade and Europe's geography. In effect, European geography demands multimodal transport.[68] A glance at the map of Europe shows that some countries are islands, like England, Ireland and Malta.[69] Some countries, like Scandinavia, are divided by straits from the rest of the continent or have river boundaries.[70] Very often, therefore, road carriers may have to make temporary use of other modes of transport, such as railways or ferries to cross these bodies of water.[71]

EU law prohibits multimodal transport price-fixing between liner conferences and inland carriers. The European Commission has rejected the possibility of granting a group exemption in respect of the fixing of inland transport rates by conferences and it has adopted formal decisions prohibiting such rate fixing by conferences.[72] However, the possibility of granting individual exemptions to conference members for inland price-fixing arrangements under Article 81(3) of the *EC Treaty* is not ruled out provided that the four conditions set by this Article are fulfilled.[73] In this way, the European Commission accepts that individual exceptions can be envisaged in the event that inland services are organized individually or jointly by the maritime companies of a conference if this improves transport conditions and lowers costs without abusively reducing competition.[74]

The prohibition of inland price-fixing by conferences at the EU level was meant to protect shippers since the European Commission is not known to sympathize with horizontal price-fixing. When the conferences' antitrust immunity was still in force, opponents of the Commission's decision to prohibit inland price-fixing were arguing that multimodal transport operations and "through" (door-to-door) rate fixing were an integral part of the conferences activities and were already covered by the European Regulation 4056/86 conference block exemption.[75] They stated that to deny application of the conference block exemption to intermodal transport would be unduly restrictive.[76] The repeal of the European Regulation 4056/86 and the subsequent abolition of the liner conferences' block exemption weakens the authority of this argument.

THE U.S. ANTITRUST LAWS APPLICABLE TO LINER CONFERENCES

In the United States, the 1998 *Ocean Shipping Reform Act* (OSRA)[77] maintained liner conferences' antitrust immunity for international transportation but introduced independent service contracting, the terms of which may be kept confidential and against which conferences are not permitted to take any punitive action.[78] Thus, contrary to EU law, conferences in the United States may collectively fix rates and other terms of carriage even though such agreements are no longer binding.[79] In this way, members of a conference may share price information, agree to non-binding guidelines for rates and terms of service, adopt non-binding tariffs and enter into confidential contracts with shippers.

Moreover, under the *OSRA*, a conference or two or more ocean carriers acting jointly can negotiate price-fixing agreements with inland carriers.[80] However, such negotiations and resulting agreements are not exempt from antitrust laws.[81] This is contrary to EU law that does not allow conferences to enter into price-fixing agreements with inland carriers.

Despite the fact that the *OSRA* maintained liner conferences' antitrust immunity contrary to EU law, with the passage of this Act the conference system has virtually collapsed in the United States.[82] In effect, the OSRA struck a blow to the 140-year-old liner conference system in trying to compromise shipper and carrier interests by introducing confidential contracting in favor of shippers while keeping the immunity from antitrust laws to benefit carriers.[83] According to a U.S. Senate report: "[the change was made] to foster intra-agreement competition, promote efficiencies, modernize ocean shipping arrangements, and encourage individual shippers and carriers to develop economic partnerships that better suit their business needs."[84]

It is said that the independently negotiated rates and price competition introduced by the OSRA are probably available only to shippers large enough to exert influence in negotiation with individual carriers.[85] However, so far, the OSRA reform is said to have created a more competitive environment, and to have benefited commercially both carriers and shippers and improved relations between them.[86] Confidential contracts are now the preferred business arrangement for both carriers and shippers.[87] Competitive forces and not liner conferences play a key role in establishing liner shipping rates.

By maintaining the antitrust immunity for conferences and permitting inland price-fixing, the OSRA is not as radical as the recent EU reform. With the EU repeal of antitrust immunity for liner conferences, the question arises as to whether the United States will rethink its antitrust immunity laws that ocean carriers retain under the OSRA.[88] Commentators argue that it is difficult to envision a perpetual U.S.-sponsored carrier antitrust immunity given that the United States no longer owns any major steamship lines.[89] They explain that allowing the antitrust immunity to exist will essentially protect only foreign carriers to ship to and from the earth's largest market.[90] This is probably why a report released on April 3, 2007 by the U.S. Antitrust Modernization Commission recommended that the antitrust immunity afforded to liner carriers be repealed in the United States to achieve greater public benefit.[91] Carrier and shipper interests also agree that some measure of change of the existing regime is needed in the United States but their views differ on what the content of the reform should be.[92]

Commentators argue that it is questionable whether the U.S. Congress will take an interest in liner conferences' antitrust immunity in view of the recent economic recession.[93] In addition, the members and staff who championed the OSRA ten years ago are no longer on Capitol Hill.[94] Time may be needed to effectively wean liner conferences away from carrier collective rating but principles of worldwide uniformity should, in the end, be the primary concern of U.S. legislators.[95]

NOTES

1. EU, *Maritime Transport: Blue Horizons of Commitment*, 2008. http://europa.cu/rapid/pressReleasesAction.do?reference=IP/08/760&format=HTML&aged=0&language=EN&guiLanguage=en

2. *Ibid.*

3. The EU—previously known as the European Economic Community (E.E.C.)—is an institutional framework for the construction of a united Europe. A brief account of the history of the European Union can be found at: EU, *The History of the European Union*, 2009. http://europa.eu/abc/history/index_en.htm. Twenty-seven European countries are currently members of the EU: Austria, Belgium, Bulgaria, Cyprus, Czech Republic, Denmark, Estonia, Finland, France, Germany, Greece, Hungary, Ireland, Italy, Latvia, Lithuania, Luxembourg, Malta, Netherlands, Poland, Portugal, Romania, Slovakia, Slovenia, Spain, Sweden, United Kingdom. See also: EU, *European Countries*, 2009. http://europa.eu/abc/european_countries/index_en.htm

4. EU, *Maritime Transport: Blue Horizons of Commitment*, 2008. http://europa.eu/rapid/pressReleasesAction.do?reference=IP/08/760&format=HTML&aged=0&language=EN&guiLanguage=en

5. Chris Sagers, "The Demise of Regulation in Ocean Shipping: A Study in the Evolution of Competition Policy and the Predictive Power of Macroeconomics," *Vand. J. Transnat'l L.* 39 (2006): 779, note 20, and accompanying text.

6. EU, *Competition: Commission Welcomes Council Agreement to End Exemption for Liner Shipping Conferences*, 2006. http://europa.eu/rapid/pressReleasesAction.do?reference=IP/06/1249&format=PDF&aged=0&language=EN&guiLanguage=en

7. Canadian Transportation Agency, "What is a Shipping Conference?" 2009. http://www.cta-otc.gc.ca/doc.php?sid=1156&lang=eng. In 1875, six years after the opening of the Suez Canal, British ship owners operating between the United Kingdom and Calcutta reacted to the prevailing fierce competition by concluding an agreement setting a uniform tariff and establishing a common schedule of sailings. The British initiative has had, since 1875, extraordinary success around the world. See: Nikolaos E. Farantouris, *European Integration and Maritime Transport* (Athens & Thessaloniki: Ant. N. Sakkoulas, 2003), 344-5. Liner conferences are most prevalent on routes between Europe, on the one hand, North America and the Far East, on the other hand.

8. Definition based on the one forwarded by OECD, *Glossary of Statistical Terms*, 2002. http://stats.oecd.org/glossary/detail.asp?ID=3284

9. *Treaty for the Establishment of the European Economic Community*, March 25, 1957, 298 U. N. T. S. 11. The 1957 *EC Treaty*—signed by France, Germany, Italy, Belgium, the Netherlands and Luxembourg—established the European Economic Community (E.E.C.). It has been amended numerous times, and its 1992 amendment through the Maastricht Treaty transformed the E.E.C. to the EU. The new and much debated 2007 Treaty of Lisbon further amends the *EC Treaty*.

10. EU, *Antitrust, Overview,* 2008. http://ec.europa.eu/comm/competition/antitrust/overview_en.html

11. On the definition of "antitrust laws," in general, see *ibid*.

12. *Ibid.*

13. *Ibid.*

14. *Ibid.*

15. *Ibid.* Article 82 will not be commented herein.

16. Chris Sagers, "The Demise of Regulation in Ocean Shipping: A Study in the Evolution of Competition Policy and the Predictive Power of Macroeconomics," *Vand. J. Transnat'l L.* 39 (2006): 779, 780.

17. *Ibid.*

18. A common policy is defined as a set of decisions, measures (such as Regulations, Directives and Decisions), rules and codes of conduct adopted by the common institutions set up by a group of states and implemented by these common institutions and the member states. A "real" common policy (to be distinguished from a so-called one) has to be implemented by all the participants and, therefore, needs to be monitored by supranational executive and judiciary authorities. Hence, by adopting a common policy, the participants agree to transfer some of their sovereign powers to common supranational institutions. This transfer of sovereign rights in the framework of common policies is the main drawback but also the fundamental characteristic of multinational integration. It explains why common policies are difficult to adopt, but also why, once adopted, they are the binding (or integrating) elements of the whole multinational structure. Common policies, thus, distinguish multinational integration from intergovernmental cooperation and explain nationalistic skepticism toward the former. See: EU, *An Empirical Approach to European Multinational Integration*, 2009. http://www.europedia.moussis.eu/books/Book_2/2/1/1/02/index.tkl?lang=en&all=1&pos=6&s=1&e=10

19. The European Council is the main decision-making body of the European Union. It: 1. is responsible for decision-making and co-ordination; 2. passes laws, usually legislating jointly with the European Parliament; 3. co-ordinates the broad economic policies of the Member States; 4. defines and implements the EU's common foreign and security policy based on guidelines set by the European Council; 5. concludes, on behalf of the Community and the Union, international agreements between the EU and one or more states or international organizations; 6. co-ordinates the actions of Member States and adopts measures in the area of police and judicial co-operation in criminal matters; 7. constitutes the budgetary authority that adopts the Community's budget (EU, The Council of the European Union, 2009). http://consilium.europa.eu/cms3_fo/showPage.asp?id=242&lang=en&mode=g

20. This is the only provision that the *EC Treaty* has dedicated to sea transport. Mario Riccomagno, "The Liberalization in Access to Maritime Transport Markets in the European Union," *E. T. L.* 32 (1997): 537, 538.

21. French Senate, *La Difficile Naissance de la Politique Commune des Transports*, 2000-2001. http://www.senat.fr/rap/r00-300/r00-3001.html#toc9

22. Helmut Kreis, "European Community Competition Policy and International Shipping," *E. T. L.* 27 (1992): 155, 156-57.

23. *Ibid*, 157.

24. *Merchant Vessel*, 2009. http://en.wikipedia.org/wiki/Merchant_ship

25. V. Power, *European Union Shipping Law* (1995), 43-48. http://books.google.com/books?id=qFJrCf2diuIC&pg=PA48&lpg=PA48&dq=4057/87+unfair+pricing&source=web&ots=Uyi73kmTfR&sig=w9YuELJ0FIcOgavWwujUAW-dL-A&hl=en&sa=X&oi=book_result&resnum=1&ct=result#PPA9,M1

26. Nikolaos E. Farantouris, *European Integration and Maritime Transport* (Athens & Thessaloniki: Ant. N. Sakkoulas, 2003), 313-14.

27. For a summary of these regulations, see: *Summaries of Legislation Freedom to Supply Services, Competition, Unfair Pricing Practices and Free Access to Ocean Trade*, 2007. http://europa.eu/scadplus/leg/en/lvb/l24064.htm. Also, V. Power, *European Union Shipping Law* (1995), 43-48.

28. Tramp services concern the non-regular maritime transport of bulk cargo that is not containerized and include a range of economically important services, such as the

transport of oil, agricultural and chemical products. See: *Antitrust: Guidelines on the Application of Competition Rules in the Maritime Sector—Frequently Asked Questions*, 2008. http://www.edubourse.com/finance/actualites.php?actu=43056

29. Helmut Kreis, "European Community Competition Policy and International Shipping," *E. T. L.* 27 (1992): 155, 157.

30. See also: *Ibid* (1992): 158; and Nikolaos E. Farantouris, *European Integration and Maritime Transport* (Athens & Thessaloniki: Ant. N. Sakkoulas, 2003), 347. Some restrictions to this exemption applied based on Article 4 of the European Regulation 4056/86.

31. Helmut Kreis, "European Community Competition Policy and International Shipping," *E. T. L.* 27 (1992): 155-58.

32. Cabotage services are maritime transport services, either scheduled (i.e., liner) or unscheduled (i.e., tramp) shipping that take place exclusively between ports in the same EU Member State. See: *Antitrust: Guidelines on the Application of Competition Rules in the Maritime Sector—Frequently Asked Questions*, 2008. http://www.edubourse.com/finance/actualites.php?actu=43056. For the definition of tramp services, see supra note 28.

33. D. Waelbroeck, *An Introduction to European Competition Rules and Their Impact on Shipping Law* (1995), 157, 164. http://books.google.com/books?id=qFJrCf2diuIC&pg=PA166&lpg=PA166&dq=%22individual+exemptions%22+inland+price+fixing&source=web&ots=Uyi63ll_cP&sig=ZOs_lleaPFR0N8S3jNTm5zzvzlA&hl=en&sa=X&oi=book_result&resnum=3&ct=result#PPA166,M1

34. *Ibid.* The European Commission (hereinafter Commission) was created to represent the interests common to all Member States of the EU. It is composed by Commissioners (one for each Member State) and has four main roles: 1. to propose legislation to Parliament and the Council; 2. to manage and implement EU policies and the budget; 3. to enforce European law (jointly with the Court of Justice); 4. to represent the European Union on the international stage, for example, by negotiating agreements between the EU and other countries. See: EU, *European Commission*, 2009. http://europa.eu/institutions/inst/comm/index_en.htm

35. D. Waelbroeck, *An Introduction to European Competition Rules and Their Impact on Shipping Law* (1995), 157, 164.

36. Nikolaos E. Farantouris, *European Integration and Maritime Transport* (Athens & Thessaloniki: Ant. N. Sakkoulas, 2003), 345. On the other hand, shippers have always complained that the liner conferences have enjoyed *carte blanche* to determine the price, quality and quantity of supply in the market for carriage services. *Ibid.*

37. *Ibid*, 348-65, and Rawindaran V. N. P. Nair, Bernard M. Gardner and Ruth Banomyong, *Theories and Practices of Multimodal Transport in Europe*, 2001. http://www.bus.tu.ac.th/usr/ruth/file/theory.pdf. See also: EEC, *Council Regulation No. 4056/86 of 22 December 1986*, 1986. http://ec.europa.eu/comm/competition/antitrust/legislation/405686_en.html. For instance, there was a condition of non-discrimination that conference members had to respect in order to benefit from the conference block exemption under European Regulation 4056/86: conference members could not discriminate between ports or transport users by applying different rates and conditions of carriage for the same goods carried in the same area unless these could be justified economically.

38. The EU Competitiveness Council ensures an integrated approach to the enhancement of competitiveness and growth in Europe. In that spirit, it reviews on a regular basis both horizontal and sectoral competitiveness issues on the basis of analyses provided by the European Commission and gives its views on how competitiveness issues can be properly taken into account in all policy initiatives which have an impact on enterprises. The Council also deals with legislative proposals in its different fields of activ-

ity where it decides by qualified majority, mostly in co-decision with the European Parliament (Competitiveness Council, 2009). See also: http://consilium.europa.eu/cms3_fo/showPage.asp?id=412&lang=en

39. EU, *European Regulation No 1419/2006* (September 25, 2006). http://eur-lex.europa.eu/LexUriServ/LexUriServ.do?uri=OJ:L:2006:269:0001:0003:EN:PDF. *Antitrust: Commission Adopts Guidelines on Application of Competition Rules to Maritime Transport Services*, 2008. http://europa.eu/rapid/pressReleasesAction.do?reference=IP/08/1063&type=HTML&aged=0&language=EN&guiLanguage=en. European Regulation No 1419/2006 (September 25, 2006) repealed Regulation No 4056/86 laying down detailed rules for the application of Articles 81 and 82 of the *EC Treaty* to maritime transport and amended Regulation No 1/2003 as regards the extension of its scope to include cabotage and international tramp services. See: Submission to the EC Directorate General for Competition's Issues Paper Re: the (revised) ELAA proposal following the forthcoming repeal of *Council Regulation No 4056/86*, 2006. http://ec.europa.eu/competition/antitrust/others/maritime/dynamar_bv.pdf

40. *European Regulation No 1419/2006* (September 25, 2006) http://eur-lex.europa.eu/LexUriServ/LexUriServ.do?uri=OJ:L:2006:269:0001:0003:EN:PDF; *Competition: Repeal of Block Exemption for Liner Shipping Conferences—Frequently Asked Questions*, 2006. http://europa.eu/rapid/pressReleasesAction.do?reference=MEMO/06/344&format=HTML&aged=1&language=EN&guiLanguage=fr

41. *European Regulation No 1419/2006* (September 25, 2006). http://eur-lex.europa.eu/LexUriServ/LexUriServ.do?uri=OJ:L:2006:269:0001:0003:EN:PDF. *Antitrust: Guidelines on the Application of Competition Rules in the Maritime Sector—Frequently Asked Questions*, 2008. http://europa.eu/rapid/pressReleasesAction.do?reference=MEMO/08/460&format=HTML&aged=0&language=EN&guiLanguage=en

42. Consultation paper on the review of Council Regulation (EEC) No 4056/86 laying down detailed rules for the application of Articles 81 and 82 of the *EC Treaty* to Maritime Transport. http://ec.europa.eu/comm/competition/antitrust/legislation/maritime/en.pdf

43. *Ibid.*

44. *Ibid.*

45. *Ibid.*

46. EU, *Competition: Repeal of Block Exemption for Liner Shipping Conferences—Frequently Asked Questions*, 2006. http://europa.eu/rapid/pressReleasesAction.do?reference =MEMO/06/344&format=HTML&aged=1&language=EN&guiLanguage=fr

47. *Ibid.*

48. *Ibid.*

49. Watson, Farley and Williams, *EU and Competition: All Change at Sea*, 2007. http://www.legalweek.com/Company/386/Navigation/18/Articles/1007278/EU+and+Competition+All+change+at+sea.html. Prior to the introduction of the new Council regulation, cabotage and tramp services were the only remaining sectors to be excluded (as opposed to exempted) from the EU's competition implementing rules. *Ibid.*

50. *Ibid.*

51. *Explanatory Memorandum to the Merchant Shipping (Liner Conferences) Act (1982) Repeal Regulations*, 2008. http://www.opsi.gov.uk/si/si2008/em/uksiem_20080163_en.pdf. The Competitiveness Council of the European Union has decided to extend the scope of the procedural antitrust rules to cabotage and tramp shipping services. This means that the Commission now enjoys the same investigation and enforcement powers as regards cabotage and tramp services as in all other economic sectors. *Antitrust: Commission adopts Guidelines on application of competition rules to maritime transport services*, 2008. http://europa.eu/rapid/pressReleasesAction.do?reference=IP/08/1063&type=HTML&aged=0&language=EN&guiLanguage=en

52. Consortia is an association of two or more individuals, companies, organizations or governments (or any combination of these entities) with the objective of participating in a common activity or pooling their resources for achieving a common goal (Consortia, 2008). http://en.wikipedia.org/wiki/Consortium

53. *Competition: Repeal of Block Exemption for Liner Shipping Conferences— Frequently Asked Questions*, 2006. http://europa.eu/rapid/pressReleasesAction.do? reference=MEMO/06/344&format=HTML&aged=1&language=EN&guiLanguage=fr. Jürgen Mensching, *Liner shipping: Examining the Development and Impact of European Legislation*, 2000. http://ec.europa.eu/comm/competition/speeches/text/sp2000_001_en. html. The consortia block exemption was originally granted by Commission Regulation 870/95 and was renewed by Regulation 823/2000 since the original measure was only applicable for five years. The application of Regulation 823/2000 was extended in 2005 for another five years. On October 22, 2008 the European Commission opened consultations on a draft Regulation on the liner shipping consortia exemption proposing to continue to allow for such co-operation within a new legislative and economic environment. *Antitrust: Commission Opens Consultations on Review of Block Exemption for Liner Shipping Consortia*, 2008. http://europa.eu/rapid/pressReleasesAction.do? reference=IP/08/1566&format=HTML&aged=0&language=EN&guiLanguage=en

54. Nikolaos E. Farantouris, *European Integration and Maritime Transport* (Athens & Thessaloniki: Ant. N. Sakkoulas, 2003), 365. Consortia are fairly recent phenomena born out of the container revolution which called for the building of much larger ships to effect economies of scale and increase productivity. *Ibid.*

55. *Competition: Repeal of Block Exemption for Liner Shipping Conferences— Frequently Asked Questions*, 2006.

56. *Ibid.*

57. Holman, Fenwick and Willan, *Comments on Maritime Guidelines*, 2007. See: http://ec.europa.eu/comm/competition/antitrust/legislation/maritime/holman.pdf

58. *Guidelines on the Application of Article 81 of the EC Treaty to Maritime Transport Services*, 2007. See: http://eur-lex.europa.eu/LexUriServ/LexUriServ.do?uri= CELEX:52007XC0914(01):EN:NOT

59. *Guidelines on the Application of Article 81 of the EC Treaty to Maritime Transport Services*, 2008. See: http://ec.europa.eu/competition/antitrust/legislation/maritime/ guidelines_en.pdf. *Antitrust: Commission Adopts Guidelines on the Application of Competition Rules to Maritime Transport Services*, 2008. http://europa.eu/rapid/press Releases.Action.do?reference=IP/08/1063&type=HTML&aged=0&language=EN&guiLa nguage=en. See also: *Shipping Briefing: Tramp Pools and Liner Consortia*, 2008. http://www8.legal500.com/images/stories/firmdevs/thom10555/newsletter_shipping_nov 08.pdf and the speech of Olivier Guersent, *The Guidelines on Maritime Transport Services*, October 24, 2008. http://ec.europa.eu/competition/speeches/text/sp2008_12_ en.pdf

60. *Guidelines on the Application of Article 81 of the EC Treaty to Maritime Transport Services*, 2008.

61. *Ibid.*

62. Christopher Clott and Gary S. Wilson, "Ocean Shipping Deregulation and Maritime Ports: Lessons Learned from Airline Deregulation," *Transp. L. J.* 26 (1999): 205-210.

63. Chris Sagers, "The Demise of Regulation in Ocean Shipping: A Study in the Evolution of Competition Policy and the Predictive Power of Macroeconomics," *Vand. J. Transnat'l. L.* 39 (2006): 779-802.

64. Christopher Clott and Gary S. Wilson, "Ocean Shipping Deregulation and Maritime Ports: Lessons Learned from Airline Deregulation," *Transp. L. J.* 26 (1999): 205, 209.

65. *Competition: Repeal of Block Exemption for Liner Shipping Conferences—Frequently Asked Questions*, 2006.

66. *Ibid.*

67. Definition based on the one forwarded by W. Brad Jones, Richard Cassady and Royce O. Bowden, "Symposium on Intermodal Transportation: Developing A Standard Definition of Intermodal Transportation," *Transp. L. J.* 27 (2000): 345, 349.

68. Rolf Herber, "The European Legal Experience with Multimodalism," *Tul. L. Rev.* 64 (1989-1990): 611.

69. *Ibid*, 615.

70. *Ibid.*

71. *Ibid.*

72. See i.e., the *Transatlantic Agreement (TAA)* (1994), OJ L376/1; *Far Eastern Freight Conference (FEFC)* (1994), OJ L378/17; and the *Transatlantic Conference Agreement (TACA)* (1999), OJ L95/1 decisions. Nikolaos E. Farantouris, *European Integration and Maritime Transport* (Athens & Thessaloniki: Ant. N. Sakkoulas, 2003), 358-9. See also: *Competition: Repeal of Block Exemption for Liner Shipping Conferences —Frequently Asked Questions*, 2006.

73. Nikolaos E. Farantouris, *European Integration and Maritime Transport* (Athens & Thessaloniki: Ant. N. Sakkoulas, 2003), 358. For the four conditions under Article 81(3), see supra 8.

74. In other words, if it is the same conference members that extend their co-operation to inland transport, the Commission may consider an exemption in view of the benefits to users resulting from the "door-to-door" transport. See: D. Waelbroeck, *An Introduction to European Competition Rules and Their Impact on Shipping Law* (1995), 157-66.

75. Helmut Kreis, "European Community Competition Policy and International Shipping," *E. T .L.* 27 (1992): 155, 167.

76. Nick Maltby, "Multimodal Transport and EC Competition Law," *L. M. C. L. Q.* 79 (1993): 83-84.

77. *Ocean Shipping Reform Act* (OSRA) Pub. L. 105-258 (46 U. S. C. ss 1701-18) (1998). The legislative procedure for the adoption of the OSRA started in 1995 with adoption of the OSRA 1995 by the House of Representatives. The legislation was stalled in the Senate that finally adopted an amended version of the Act on October 9, 1998. The text finally adopted by the House of Representatives and the Senate is known as the OSRA 1998.

78. OSRA, Sections 4 and 5. *Ocean Shipping Reform Act*, 1998. http://www.hanjin.com/en/container/shipping/osra_1998.pdf and Chris Sagers, "The Demise of Regulation in Ocean Shipping: A Study in the Evolution of Competition Policy and the Predictive Power of Macroeconomics," *Vand. J. Transnat'l. L.* 39 (2006): 779, 801.

79. Chris Sagers, "The Demise of Regulation in Ocean Shipping: A Study in the Evolution of Competition Policy and the Predictive Power of Macroeconomics," *Vand. J. Transnat'l. L.* 39 (2006): 779-801.

80. OSRA, Section 10C (4). *Ocean Shipping Reform Act*, 1998. http://www.hanjin.com/en/container/shipping/osra_1998.pdf. Transport Canada, *Regulation of Liner Conference in Canada and the United States*, 2007. http://www.tc.gc.ca/pol/en/acf/scea/comparativeInformationPaper.htm

81. *Ibid.*

82. Chris Sagers, "The Demise of Regulation in Ocean Shipping: A Study in the Evolution of Competition Policy and the Predictive Power of Macroeconomics," *Vand. J. Transnat'l. L.* 39 (2006): 779, 815.

83. R. G. Edmonson, *Ocean Shipping Reform Act Changed the Industry Forever*, 2008. http://www.bawtc.com/whatsnew_article.asp?WhatsNewID=1276. In considering

OSRA, Congress was faced with the challenge of balancing the need to deregulate the maritime shipping industry with the requirement to provide oversight of ocean carrier practices. See also: David B. Vellenga, *The Ocean Shipping Reform Act of 1998*, 2000. http://www.allbusiness.com/operations/shipping/655723-1.html

84. As quoted by the Federal Maritime Commission, *Ocean Common Carrier and Marine Terminal Operator Agreements Subject to the Shipping Act of 1984*, 1998. http://www.fmc.gov/Dockets/98-26.htm

85. Chris Sagers, "The Demise of Regulation in Ocean Shipping: A Study in the Evolution of Competition Policy and the Predictive Power of Macroeconomics," *Vand. J. Transnat'l. L.* 39 (2006): 779, 817.

86. Statement of Mr. Michael Berzon on behalf of the National Industrial Transportation League, 2008. http://www.nitl.org/testimony6-19-08.pdf

87. *Ibid.* Richard K. Bank, Ashley W. Craig and Edward J. Sheppard IV, *Shifting Seas: A Survey of US and European Liner Shipping Regulatory Developments Affecting the Transatlantic Trades*, 2005. http://www.palgrave-journals.com/mel/journal/v7/n1/full/9100124a.html#ftnote18

88. R. G. Edmonson, *Ocean Shipping Reform Act Changed the Industry Forever*, 2008. http://www.bawtc.com/whatsnew_article.asp?WhatsNewID=1276

89. Steve W. Block, *Carrier Antitrust Immunity Revisited: The Continent Abolishes It; Is Uncle Sam Next?*, 2006. http://www.forwarderlaw.com/library/view.php?article_id=409

90. *Ibid.*

91. Statement of Mr. Michael Berzon on behalf of the National Industrial Transportation League, 2008. http://www.nitl.org/testimony6-19-08.pdf

92. Steve W. Block, *Carrier Antitrust Immunity Revisited: The Continent Abolishes It; Is Uncle Sam Next?*, 2006. http://www.forwarderlaw.com/library/view.php?article_id=409

93. R. G. Edmonson, *Ocean Shipping Reform Act Changed the Industry Forever*, 2008. http://www.bawtc.com/whatsnew_article.asp?WhatsNewID=1276

94. *Ibid.*

95. Steve W. Block, *Carrier Antitrust Immunity Revisited: The Continent Abolishes It; Is Uncle Sam Next?*, 2006. http://www.forwarderlaw.com/library/view.php?article_id=409

PART IV

Caribbean Competitiveness Aspects

Chapter 11
Promoting Export Competitiveness in CARICOM: Issues and Challenges

Marie Freckleton

INTRODUCTION

Export competitiveness is critical for the survival of the small economies of the Caribbean Community (CARICOM) in an increasingly competitive global economy. Given the limited resource endowments of CARICOM economies they are dependent on export earnings for growth and development. Increased foreign exchange inflows from exports are necessary to procure imports of capital goods, technology and services required to sustain higher levels of economic growth. Increasing export market shares is also essential for these economies to surmount the economic constraints imposed by small domestic markets. Furthermore, for the majority of CARICOM states export earnings are urgently needed to service burdensome external debt.[1]

It is important to note that export competitiveness encompasses more than the ability to increase export earnings. According to UNCTAD (2002: 117):

> Export competitiveness has many facets, the most obvious implying higher exports. But it also means diversifying the export basket, sustaining higher rates of export growth over time, upgrading the technological and skill content of export activity and expanding the base of domestic firms able to compete globally; thus, competitiveness is sustained and is generally accompanied by rising incomes.

Recognizing the important role of export earnings in promoting economic growth and development, CARICOM governments have implemented various policies over the last two decades intended to stimulate export growth. The policies that have been introduced include the establishment of trade promotion organizations, provision of tax incentives to attract foreign investors, establishment of export processing zones, and export financing schemes. However, the relatively poor export performance of CARICOM countries suggests that these policies, while necessary are not sufficient to promote export competitiveness.

This chapter examines the constraints on export competitiveness in CARICOM and assesses the prospects for enhancing competitiveness. The chapter is organized as follows: Section 2 provides an overview of CARICOM's export performance over the past two decades. This is followed by an analysis of the constraints on export competitiveness in the region. The next section addresses policy measures for improving export competitiveness. Conclusions are presented in the final section.

CARICOM EXPORT PERFORMANCE

For the decade of the 1990s, the merchandise exports of most CARICOM countries recorded sluggish growth (Table 11.1). Export growth in the period 2000-2005 exhibited a similar pattern, with the average annual growth rate of merchandise exports exceeding 5 percent in only five CARICOM countries compared to 13.4 percent for middle income developing countries and 11.9 percent for developing economies excluding China. In addition to growing slowly, merchandise exports remain concentrated in a narrow range of primary products, resource-based manufactures, and low technology manufactures.[2] Furthermore, the traditional merchandise exports are dependent on preferential market access due to lack of competitiveness.

Developing countries benefit from the Generalized System of Preferences (GSP) provided by developed countries. In addition, CARICOM countries have successfully negotiated other preferential trade arrangements. In the case of the Canadian market, CARICOM benefits from the Canada-CARICOM (CARIBCAN) Agreement that provides duty free access to all products except textiles and clothing, footwear, leather goods, and methanol. The Caribbean Basin Initiative (CBI) allows duty free treatment for Caribbean exports excluded from the United States' GSP. These include beef, veal, rum, tobacco, iron, steel, and pharmaceutical products. The CBI excludes petroleum products, footwear, canned tuna, and textiles and apparel. However, textiles and apparel are given special quotas under the *807 Program*. In 2000, the United States-Caribbean Trade Partnership Act improved the CBI by providing duty free access to products excluded under the CBI. This was intended to give CARICOM countries parity with Mexico, which has duty free access to the U.S. market under the North American Free Trade Agreement (NAFTA). Preferential access to the European Union (EU) market has been available since 1975 under the *Lomé* Conventions, and the subsequent *Cotonou* Agreement and Economic Partnership Agreement.[3]

CARICOM's dependence on preferential market access is particularly severe in the cases of the major agricultural exports—sugar and bananas—that are unable to compete without the preferential access offered by the European Union. The erosion of preferential margins brought about by multilateral trade liberalization and the proliferation of free trade agreements therefore constitutes a serious threat to the survival of uncompetitive merchandise exports. In the case of sugar the viability of the industry is further threatened by a 36 percent reduction in the guaranteed price paid by the EU. The banana industry also faces an uncertain future due to the WTO ruling that the preferential quotas for African, Caribbean, and Pacific (ACP) bananas should be replaced by a single tariff for bananas imported into the EU.

Given the poor prospects for merchandise exports, diversification efforts have focused on the expansion of the tourism industry and the development of other service exports. Services account for more than half of total exports of goods and services in all CARICOM member states except Guyana, Haiti, Suriname, and Trinidad and Tobago (Table 11.2). The Bahamas and the Eastern Caribbean islands are most heavily dependent on service exports with services accounting for 70 percent or more of total exports of goods and services in those countries in 2008. Available data indicates that tourism accounts for 70 percent of the region's total exports of goods and services.[4] While expansion of tourism has been successfully achieved, the heavy dependence on this volatile industry increases the vulnerability of CARICOM economies. Hence, it is imperative that the region achieves international competitiveness in non-tourism services. Attempts to develop non-tourism services have focused on financial services, information enabled services, and recreational and cultural services. However, except in the case of The Bahamas, which has a well-developed financial services export sector, non-tourism services exports are relatively underdeveloped within CARICOM.

TABLE 11.1
CARICOM Annual Average Growth Rates of Merchandise Exports (%)

Country	1990-2000	2000-2005	2007
Antigua & Barbuda	0.4	0.9	..
The Bahamas	8.5	-4.1	*7.4
Barbados	3.9	4.8	8.7
Belize	4.9	2.3	0.1
Dominica	0.5	-4.6	*-6.5
Grenada	9.0	-17.9	*47.3
Guyana	8.3	3.2	*14.3
Haiti	12.2	9.7	*-0.1
Jamaica	2.2	3.4	*15.9
Montserrat	5.4	21.5	*65.2
St Kitts & Nevis	8.9	2.2	*5.7
St Lucia	-9.7	9.3	*10.5
St Vincent & the Grenadines	-5.3	-4.2	*32.2
Suriname	3.2	28.0	..
Trinidad &Tobago	6.8	17.2	*-16.7
Middle-income developing countries	7.5	13.4	16.5
Developing countries excluding China	8.5	11.9	12.3

.. Not available   * Estimate
Source: UNCTAD, Handbook of Trade Statistics, 2008.

TABLE 11.2

CARICOM Exports of Commercial Services as Percentage of Total Exports of Goods and Services

Country	1996	2000	2008
Antigua & Barbuda	90.5	88.6	85.0
The Bahamas	89.6	77.2	74.3
Barbados	76.2	79.5	*77.8
Belize	42.7	38.2	56.0
Dominica	56.8	62.1	69.6
Grenada	84.0	75.2	85.3
Guyana	20.4	25.3	*17.8
Haiti	53.6	33.2	29.4
Jamaica	53.2	60.4	52.6
Montserrat	..	..	..
St Kitts & Nevis	79.8	74.2	80.4
St Lucia	76.9	88.3	75.1
St Vincent & the Grenadines	67.6	72.8	79.1
Suriname	18.1	17.6	12.0
Trinidad & Tobago	15.2	11.3	*6.4

.. Not available *2007 data
Source: Author's calculations based on WTO (2008).

CONSTRAINTS ON EXPORT COMPETITIVENESS WITHIN CARICOM

CARICOM's export performance over the last decade suggests that there has been some success in expanding tourism. However, efforts to develop exports of non-tourism services have been less successful and merchandise exports remain concentrated in a narrow range of products. The failure to achieve significant export growth despite preferential access to major export markets suggests that lack of competitiveness is a serious problem for CARICOM countries. Competitiveness is determined by a wide range of factors that affect productivity.[5] In addition, the requirements for competitiveness will vary with the level of development of the country (World Economic Forum 2009: 7). This section examines the major constraints on the competitiveness of CARICOM countries.

A significant obstacle to competitiveness is lack of access to capital. CARICOM economies have relatively low levels of domestic savings that have resulted in a shortage of the capital required for investment. This problem is compounded by underdeveloped financial markets. These underdeveloped markets are characterized by small equity markets, few venture capital institutions, and risk averse banks. This restricts the ability of exporters to access the financing required to improve productivity or to develop new exports. Given the limited availability of capital, exporters are forced to rely on commercial banks. Access to bank credit is constrained by the preference of commercial banks for financing of consumer loans and investment in government securities that are perceived to be relatively low risk. This problem is aggravated by the inability of some exporters to provide the collateral required by commercial banks as only a limited range of assets is accepted as collateral. Moreover, available credit in some CARICOM countries is obtained at relatively high cost due to limited competition in the banking sector.[6]

Recognizing that lack of access to financing impedes export competitiveness, some governments of the region provide export financing.[7] However, export finance schemes help to satisfy the short term credit needs of exporters but do not address the need for risk capital. Lack of access to capital therefore continues to restrict competitiveness.

The unavailability of adequate human capital is another major constraint on CARICOM export competitiveness. The region produces a limited supply of human capital. According to the World Bank (2005a) enrollment in tertiary education within the region is approximately 15 percent compared to average enrollment of 24 percent for middle income developing countries. Moreover, the limited supply of highly skilled labor produced in the region is consistently depleted by the brain drain to developed countries. According to the International Monetary Fund (2005: 75), Caribbean countries are among the twenty countries in the world with the highest rates of emigration of workers with tertiary education. The shortage of human capital restricts the ability of CARICOM countries to undertake the technological upgrading required to improve productivity. While technology can be imported, adequate human capital with the knowledge and skills to adapt technology to local conditions is necessary for successful technological advancement. Insufficient human capital also limits the region's capacity to take advantage of new export opportunities opening up in knowledge intensive industries.

Good infrastructure is a basic requirement for international competitiveness (World Economic Forum 2009). Deficient infrastructure constrains export competitiveness by reducing efficiency and increasing production costs. The majority of CARICOM countries face serious infrastructural deficiencies particularly in the vital areas of energy, transportation, and telecommunications. The poor quality of infrastructure is partly due to the fiscal constraints facing governments of the region.

The quality of institutions is another important determinant of international competitiveness (World Economic Forum 2009; World Bank 2005). Institutional deficiencies within CARICOM that adversely affect competitiveness include inefficient judicial systems, corruption, incompetent public administration, and lack of security. Inefficient judicial systems result in costly delays in the enforcement of contracts. Trinidad and Tobago, for example, is ranked at 169 out of 183 countries with respect to the ease of enforcing contracts (World Bank 2009).[8] Corruption is a serious problem in CARICOM. The 2008 Transparency International Corruption Perception Index ranked Haiti at 177 out of 180 countries while Guyana was ranked at 126.[9] Cumbersome administrative procedures in government agencies also increase the costs of doing business. Tax administration for example is particularly problematic in some CARICOM countries. In addition, the region has a relatively high crime rate compared to other parts of the world. One recent study found that the Caribbean with its murder rate of 30 persons per 100,000 per year is the region with the highest murder rate in the world (UNODC 2007). The high crime rate imposes high security costs on business and discourages investment.

Finally, international competitiveness has been undermined by weak private sectors. The domestic entrepreneurial class within CARICOM is underdeveloped and lacking in dynamism. This is mainly due to the fact that this class is dominated by merchant capitalists with limited capacity or willingness to undertake the challenge of penetrating export markets. Furthermore, domestic entrepreneurs in the region's export industries have had little incentive to promote competitiveness as they have been sheltered from international competition by an abundance of preferential trade arrangements.

POLICY RECOMMENDATIONS

In order to respond to the increasingly competitive international environment CARICOM governments need to intensify efforts to enhance international competitiveness. Increasing investment in human capital has to be given priority if the region is to achieve the technological upgrading required to improve productivity. However, the fiscal constraints facing governments means that the state is not well positioned to undertake the increased investment required. This problem can be addressed by stimulating increased private sector investment in education and training. Given the shortage of capital within the region it will also be necessary to promote increased foreign investment in education and training.

The shortage of human capital reflects both fiscal constraints and the effects of the brain drain but there are limited prospects for reducing the brain drain in the short term. Nevertheless, CARICOM countries need to continue to collaborate with other developing countries to negotiate for the liberalization of temporary movement of natural persons in the multilateral negotiations on trade in services. If this is achieved then opportunities for temporary movement may reduce the permanent emigration of educated workers over the medium term.

Increased availability of risk capital is critical for export competitiveness. The scarcity of venture capital institutions within the region is a clear case of market failure that needs to be corrected by governments. This can be achieved directly by establishment of venture capital funds by state-owned development banks or indirectly through the provision of incentives to private investors for the establishment of venture capital funds. It is important to note however that, with the exception of oil rich Trinidad and Tobago, the ability of CARICOM governments to finance venture capital funds is dependent on their ability to obtain assistance from multilateral lending agencies.[10] Improved access to bank credit has to be facilitated as well. Hence, reform of collateral regulations needs to be implemented to allow a wider range of assets to be used as collateral.

With respect to improving the quality of infrastructure, the fiscal burden can be reduced by means of partnerships with private investors. This strategy has been successfully employed in Jamaica where the government entered into build-operate-transfer contracts with foreign investors to upgrade the country's road network.

Finally, given the weakness of the domestic entrepreneurial class and the shortage of capital attracting increased inflows of foreign direct investment is vital if enhanced international competitiveness is to be achieved. It is recognized however that increasing globalization is intensifying competition for foreign direct investment (FDI). Furthermore, the current global recession has reduced FDI inflows into developing countries. Under these conditions, fiscal incentives traditionally relied on by CARICOM countries to attract FDI are not sufficient. The region has to address the institutional deficiencies including corruption and high crime rates that reduce the ability to attract foreign investors. Good infrastructure and an adequate supply of skilled workers are also important determinants of FDI.

To the extent that the region is able to attract FDI, maximizing the impact of FDI on competitiveness will require strengthening of domestic firms so that they can integrate into the international production networks of transnational corporations. As noted by UNCTAD (2002: 141), export competitiveness is more likely to be sustained if domestic firms are able to improve their competitiveness by establishing linkages with transnational corporations.[11]

CONCLUSIONS

Despite preferential market access the export performance of CARICOM countries over the last two decades has been relatively poor. This suggests that promoting export competitiveness is essential in order to earn the foreign exchange needed to finance economic growth and development in this trade dependent region.

The policy measures used to promote export development within CARICOM have failed to address the structural and institutional constraints that undermine export competitiveness. Major obstacles to competitiveness include lack of access to capital, insufficient supply of human capital, poor infrastructure, deficient institutions, and weak private sectors.

Prospects for improved competitiveness depend on the extent to which governments are able to implement policy measures designed to relax existing constraints. Given the limited financial resources available to most governments of the region, private public partnerships, foreign direct investment, and access to external financing are essential.

NOTES

1. At the end of 2005, external debt exceeded gross national income (GNI) in the cases of Guyana and Belize and amounted to more than two-thirds of GNI in Dominica, St Kitts & Nevis, and St Vincent. For further details see World Bank 2007.

2. Based on CARICOM Secretariat data, the major primary exports are petroleum, natural gas, aluminum ores, sugar, bananas, and rice. The major resource based manufac-

tures including ammonia, methanol, and urea are exported by Trinidad and Tobago. Low technology manufactures include garments, beverages, medicaments, and paper products.

3. While the *Lomé* Conventions and *Cotonou* Agreement offered non-reciprocal preferential access to the EU market, the Economic Partnership Agreement signed in October 2008 is a reciprocal free trade agreement. Under the terms of this agreement, CARICOM countries have duty free access to the EU market but are required to grant duty free access to imports from the EU on a phased basis.

4. Author's calculations based on World Trade Organization statistics database available at http://www.wto.org.

5. See for example: World Economic Forum 2009; UNCTAD 2002; and Porter 1998.

6. This is particularly true in the case of Jamaica where the banking sector is dominated by two large banks.

7. In the cases of Jamaica and Trinidad and Tobago state-owned export-import banks have been established to provide trade financing. The export finance facilities offered by these institutions include foreign currency lines of credit, pre-shipment financing, post-shipment financing, and export credit. In the case of Barbados, there is no export-import bank but similar facilities are provided through the Central Bank.

8. Other CARICOM countries with low rankings include Belize 168, St Lucia 165, and Jamaica 128.

9. St Lucia and Barbados which were ranked at 21 and 22 respectively are perceived to be the least corrupt countries in the region.

10. The Government of Jamaica is seeking financial assistance from international lending agencies to establish a venture capital fund for the tourism sector. Meanwhile, the Government of Trinidad and Tobago has announced a venture capital incentive program that will offer tax credits to investors in venture capital funds.

11. Initial steps toward strengthening domestic firms are being funded by the EU under its Private Sector Development Program but much more remains to be done.

REFERENCES

CARICOM Secretariat. *Caribbean Trade and Investment Report*. Kingston: Ian Randle Publishers, 2005.

International Monetary Fund. *World Economic Outlook*. Washington, DC: IMF, 2005.

Porter, M. E. *The Competitive Advantage of Nations*. London: Macmillan, 1998.

Transparency International. *Corruption Perceptions Index*, 2008. Available at: http://www.transparency.org/policy_research/surveys_indices/cpi

UNCTAD. *Handbook of Trade Statistics*. Geneva: United Nations, 2008.

——— . *World Investment Report*. Geneva: United Nations, 2002.

United Nations Office on Drugs and Crime. "Crime, Violence and Development: Trends, Costs, and Policy Options in the Caribbean," UNODC, 2007. Available at: http://unodc.org/pdf/research/Cr_and Vio_car_E.pdf

World Bank. *Doing Business 2010*. Washington, DC: World Bank, 2009.

——— . *Global Development Finance*. Washington, DC: World Bank, 2007.

——— . *World Development Report*. Washington, DC: World Bank, 2005.

——— . *A Time to Choose: Caribbean Development in the 21st Century*. Washington, DC: World Bank, 2005a.

World Economic Forum. *Global Competitiveness Report 2009-2010*, 2009. Available at: http://www.weforum.org/pdf/global_competitiveness_reports

Chapter 12
Boosting Private Sector Competitiveness for Development in the Caribbean

Dillon Alleyne

INTRODUCTION

This chapter provides an overview of the private sector in the Caribbean[1] and examines the policy environment that fosters its development. The chapter also examines the prospects for developing competitive firms and activities. Caribbean firms face many challenges which are the result of closer regional integration due to the signing of the CARICOM single market and economy (CSME), and the new global trade arrangements. The completion of the Uruguay Round and the establishment of the WTO have emphasized the widening and deepening of the process of globalization and trade liberalization. New pressures have emerged as non-trade elements such as labor, environmental and phytosanitary standards, have been included in the institutional framework of the international trading system. The revision of the *Lomé* Accord which was encapsulated in the *Cotonou* agreement and the signing of the European Partnership Agreement (EPA) virtually brought to an end, traditional preference arrangements (Barclay et al. 2001).

In this context, the Caribbean firms must compete to survive. Given the high level of substitutability among goods produced in the region, full integration of the regional market as envisaged by the CSME will bring only limited gains (IDB 2006a: 3). The issue then is how to rationalize traditional areas of economic activity, and how new ones can be financed and developed within the private sector.

The public policy has been on reducing market distortions and improving efficiency. An expression of this approach has been the decline in government's role in business activity in most countries of the region.[2] Much progress has also been made by reducing regional tariff barriers and improving the regional market for trade through the limited movement of labor and capital.

At the micro level, firms must now reorient their production from low technology exports of goods and services to high value added production.[3] Secondly, labor productivity must increase if firms are to be internationally competitive. Thirdly, firms need to invest more in research and development to improve the capacity for innovation. Firms must also develop industry clusters to reap the benefits of agglomeration due to small size and scale.

At the macro level, evidence of declining competitiveness has manifested itself in the expanding deficit on the current account of the balance of payments of several countries in the region (Alleyne and Francis 2007). Figure 12.1 shows that, except for Trinidad and Tobago and Suriname, most other countries have accumulated deficits in excess of 10 percent of their GDP (ECLAC 2006).

FIGURE 12.1
Current Account Balance 2002-2009 and Public Debt as Percentages of GDP, 2009

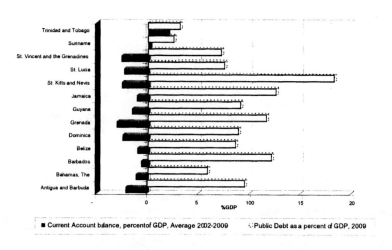

In addition, some Caribbean countries face a substantial debt burden with the debt-to-GDP ratio often in excess of 100 percent (Perez 2006).[4] Given the openness of Caribbean economies, firms help to reduce the balance of payments constraint by export expansion and efficiency in the use of imports, that is increasing import capacity.[5] To this end, firms can be distinguished between those that exhibit dynamic competitive advantage relative to those that are engaged in import-intensive and price-taking activities. The first group of firms are efficient in their foreign exchange use (their import productivity),[6] and the extent to which they develop the capacity to innovate. They adjust through the intensive use of domestic capital,[7] the flow of work,[8] and import efficiency. The next section presents an overview of the private sector in the region by examining the number and types of firms, their size, and activity.

BASIC INFORMATION ON THE PRIVATE SECTOR IN THE CARIBBEAN

Types of Firms by Legal Status and Ownership Structure

The Caribbean private sector is made up of a variety of enterprises ranging from single-owned firms and small operators to multinational corporations. We have identified four types of firms based on their legal status and organizational structure. There are local and regional formal enterprises, foreign enterprises and affiliates, and domestic informal enterprises.

Formal Private Sector

Domestic firms: In this category are the traditional private sector firms which are registered and operate in all sectors of the economy. The most popular form of organization are the private held companies or limited liability companies, partnerships, cooperatives, and publicly held companies. Traditionally, Caribbean firms have either been organized as partnerships or privately held companies, and although publicly held corporations limit personal financial liability of shareholders and directors, private ownership has been seen as a means of maintaining control of firms (CTIR 2005).

It is recognized that most domestic firms in the Caribbean are of small and medium size with a relatively few large ones.[9] When the top twenty firms in the Caribbean were compared with firms in Latin America, Canada, Europe, and the United States for 2009, the results were revealing. While revenues varied between US$ 1.91 billion and US$ 5.42 billion for the Caribbean top twenty firms, for Latin America revenues varied between US$ 4.28 and US$ 104.81 billion, for Europe it was between US$ 49.27 billion and US$ 109.57 billion, for the United States it was between US$ 35.53 billion and US$ 115.63 billion, and for Canada between US$ 11.19 billion and US$ 35.41 billion (www.Forbes.com 2010). One estimate was that 70-85 percent of all business activity in the Caribbean was conducted by firms employing less than twenty-five persons (ILO 2000: 7).

Non-resident non-Caribbean private sector: The non-resident, non-Caribbean private sector was made up of transnational corporations or affiliates involved in various areas of the economy. They operate in banking and finance, mining, oil and gas, telecommunications, power generation, and large-scale tourism activities. In recent years, there has been the diversification of activity into information technology, telecommunications and other services.[10] There has also been increased use of franchises and licensing arrangements in the Caribbean, especially in the fast food sector (Best 2006). These firms may operate under special concessions and their marketing networks and international linkages gave them considerable advantages over local firms in cases where there were competitors.

The majority of firms operating in the region tended to originate from a few countries. Of the sixteen largest foreign affiliates located in Barbados, five were from the United States; four from Canada; three from the United Kingdom; and Germany, Italy, Finland, and Bermuda had one each. Of the top five in Belize, two were from the United States; and Canada, Denmark, and Panama had one each. Of the top eight in Guyana, four were from the United States; two from the United Kingdom; and two from Canada. In the case of Jamaica, of the twenty-five top foreign affiliates, thirteen were from the United States; three from Canada; three from Switzerland; and Spain, the Netherlands, Germany, and the United Kingdom had one each (CTIR 2005).[11]

In the case of Trinidad and Tobago, of the fourteen largest affiliates, five were from the United States; two from the UK; and one each from Canada, Venezuela, Japan, Italy, France, Germany, and Switzerland. It appears that, over time, there was diversification in origin of firms from traditional sources such as Canada, the United States, and the UK,[12] but this has been limited.

In a study of subsidiaries in the Caribbean, regardless of their country of origin, it was found that 52 percent were privately held companies with limited liability and publicly listed companies were 36 percent, while companies with other forms of legal status as partnerships and cooperatives were only marginally represented (World Bank 2004).

Cross-border investment and regional firms: The liberalization of the foreign exchange markets in many Caribbean economies and the implementation of the common external tariff plus recognition of the right of establishment under the rules of CARICOM Single Market and Economy have led to the emergence of several regional firms that are engaged in cross-border investment to service domestic markets. Some firms have even begun to develop links extra-regionally as well. One expression of this regional thrust was the development of individual stock markets and cross-listing of firms across markets. The markets lacked depth and none of the exchanges include a large number of firms despite the fact that some markets have been established for some time.[13]

TABLE 12.1
Number of Domestic and Cross-listed Firms, December 2005 and 2009

Stock Exchange of	No of Firms		No of Local Firms		No of Firms Cross-listed		% of Firms Cross-listed	
	2005	2009	2005	2009	2005	2009	2005	2009
Trinidad & Tobago	34	38	25	26	8	12	24	32
Barbados	23	25	18	20	5	5	5	20
Jamaica	44	46	40	43	4	3	9	7
Eastern Caribbean	9	14	7	11	2	3	22	21
Bahamas Int'l	19	19	18	17	1	2	1	11
Guyana	...	14	...	13	...	1	...	7

... Not available
Source: Individual Stock Exchanges, CARICOM Cross-Border Equity Flows, 2005 and 2009.

In 2005, there were eighteen firms each on the stock markets of The Bahamas and Barbados (CTIR 2005). For the Eastern Caribbean Stock Exchange (ECSE) it was seven, for Trinidad and Tobago it was twenty-five, and for Jamaica it was forty, the largest number of publicly listed firms for a single country in the Caribbean up to that period (CTIR 2000; 2005). In the case of Guyana, while several firms were allowed to trade, they were not listed.

Among the publicly listed firms some were also cross listed, however, these were a few of the larger firms that conducted business in several jurisdictions.[14] The number of firms with multiple listings was even smaller. As of December 2005, on the Bahamas International Securities exchange only one firm was cross -listed. For the ECSE it was two, for the Barbados stock exchange it was five. The largest number of cross listed firms was from Trinidad and Tobago, which was 24 percent or a mere eight firms.[15] The situation had not changed significantly in 2009.

TABLE 12.2
Selected Numbers of Domestic and Cross-Listed Firms by Sector,
December 2009

Sector	The Bahamas	Barbados	Eastern Caribbean	Guyana	Jamaica	Trinidad & Tobago
Finance	5	6	5	6	15	8
Com/cations	1	...	...	...	3	...
Health Care	1	...	...	...	...	...
Industrial	4	..	...	...	...	...
Insurance	3	2	...	...	2	...
Investment	1	...	...	...	...	...
Manufacturing	...	4	1	6	10	10
Property	2	...	1	1		1
Retail	1	...	...	1	2	...
Second Tier	...	...	...	...	...	2
Tourism	...	1	...	...	3	...
Trading	...	2	...	...	...	11
Utilities	...	2	4	...	...	...
Other	...	1	...	...	6	...
TOTAL	18	18	11	14	45	34

... Not available
Source: CARICOM Cross-Border Equity Flows, on the basis of individual stock exchanges.

In examining the activities of firms by sector, in Jamaica, and Trinidad and Tobago, manufacturing, tourism, and finance had a majority of firms. This was not surprising since these were countries with fairly large manufacturing sectors. In Barbados, the range was more varied but manufacturing and finance were important. Given the large financial services sector it was not surprising that on the Bahamas stock exchange, a majority of firms were in financial services. In the ECSE a majority of firms were in utilities and financial services.

Average capitalization, for the markets of Bermuda, Jamaica, St Kitts and Nevis, and Trinidad and Tobago, declined from US$ 8 billion in 2005 to US$ 6 billion in 2009, with the decline in 2009 due directly to the global recession and a softening of the appetite for risk. The demise of Colonial Life Insurance Company (CLICO), which was a major Trinidad and Tobago conglomerate in the Caribbean, may have also dampened the trend in cross-border investment with tougher regulation promised to reduce future systemic risk. It can be concluded that while public listings were a relatively new development for the Caribbean private sector, it motivated the interest of the larger companies in the region rather than the small and medium size operations that are the bulk of regional firms.

Informal Private Sector

The informal sector employed a large number of individuals and was especially significant in the economies of Jamaica, Haiti, Barbados, Guyana, and Suriname. Sole proprietorship was the dominant form of ownership and many of these businesses operated from homes (ILO 2000: x1).

In Suriname the sector was estimated at 16 percent of GDP, while in Jamaica it is estimated as between 40 to 43 percent of GDP (IDB 2006a; 2006b). Vuletin (2006) estimated the size of the informal sector for a number of Caribbean countries.[16] For example, in the case of The Bahamas it was 11-15.9 percent, for Barbados 24.3-36.6 percent, for Jamaica 35.0 percent, and for Guyana 36.7-57.3 percent.

Informal activities were present in various labor intensive activities in the Caribbean. Data on Jamaica showed that 60 percent of workers were in wholesale/retail trade or agriculture with manufacturing at 9 percent (IDB 2006b). Most studies suggest that women make up a large percentage of the sector (IDB 2006b; ILO 2000). In Jamaica, some 56 percent of workers in this sector are women relative to 50 percent in the formal sector.[17] As was typical, most workers did not have formal contracts, which reflected the dual nature of the labor market (see James 2006b). The next section of this chapter identifies the size and structure of the private sector in a number of Caribbean economies.

NUMBER OF FIRMS, SIZE OF EMPLOYMENT, AND OUTPUT STRUCTURE OF THE PRIVATE SECTOR

In trying to characterize the private sector, at the country level, several hurdles must be overcome. First, there were no easily available registers of firms for several countries and what information was available may be dated. Secondly, registered firms represented only one aspect of the characterization because of the large informal sector which existed in many Caribbean countries. A first step was to examine the distribution of firms for Jamaica, Barbados, Trinidad and

Tobago, St Lucia, the British Virgin Islands, and The Bahamas, and to develop some stylized facts about the size of Caribbean firms.

The Number and Distribution of Firms by Sector and Employment

The first pattern observed was that the largest numbers of firms were in the service sector as the percentage of firms in this sector varied between the range of 64 percent and 89 percent. Secondly, the number of firms in the mining and quarrying sectors was small, even in the case of Trinidad and Tobago which had the largest mining sector of the countries being examined. The numbers of firms in the sectors agriculture, manufacturing, and construction were also significant. When the numbers of registered firms in the six countries were combined, they represented some 89,204 firms overall. Most of the employment occurred in the tertiary sector where the majority of firms were concentrated. The primary sector employed the least number of workers, except for Trinidad and Tobago where the primary sector, mainly petroleum production, was relatively large.

TABLE 12.3
Caribbean Business Enterprises: Percentage of Firms and Employment by Sector

	Jamaica	Barbados	T&T	St Lucia	BVI	Bahamas
No of Firms	2005	2006	2004	2006	2006	2005
AFF	4.5	6.1	**0	3.9	2.5	
MQ	**0.17	**0.4	1.5		**0.1	
MAN	7.07	11.4	6.9	31.9	8.4	6.2
CON	5.41	6.5	6.4		14.8	4.6
IFI	4.50	2.0	10.8	1.1	1.3	
WR				16.9	15.0	33.2
TS	79.12	75.4	85.2	64.2	74.3	89.2
Total	46067.0	7021.0	29418.0	3027.0	1624.0	*5625.0
EMP						
PRIM	2.3	4.3	17.3	11.9	1.3	6.0
SEC	29.9	21.4	17.8	20.8	16.3	15.0
TERT	67.8	74.3	64.8	67.3	82.3	79.0
	100.0	100.0	100.0	100.0	100.0	100.0

AFF: Agriculture, Forestry & Fishing (%); MQ: Mining & Quarrying (%); MAN: Manufacturing (%); CON: Construction (%); IFI: Investment, Finance & Insurance (%); WR: Wholesale & Retail (%); TS: Total Services (%); Total: total number of firms; EMP: Employment; PRIM: Primary (%); SEC: Secondary (%); TERT: Tertiary (%).
* Offshore financial services are not included. ** Less than 1%.
Sources: Registers of firms and employment from country sources.

Information on employment by firms was available for Trinidad and Tobago, St Lucia, and The Bahamas. In respect of Trinidad and Tobago, of the 29,418 registered firms in 2004, 9,399 or 31.9 percent did not report their level of employment. Of those that reported, 69 percent employed between zero to four workers, while 24.8 percent employed between five and ninety-nine workers. The rest of the firms employed one hundred or more workers, and only about 6 percent of the firms reporting were in the latter category. In fact, there were only eleven firms employing 1,000 workers and over. In addition, of the total number of firms, only 2.7 percent were branches of other entities.

The results for St Lucia provided an example of extremely small firms in the private sector of the Caribbean. Small firms were defined as those employing less than ten persons, medium size firms were those employing ten to twenty persons, and large firms were those employing in excess of twenty persons. The total number of registered firms was 3,027 of which 52 percent were small according to the definition, 44.3 percent were medium, and the rest were large. In effect, nearly 97 percent of the firms employed between one and twenty persons, and less than three percent were defined as large.

In The Bahamas, of the firms registered in 2005, 47 percent employed less than ten persons, 26 percent employed between ten and nineteen persons, and another 26 percent employed between twenty and forty-nine persons.[18]

The results revealed two important facts. Firstly, firms in the Caribbean were small or medium size enterprises; and, secondly, the bulk of regional employment occurred in such enterprises. The implication was that due to the problem of scale firms will benefit from being part of value chain clusters and reap considerable benefits from the sharing of information, factory space, and other facilities which help to overcome the limitations of size.

The Structure of Output of the Private Sector in the Caribbean

In examining the structure of private sector output in the Caribbean, two issues must be raised. First, there was a danger in aggregating output across Caribbean countries because there were striking differences between the OECS countries and the rest.[19] Secondly, issues of scale tended to mask the difference between the smaller and larger economies.[20] The objective of the exercise was to show where there was the greatest concentration of private sector output in the region and what sectoral shifts have occurred over time.

Table 12.4 examines the private sector contribution to output, disaggregated by services and non-services, for the years 2005 and 2009. For The Bahamas, Barbados, Grenada, and St Lucia, the share of non-services declined relative to services between the two periods, reflecting the drift to services in these economies.[21] This was due to the secular decline in agriculture and manufacturing in these countries. Guyana, Trinidad and Tobago, Suriname, Dominica, and Belize had relatively large non-service sectors, including mining, agriculture, and manufacturing. Thus, the Caribbean private sector contribution to GDP tended to vary by country. The results for Table 12.4 represent only a rough approximation since government participation tended to be significant in some activities as in sugar production in Guyana and mining in Jamaica.

TABLE 12.4
Sectoral Composition of Real GDP by the Private Sector, 2005 and 2009

| Country | Private Sector Composition of GDP | | | |
| | 2005 | | 2009 | |
	Non-Service	Service	Non-Service	Service
Antigua & Barbuda	23.2	60.4	23.7	59.8
Bahamas, The	15.5	64.6	11.7	69.3
Barbados	19.5	49.3	15.2	...
Belize	29.7	55.5	28.4	62.7
Dominica	31.3	49.3	29.7	50.7
Grenada	27.3	60.7	18.2	68.3
Guyana	55.0	32.1	51.0	37.5
Jamaica	26.8	61.3	23.7	64.1
St Kitts & Nevis	32.0	53.0	27.3	55.9
St Lucia	17.8	70.0	15.8	70.0
St Vincent & Gren.	25.0	59.4	24.5	59.0
Suriname	32.5	54.3	31.0	56.9
Trinidad & Tobago	47.2	47.5	49.9	45.6

Notes: ... Not available. For Bahamas, Barbados, Belize, and Suriname, "Community, Social & Personal Services" are used to represent Government services. "Construction & Quarrying" are listed under services in Trinidad & Tobago.
Source: ECLAC on the basis of official data.

THE EXISTING POLICY FRAMEWORK

Evolution of Domestic Policy Toward the Private Sector in the Caribbean

The evolution of public policy in the Caribbean has had a direct impact on the nature and development of private sector activity. In the immediate post independence period there was general agreement that the lack of savings to meet the investment requirements for growth and development required large inflows of foreign direct investment (FDI).[22]

A particular interpretation of the Lewis (1950) model, referred to as Import Substitution Industrialization (ISI), was employed in the late 1960s. While courting FDI, high tariffs walls and a variety of incentives were provided to help develop local industry and protect them while they developed (CTIR 2005: 412).

The regional expression of this approach to industry was seen in the series of agreements in CARICOM designed to create a common industrial strategy. Under the *Treaty of 1974*, the trade regime was to provide protection against external regional products through the Common External Tariff. Secondly, there were a set of incentives made available to promote industrial development. Among these were the Agreement on Harmonization of Fiscal Incentives (HFI) and the Industrial Allocation Scheme for the OECS states.[23] The objectives of these agreements were to encourage new manufacturing enterprises and reduce the competition among CARICOM states for new investment (McIntyre 1995: 60).

There was little monitoring to see whether firms were adhering to the conditions for the incentives and the program encouraged footloose enterprises which were encouraged by the provision of cheap factory space, and infrastructural requirements. The tax holidays also were biased against firms that had a long gestation period before becoming profitable.[24] As this program began to exhaust itself, there was an expansion of state enterprises and state trading corporations,[25] and the emergence of Development Banks to create opportunities for credit expansion to particular sectors and industries. This process was helped initially by the increase in commodity and metal prices which brought some windfall revenue and more opportunities for fiscal expenditures. Extreme expressions of this approach were the policies pursued by Jamaica, Guyana, and Trinidad & Tobago, but less severe variants were practiced elsewhere. By 1980 for example, the Jamaica Government owned 50 percent of hotel room capacity, and eight out of twelve sugar factories. In Guyana, the government owned a large number of enterprises in all areas of the economy including sugar, bauxite, manufacturing, and banking (ECLAC 2001).

This period created considerable strains on the private sector especially in economies where state expansion was greatest and with the series of international oil crises many Caribbean countries began to experience balance-of-payment problems complicated by high debt-to-GDP ratios, fiscal deficits, and current account imbalances. These difficulties forced many Caribbean countries to enter a series of stabilization agreements and structural adjustment programs (SAPs) under the IMF and the World Bank. The SAPs focused on reducing the public sector deficit by reducing employment in the state sector, the removal of price controls, and other macroeconomic reforms. Countries that had to undergo intense adjustment at various stages were Jamaica, Guyana, Trinidad and Tobago, and to a lesser extent Barbados. By the early 1980s, there was the recognition that the international business landscape had changed and the push for privatization, liberalization, and the removal of price controls and exchange rate restrictions began to create more room for private sector expansion.

In order to boost the weak export performance of these economies, the U.S. and Canadian Governments through the 1983 Caribbean Basin Initiative (CBI) and its successor agreements, the Caribbean Basin Trade Partnership Agreement (CBTPA) in 2000 and CARIBCAN in 1986 respectively, provided duty-free access for a range of Caribbean goods. These agreements together with a generous incentive structure in manufacturing and tourism set off a new inflow of foreign direct investment especially in the garments sector, electronics, and information processing.[26]

Liberalization was not a smooth process, and in several countries the liberalization of the exchange and capital accounts, and other changes, without appropriate legal and monitoring safeguards, led to instability in financial markets. Banking crises developed in countries like Jamaica, Trinidad and Tobago, Antigua and Barbuda, and Guyana. These crises exposed the need to examine more carefully issues of corporate governance in order to inspire public confidence in the private financial sector. The crises saw the consolidation of banks and a renewed expansion of the financial sector in the Caribbean.

The subsequent lowering of tariffs and a flexible exchange rate regime in some countries affected firms in manufacturing as many in the exporting processing zones and elsewhere found it difficult to continue in business. While the recent emphasis has been on creating a better business environment, the generous incentive regime persists. The implication was that industry specific incentives may have laid the foundations for the focus of investment in low technology-related areas. A number of countries have begun to re-examine the incentive structure to negate the sector-specific effects and to create a better environment for backward and forward linkages between local and foreign firms. In the next section, the role of private sector organizations is explored.

The Role of Private Sector Organizations and Agencies

Private sector organizations operate at the regional, national, and sub-national levels. At the regional level, two major organizations are the Caribbean Association of Industry and Commerce (CAIC) which focuses on the larger private sector businesses, and the Caribbean Association of Small and Medium Enterprises Inc. (CASME), the small business counterpart to the CAIC. Both are emerging from an environment in which firms have been protected at home from competition to one in which the private sector must expand in a competitive environment.

The CAIC began as early as 1955 and has members in twenty countries within the Caribbean. These countries comprise the CARICOM member states plus Cuba, the Dominican Republic, Guadeloupe, the British Virgin Islands, and the Netherlands Antilles. Its membership covers all the national private sector organizations in the Caribbean, transnational corporations with offices across the Caribbean, and local companies operating in a single country. Its activities are wide ranging, covering trade facilitation, advocacy, and training and information dissemination.

The CASME, a non-profit entity, held two round tables, one in Jamaica in 2005 and another in Guyana in 2006, to discuss strategies to promote the SME sector. The CASME was formed through the initiative of seven Small Business Associations in the region and its mandate was to enhance the SME sector in the Caribbean to make it an important engine of growth. Its primary roles are advocacy, education and development, and the facilitation of regional and international trade among members. At the last round table, a strategic plan was developed with a series of goals and priority areas. The important areas of interest were financing of the sector, legislative issues, institution capacity building, the use of information and communication technology, marketing, and management and development. Under the area of marketing, an important aspect of the Association's work was to develop some five to ten business clusters, both local and regional, in the major industry areas by 2008. The possible areas were agro-processing, craft, and ITC (CASME *Strategic Plan* 2007).[27]

At the country level, there are a number of private sector organizations catering for all sectors in some cases and particular interests in others. Appendix 1 reports a sample of the major private sector organizations in the region, their area of activity, and membership base. In a study of some private sector organizations surveyed in the Caribbean in 2005,[28] some 24 percent were Chambers of Commerce with at least one chamber present in each territory. The second largest group constituted hotel associations (13 percent), followed by small business associations (11 percent), and manufacturing associations (9 percent). Interestingly, some 43 percent or the rest of the sample was made up of construction, farmers and employers' organizations (IDB/CAIC 2006: 16).

It appears that the majority of the private sector organizations were about forty years old (IDB/CAIC 2006: 16), and some organizations worked with both regional governments and international organizations to craft domestic and regional policy for the private sector. Most of the private sector bodies are non-profit organizations (73 percent), and their major emphasis has been on advocacy. Because their financial support was largely based on membership fees, they often lacked the capacity to upgrade the skills of their personnel and those of their clients.

One of the important findings was there were gaps in the human resources necessary to carry out their functions and to advise their clients on the latest developments in trade and business practices regionally and internationally. In addition, many of the staff had general training but were not highly trained in specific areas of business development. This comment related not only to the smaller organizations but several of the larger and more organized as well. This may reflect the oligopolistic nature of many Caribbean markets where market share was well defined and there was no motivation to innovate.

COMPETITIVE ANALYSIS OF THE REGIONAL
PRIVATE SECTOR

Levels of Investment and Industrial Specialization

The role of firms in generating growth lies in their ability to create productive investment. The data on domestic investment were not easily available but what data exist showed that generally domestic investment spending constituted the largest share of total investment in the Caribbean region.

In Haiti and Suriname, because of the precipitous decline in FDI, private domestic investment was relatively larger. Public investment was also large in such countries as Guyana, Grenada, and Belize.[29] Policies toward FDI have influenced the patterns of investment and production specialization in the region.[30] The objectives of FDI[31] and the structure of incentives offered by regional governments have also impacted on the degree of complementarity between foreign and local firms. Except for investment in services, the bulk of FDI was in resource abundant export-oriented sectors characterized by price-taking activities (World Bank, *A Time to Choose*, 2006: 47).

Because of its volatility, data on net FDI flows were aggregated over the periods 1989-1997, 1998-2006, and 2007-2008. Between 1989 and 1997, some US$ 9,166 million in net foreign investment flowed to the Caribbean (see Table 12.5).[32] This distribution of FDI was however uneven since most of the FDI went to a relatively few countries. Thus, Trinidad and Tobago received 34.4 percent, followed by Dominican Republic which received 20.7 percent, and Jamaica 13.2 percent. These three countries together received about 68.3 percent of the total inflows. Of the other countries, The Bahamas and Guyana got slightly over 5 percent each, while the others received less.

TABLE 12.5
Average Foreign Direct Investment, 1989-1997, 1998-2006, 2007-2009,
US$ million and Percentage Share

Country	1989-1997	% Share	1998-2006	% Share	2007-2008	% Share
Antigua/Barbuda	292.0	3.2	724.4	2.6	329.8	4.5
Anguilla	122.0	1.3	419.1	1.5	105.3	1.4
Dominica	194.5	2.1	177.4	0.6	60.3	0.8
Grenada	171.2	1.9	466.4	1.7	166.8	2.3
Montserrat	44.4	0.5	21.0	0.1	3.9	0.1
St Kitts & Nevis	228.0	2.5	584.9	2.1	128.9	1.8
St Lucia	335.8	3.7	711.0	2.5	216.7	3.0
St Vincent & Grs	285.2	3.1	467.6	1.7	108.1	1.5
The Bahamas	462.2	5.0	1869.9	6.7	870.0	11.9
Barbados	103.6	1.1	227.9	0.8	183.3	2.5
Belize	139.2	4.5	· 560.9	2.0	168.5	2.3
Guyana	508.3	5.5	433.7	1.6	165.2	2.3
Haiti	18.1	0.2	269.8	1.0	52.2	0.7
Jamaica	1212.6	13.2	5082.0	18.1	838.5	11.5
Dominican Rep.	1895.0	20.7	8714.9	31.1	2231.5	30.6
Trinidad/Tobago	3154.6	34.4	7307.0	26.1	1665.0	22.8
Total	9166.6	100.0	28038.0	100.0	7293.7	100.0

Source: ECLAC on the basis of official data.

Over this period, the amount received by the Dominican Republic surpassed that of Trinidad and Tobago. While it may be the case the other countries received smaller amounts, the issue of scale is important since the size of the investment relative to gross fixed capital formation (GFCF) was key to understanding how important FDI was to the economy.

When FDI as a ratio of GFCF is examined (CTIR 2005: 144), they were quite large for several countries. Thus, for Trinidad and Tobago the ratio was 39.7 percent in 2003, and 42.5 percent in 2005 (UNCTAD 2006), while for Jamaica it was 29.6 percent and 20.8 percent respectively. With the exception of Montserrat, the Dominican Republic, Grenada, Suriname, and Haiti, for most other Caribbean countries the ratio was in excess of 20% in 2005.

The bulk of investment occurred in export-oriented[33] resource based industries (ECLAC 2003; World Bank, *A Time to Choose*, 2006) in Guyana, Trinidad and Tobago, and Suriname. In recent years, there has also been a shift to market-seeking activities as in tourism and telecommunications following the demonopolization of that sector in many countries in the region.[34]

The Caribbean has done well in attracting FDI. According to the UNCTAD's FDI performance index,[35] the region has received two to three times more investment than predicted by its relative economic activity except in the late 1980s when there was a decline. In addition, the index also showed for 2002-2004 that the Dominican Republic, and Trinidad and Tobago were among the high performers, Guyana and Jamaica were above potential, while Haiti was an underperformer.

Barclay (2003) has argued that the limited technology spillovers between FDI and local firms were due to the lack of enabling environment[36] and a clear policy of technology transfer that would allow local firms to benefit from the presence of FDI. For instance, the level of local capacity for upstream innovation in the petrochemical industry in Trinidad and Tobago was limited despite the considerable presence of FDI in the petroleum sector (Barclay 2003; Fairbanks et al. 2006). The same could be said for bauxite in Jamaica, Suriname, and Guyana. The evidence also was that the level of technology licensing, which was a way of securing technology transfer between firms or U.S. patents to the resident population was very low in the Caribbean (Ferranti et al. 2003).

In a study of the impact of FDI in Latin America and the Caribbean (ECLAC 2004: 145), it was argued that the benefits of FDI were greater, the higher the level of human capital in the host country. This was confirmed in a study of FDI and productivity growth in the Latin America and the Caribbean (Alleyne and Freckleton 2010). The Caribbean has been hamstrung in this respect due partly to several factors: the outmigration of large numbers of highly trained individuals many of whom were young people (Mishra 2006); the limited investment of local firms in research and development; public research and development programs that are not driven by market signals; and the high level of import-intensive price-taking activities among foreign firms, which limit spillover effects. In a study of investment in the Caribbean, Roache (2006) concluded that private domestic investment did not respond to public investment or

FDI, and that the costly fiscal incentives were not effective in creating this response.

Firm Technology Absorption and Technology Readiness

The structure of Caribbean exports reflected the level of technical sophistication of the economy. Alcorta and Peres (1995) suggested that while this was not always the case, technological capabilities for the domestic market should eventually reflect itself in the export sector. Since Caribbean economies have focused on an export strategy the biggest gains lay in sectors where local technical capabilities translated into a rising share of exports in dynamic markets. A measure of technological specialization, the technology specialization index (ITS) showed the extent to which the level and composition of exports was changing in world trade.[37] When the index was less than one, it meant that a country's exports share of high-technology markets was bigger than its export share in low-technology markets. An increasing value over time showed a growing share of high technology markets. Alcorta and Peres (1995) reported the ITS for Latin America and the Caribbean, and for the Tigers which include Korea, Taiwan, Hong Kong, and Singapore.

The results show an increase in the index for the Caribbean in the 1980s followed by stagnation in the 1990s. This level of technology intensity was also replicated when the export structure was broken down by type of exports. For example in 1985 and 2000, CARICOM exports of primary products were 41.7 percent and 37.4 percent respectively (Table 12.6).

TABLE 12.6
Export Structure by Technological Intensity (% of Exports)

	Primary Products		Natural Re-based Man[1]		Low-tech Man[2]		Int'te-tech Man[3]		High-tech Man[4]	
	1985	2000	1985	2000	1985	2000	1985	2000	1985	2000
CCOM	41.7	37.4	39.3	34.9	5.4	10.2	5.7	11.6	6.0	1.4
CR	67.2	29.1	7.9	8.5	14.5	17.1	6.5	8.3	3.2	34.3
Haiti	18.4	8.9	4.5	2.9	52.8	85.2	14.3	1.0	0.8	0.4
DR	23.7	4.9	24.3	8.6	28.2	62.7	9.9	17.5	1.1	2.6
Taiwan	5.0	1.3	9.1	4.8	48.2	21.8	20.7	25.0	15.9	45.5

Notes: The totals do not add up to 100% as the residual is accounted for by unclassified products. CCOM: CARICOM; Taiwan: Taiwan Republic of China; CR: Costa Rica; DR: Dominican Republic; [1] Natural Resource-based Manufactures; [2] Low-technology Manufactures; [3] Intermediate-technology Manufactures; [4] High-technology Manufactures.
Source: ECLAC 2003d.

For similar years, natural resource-based manufacturers were 39.3 percent and 34.9 percent respectively. On the other hand, the share of lower technology manufacturers, intermediate manufacturers, and high technology manufacturers were quite small in terms of their technology content. In contrast, the Taiwan Republic of China had considerably higher ratios for low, intermediate, and high technology exports relative to other exports. When the technology content of intra-regional merchandise exports was examined, the results were slightly different. Primary products in 2003 were 8 percent in terms of technology content, resource-based manufacturers were 69.9 percent, and low tech manufacturing was 11.5 percent (IDB 2006a). These results suggested the need for great emphasis on domestic capital formation at the firm level in order to raise the share of exports in growing and dynamic sectors. This requires building a national system of innovation that would help to complement and intensify firm-level innovation.

Technology readiness requires building a system of innovation through education and training, not just for creating knowledge but through learning and innovation. The Caribbean spent a great deal through public education but the quality of education has come under scrutiny. Caribbean governments on average spent a record of 6.6 percent of GDP on education, and for the OECS 7.1 percent, but there were wide variations in expenditure by country (World Bank, *A Time to Choose*, 2006: 147). For example, in 2000, for Belize it was 6.2 percent, Barbados 7.3 percent, Dominica 6.7 percent, Dominican Republic 2.3 percent, Grenada 6.8 percent, Guyana 7.3 percent, Jamaica 7.2 percent, St Kitts and Nevis 6.2 percent, St Lucia 6.6 percent, and St Vincent and the Grenadines 5.8 percent (McArdle 2006). The evidence also showed that except for the Dominican Republic, the Caribbean was a high wage area with declining productivity.[38]

The development of a pool of skilled workers was an incentive for firms to locate in particular areas, and even in the case of extra-regional corporations, to transfer high quality research facilities to those areas. Thus, regional universities and other related institutions need to create training programs which generate these skill sets. The current emphasis on public funding of major universities without requirement for particular skill generation to meet industry needs must be reformed. More competitive bidding for research funds and greater private sector participation in funding will help to correct this.[39]

At the firm level, Caribbean firms trained their workers less on average than those in Latin America. For example, according to McArdle (2006: 37), while the Latin American average was 75 percent, for the Caribbean it was 67 percent. There was also considerable variation by individual countries. Thus, for Belize 65 percent of firms trained their workers, for Haiti it was 54 percent, for Trinidad and Tobago it was 41 percent, and for Jamaica it was over 90 percent. The small number of firms training workers was probably attributable to the low perceived need for such training. This may also be reinforced by the oligopolistic nature of some markets.

The analysis suggests that training agencies in the public sector should reorient some of their activities on the basis of market signals and, given the movement of labor across the region, training programs need to have a greater focus on regional technology upgrade.

Innovation, Company Spending on Research and Development

The building of a national system of innovation was important for developing the capacity to compete in high value-added products and activities.[40] Such a system required the joint effort of the private sector and government institutions to translate scientific knowledge into commercial benefits. The institutions reported in Appendix 2 were all national or regional government institutions, and were the core research agencies in the region.[41] It was clear however that strong research capabilities have not been developed in the private sector and there was anecdotal evidence that expenditures on research and development are not significant. The existing data showed, for example, that while Latin America and the Caribbean contributed 1.6 percent to world expenditure on R&D in 2002, Jamaica's share of gross R&D expenditure in Latin America and the Caribbean was 4.6 percent, and that of Trinidad and Tobago 8.6 percent (Cimoli et al. 2005: 24). In terms of the share going to GDP, in 2002, it was 0.08 percent for Jamaica, and 0.14 percent for Trinidad and Tobago.

The costs of setting up research facilities and attracting highly skilled personnel were prohibitive for many small and medium size firms in the Caribbean, thus, collaboration and information sharing was important. The bulk of R&D spending still flowed from the state sector and in 2002 in the case of Trinidad and Tobago, 48.2 percent of R&D expenditure was from the public sector, 34.5 percent from enterprises, and 17.3 percent was spent by higher education institutions (Cimoli et al. 2005: 25).

While the Caribbean always pursued technology policies and has a high level of expenditure on education, there has not been a consistent policy toward innovation in the region.[42] During the ISI phase, a linear supply model of technology prevailed as the public sector played a major role in identifying priorities and intervening in Science and Technology (S&T) activities with the hope of interesting the private sector (Cimoli et al. 2005). The aim was to expand local production and develop an autonomous technical capacity. The objectives however were based on government priorities with innovations flowing one way from the supply to demand side.

However, in only a few cases did scientific progress translate into technological innovation. In addition, the specialization of production in import intensive sectors allowed for limited endogenous technical change (ECLAC 2003: 11; Kawa and Ramkissoon 2005: 81).

In the period of liberalization and structural adjustment, technology policies were relaxed and state enterprises focusing on research and development were downgraded. Regional and local firms that positioned themselves in the global value chains mainly performed material assembly based on static comparative advantage. In addition, the decline of some areas of manufacturing in the Caribbean affected the level of research conducted by some institutions.

At the regional level, as early as 1984, the CARICOM Ministerial Subcommittee on Science and Technology coordinated the preparation of S&T policy and plans for the Caribbean region. There were national consultations between 1987 and 1992 to develop an S&T policy for the region but it appears that there was no coordinated regional policy (ECLAC 2005). The task force on information and communication technology (ICT) policy replaced the CARICOM Sub-committee on S&T.

There has been renewed interest in S&T policy at the national level in some countries as Jamaica has completed a six-year plan for its national Commission on S&T, and Trinidad made S&T an important part of its vision 20/20 development plan. The approach to technology development in the 1990s focused on a horizontal perspective in which incentive based mechanisms were pursued, with emphasis on the role of private sector agencies in financing and commercializing research (Cimoli et al. 2005: 17). This approach sought to incorporate both demand-pull and technology-based incentives, and coordination between the private and public sector, and an emphasis on commercialization of technology services.

Crucial to technology upgrading was the management of intellectual property (IP) systems to enhance knowledge generation and diffusion. The changes in IP regimes through legislation and enforcement[43] must be integrated with patenting local cultural and indigenous products, natural resources, and local tacit knowledge which are major exploitable resources. Ways must also be found to avoid the hurdles posed by restrictions on reverse engineering and imitation which was important to the catch up of South East Asia.

Globalization and regionalism have altered the incentives and threats which firms face and have widened the sphere for decision making. Dynamic technology upgrading is now necessary for local firms, and research and development expenditure needs to be increased for two reasons. Local firms need to compete in dynamically expending sectors, and, secondly, increasing local technological capability will increase the opportunity for benefiting from the outsourcing of research and development of transnational firms.

In light of these several challenges, a regional approach to technology policy and IP protection is an important way of deepening the integration process for technology upgrading, through national and regional institutions in both the private and public sector.

Business Sophistication: Networks and Supporting Industries

It is now well recognized that country-wide competitiveness requires changes at both the macro and micro economic levels. The global competitiveness index (GCI) of the World Economic Forum (WEF) gauges the progress countries have made toward developing competitive economies. The changes needed must occur at both the macro and micro levels of the economy. The GCI was based on the twelve so-called pillars of competitiveness, and among these are: macroeconomic stability, technical readiness, the quality of human capital, and business sophistication. In addition, they have identified stages of development and how transformation can occur at each stage. The Caribbean firms are clearly seeking to move from a production function rooted in price-taking activities to a phase of increasing product quality and innovation. The indices reported in Table 12.7 cover only some Caribbean countries.

TABLE 12.7
Indices of Competitiveness Based on the Global Competitiveness Index for the Caribbean

Various Indices	Barbados	Guyana	Jamaica	Trinidad & Tobago	Latin America & Caribbean *
Rank	5.34	3.89	3.92	4.7	4.32
Institutions	5.2	3.54	3.66	3.89	3.58
Infrastructure	5.37	2.92	3.91	4.53	3.71
Macro stability	4.3	3.52	2.93	4.59	4.40
Health & Primary Ed	6.48	5.55	5.19	5.78	5.49
Higher Ed & Training	4.97	3.91	3.92	4.25	3.94
Goods Market Efficiency	4.27	3.88	4.04	3.94	3.84
Labor Market Efficiency	4.6	4.08	4.23	4.25	3.93
Financial Market Devel.	4.61	3.7	4.49	4.57	4.00
Technological Readiness	4.98	3.05	3.76	3.92	3.52
Market size	1.91	1.96	2.94	2.78	3.65
Business Sophistication	4.07	3.61	3.72	3.83	3.69
Innovation	3.32	2.65	2.9	2.9	3.02
GCI-aver. 2010	4.57	3.55	3.81	4.14	3.93

* denotes average.
Source: The Global Competitiveness Report, *Basic Requirements 2010-2011*, World Economic Forum.

The results were compared with the averages for Latin America and the Caribbean. What was most striking was that Guyana scored very low on innovation relative to Trinidad and Tobago, Barbados, and Jamaica. In terms of overall rank, Barbados, and Trinidad and Tobago scored higher than Latin America and the Caribbean but Jamaica and Guyana were below.

To compete, dynamic market clusters of related and supporting firms were the building blocks of a competitive economy (Fairbanks et al. 2006). In such clusters were small and large firms engaged in delivering a specific set of services or products to customers. Regional clusters should be pursued especially in a context of small scale and limited resources. This offered great opportunities for information flows and technical complementarities in economies in which enclaves have been developed in certain sectors with limited spin-offs among related firms. Cluster relationships helped to create greater links between large,

Alleyne

small, and medium size firms which permitted outsourcing and complementarities.

The role of clusters was captured in the category business sophistication which measured the degree of interconnectedness among geographically proximate groups of companies, their suppliers, service providers, and institutions. Barbados, and Trinidad and Tobago scored well in the category, while Jamaica and Guyana lagged behind. Despite these scores, many medium size firms in the Caribbean tended to engage in multiple activities usually as affiliates, but left little room for diversification of supplies and the development of strong value chains. There was evidence of few business clusters in the Caribbean (IDB 2006b: 36).

TABLE 12.8
Doing Business Index for 2009-2010 and Other Characteristics for 2009

Country	Ease Bus		St	Lc	E	RP	CR	PRI	TA	BO	COS	CL
	09	10	09	09	09	09	09	09	09	09	09	09
St Lucia	34	36	36	13	23	66	84	24	29	80	161	45
Puerto Rico	35	35	9	144	39	122	12	15	98	101	97	28
Aruba/Barbados	42	50	45	22	46	97	109	24	136	46	73	61
The Bahamas	55	68	45	92	44	143	68	104	39	51	120	29
Jamaica	63	75	11	49	32	109	84	70	173	100	127	22
St Vincent & Gr.	66	70	39	1	41	129	84	24	76	72	109	181
St Kitts & Nevis	67	76	72	6	22	146	84	24	95	27	114	181
Dominica	74	83	21	24	61	103	68	24	63	82	164	181
Belize	78	80	139	2	25	121	84	113	53	114	168	24
Trinidad & Tob.	80	81	56	84	36	164	28	18	51	47	167	181
Grenada	84	91	40	16	51	156	68	24	74	63	163	181
Dominican Rep.	97	86	84	77	97	106	68	126	72	32	83	144
Guyana	105	101	100	37	72	63	145	70	108	113	73	126
Suriname	146	155	170	95	53	136	131	178	26	98	177	147
Haiti	154	151	176	126	35	128	145	164	91	146	92	153

Notes: **Ease Bus**: Ease of Doing Business rank; **St**: Starting a Business; **Lc**: Dealing with Licenses; **E**: Employing workers; **RP**: Registering Property; **CR**: Getting credit; **PRI**: Protecting investors; **TA**: Paying Taxes; **BO**: Trading Across Borders; **COS**: Enforcing Contracts; **CL**: Closing a business.
Source: World Economic Forum, Doing Business Index 2009 and 2010, WEF.

The impact of institutions can be examined more clearly in the World Bank's report on doing business and creating an enabling environment. The countries at the bottom tend to rank poorly on several indicators. Overall rankings tend to hide the distribution of individual characteristics. For example, most countries except Jamaica did poorly with respect to starting a business or St Vincent and the Grenadines with respect to dealing with licenses. The individual country score clearly suggests that more needs to be done in order to create a better business environment.

RECOMMENDATIONS FOR INCREASING PRIVATE SECTOR COMPETITIVENESS

The above analysis identified a number of areas where the private sector encountered difficulties. The fundamental challenge at the level of production was to use domestic capital more intensively to enhance competitiveness. This cannot occur however, without major technology upgrades and investment in research and development and the utilization of local knowledge both tacit and codified in areas where there was competitive advantage.

The removal of trade preferences emphasizes the need to rationalize production in price-taking activities[44] for countries that are uncompetitive in these areas, and to develop new areas of advantage. The rising importance of the music and entertainment industry, cultural products, and their links with the tourism sector point to the need to finance new activities.

The fact that most Caribbean firms were small means that every opportunity to reap the benefits of agglomeration must be pursued. The formation of industry clusters and the creation of better linkages among value chains are necessary. The movement of labor and capital across the region under the CSME has already helped to facilitate more cross-border investment and increased the share of Caribbean firms in FDI. The regional trade flows are however still small, and Caribbean countries rely heavily on extra regional trade.

Many of the features identified required intervention by government beyond creating an enabling environment. According to Altenberg and Drachenfels (2005), the current approach to private sector development[45] premised on the proliferation of copyrights and higher levels of formality, credit access, simplification of business procedures,[46] and regulations and the provision of competitive markets for non-financial business services though necessary are not sufficient to solve many developmental problems.

In addition, the low level of research and development, and lack of strong linkages between large and small businesses and the public sector may require government's participation to start the processes by removing some market failures. UNIDO (2001: 3) pointed out however that intervention required is different from what was obtained in the past under the ISI phase before the mid-1980s or the more recent period of deregulation and liberalization. They pointed out that SMEs will need support since the process of market-based adjustment may be too slow, and many such firms may not have the resources for restructuring.

In relation to ways in which businesses can upgrade in national and regional value chains, business organizations need to focus on developing more business clusters among SMEs to allow for the following:

- joint buying and selling
- product development
- process improvement
- recognition of joint standards and codes
- collaboration through network facilities and learning networks.

These arrangements will allow SMEs to reap the benefits of cooperation while reducing the costs of trading with many small entities. According to UN-IDO (2001), at a minimum, they gain from the unintended consequences of proximity. Therefore, they can draw on a common labor pool, infrastructure, and business services, which can be provided at lower costs to a group.

In relation to the development of competitive sectors, a number of key programs may be identified, which involve joint public and private sector involvement. These are as follows:

- improve the condition for competitiveness of key business clusters through the use of domestic capital and upgrading of skills of workers and management;
- public research and development institutions both local and regional must collaborate more directly and respond to market signals by meeting private sector needs;
- diversify from existing activities that are import intensive and create more high value up-stream processing;
- create digital links between industry clusters, customers, and suppliers, both nationally and regionally under the CSME; and
- improve the capacity of private sector institutions to move beyond advocacy to understand the opportunities for firms in global markets and to help to build industry clusters.

These are key considerations that should underpin the development of new competitive sectors and firms in the Caribbean in order to meet the challenges ahead.

APPENDIX 1
Selected Private Sector Organizations in the Caribbean

Private Sector Organizations	Location	Sphere of Activity	Year Establ.	No of Members	Sector of Interest
CAIC	Trinidad & Tobago	Regional	1955 1962 1970	NA	All Sectors
The Caribbean Association of Small & Medium Enterprises Inc.	Jamaica	Regional	2005	NA	Small Business Sector
Association of Caribbean Farmers	St Vincent & Grenad.	Regional	1982	1500	Primary Sector
National Organizations					
Chamber of Commerce & Industry	Suriname	National	1950	200	All Sectors
Suriname Trade & Industry Association	Suriname	National	1950	200	All Sectors
Associate Klleine En Midden Gnote Bedryven in Suriname	Suriname	National	2001	106	Primary, Secondary & Professional Services
National Development Foundation	Montserrat	National	1988	145	All Sectors
Antigua Hotels & Tourism Association	Antigua	National	NA	89	Services
Small Business Association of The Bahamas	Bahamas	National	2003	30	Services
Grand Bahamas Chamber of Commerce	Bahamas	National	1982	214	Services
Bahamas Chamber of Commerce	Bahamas	National	1899 1966	360	Services
Bahamas Hotel Association	Bahamas	National	1952	200	Services
Bahamas Real Estate Association	Bahamas	National	1916	410	Real Estate Information Services
Nassau Tourism Development Board	Bahamas	National	1914	75	Business Information
The Georgetown Chamber of Commerce & Industry Inc.	Guyana	National	1889	100	All Sectors
Guyana Small Business Association	Guyana	National	1992	100	All Small Business Sectors
Private Sector Commission of Guyana	Guyana	National	1992	27	All Sectors
Tourism & Hospitality Association of Guyana	Guyana	National	1991	50	Tourism Services
Berbice Chamber of Commerce & Development Association	Guyana	Sub-national	1931	38	Services
Guyana Manufacturing & Services Association	Guyana	National	1961	104	Primary & Secondary Sectors

Institute of Private Enterprise Development	Guyana	National	1985	5,000	All Sectors
Shipping Association of Guyana	Guyana	National	1995	15	Services related to Shipping
National Association of Chamber of Commerce	Guyana	National	1985	1,400	All Sectors
Women's Business Owners (Ja) Ltd.	Jamaica	National	2003	22	Business Services
Hardware Merchants Association	Jamaica	National	1957	100	Construction Distribution
Jamaica Chamber of Commerce	Jamaica	National	1779	200+	All Sectors
Jamaica Employers Federation (JEF)	Jamaica	National	1948	321	Trade & Business Services
Jamaica Exporters' Association (JEA)	Jamaica	National	1966	205	Manufacturing & Services
Jamaica Hotel and Tourist Association	Jamaica	National	1961	250	Services
The Jamaica Manufacturers' Association Ltd.	Jamaica	National	1947	275	Secondary Sector
Small Businesses Association of Jamaica	Jamaica	National	1947	116	Business Services
The Private Sector Organization of Jamaica	Jamaica	National	NA	NA	All Sectors
St Vincent & Grenad. Chamber of Industry & Commerce	St Vincent	National	1925	105	All Sectors
St Vincent & Grenad. Construction Assoc/tion	St Vincent	National	2002	13	Construction
St Vincent Employers' Federation	St Vincent	National	1965	48	Services
St Vincent & the Grenadines Hotel & Tourism Association	St Vincent	National	1968	NA	Services
Small Manufacturers Association	St Vincent	National	1995	22	Primary & Secondary
Shipping Association of Trinidad & Tobago	Trinidad & Tobago	National	1938	67	Shipping Services
San Juan Business Association	Trinidad & Tobago	National	1990	140	All Sectors
Trinidad & Tobago Chamber of Industry & Commerce	Trinidad & Tobago	National/ Sub-national	1879	460	All Sectors
Trinidad Hotels, Restaurants & Tourism Association	Trinidad & Tobago	National	1963	93	Services
Trinidad & Tobago Manufacturers' Association (TTMA)	Trinidad & Tobago	National	NA	350	Manufacturing
Trinidad & Tobago Chamber of Industry & Commerce – Tobago	Trinidad & Tobago	National/ Sub-national	1936	35	Secondary & Tertiary Sector
Tobago Hotel Association	Tobago	National	NA	160	Finance & Tourism
S. Trinidad Chamber of Industry & Commerce	Trinidad & Tobago	National	1961	182	All Sectors

Source: CAIC/IDB 2005.

APPENDIX 2
Selected Regional Research and Administrative Institutions by Activity and Year of Establishment

Establishment	Location: Major Activity	Year Establ.
Domestic Institutions		
Central Agricultural Station	Nassau, Bahamas: Agricultural research	NA
Agricultural Research Center	North Andros, Bahamas: Agricultural research	NA
Research & Development Unit	Barbados: Research in agricultural engineering, agronomy and plant protection	NA
Central Farm Research Station	Belize: Plant protection	NA
National Agricultural Research Institute	Guyana: Agricultural research	NA
Department of Science, Technology, Research & Development	Jamaica: Agricultural research	NA
Central Experiment Station	Trinidad & Tobago: Agricultural research	NA
National Commodity Institutions		
Sugar Cane Feed Center	Trinidad & Tobago: Mainly beef production	NA
GUYSUCO Agricultural Research & Development Division	Guyana: Sugar cane	NA
GUYSUCO Other Crops Division	Guyana: Non-sugar cane	NA
Guyana Rice Board (Research & Extension Division)	Guyana: Research and extension services	NA
San Roman Experiment Station	Belize: Sugar cane	NA
Citrus Research & Education Institute	Belize: Citrus research	NA
Toledo Rural Development Project	Belize: Rice	NA
Sugar Industry Research Institute	Jamaica: Sugar	NA
Banana Board of Jamaica	Jamaica: Bananas	
Coconut Industry Board	Jamaica: Coconut	
Coffee Industry Board	Jamaica: Coffee	
Scientific Research Council	Jamaica: Agricultural research, food technology, microbiology, etc.	1960
Institute of Applied Science & Technology	University of Guyana: Research in a wide range of areas	NA
Institute of Marine Affairs (IMA)	Trinidad and Tobago: R&D in marine fisheries, aquaculture, etc.	NA
International Center for Environmental & Nuclear Sciences (ICENS)	University of the West Indies (UWI), Jamaica: Development of spatial data bases and nuclear energy applications	NA
Center for Resource Management & Environmental Studies (CERMES)	UWI Barbados: Research in marine resource and environmental management	NA
Bureau of Standards	Exist in most CARICOM countries	NA
Regional Institutions		NA
Caribbean Council for Science & Technology	Developing science and technology policy for the Caribbean	
Windward Island Banana Development Company Research Station	St Lucia: Serving the Windward Islands.	NA
Sugarcane Breeding Station	Barbados: Serving Barbados, Belize, Guyana, Jamaica, and Trinidad & Tobago	NA
Caribbean Rice Improvement Network	Guyana: serving the rice growing areas in the region	NA
OECS Fisheries Unit (Part of Caribbean Regional Fisheries Mechanism)	Belize: Serving the OECS	NA

CARICOM Regional Organization for Standards & Quality	To promote the development of standards and quality	2002
Caribbean Agriculture Research & Development Institute (CARDI), University of the West Indies	Trinidad & Tobago: Agricultural research and development based on R&D on natural products and food, and biochemistry technologies	1975
Cocoa Research Unit	UWI Trinidad & Tobago: Cocoa	
Caribbean Epidemiology Center (CAREC)	Caribbean disease monitoring and prevention	1975
Caribbean Industrial Research Institute (CARIRI), University of the West Indies	UWI Trinidad & Tobago: Laboratory-based testing and consultancy	1970
Inter-American Institute for Co-operation on Agriculture (IICA)	Agricultural sector development and modernization	1978
Caribbean Tourism Organization	Research and consulting	NA
Caribbean Export Development Agency	Barbados: Research, financing, export development, and promotion	1996
Caribbean Music Exposition	Music/Entertainment industry research, advocacy, and export promotion	
CARICOM Secretariat	Guyana: Research, administration, and intra-regional trade promotion	1973
Caribbean Meteorological Institute (CMI)	Meteorological research; training	NA
Caribbean Environmental Health Institute (CEHI)	Environmental health research; training	NA
Caribbean Regional Center for the Education & Training of Animal Health and Veterinary Public Health Assistants (REPAHA)	Research and training	NA
Caribbean Center For Developmental Administration (CARICAD)	Research on development administration	NA
Caribbean Food & Nutrition Institute (CFNI)	Jamaica: Research on food and nutrition; food standards; poverty; training	NA
Caribbean Development Bank (CDB)	Barbados: Financing; project development/management	NA
Caribbean Law Institute/Caribbean Law Institute Center (CLI/CLIC)	Legal research	NA
International Institutions		NA
CAB International	Trinidad & Tobago: Evolved out of the Commonwealth Institute of biological control	NA
PROCICARIBE	Network of agricultural networks and is coordinated by CARDI	NA
Iworkama International Center for Rain-forest Conservation & Development	Guyana: Studies issues of rainforests	NA
Local & Regional Universities		
University of Suriname	Suriname: Teaching and research	
University of Technology	Jamaica: Teaching and research, began 1958 as College of Arts, Science and Technology	1995
University of Guyana	Guyana: Teaching and research	1963
University of Belize	Belize: Teaching and research	2000
University of the West Indies	Jamaica, Barbados, and Trinidad & Tobago: Major research and teaching institution in various fields	1960
University of Trinidad & Tobago	Trinidad & Tobago: To examine hydrocarbon and energy-based industries	2005

Universidad Autonoma de Santo Domingo	Dominican Republic: Teaching and research	

NA: not available

Source: ECLAC, Report on Science and Technology Infrastructure and Policy in Selected Member and Associate Member Countries of the CECS, LC/CAR/l.45, 2005.

NOTES

1. This study deals basically with the CARICOM member states. The treaty establishing CARICOM (1973) provided for the creation of two distinct entities: the Caribbean Community and the Common Market. The Caribbean Community (CARICOM) has fifteen member states (Antigua and Barbuda, The Bahamas, Barbados, Belize, Dominica, Grenada, Guyana, Haiti, Jamaica, Montserrat, St Kitts and Nevis, St Lucia, St Vincent and the Grenadines, Suriname and Trinidad and Tobago). The Bahamas is not a member state of the Common Market. CARICOM has five associate members (Anguilla, Bermuda, British Virgin Islands, Cayman Islands, and Turks and Caicos Islands). Aruba, Mexico, Venezuela, Colombia, the Netherlands Antilles, the Dominican Republic, and Puerto Rico are observers. Six member states are considered more developed countries (The Bahamas, Barbados, Guyana, Jamaica, Suriname, and Trinidad and Tobago) and eight countries are considered less developed countries (Antigua and Barbuda, Belize, Dominica, Grenada, Haiti, St Lucia, St Kitts and Nevis, and St Vincent and the Grenadines).

2. The exception might be Suriname which has a large public sector with as much as 120 state enterprises.

3. Following a stages approach to development firms must now enter the efficiency driven and innovation phases of development (Porter 2005).

4. The average current account deficit to GDP in CARICOM 2005 was 17.4 percent, while the average debt-to-GDP ratio between 2000-2005 was 83.7 percent.

5. One rough measure of import productivity is the ratio of GDP to capital and intermediate goods imports.

6. James 2006a.

7. Domestic capital is defined as the means of production created within a society (James 2006a; Barclay et al. 2006). This includes supporting institutions (for example, education, financial, and technical) that expand the production capabilities of Caribbean society. This is differentiated from imported equipment and tools which represent capital created elsewhere.

8. Following James (2006a), the flow of work is the number of effective units of labor, and these increase with the growth of human and institutional capital.

9. There is no universally accepted definition of a small enterprise and different countries may apply different definitions according to their circumstances. A working definition would be the number of firms with less than ten workers although a cut off of five is also used (Harris 1998; ILO 2000). An examination of the ten largest firms in CARICOM with those of Canada, United States, and Latin America, has prompted one author to describe Caribbean firms as "nano-firms" since they are extremely small in terms of their revenue, asset base, and employment generation (Bernal 2006).

10. This reflects a move from purely resource seeking to market seeking activities as in the Dominican Republic, Jamaica, and the OECS states.

11. These data were also in line with a World Bank survey of firms in which 45 percent of firms had headquarters in North America. Latin America and the Caribbean accounted for 40 percent. The remaining 15 percent originated from Europe and one from Japan. There were also differences between sources of investment in terms of size and export orientation. While European firms are capital intensive reflecting their involvement in oil and gas, American companies are more labor intensive due to their presence in apparels, food processing, and electronics manufacturing.

12. There were variations by country. For Antigua and Barbuda, of the firms identified by origin between 1998-2003, 27.1 percent were from the United States, 27.4 percent from the Caribbean, and 4.5 percent from China. For Grenada in 2001, the shares were 11

percent United States, 6 percent Europe and the UK, and 82 percent Caribbean, while in 2004 the shares were 54 percent, 28 percent, and 17 percent respectively. For St Lucia in 2003, the shares were 12 percent United States, 47 percent UK, 6 percent Caribbean, and 35 percent other (OECD, *Investment Policy Reviews, Caribbean Rim, Antigua and Barbuda, Grenada and St Lucia*, 2006). In the Dominican Republic, 26 percent of FDI inflows was from Spain, 21.2 percent from the United States, 19.7 percent from Canada, and 8.0 percent from the Cayman Islands (OECD, *Caribbean Rim Investment Initiative: Dominican Republic*, 2003).

13. The Jamaica stock exchange was set up in 1968 while the Barbados stock exchange was set up 1982 under the Securities Exchange Act and began trading in 1987. The Trinidad and Tobago Stock Exchange was set up under the 1981 Securities Industry Act. The stock exchange in the Dominican Republic opened for trading in 1991. The Bahamas stock exchange was set up in 1999 and started listing and trading in 2000. The ECSS was set up in 2001.

14. Although the requirements for cross-listing, such as capital requirements, the allocation of shares for trading, and the standards of financial reporting vary by stock exchange. They are not onerous and over time may be standardized in a regional stock market.

15. The reporting requirements, for listing on the stock exchange, are often regarded as an encumbrance in cases in which there is some level of informality in operations and there are opportunities for tax evasion. It is also recognized that several local firms may be branch plants of transnational corporations or may be local affiliates in which case there may be strategic decisions not to list on the exchanges in the region.

16. These estimates seem reasonable except for Barbados.

17. The study also found that only 35 percent of medium and small scale enterprises (MSEs), meet all legal requirements.

18. Data for The Bahamas came from the *Business Establishment Survey 2005*; and The Bahamas, *A Road Map for Improving the Business Climate for SMEs*, 2007. Hotels were not included in the service sector.

19. Many of the OECS states have moved away from primary and secondary production and have concentrated on services, mainly tourism. For example, as a group between 1993 and 2003, services—mainly tourism—were 70 percent of their exports.

20. A division often used categorizes the CARICOM states as MDCs and LDCs.

21. The services sector is made up of electricity, gas and water, transport, storage and communication, commerce, restaurant and hotels, financial institutions, insurance, real estate, and business services. The non-service sector is made up of agriculture, mining, manufacture, and construction.

22. Underpinning this approach was the work of Arthur Lewis (1950) who saw industrialization as a way to developing both agriculture and industry in the Caribbean. The expansion of industry would absorb labor in the agricultural sector raising its productivity. Because of small internal markets and scale issues, the countries would export their excess manufactures and agriculture as the expansion of output continued. In order to get the process moving, it was suggested that foreign companies could be induced to operate in the Caribbean as catalysis for the process. In the interim, they would also transfer technology and allow for local technical development.

23. While much harmonization did not occur the incentives were not freely available to all firms and were restricted to approved products and producers. Countries engaged in a wide range of incentives and regulations and among these were foreign exchange controls, quotas, tariffs, import licensing, and a variety of other industrial incentives.

24. The World Bank (1990) pointed out that the incentives had resulted in a distinctly pro-manufacturing bias, and did not distinguish between firms serving the domes-

tic and export market, served as barriers to entry thereby reinforcing oligopolistic behavior, and lacked transparency because of multiple qualifying criteria.

25. The trading corporations were import monopolies. In Dominica for example, there was the public sector agency as the sole importer of sugar and rice. In Antigua, the Central Marketing Corporation (CMC) was the sole importer of certain food items. In Jamaica, there was the Jamaica Commodity Trading Corporation (JCTC) which was the sole importer of some thirty-four key product groups.

26. Incentives include tax holidays on corporate profits and dividends, customs duty and value-added or consumption tax-free imports of plant, equipment, components, and inputs, waiver of land transfer taxes, stamp duties, land and property taxes as well as low interest rate loans in a few instances. Other incentives offered include varying basic corporate profit tax rates (depreciation methods and schedules), loss carry-forward allowance, dividends and interest tax, tax rates on royalties and management fees, and personal income taxes for domestic and expatriate personnel (CTIR 2005: 453). Many of these incentives may violate WTO Trade Related Investment Measures (TRIMS), and may come under scrutiny in the future.

27. Of course, issues of formalization of the informal sector and ways to interconnect with the large private also need to be examined.

28. This was not the sum total of all organizations.

29. Roache (2006) has reported investment for the sub-periods, 1985-1989, 1990-1994, 1995-1999, and 1999-2000. Over succeeding sub-periods, there has been a decline in government share of investment for Barbados, Trinidad and Tobago, and Jamaica. The share of private domestic investment declined in the last sub-period. In the case of FDI, there has been a consistent increase over time. In the Eastern Caribbean Currency Union (ECCU) countries, government investment has been stable but the shares of FDI and PDI have tended to increase over the sub-periods.

30. The role of foreign firms and their affiliates has been important in shaping investment dynamics in the Caribbean. Caribbean public policy has focused heavily on attracting private sector investment mainly from extra regional sources. The rationale usually is that FDI can potentially contribute more to growth than domestic investment since it augments the capital stock and facilitates the diffusion of technology and management policies (World Bank, *A Time to Choose*, 2006). It is also argued that spillovers are larger where the investment climate is liberal since it may cause a clustering of firms creating backward and forward linkages.

31. These could be natural resource seeking, market seeking, or efficiency seeking objectives.

32. In the case of Suriname, the figure was negative for most of the period.

33. These strategic locations of firms were based on resource abundant comparative advantage.

34. The strategy of firms varied over time. For example, the strategy with respect to Guyana, Jamaica, Trinidad and Tobago, and Suriname has been in resource seeking activities in the primary sector, despite the decline in this sector's share of GDP. In manufacturing, the strategy has been market efficiency largely in apparels in Jamaica, the Dominican Republic, and Haiti. In a number of countries, the emphasis has been on market access in finance, tourism, telecommunication, power generation, and information technology (ECLAC 2003: 16).

35. The FDI performance index is the ratio of a country's FDI inflows as a proportion of the world's inflows divided by the ratio of a country's GDP to global GDP. A ratio greater than one reflects a proportionally higher FDI relative to GDP.

36. This may be interpreted as a low level of domestic capital formation in some sectors.

37. The index is computed as follows:

$$MS_i^H = \frac{\sum\limits_{j\in H} X_{ij}}{\sum\limits_{j\in H} X_j} \; ; \; MS_i^L = \frac{\sum\limits_{j\in L} X_{ij}}{\sum\limits_{j\in L} X_j} \text{ and the } ITS = \frac{MS_i^H}{MS_i^L}$$

H is the high-technology SITC products and L is the low-technology SITC products (see Alcorta and Peres 1995).

38. There was evidence that several Caribbean countries are falling behind in improving educational attainment (Barro and Lee 2002), and the world ranking of several countries, in terms of years of schooling, except for Barbados were in decline.

39. The World Bank (*A Time to Choose*, 2006: 165) points out that most programs for training were provided by government agencies as in Jamaica (HEART/NTA), Barbados TVET, and the National Training Agency, Trinidad and Tobago, or the Ministry of Education in Barbados and the OECS. However, in the Dominican Republic and Barbados, a significant part of their budget is dedicated to private sector driven and incentive-training schemes.

40. According to the literature on national innovation systems, innovation is interaction that occurs in an environment when agents respond to incentives and cooperate (Cimoli et al. 2005: 33).

41. There were a variety of other institutions that were important to science and technology: the Sir Arthur Lewis Community College (St Lucia), the College of The Bahamas, Barbados Community College, College of Science Technology and Applied Arts (Trinidad and Tobago), the University of Technology (Jamaica), Belize College of Agriculture and Central American Health Science University (Belize Medical College) allow students to complete the preliminary portion of their degrees before going on to university (Kawa and Ramkissoon 2005: 77).

42. Much of the early R&D research was focused on agricultural development given the historical role of the natural resource sector in investment. R&D operations have taken place in agricultural related activities though agricultural and fisheries institutions, national commodity institutions, regional and sub-regional and international institutions operating in the region.

43. The Caribbean Court of Justice is a step in this direction.

44. Among these products are sugar and bananas.

45. They refer to this as the "New Minimalist Approach (NMA)."

46. These are exemplified by the World Bank's *Doing Business Report.*

REFERENCES

Alcorta, L. and W. Peres. "Innovation Systems and Technological Specialization in Latin America and the Caribbean." *United Nations University/Institute for New Technologies Discussion Paper Series*. ECLAC/UNDP Regional Project RLA/88/039, 1995.

Alleyne, D. and A. Francis. "Balance of Payments Constrained Growth in Developing Countries: A Theoretical Perspective." *Metroeconomica* 59, no. 2 (2007): 189-202.

Alleyne, D. and M. Freckleton. "FDI and Import Productivity Growth in Latin America and the Caribbean: The Role of Threshold Effects." Unpublished, 2010.

Alentberg, T. and C. von Drachenfels. Paper presented at the 11th EADI General Conference, Workshop Group: Industrialization Strategies, Bonn, September 21-24, 2005.

Barcaly, L. A. "FDI-facilitated Development: The Case of Natural Gas in Trinidad and Tobago." UTRECH Institute for New Technology, *Discussion Paper Series #2003-7*, 2003.

Barclay, L. A., Henry, R. and V. James. "Trade Policy and Caribbean Development Prospects and Options: A Summary." Submitted by Kairi Consultants Ltd. to Caribbean Development Bank, 2001.

Bernal, R. L. "Nano-firms, Regional Integration and International Competitiveness: The Experience and Dilemmas of the CSME." In *Production Integration in CARICOM: From Theory to Action*, edited by D. Benn and K. Hall. Kingston: Ian Randle Publishers, 2006.

Best, R. and L. Placida. "An Assessment of the Agro-food Distribution Services Industry in CARICOM," IDB/MIF, 2006.

Bynoe, M. "Diagnosis of Caribbean Private Sector Organizations and their Trade-related Services." Prepared for the IDB and the CAIC, 2006.

CARICOM Trade and Investment Report (CTIR). *Dynamic Interface of Regionalism and Globalization*, Caribbean Community Secretariat, 2000.

————. *Corporate Integration and Cross-border Development*, Caribbean Community Secretariat, 2005.

CARICOM Secretariat and CASME. "Strategic Plan and Coordinating Mechanism for Small and Medium Enterprises." The CARICOM Secretariat in association with the Caribbean Association of Small and Medium Enterprises, 2007.

Cimoli, M., Ferraz, J. C. and A. Primi. "Science and Technologies in Open Economies: The Case of Latin America and the Caribbean." Santiago de Chile: CEPAL, 2005.

Caribbean Trade and Adjustment Group (CTAG). "Improving Competitiveness for Caribbean Development." Prepared for the CARICOM Secretariat and the Caribbean Regional Negotiating Machinery (RNM), 2001.

Delloite and Touche. "Caribbean Tourism Sector Study," 2005.

Economic Competitiveness Group. "Ecotourism Profile—Guyana." Report for USAID under USAID-GTIS Project, 2005.

Fairbanks, D., Rabkin, D., Ecobari, M. and C. Rodriguez. "Building Competitive Advantage." In *From Growth to Prosperity: Policy Perspectives for Trinidad and Tobago*, edited by L. Rojas-Suarez and C. Elias, Inter-American Development Bank, 2006.

de Ferranti, D., Perry, G. E., Gill, I., Luis Guasch, J., Maloney, W. F., Sanchez-Paramo, C. and N. Schady. "Closing the Gap in Education and Technology." *World Bank Latin America and Caribbean Studies*. Washington, DC: World Bank, 2003.

Forbes Global 2000, 2010. www.Forbes.com

Harris, M. "Report on The Current Situation of Small and Medium-sized Industrial Enterprises in Trinidad and Tobago, Barbados and St Lucia." CDC 15320, 1998.

International Labour Organisation. "Small Enterprise Development in the Caribbean." *ILO Caribbean Studies and Working Papers* No 3, 2000.

Inter-American Development Bank. *Regional Strategy for Support to the Caribbean Community 2007-2010*, IDB, 2006a.

————. *Informal Sector in Jamaica*, IDB, 2006b.

IDB and CAIC. "Diagnosis of Caribbean Private Sector Organizationa and their Trade-related Services," ATN/FC-8788-RG, 2006.

James, V. "Labor, Domestic Capital and Growth: Key Developments and Implications for Regional Industrial Integration." In *Production Integration in CARICOM: From Theory to Action*, edited by D. Benn and K. Hall. Kingston: Ian Randle Publishers, 2006a.

————. "Externalities, Earnings, and Labor Surplus in Jamaica." School of Labour Studies and Mona School of Business, Mona, Jamaica, October 2006 (2006b).

————. "Import Productivity Growth, Capital Deepening and Caribbean Development: Some Theoretical Insights." In *Finance and Development in the Caribbean*, edited by A. Birchwood and D. Seerattan. St Augustine, Trinidad: UWI Caribbean Centre for Monetary Studies, 2006c.

Kawa, I. and H. Ramkissoon. "The CARICOM Countries," UNESCO Science Report, UNESCO Publishing, 2005.

Lewis, A. "Industrialization of the British West Indies." *Caribbean Economic Review* 2, no. 1 (1950): 1-61.

Marquez, G. "Training the Workforce in Latin America: What Needs to Be Done." *Labor Market Policy Briefs Series*, IDB, Sustainable Development Department, Social Development Division, 2006.

McArdle, T. "Firm and Worker Training in the Caribbean: A Report for the World Bank." Washington, DC: World Bank, 2006.

McIntyre, A. *Trade and Economic Development in Small Open Economies: The Case of the Caribbean Countries*. Westport, CT & London: Praeger, 1995.

Mishra, P. "Emigration and the Brain Drain: Evidence from the Caribbean." *IMF Working Paper* WP/06/25, IMF, 2006.

Nurse, K. "The Cultural Industries in CARICOM. Trade and Development Challenges." Draft Report prepared for the Caribbean Regional Negotiating Machinery, 2006.

OECD. *Investment Policy Reviews: Caribbean Rim, Antigua and Barbuda, Grenada and St Lucia*, 2006.

————. *Caribbean Rim Investment Initiative: Business Environment Report*. Dominican Republic, April 2003.

Perez, E. "Debt Accumulation in the Caribbean: Origins, Consequences and Strategies." Port-of-Spain, Trinidad: ECLAC, Economic Development Unit, 2006.

Planning Institute of Jamaica (PIOJ). *Economic and Social Survey – Jamaica*. Kingston: PIOJ, 2006 and 2009.

Porter, M. "Building the Microeconomic Foundations of Prosperity: Findings from the Business Competitiveness Index." *The Global Competitiveness Report 2004*. World Economic Forum, Palgrave Macmillan, 2004.

Roache, S. K. "Domestic Investment and the Cost of Capital in the Caribbean." *IMF Working Paper* WP/06/152, 2006.

Schnewly, P. "The Bahamas: A Road Map for Improving the Business Climate for the SMEs." First Draft, June 2007.

United Nations Industrial Development Organization. "Integrating SMEs in Global Value Chains: Towards Partnership for Development." UNIDO, 2001.

United Nations Economic Commission for Latin America and the Caribbean (ECLAC). "Competitiveness of the Manufacturing and Agro-industrial Sector in the Caribbean with a Focus on Dominica, Guyana, St Vincent and the Grenadines, and Trinidad and Tobago." UN-ECLAC, Sub-regional Headquarters for the Caribbean, Economic Development and Cooperation Committee, 1999.

————. "Impact of Privatization on the Banking Sector in the Caribbean." Sub-regional Headquarters for the Caribbean, Economic Development and Cooperation Committee, 2001.

————. "The Impact of Foreign Direct Investment on Patterns of Specialization in the Caribbean." ECLAC, 2003.

————. "The Impact of FDI on Patterns of Specialization in the Caribbean." Sub-regional Headquarters for the Caribbean, Economic Development and Cooperation Committee, *General LC/CAR/G.*718, January 2003.

————. "Caribbean Tourism, Trends, Policies and Impacts: 1985-2002." Sub-regional Headquarters for the Caribbean, 2003.

————— . "Productive Development in Open Economies." Thirteenth Session of ECLAC, San Juan, Puerto Rico, June 28-July 2, 2004.

————— . "Foreign Investment in Latin America and the Caribbean," 2005.

————— . "Report on Science and Technology Infrastructure and Policy in Selected Member and Associate Member Countries of the CDCC," June 25, 2005.

————— . *Economic Survey of the Caribbean 2005-2006.* Sub-regional Headquarters for the Caribbean, 2006.

Vuletin, G. "What is the Size of the Pie? Measuring the Informal Economy in Latin America and the Caribbean." Washington, DC: IMF, November 2006.

World Bank. "The Caribbean Common Market: Trade Policies and Regional Integration in the 1990s." *CRG Report No* 8381, 1990.

————— . *Caribbean Countries Policies for Private Sector Development*, April 1994.

————— . "Benchmarking FDI Climate in the Caribbean." FIAS a joint service of the IFC and the World Bank, Washington, DC: World Bank, 2004.

————— . *A Time to Choose.* Washington, DC: World Bank, 2006.

World Economic Forum. *Global Competitiveness Report 2006-2007*, WEF, 2006.

Chapter 13
Improving the Competitiveness of the Caribbean Tourism Model

Anthony Clayton, Nikolaos Karagiannis &
Jessica M. Bailey

ABSTRACT

The line of argument of this chapter describes a means of improving the competitiveness of Caribbean tourism. The first section analyzes the Caribbean tourism industry according to its principal characteristics, and sets the sector in the context of endogenous development. The second section discusses developmental, economic, social, and environmental impacts and challenges that emanate from tourism growth in the Caribbean. The combination of these factors would largely define a new policy framework of an alternative tourism model for Caribbean territories. Strategic requirements and policy considerations for such an alternative framework are offered in the final section of the chapter.

INTRODUCTION: THE CARIBBEAN CONTEXT

The Caribbean region presents a wide diversity of historical and cultural backgrounds. Most of the Caribbean territories were formerly administered by various colonial powers. This era ended half a century ago, but the legacy can still be seen in their political, institutional, and economic structures. So, the region today is the complex result of a mixture of the residual effects of colonialism and a complex network of relations between external agents and the internal elites that now dominate political and economic life. A number of Caribbean states have serious problems with corruption, a few also have very high levels of violence, and the internal elites are sometimes implicated in both; raising serious questions about the nature and quality of the governance.

Many of the islands still have a narrow economic base, and are therefore vulnerable to changes in external market prices, although some have built a strong, competitive presence in services such as tourism and finance. An examination of the patterns of trade makes the dependence of the Caribbean on the outside world most apparent, as foreign decisions with regard to tourism destinations, financial regulations, and commodity prices (especially food and energy) have a marked and immediate impact on the Caribbean economies. This pattern of external dependency, the dominance of internal elites, and the context of crime and violence has led to the development of enclave tourism resorts, which reflect the highly unequal economic and cultural relations which structured tourism development in less-developed and small island states, and have typically resulted in few or weak linkages to local communities and low levels of economic diversification.

This has led some to argue that tourism is equivalent to a new type of "plantation economy," and that the needs of the metropolitan countries are being met by Caribbean and other developing countries (i.e., the "pleasure periphery"), where the wealth generated is transferred from the periphery to the core. However, this is to underestimate the role of the local elites, which have also benefited greatly, although relatively little of this wealth trickles down.

The controlling and integrating force in international tourism is the large firms that control cruise lines, airlines, tour wholesaling, and hotel chains. These multinational companies are able to create, coordinate, and market the main components of the industry to develop a tourism product. They typically control tourism technology (communications, ITC), industry expertise, product design, pricing, and economies of scale. Their control over financial resources, managerial expertise, and especially their ability to influence consumer demand through marketing and promotion, endows them with an overwhelming competitive advantage. This can be seen, in its most extreme form, in the cruise industry, which uses flags of convenience to evade almost all national regulation and taxes.

CARIBBEAN TOURISM PERFORMANCE

Tourism has had nearly sixty years of almost uninterrupted growth, which has made it one of the world's largest industries. There have been wars, terrorist attacks, and other crises, but these have generally resulted in flows being rerouted—as people switched destinations—with no lasting effect on total demand. According to the World Travel and Tourism Council (WTTC), the travel and tourism industry now generates about 11.5 percent of world GDP and accounts for some 12.5 percent of all employment. International arrivals rose from 594 million in 1996 to 700 million in the year 2000, and should reach 1 billion in 2010. The vast majority of tourists currently come from the developed world, but rising incomes in countries such as China, India, and Brazil mean that these countries will make an increasing contribution in the future. Current projections of an annual increase of about 4 percent in international tourist arrivals and expenditure suggest that by 2010 world tourism should generate nearly US$10 trillion (World Tourism Organization [WTO] 2006).

Caribbean tourism is the region's most globally competitive industry (Boxill et al. 2003). This status is now openly acknowledged; over the last decades, tourism has been recognized as the main economic engine in many of the Caribbean island states. The World Travel and Tourism Council estimates for 2002 indicated that the regional industry would generate US$34.3 billion in economic activity, contribute US$7 billion to GDP, produce 2.1 million jobs and account for US$7 billion in capital investment (WTTC 2002). The WTTC also projected that this contribution would continue to grow.

The performance of Caribbean tourism, which is predominantly based on a warm climate, fine beaches, and attractive scenery, has exceeded the world average. The region's international tourist arrivals and receipts have been increasing since the 1950s (WTO 1998a). By 1980, there were six million tourist arrivals in the region. By 1990, this had risen to over ten million. By 2000, the region had over twenty million tourist arrivals, with more than twelve million cruise passenger arrivals, and recorded over US$18 billion in tourism receipts (Caribbean Tourism Organization [CTO] 2001). The Caribbean has been increasing its share of world tourism since 1980; it was 2.11 percent in 1980, reached 2.41 percent in 1987, declined slightly to 2.34 percent by 1990, and reached 3.2 percent in the late 1990s (CTO various issues), even though there is significant variation by country (see Tables 13.1, 13.2, 13.3, and 13.4).

TABLE 13.1
Tourism Arrivals and Receipts Growth Rates, 1950-2000

Decade	Arrivals (Average Annual Increase %)	Receipts (Average Annual Increase %)
1950-1960	10.6	12.6
1960-1970	9.1	10.1
1970-1980	5.6	19.4
1980-1990	4.8	9.8
1990-2000	4.0	6.5

Source: WTO 1999a.

TABLE 13.2
Top Job Creators in the Caribbean, 2002-2012

Country	Job Creation 2002-20012
Cuba	262,800
Dominican Republic	216,500
Jamaica	111,600
Haiti	75,800
The Bahamas	40,400
Puerto Rico	26,500
Curacao	23,800
Barbados	16,900
Trinidad & Tobago	12,800
Guadeloupe	11,400

Source: WTTC 2002: Chart 5.

TABLE 13.3
Stopover Arrivals in the Caribbean's Major Destinations, 1990-2009

Country	1990	1995	2005	2009
Antigua & Barbuda	184,248	191,401	198,084	211,107
Aruba	391,443	454,892	642,627	812,623
The Bahamas[a]	1,561,600	1,598,135	1,561,312	[d]1,524,442
Barbados	432,092	442,107	497,899	518,564
Bermuda	414,097	387,535	283,967	235,860
Cayman Islands	253,158	361,444	302,797	271,958
Cuba	N/A	519,400	1,686,162	2,429,809
Curacao	207,695	223,788	217,963	333,866
Dominican Republic	1,533,000	[b]2,334,493	2,793,581	3,992,303
Jamaica	840,777	1,018,946	1,266,366	1,831,097
Martinique	280,644	381,019	447,891	443,202
Puerto Rico	511,382	730,250	1,279,761	1,082,423
St Lucia	141,314	230,805	253,463	278,491
St Maarten/St Martin	393,962	323,571	380,301	440,185
Trinidad & Tobago	158,982	132,845	[c]383,101	251,975
US Virgin Islands	691,772	499,913	597,958	666,051

Notes: [a] There is a significant difference between the numbers published by the Ministry of Tourism and the Central Bank of The Bahamas and those included in the *Economic and Social Survey Jamaica*, Planning Institute of Jamaica (PIOJ), possibly because of varying definitions. [b] 1998 figure. [c] 2001 figure. [d] 2007 figure.
Sources: Planning Institute of Jamaica, Economic and Social Survey Jamaica, various years; Caribbean Tourism Organization, Tourism Statistics, various years.

TABLE 13.4

Cruise Ship Arrivals in the Caribbean's Major Destinations, 1990-2009

Country	1990	1995	2005	2009
Antigua & Barbuda	182,621	171,845	227,757	539,924
Aruba	122,511	150,776	392,036	441,288
The Bahamas[a]	1,853,897	1,543,495	3,360,012	2,902,321
Barbados	362,611	484,670	393,052	635,746
Bermuda	112,551	168,452	72,662	318,528
Cayman Islands	361,712	682,885	1,401,619	1,520,372
Cuba	N/A	N/A	N/A	N/A
Curacao	158,552	155,115	279,477	359,601
Dominican Republic	N/A	N/A	289,805	374,284
Jamaica	385,771	605,178	865,419	922,349
Martinique	421,259	428,032	94,262	69,749
Puerto Rico	599,755	773,267	634,326	1,045,459
St Lucia	101,948	193,912	299,315	699,306
St Maarten/St Martin	N/A	410,235	723,942	1,215,146
Trinidad & Tobago	26,928	N/A	40,941	163,713
US Virgin Islands	1,119,569	920,931	1,282,830	1,582,264

Notes: [a] There is a significant difference between the numbers published by the Ministry of Tourism and the Central Bank of The Bahamas and those included in the *Economic and Social Survey Jamaica*, Planning Institute of Jamaica (PIOJ), possibly because of varying definitions. [b] 1998 figure. [c] 2001 figure. [d] 2007 figure.
Sources: Planning Institute of Jamaica, Economic and Social Survey Jamaica, various years; Caribbean Tourism Organization, Tourism Statistics, various years.

Tourism earnings now account for approximately 25 percent of the Caribbean's GDP. The industry generates a larger ratio of both GDP and employment in most Caribbean islands than in other countries, as the region is now the most tourism-dependent region of the world. Also, tourism is a labor-intensive industry, and its role in generating direct and indirect employment in otherwise fragile Caribbean economies is regarded as one of its most important immediate economic benefits, although there are wide variations throughout the region in the proportionate importance of tourism in employment (Poon 1993: 266). In The Bahamas, for example, tourism accounts for around 70 percent of the country's national income, directly and indirectly, while the employment contribution, directly and indirectly, is between 50 and 60 percent of the labor force.

Jamaica's tourism reflects the regional profile, having grown strongly since the early 1980s. Apart from a poor performance in 1985 and a major setback in 1988 (due in part to the effects of hurricane Gilbert and the impact of the stock market crash the previous year, which caused a sharp decline in U.S. arrivals), Jamaica more than doubled its number of stopover arrivals over the last three decades and maintained its fourth position ranking during the period (PIOJ various years; Jamaica Tourism Board [JTB] various issues). Caribbean Tourism Organization data shows that visitor expenditure in 2000 ranged from 3.59 percent of GDP in Trinidad and Tobago (which has a large oil and gas industry) to 83.06 percent of GDP in Anguilla (which has little other industry). Estimates of total visitor expenditure in the region for the same period were US$19.9 billion; about US$979 per tourist. Vaugeios (2002) noted that this represented 50-70 percent of the region's hard currency earnings, and pointed out that this contribution had grown dramatically; tourism was the only sector of regional GDP that had consistently increased its share of total income during the past twenty-five years, reflecting both the success of the industry and the decline of other traditional local activities.

However, the terrorist attacks of September 11, 2001 in the United States impacted on existing projections. Although the worldwide decline in travel and tourism demand was 8.5 percent, the loss in the Caribbean was 13.5 percent, which translated into a temporary loss of some 365,000 jobs. The WTTC analysis found that the greatest job loss was in the Dominican Republic (192,800), followed by Cuba, Jamaica, Haiti, and Puerto Rico, whereas The Bahamas was placed sixth with 10,200 job losses. WTTC also found that the greatest revenue losses were sustained by the Dominican Republic ($837.2 million) and Puerto Rico ($589 million), followed by Jamaica ($299 million), The Bahamas ($282.5 million), Cuba ($281 million), Barbados ($169 million), Aruba ($141 million), Bermuda ($133 million), Trinidad & Tobago ($116 million), and Curacao ($113 million) (WTTC 2002: Chart 2). This reflected the extent to which Caribbean islands rely on the U.S. market. Many Americans were reluctant to fly after 9/11, whereas Europeans were relatively unaffected, so countries that relied more on European visitors did not suffer to the same extent.[1] The reaction to 9/11 illustrated the importance of the industry to the regional economies as well as their vulnerability. In addition, figures and relevant statistical information clearly illustrate that Caribbean tourism performance has declined during the last three years due to the recent ugly financial crisis (CTO various issues; PIOJ various years).

Tourism earnings are a critically important source of hard currency, and vital for the region's balance of payments. Tourism receipts rose from just under 18 percent of current account receipts in 1980 to around 37 percent in the 1990s. The total accumulated deficit on the current account of Caribbean economies would rise significantly if tourism receipts were excluded. This is true in spite of the leakage of gross foreign exchange earnings, which probably averages around 40 percent, with wide variations between local economies (EIU 1993; quoted in Karagiannis 2002).

The Caribbean's proximity to the United States gives it a natural advantage, as the United States has always been the largest generating market to the Caribbean, providing well over half the total arrivals in the region. The United States remains the single most important origin market for Bahamian and Jamaican tourism, for example, with arrivals exceeding 85 percent and 60 percent (on average) of their total respectively during the 1980s, 1990s, and 2000s. However, the number of visitors from Europe has grown rapidly since the late 1980s, increasing its share of arrivals in the region and, consequently, the European market has provided the main growth impetus for Caribbean tourism. Indeed, the European market has been increasing strongly mainly due to a flourishing charter business, as have some newer markets (CTO various issues; PIOJ various years).

Therefore, tourism has become an indispensable source of livelihoods, tax revenues, and foreign exchange, and makes an equally indispensable contribution to the balance of payments. Fortunately, the industry has significant potential for further growth, as the demand for tourism services appears to be both expandable (it is possible to add new products) and elastic (as the price of airfares, for example, has declined, demand for air travel has increased even more rapidly). Besides, tourism drifted into its current prominence as a result of steady growth over decades, and as economic sectors like agriculture and manufacturing shrank in the face of growing global competition.

According to Jayawardena (2002), this success, in general, cannot be attributed to any good strategic decisions or wise planning by Caribbean governments. In the early days of tourism, most Caribbean governments were generally satisfied to play a non-interventionist role which was largely limited to legislation, coordination, and the promotion of the various destinations. Most of the tourism legislation in the region, even today, pertains to the establishment of National Tourism Organizations (NTOs) and specifies their roles and functions within the industry (McDavid 2002).

DEVELOPMENTAL, ECONOMIC, SOCIAL, AND ENVIRONMENTAL IMPACTS

The Flying-Geese Pattern

Some recognize that Caribbean islands follow a "flying-geese pattern of tourism growth," in which countries gradually move up in tourist product development and service quality by following in the pattern of countries ahead of them (say, The Bahamas) in the growth process. There is no doubt that the growth of tourism in the post-war period has brought a measure of prosperity to several countries, both in the developed and developing world. This is no better illustrated than in The Bahamas where the traditionally high foreign ownership pattern enmeshed with a web of international structures relating to all aspects of the sector. On the other hand, the growth of tourism in The Bahamas has relied heavily on government's efforts that have been directed toward providing and maintaining certain basic infrastructures within its limited financial capacity and external promotion. The tendency has been to attract more tourists and business and to increase expenditure *per tourist*.

While The Bahamas has always had its "sun, sand and sea," it is only in the period following World War II that tourism grew to a position of any preeminence. In fact, the growth of tourism in the country has been the consequence of several factors. One of the most important has, undoubtedly, been the tremendous promotional campaign which successive administrations have pursued since the early 1950s in overseas efforts aimed at attracting both visitors and investors. Another important and critical factor, which added impetus to the Bahamian tourism industry, was the establishment of modern airport facilities and the initiation of regular air links with population centers in North America and Europe. A third and fortuitous development was the isolation of Cuba from the inter-American system in the early 1960s. The inability of Americans to travel to that country and the almost simultaneous introduction to casino gambling in The Bahamas diverted a great part of the Cuban business to The Bahamas which was already beginning to attract the attention of American holiday and pleasure seekers. A fourth, and not the least important of the factors mentioned, has been the role of foreign private capital in the whole post-war effort, starting with the inflow of British capital just after the end of World War II and later with the influx of finance from other sources (particularly the United States). In addition, the experience of The Bahamas since the 1970s has been affected not only by the nature of the activities which formed the basis of the 1960s boom but also by the policy framework within which the whole process has taken place.

Therefore, in the case of Caribbean tourist destinations, the concept of "flying-geese pattern" may be relevant and applicable. To some degree, the flying-geese pattern is a result of market forces: Caribbean nations with unemployed or under-employed labor forces become internationally competitive in this labor-intensive low-skill industry, and graduate to more learning and knowledge-based initiatives as education deepens the availability of capital and skilled labor force. Caribbean governments also try to support tourism with various policies and incentives. However, tourism is highly determined by multinational agents and corporations, and IT technology created in leading industrial nations.

The flying-geese pattern of growth assumes that the sophistication of domestic tourism will advance one position at a time. Thus, a nation is not likely to remain at the initial stage; education, learning, and additional investment will lead to more sophisticated tourist products and better operations quality. On the other hand, in this one sector (i.e., tourism) may lay much of the economic survival of Caribbean islands.

Investments and Incentives

The limited availability and relatively high capital cost in addition to the general short-termism of financial institutions can make it difficult for an entrepreneur to raise the investment capital required (Economic Intelligence Unit [EIU] 1993; Poon 1993: 269). To overcome this significant impediment, countries like Jamaica support investment in tourism via direct support (national advertising), investment in infrastructure, and generous tax breaks for investors. The latter can be used as a revolving subsidy, as each hotel extension qualifies for tax relief. However, various forms of support and subsidy may be insufficient to offset some of the general disadvantages of some Caribbean countries in attracting investment. Bureaucratic inefficiencies, slow and dysfunctional planning procedures, inconsistent regulatory requirements, corruption and extortion, a lack of transparency in incentive decisions, high operating costs, poorly maintained tourism attractions and supporting infrastructure, and the general difficulties of achieving scale economies in small islands add to the construction, security, overhead, management, and administrative costs faced by hoteliers.

Incentives in general probably do little to influence investment decisions. Studies in other countries of investment incentives, often allied to regional policy, have cast similar doubts on the effectiveness of incentive regimes as core factors like the general business and investment climate, a government's proactive business attitude, openness to foreign investors and economic policies, political and economic stability, operating costs, and location (e.g., proximity to supplies and markets) usually have a greater role in the investment decision. Once a broad decision has been taken on investment location, the incentives available may play a secondary role in decision making, but they are rarely the deciding factor.

Ownership Structure: Size Matters

The increasingly important role of foreign capital and ownership in the industry began in the early 1970s, when regional governments took the decision to allow the construction of all-inclusive resorts. Two of the earliest and most successful pioneers were Jamaican. In general, however, the capital needed to execute these projects was not readily available in the domestic capital markets. As a consequence, it was foreign-owned hotel chains that increasingly came to build, participate in the ownership of these enclave resorts, and dominate the industry (Barberia 2003). These hotel chains consistently maintain higher occupancy levels and profits, probably because they offer a convenient, comfortable, secure package that fits into the modern lifestyle. This trend is likely to continue, so that the market will be increasingly dominated by large all-inclusive resorts.

Indeed, a number of large tourism corporations have operations in the Caribbean, and these generally control their own marketing because they have a number of advantages: a strong cash flow and capital base, managerial expertise, ability to influence consumer demand through marketing and promotion, and links with tour operators. The last two factors give them a substantial competitive advantage, as most holidays are booked as packages in the originating country, and sales are heavily influenced by the way that particular products are bundled and by marketing and continuous positive exposure (EIU 1993). Some of the large hotels, resorts, and chains are locally owned, but most are foreign owned usually focusing their promotion in their home base. This too gives them an advantage compared to local tourism enterprises in the destination countries themselves.

However, as Karagiannis (2002: 156) noted, there are still a large number of small locally owned hotels. Many of them find it increasingly difficult to compete with the large transnationals; but it is partly because of these smaller properties that locals can feel that they have a greater stake in the sector. This, of course, raises the question: what would happen if these small properties were to disappear? There can be no definitive answer to this question; this might create a similar situation to that of Riviera Maya, Mexico, where small entities are marginalized, the industry is dominated by large international chains, and local resentment and hostility is correspondingly high (Boxill and Hernandez 2002). This could be replicated in the Caribbean. For instance, a study by Boxill and Frederick (2002) for Antigua found that there can be serious tension when foreign investors develop tourism projects without consulting locals in the planning process.

The real disparity, however, is not between domestic and foreign operators, but between large and small competitors. There are a lot of small hotels and guest houses in the region, and most of these do not have the necessary skills or the budgets to finance a major marketing push.[2] So, the small hotels and resorts generally have to rely on the generic promotions run by the national tourist offices/boards, and occasional attendance at tourism events. Some of them have links with tour operators and wholesalers, who will typically market them as part of a package. National governments may again be confined to promotional activities and the provision of investment for infrastructure development around tourism enclaves. This might actually be a positive development, given the lackluster performance of the government agencies, but could still impact negatively on the smaller units that rely more on external advice and support.

Increasing Competition–Higher Costs

The market for Caribbean destinations can be categorized in many ways, based on a variety of market segments being served. Geographic segmentation, which used to be confined to the United States, Canada, and Europe, must be expanded to include Japan, China, and some nations of South America. Seasonal segmentation, which includes summer and winter months, attracts two distinct income brackets and must, of necessity, employ vastly different media. Similarly, age segmentation is also apparent as younger, less affluent tourists seek recreation, fun and sports entertainment, while older travelers seek upscale shopping, arts-related enclaves, and more serene entertainment.

This range of international travelers and market niches represents a form of diversification, which helps to both reduce risk and distribute income over the year. In practice, however, it also presents the Caribbean islands with conflicting signals as to how tourism should be marketed, the facilities required, the way in which the industry should relate to the rest of the economy, and the overall strategy for the industry. In addition, Caribbean tourism is facing increased competition from other destinations including some well-established ones, such as the Florida coast, and various resorts of Mexico and the Mediterranean.[3] However, its greater threat may be from emerging rivals, not yet well-established on the international tourist scene, like the Far East and Central America. These newer tourism products offer a diversity that directly responds to broader demands of the traveling public.

The challenge facing many Caribbean nations is that small islands suffer from poor economies of scale in the provision of essential utilities like water and electricity. The relatively high import requirements that sustain tourism in the region translate into more expensive products than those of many competitors, with a greater price differential between winter and summer months. In addition, employment costs are relatively high in the region; although wage rates are relatively high, labor productivity tends to be low.

The Import Content of Caribbean Tourism, Linkages and Leakages

Researchers have repeatedly argued that, because of the relatively high import content of tourism, much of the revenue earned from the industry does not remain in local economies. Estimates by the World Bank (2003) suggested that approximately 55 percent of tourism receipts earned by developing countries are accrued overseas. The position with respect to Caribbean island states is not dissimilar as one of the major criticisms usually directed at Caribbean tourism relates to the high import content of the industry and its attendant low net foreign exchange benefits accruing to the region. According to the Organization of American States (OAS), some 30 to 50 percent of the revenue earned by the regional industry is accrued overseas, and in particular to developed countries. Other researchers place the average import content at 53 percent or higher.

Obviously, this is not typical of all countries in the region as there are a few destinations such as Trinidad & Tobago (22 percent) and St Vincent & the Grenadines (33 percent) with relatively lower leakage rates. However, the prevailing trend clearly suggests that the vast majority of destinations are saddled with an industry that depends heavily on imports to satisfy tourist needs. Nine Caribbean countries have rates ranging from 45 to almost 90 percent, with Dominica and The Bahamas representing the lower and upper limit of this range respectively, while the others are either in the 50 or 60 percent region (Ramjee Singh 2003; 2006). There is little doubt that the import content of the tourist industry in these island states is exceptionally high, especially when compared to other well-established and mature destinations outside of the region. For example, destinations such as New Zealand and Philippines have rates varying between 11 and 20 percent while those for Kenya and South Korea fluctuate between the 20 and 22 percent range.

Besides impacting on the tourism industry's net earnings, the leakage rate to a large extent influences the size of the tourism income multiplier. Available statistics and research amply demonstrate that the import content and the size of the tourism multipliers are inversely related. That is to say, countries (like The Bahamas) with high leakage rates tend to end up with small multipliers and relatively insignificant ripple effects from tourist spending. Research revealed that seven Caribbean destinations are expected to generate 39 cents or less in income from every dollar of tourist expenditure while only four countries (St Lucia, Dominica, St Vincent & the Grenadines, and Trinidad & Tobago) would produce an additional $0.56, $0.59, $0.79, and $1.00 respectively per dollar of tourist spending.

The question that next arises is: what factors are likely to explain the differences in the import content (leakage rate) of the tourism industry among regional destinations? First, it is argued in the literature that small island economies tend to rely more on imports to meet the diverse needs of tourism, because they do not have the capacity to produce the goods and services that are required to meet the demand of the industry. This position is supported by an UNEP (2002) study which suggested that the leakage rate tends to be higher among small island economies because of major resource constraints. In contrast, larger island states do not face these resource constraints and are expected to develop stronger intersectoral linkages between tourism and the rest of the domestic economy.

Secondly, physical infrastructure is one of the main pillars of economic development for any economy. The level of infrastructural development determines the diversity and speed of economic development. A well developed infrastructure is expected to improve the production possibilities of domestic industries, develop stronger intersectoral linkages within the economy, provide the platform for the efficient distribution of goods and services, and allow domestic industries to try to compete successfully with their overseas counterparts. These factors taken together are most likely to improve the ability of the domestic economy to increase its inputs into tourism.

Thirdly, the Caribbean area today hosts about 700 million tourists per annum (CTO 2009). The phenomenal increase in tourist arrivals over the last years was due primarily to the decision of most regional destinations to engage in mass tourism. A massive influx of tourists to a destination, however, increases the demand for goods and services. To satisfy this demand, most destinations invariably turn to imports.

Lastly, Caribbean economies are open, export-oriented, dependent structures. This export focus coupled with overemphasis on tourism growth over the years has not stimulated an autonomous path of development, and has resulted in the neglect of local agriculture and manufacturing industry. It is not surprising that the local agricultural sector has remained inefficient and is unable to provide the required volume of output at competitive prices to tourism. Hence, the continued underdevelopment of domestic agriculture contributes to the import content of tourism, and the region has become highly dependent on food imports. That is to say, the more underdeveloped a country's domestic production the higher the tourism industry's import content. Instead, domestic production should be oriented toward satisfying domestic demand in the first instance, with export specialization occurring as an extension of this.

Scientists have pointed to the potential mutual benefits between local agriculture and tourism. Most Caribbean governments disregard this advice and seem to ignore developmental requirements and domestic needs. Identifying the factors that lead to the differential in leakage rates has become a critical issue for small island states, and especially those that are characterized as tourism-dependent economies. In many cases, the mere survival of these economies will depend on their abilities to retain more of the tourism industry's earnings. Without a doubt, the quest to reduce the leakage level of tourism receipts and, by extension, to increase the benefits accruing from tourism presents a major challenge.

This problem exists due to a serious lack of diversification in local production coupled with a lack of linkages between tourism and the rest of the economy. The industry imports much of its supplies, largely because local manufacturers, farmers, and distributors can find it difficult to organize the quantity and quality of goods required. The level of leakage varies significantly from country to country, depending on the extent to which the domestic economy is able to meet the needs of the industry.

Tourist receipts leak at several different stages. First round leakages stem from the direct imports required by the industry and the visitors. Second round leakages arise from the import content of investment and overall consumption. Third round leakages refer to expenditure by governments, national tourism organizations, and individual firms on overseas promotion in order to sell the destination (Karagiannis 2002). This sequence could have several negative effects. One is that the number of linkages into the local economy is likely to decline; consequently, the indirect benefits of the industry could decline even as the industry grows.

The cost of building new hotels and the refurbishment of old ones is significantly affected by the high import content, as well as by local factors such as extortion, a major factor in some of the islands. This is a particular problem for the older and smaller hotels, which are typically old-fashioned, family-run, and in need of major reinvestment. However, the initial capital costs can be less significant than ongoing operating costs, with the importation of management services, spare parts, and replacement goods. As a result, strong revenues do not necessarily mean large profits.

One policy option is to reduce tariffs and thereby lower the cost of imports for construction and consumer goods. However, in a situation where the rates of leakage are already exceptionally high, tariffs may represent a significant source of government revenue from the industry. Reduced tariffs might also lead to even higher levels of capital outflow from the region. Consequently, any reduction in tariffs would have to be accompanied by parallel measures to raise new revenue and thereby ensure that the host country was able to derive some benefit from the industry.

Finally, mass tourism associated with all-inclusive resorts could perpetuate or even exacerbate the Caribbean dependency on specific markets, while the concentration of ownership could narrow the local distribution of benefits. The ownership structure of the industry has given particular impetus to concerns about high rates of leakage, the loss of tourist dollars on imports, and repatriated profits (UNEP 1996). Current data on the leakage rate for the industry are only available for eleven countries in the region (Table 13.5). With the exception of Trinidad & Tobago, the leakage rates for the rest of these economies are particularly high. In most of these cases, over half of the industry's earnings flow out of the local economy. This is driven mainly by the exceptionally high import content of tourism, the relatively little local supply, and the relatively few inter-sectoral linkages between the local economy and tourism.

Apart from influencing the industry's net earnings, the leakage rate also affects the tourism income multiplier. The multiplier, sometimes referred to as the ripple effect, refers to the total value of economic activity generated by the industry. The multipliers for several of the regional economies are listed in Table 13.6.

TABLE 13.5
Leakage Rates (%) in the Caribbean, 2003*

Antigua & Barbuda	56
Barbados	66
The Bahamas	85
British Virgin Islands	56
Dominica	45
Grenada	55
Jamaica	50
St Lucia	62
St Kitts & Nevis	67
St Vincent & the Grenadines	33
Trinidad & Tobago	22

Note: * Computed by Ramjee Singh 2003; 2006.
Source: Caribbean Tourism Organization (CTO), Tourism Receipts (Statistical Annex), 2002.

TABLE 13.6
Tourism Multipliers for Several Caribbean Economies*

Antigua & Barbuda (1997)	1.06
Barbados (1996)	1.19
The Bahamas (1996)	0.98
British Virgin Islands (1996)	1.16
Dominica (1999)	1.59
Grenada (1996)	1.39
Jamaica (1996)	1.35
St Lucia (2000)	1.56
St Kitts & Nevis (1998)	1.00
St Vincent & the Grenadines (2000)	1.79
Trinidad & Tobago (1999)	2.00

Note: * Computed by Ramjee Singh 2003; 2006.
Source: IMF website, Individual Country Report, 1998; 2000; 2002; 2006.

A simple comparison of Tables 13.5 and 13.6 indicates a negative correlation between the leakage rates and the tourism multipliers. For example, Trinidad & Tobago, St Vincent & the Grenadines, and Dominica have larger multipliers, essentially because they have a lower leakage rate, while the opposite is true in the case of The Bahamas, and Antigua & Barbuda. Consequently, the relatively high import content of the industry reduces the economically beneficial multiplier effect of tourist expenditure in the region. The high import level in the islands at least partially explains why a number of countries complain that they do not appear to be deriving commensurate benefit from the industry (Ramjee Singh 2006).

Air Lift

Air transport is critically important for the hotels and land-based resorts. There are frequent scheduled air connections between the Caribbean and the United States, Canada, and Europe, and a number of major international airlines serve the region. American Airlines are in a particularly strong position, because they have a major base at Miami airport which serves as the hub for much of Latin America and the Caribbean, and currently have about 70 percent of the Caribbean market. Partly as a legacy of the independence era of 1960s and 70s, there are also several relatively small regional carriers, including Caribbean Airways and Air Jamaica.

Caribbean nations are concerned about two aspects of their air links with their main markets. The first is the potential vulnerability of the region to changes in route structure, and the second is the possibility of any reductions in direct connections. There is therefore a general concern that the region does not control most of its own airlift. However, Caribbean regional carriers have proved to be exorbitantly costly status symbols since they accumulated collective losses of about US$ 1.5 billion between 1995 and 2005, a crippling burden for small island economies.[4]

More recently, the slow removal of national barriers to merger, acquisition, route planning, and cabotage have gradually started to make clear that it is increasingly inappropriate to focus on the location of the head office of an airline. As a result, a number of both small (Guyana) and medium-sized countries (Switzerland, the Netherlands) no longer believe that it is necessary to have a domestically based national carrier. For example, in 2007, Guyana made Caribbean Airways (which is based in Trinidad) its new national carrier, and Jamaica is currently negotiating for the same outcome.

It is true that the major international airlines have to take decisions on a commercial basis. It is also true that the local carriers are typically small, loss-making, subsidized, under-equipped, and have trouble in competing directly with the major airlines. There has been some discussion in the Caribbean of the need for the local airlines to cooperate, coordinate timetables, code-share both with each other and with large international carriers, and become more aggressively competitive if they are to survive in the face of global competition. Rationalization and mergers might be a partial solution. National sentiment and government ownership still play powerful roles, however, and this may make it difficult for the main regional carriers to merge.

The Cruise Industry

The increasing dominance of the cruise ship industry presents a particularly problematic challenge to the region. The cruise sector has been growing faster than international tourism in general since the mid-1980s and the Caribbean is the most important region in the world for this industry, accounting for over half of world cruise ship tourism. Barberia (2003) noted that at least 40 percent of the tourists entering nine of the region's leading destinations arrived via cruise ship. Recent forecasts suggest that the growth rate of the industry will continue to outstrip that of the stopover business for the foreseeable future. The North American market dominated the cruise ship industry, accounting for over 80 percent of all cruise passengers during the 1990s (Table 13.7).

TABLE 13.7
Growth of the Cruise Industry Worldwide, 1980-2000

Country of Passenger Origin	1980	1985	1990	2000
N. America (USA/Canada)	1,431	2,152	3,640	...
Germany (former West)	160	150	184	...
UK	115	92	186	...
Australia	90	100	79	...
Italy	...	55	75	...
France	...	55	112	...
Rest of Europe/Scandinavia	...	80	110	...
Others (including Far East)	...	50	75	...
TOTAL	...	**2,734**	**4,461**	...

Note: ... denotes lack of data.
Source: EIU, Special Report No 2104, Table 2, January 1992.

Caribbean islands have four main areas of concern about the cruise industry. One is the impact that the ships have upon the environment (via, for example, illegal discharges of oily waste and garbage). The other three relate to the relatively poor net economic benefits derived from the cruise ship business compared with those derived from stopover tourism. These are:

- The low level of on-shore expenditure per cruise ship visitor.
- The low level of direct government revenues generated by the cruise ship industry, which pays remarkably little tax to any jurisdiction.
- The competition offered by on-board shops to shopping facilities on-shore.

The Caribbean Tourism Organization (2001) estimates that cruise ship travelers spent well over half a billion U.S. dollars during the 1990s in the region. The CTO points out, however, that stopover visitors accounted for around 94 percent of total tourism spending, while cruise ship passengers accounted for just 6 percent. No statistics exist in detail on leakage of cruise ship passengers' spending but it is widely reported that the bulk of on-shore purchases are duty-free goods or small souvenirs with relatively low local value-added. In general, it is clear that spending by cruise ship tourists at a destination is significantly lower than stopover tourists, as CTO estimates indicate that stopover tourists spend on average ten to seventeen times more than cruise ship tourists. The reason is simple: the cruise ship is an all-inclusive floating hotel, so all meals, entertainment, and so on are purchased in advance as part of the package. The island destinations provide little more than occasional variations in scenery, so less than half of the passengers bother to disembark.

The cruise industry is also exceptionally skilled at utilizing legal loopholes. The use of flags of convenience, in particular, allows some firms to operate on an almost entirely unregulated and untaxed basis. The industry has also, on several occasions, demonstrated that it has significantly more leverage than most island governments. Several governments have tried to impose a head tax on cruise tourists, but the threat to take the business elsewhere has obliged the governments to capitulate.

Social and Cultural Impacts

Further to the material relations of highly unequal exchange perpetuated by tourism in the periphery, other authors have likened tourism to a form of "cultural imperialism" or rather the "hedonistic face of neocolonialism." Some have argued that tourism and the institutionalization of hospitality reinforces notions of subservience, reinforced through the proliferation of mainly low grade employment for locals.

This legacy of history cannot be ignored. However, the same colonial ties also brought a diverse range of cultures, religions, values, cuisines, recreational activities, and sporting interests. The sum total is to produce a range of destinations for the leisure visitor as exciting and diverse as no other region in the world.

Amid this beautiful and powerful Caribbean culture, and despite its image as one of the world's glamorous primary destinations for the visitors, it is easy to overlook the fact that many Caribbean territories are now overpopulated but still underdeveloped countries in which prosperity coexists with squalor and deprivation. This supports the argument that most of the benefits of the industry accrue largely to small elites.

Some argue that an influx of relatively wealthy tourists into a poor country can have negative implications for social and cultural values. This is contentious, partly because all cultures are subject to multiple influences and evolve over time, and partly because definitions and measures of "good" and "bad" social change are subjective. However, tourism has in some cases clearly resulted in undesirable developments, such as children or vulnerable young adults trafficked or coerced into the sex industry and the spread of sexually transmitted diseases.

There can also be problems with resentment. These may stem from the entrenched poverty and extreme social disparities found in many developing countries, but a sense of historical grievance might appear to make tourism an obvious target, especially if many of the visitors are from the former colonial power. However, Carter (1997) found that the resentment felt by some workers in Jamaica is typically focused on their own management, rather than on the visitors, due to low pay, constant uncertainty, and long travel-to-work times.

There are still potential problems when poor local residents see the great difference between their own lifestyles and that of the affluent foreign tourist. This can be compounded by a sense that opportunities for local people are largely confined to the lower-grade jobs in hotels, while senior management positions are held by expatriate staff. The latter is not always accurate: some hotels invest significantly in staff training and local recruitment but the perception still exists.

Tourists are sometimes cheated or overcharged, and cameras or wallets might be stolen. Such incidents are upsetting but not life-threatening. The most common complaint is one of harassment, usually in the form of persistent and apparently aggressive attempts to sell something, but this does to some extent reflect cultural differences in what is perceived to be acceptable behavior. The more important problem is the rise in serious crime, like armed robbery and homicide. These do not usually affect tourists, but generally receive significant publicity when they do. As a result, many tourists prefer to stay within the confines of their all-inclusive hotels, protected by hotel security, venturing out only on organized tours, and spending little in the wider community. This serves to perpetuate the underlying problem of surrounding poverty.

Most people understand, of course, that one homicide does not make a country dangerous. The most serious cases involve a more general threat, such as terrorism.[5] However, even a few well-publicized cases can have a perceptible deterrent effect. As a result, much emphasis has been placed recently on the need for tourism awareness programs in the Caribbean to make local communities realize the economic advantages of tourism, in terms of jobs and opportunities it can offer.

A corollary to the envy felt by some of the poorer sections of Caribbean communities is the resentment felt by some members of the political elite, some of whom are irked by the contrast between their underperforming economies and the apparent vibrancy of their largest sector. More generally, some politicians have serious reservations about tourism's role as the main engine of economic growth. These reservations are generally expressed in three forms. One is the concern that tourism will result in the substitution of one type of dependence for another, as tourism could come to resemble the banana and sugar industries in small, price-taker monocrop economies. Another is the belief that tourism is a relatively volatile industry, making dependence on it risky. A third is a feeling that local culture and mores will disintegrate as other lifestyles are imported and copied by local people, especially the region's youth, and as culture becomes "objectified" by being packaged and sold as if it were just another product (Bianchi 2002: 270-71).

The first argument is, of course, an argument for diversification rather than against tourism *per se*, but highlights a potential vulnerability. The second argument is weaker, because tourism is actually less volatile than most commodities. The third argument might perhaps be stronger in countries where, for example, dances and rituals that were formerly sacred are now performed for the entertainment of visitors, but is less obviously true of the Caribbean islands, which are themselves a product of many generations of cultural fusion. This argument has also been accused of being a preoccupation of the cultural elite, rather than the actual people concerned (Clayton 2004).

Environmental Impacts

The loss of infrastructure and trade to a combination of climate change and social pressures could, potentially, result in the collapse of a number of regional economies. These daunting challenges make it essential to undertake a serious review of the nature and role of tourism in the region. In addition, mass tourism imposes various burdens on the environment and infrastructure. Many of these impacts can be mitigated or avoided, with good planning and management; but poor governance and powerful developers with a cavalier disregard for constraints can cause unnecessary damage. Dysfunctional planning processes can result in poorly managed over-development and cause unnecessary environmental damage, a combination that can eventually force the local industry into a down-market, low-margin niche. Some therefore worry that countries have become overly dependent on the industry, and that tourists are fickle and might decide to take their custom elsewhere.

The problem is exacerbated when the number of tourists hosted by a small island state is several times the size of the local population. A high tourist-to-host density ratio inevitably leads to problems, including environmental and infrastructural overloading, that would not only threaten the viability of the industry but hasten its demise. The need for Caribbean governments to develop and implement strategies that would not only counter but even reverse this trend becomes more urgent. There has to be, therefore, a growing awareness of the need to control and manage the industry to ensure its viability and sustainability in the long run.

More fundamentally, it appears likely that climate change and the frequency of severe weather conditions will have a major impact on social, economic, and environmental systems during the course of this century. As Clayton et al. (2007) note, this presents an existential challenge for small island nations. It may be necessary to relocate vulnerable infrastructure and human settlements away from high risk areas. While tourism in some countries (such as the UK) is expected to gain, the Mediterranean is projected to become increasingly arid while the Caribbean is likely to suffer from a higher intensity of hurricanes, flooding, and storm surge. It is also possible that airlines might be included in national carbon emission totals and co-opted into carbon trading schemes, which will have implications for airfares.

IMPROVING THE CARIBBEAN TOURISM MODEL: ADDRESSING THE PROBLEMS

The analysis above has focused on the problems and dilemmas associated with the operations of a large, dominant industry in a group of small island nations. Clearly, Caribbean nations have a genuine comparative advantage in tourism and have developed very successful tourism products. Tourism has delivered enormous benefits in terms of income and job creation, and is now essential to the economic survival of the region. Caribbean islands and microstates will always be vulnerable to global shifts and fluctuations in tourism and financial flows, but some of them have demonstrated a capacity to exploit, at least temporarily, some niches in globalized service markets and generate a degree of prosperity for their small populations.

This combination of issues has profound implications for the Caribbean, because it is so heavily dependent on the tourism industry. An obvious starting point is the extent of dependence. The current high level of dependence makes the region particularly susceptible to cycles in the world economy and external shocks, and could exacerbate instability in job creation and national income levels in the event of a longer-lasting recession. However, specialization in tourism tends to be less risky than specialization in a single commodity, as commodity prices can remain low for years.

Perhaps the most serious concern about tourism's role as the main engine of development is that some of the islands are excessively dependent on the industry; consequently, they are acutely vulnerable to any shock or recession in the sector, and further growth (in the absence of supply side measures) could further increase imports and exacerbate their already highly open import-dependent characteristics. It is also clear, however, that tourism has delivered only a part of its potential benefit to the region. Some aspects of this shortcoming could be easily remedied. For example, supply side measures (such as extension training, farmer cooperatives, and quality control) and intelligent changes to systems of taxes and tariffs would help to increase the economic multiplier and reduce unnecessary leakage. Better coordination between the islands, including the removal of barriers to merger and acquisition of the small airlines, would reduce duplicated effort and cut overheads.

The fact that these measures have, in general, not been pursued supports the view that the underlying problem with Caribbean tourism is that it is largely unplanned and used simply as a quick way of earning foreign exchange by some of the heavily indebted governments in the region (Hayle 2002; Karagiannis 2002; McDavid 2002). This indicates the need for a proper tourism strategy. As the dominant sector of the regional economy, tourism could be utilized to far greater effect to drive a larger development policy.

Ideally, tourism would generate significant economic benefits for both investors and hosts, while minimizing environmental impacts, respecting local people, and giving them an opportunity for advancement. This is broadly similar to the model advocated for Belize by Boxill (2003), who argued that there are four prerequisites for this more enlightened type of tourism: a regional/local approach to tourism planning; intelligent planning and regulation of the industry; a more diversified product; and greater local involvement in the process.

Some authors feel that this will not happen, however, because foreign tour companies and service providers have little regard for local socio-cultural and economic conditions, and do not have the destination community's best interests in mind. Some extend this to argue that local people and their communities have become the objects of development but not the subjects. A further extension of this argument is that international tourism is a product of metropolitan capitalist enterprise, and that "in some respects, the geography of tour company operations is the geography of dependency relationships" (Williams 1994: 115; quoted in Telfer 2002).

Some of this critique may be true, as every business tends to be primarily focused on its profits, markets, and shareholders, and cannot reasonably be expected to take on the entire responsibility for the social development of the surrounding community. However, rational self-interest also indicates that a tourism business is unlikely to thrive as an intrusion in an alienated community, and that the price of neglect will be the need to invest in high levels of security and, from time to time, to manage negative publicity when guests are the victims of violent crime.

There are some obvious remedial measures. In general, a combination of economic development (which will help to reduce levels of poverty in the surrounding community) in conjunction with some measures to promote local business and job opportunities, long-term training for more skilled positions, and sympathetic treatment of local culture and tradition, can do much to build local support. This combination can be mutually advantageous (Timothy 2002: 152; Scheyvens 1999).

Some regional coordination in tourism planning would allow Caribbean countries to pool some of their resources in areas such as marketing (Hayle 2002), and a less nationalistic approach to air traffic would encourage the small regional airlines to code-share, coordinate their timetables, and pool their maintenance, or even undertake real or virtual mergers. This would increase their load factors, reduce their maintenance costs, and reduce their overheads. This would also make them more attractive partners for the major carriers, an increasingly important factor now that the carriers are grouped into major alliances and flights are booked through the major computer reservation systems.

More generally, the building of strategic alliances and partnerships within and outside of the tourism industry is needed in order to bundle products, add value, and thereby increase the competitiveness of the sector (Poon 1993: 273). As Karagiannis (2002: 169) points out: "With cooperative arrangements and regional approaches to tourism, Caribbean islands can share the [huge] expenses of creating market intelligence systems, information technology networks, promotion, and public relations campaigns." Besides, a sophisticated marketing approach with more specialized and segmented promotional campaigns would serve the needs of the Caribbean tourist industry.

Some have also argued that proper planning and regulation of tourism is essential in order to develop a better and more sustainable product (Boxill 2000,

2002; Hayle 2002; McDavid 2002; Karagiannis 2002). McDavid (2002: 68) argues that the development of tourism cannot be left entirely to market forces, and that there is a need for selected policy interventions. Most agree that the industry would benefit from better strategic planning, instead of the current practice of largely *ad hoc* arrangements (Clayton 2001; 2004). Karagiannis suggests that this "strategic approach" would include the development of human resources, product development, and marketing, arguing that "The public and private sectors can cooperate in a range of different arrangements, each contributing what it does best and both participating in the financial returns, within the context of a socially defined development agenda" (Karagiannis 2002: 165).

A realistic question to be asked is, can Caribbean tourism achieve such a niche in this crowded market and, if so, at what cost? The increased competition can be met by an emphasis on capturing the customer service niche—one that raises the level and sophistication of customer service for all segments. More importantly, the Caribbean will have to focus strongly on improving quality standards, increasing efficiency, and offering more value for the money. As standard measures of customer service prove insufficient, investments must be made in training, technological infrastructure development and support, and marketing research.

However, for Caribbean tourism to pursue an industry-leading customer service niche, governments could face higher costs. First, establishing a customer service niche would entail investment in training, with a concomitant investment in technology development and usage. More hotels in the Caribbean would have to install new technologies and assure that their employees are trained in current utilities. That represents increased infrastructure and education costs. Second, service attitudes and skills must also be the focus of training as they are crucial to future success. Both managers and laborers must view impeccable service as important for both the internal and external components of the tourism business. Management training costs would include investment in state-of-the-art training facilities and international procurement of experienced trainers. Last, investment must be made in marketing research. Consumer surveys analyzed and interpreted by experts represent an accurate means of knowing what different market segments value. They set the stage for delivering a higher level of customer satisfaction.

But even with an industry-leading customer service, there is still the need for the Caribbean to diversify the tourism product, which still relies largely on the "sun, sea and sand" model (Boxill 2002; Nurse 2002) to give a wider range of options and thereby improve the competitive edge of the industry (Hayle 2002; Karagiannis 2002). For example, Bernal (2000: 110-11) suggests that the Caribbean should consider heritage tourism, health tourism, cultural tourism, and ecotourism (which may require different promotional appeals), while Nurse argues for the entertainment industry, stating that "the experience with festivals and other cultural events is that they tend to create a tourism demand that is resilient and less susceptible to economic downturns" (Nurse 2002: 129).

Clearly, a more diverse product would permit a wider range of training and business development options, thereby helping to secure greater local involvement in the industry. Heritage, cultural, ecological, community, and health tourism are all labor-intensive niches which require some level of knowledge and local ownership in order for them to be successfully implemented (Scheyvens 1999; Boxill 2000, 2002; Hayle 2000, 2002; Timothy 2002; Duperly-Pinks 2002). This would in turn result in a larger network of stakeholders (Boxill 2002; Hayle 2002), a wider distribution of tourism earnings, and the fostering of a more pro-tourism attitude in the region (Duperly-Pinks 2002).

As noted earlier, the linkages between tourism and local production have been relatively weak. New options such as health and heritage tourism can help to increase consumption of the region's cuisine and local products, thereby building a mutually beneficial relationship between tourism and agro-industry. However, any significant strengthening of these linkages would still require improvements in product quality, more efficient distribution systems, extension training, and access to affordable credit by local producers (Henshall-Momsen 1998).

Finally, environmental protection must be accorded a greater priority by policy makers in the Caribbean, especially as there have been some recent cases of mismanagement and unnecessarily destructive development. There is still a serious mismatch between the general recognition that environmental issues matter and the largely ineffective controls in some islands. Caribbean governments have a range of policies and legislation to protect the environment (including protected areas, land-use planning, and obligatory environmental impact analysis), but sometimes these are inconsistently enforced. More could also be done to promote effective coordination between government departments, and to encourage new approaches such as cleaner production strategies (Karagiannis 2002; Clayton et al. 2007).

CONCLUSION

This chapter sought to set Caribbean tourism in the context of endogenous development of the host nations, taking into account issues like local participation, business development, environmental concerns, greater regional cooperation, the creation of a more diversified product, and more emphasis on strategic planning. The combination of these factors would largely define a new policy framework of sustainable tourism development for Caribbean territories. This challenge is not insurmountable if Caribbean governments accept their role as change agents and seek to move the industry away from its current laissez-faire environment to one that involves serious, technically proficient planning, and coordination of the industry's needs with the rest of the domestic economy. The primary goal of such an exercise must be to implement strategies and policies that would seek to retain more of the industry's earnings in the local economy.

NOTES

1. This partly reflects the fact that many European countries have decades of experience with terrorism and, therefore, are somewhat more hardened to it. Security measures at European airports were also far more effective at the time.

2. The region's accommodation stock currently comprises a wide variety of properties including large resorts, exclusive hotels, small inns, guesthouses, and the all-inclusive resort. The latter is becoming a trademark of Caribbean tourism. A small number of mega-structures (hotels with over 500 rooms) have been built in the Caribbean, although these are still significantly smaller than the industry leader (the Venetian Hotel, in Las Vegas, which has over 7,000 rooms).

3. Florida and Mexico offer similar climatic and scenic attractions within broadly the same parameters of price and distance from the rest of the United States (EIU 1993).

4. BWIA, Air Jamaica, and LIAT. See also: Deon Green, "Virgin Takeover of Air Jamaica Route is a Backward Step," *Jamaica Gleaner*, May 24, 2007.

5. Terrorists, unfortunately, are increasingly aware of this fact, and also that tourism is both economically significant and a very soft target. The murder of seventy tourists at Luxor in 1997 is estimated to have cost Egypt about half of its tourism revenue over the following year, which appears to have been the outcome intended by the terrorist group that perpetrated the atrocity.

REFERENCES

Barberia, L. G. "The Caribbean: Tourism as Development or Development for Tourism?," 2003. www.fas.harvard.edu

Bernal, R. L. "Globalization and Small Developing Countries: The Imperative for Repositioning." In *Globalisation: A Calculus of Inequality*, edited by D. Benn and K. Hall, 88-127. Kingston: Ian Randle Publishers, 2000.

Bianchi, R. V. "Towards a New Political Economy of Global Tourism." In *Tourism and Development: Concepts and Issues*, edited by R. Sharpley and D. J. Telfer, 265-99. Clevedon: Channel View Publications, 2002.

Boxill, I. "Overcoming Social Problems in the Jamaican Tourism Industry." In *Tourism in the Caribbean*, edited by I. Boxill and J. Maerk, 17-40. Mexico: Plaza y Valdez, 2000.

——— . "Towards an Alternative Tourism for Belize." *International Journal of Contemporary Hospitality Management* 15, no. 3 (2003): 147-55.

Boxill, I. and O. Frederick. "Old Road, New Road: Community Protests and Tourism Development in Antigua." In *Tourism and Change in the Caribbean and Latin America*, edited by I. Boxill, O. Taylor and J. Maerk, 101-110. Kingston: Arawak Publications, 2002.

Caribbean Tourism Organization. *Statistical Tables 2000-2001.* Bridgetown, Barbados: CTO, 2002.

Carter, K. L. *Why Workers Won't Work: The Worker in a Developing Economy.* London: Macmillan, 1997.

Clayton, A., Wright, R., Chenoweth, J. and W. Wehrmeyer. *Energy Security for Jamaica: The Implications of Future Energy Scenarios.* In preparation.

Clayton, A. "A Policy Framework for the Sustainable Development of the Tourism Industry." In *Caribbean Tourism: Visions, Missions and Challenges*, edited by C. Jayawardeena. Kingston: Ian Randle Publishers, 2004.

————. "Sustainable Tourism: The Agenda for Tourism Professionals in the Caribbean." In *Tourism and Hospitality Education and Training in the Caribbean*, edited by C. Jayawardeena. Kingston: UWI Press, 2001.

Duperly-Pinks, D. "Community Tourism: 'Style and Fashion' or Facilitating Empowerment?" In *Tourism and Change in the Caribbean and Latin America*, edited by I. Boxill, O. Taylor and J. Maerk, 137-61. Kingston: Arawak Publications, 2002.

Hayle, C. "Community Tourism in Jamaica." In *Tourism in the Caribbean*, edited by I. Boxill and J. Maerk, 165-76. Mexico: Plaza y Valdez, 2000.

————. "Issues Confronting New Entrants to Tourism." In *Tourism and Change in the Caribbean and Latin America*, edited by I. Boxill, O. Taylor and J. Maerk, 229-72. Kingston: Arawak Publications, 2002.

The Intergovernmental Panel on Climate Change. *4th Assessment Report*, 2007.

Jayawardena, C. "Cuba: Crown Princess of Caribbean Tourism?" Paper presented at the 27th CSA Conference, Nassau, The Bahamas, 2002.

Karagiannis, N. *Developmental Policy and the State: The European Union, East Asia, and the Caribbean.* Lanham, MD: Lexington Books, 2002.

Kempadoo, K. *Sun, Sex and Gold: Tourism and Sex Work in the Caribbean.* Lanham, MD: Rowan & Littlefield, 1999.

McDavid, H. "Why Should Government Intervene in a Market Economy? A Caribbean Perspective on the Hospitality and Tourism Sector." In *Tourism and Change in the Caribbean and Latin America*, edited by I. Boxill, O. Taylor and J. Maerk, 56-81. Kingston: Arawak Publications, 2002.

Nurse, K. "Bringing Culture into the Tourism: Festival Tourism and Reggae Sunsplash in Jamaica." *Social and Economic Studies* 51, no. 1 (2002): 127-43.

Pattullo, P. *Last Resorts: The Cost of Tourism in the Caribbean.* Kingston: Ian Randle Publishers, 1996.

Pereira, A., Boxill, I. and J. Maerk, eds. *Tourism, Development and Natural Resources in the Caribbean.* Mexico: Plaza y Valdez, 2002.

Poon, A. "Caribbean Tourism and the World Economy." In *Caribbean Economic Development: The First Generation*, edited by S. Lalta and M. Freckleton, 262-79. Kingston: Ian Randle Publishers, 1993.

Ramjee Singh, D. H. "Import Content of Tourism: Explaining Differences among Island States." *Tourism Analysis* 11 (2006): 33-44.

Sharpley, R. and D. J. Telfer, eds. *Tourism and Development: Concepts and Issues.* Clevedon: Channel View Publications, 2002.

Telfer, D. J. "The Evolution of Tourism and Development Theory." In *Tourism and Development: Concepts and Issues*, edited by R. Sharpley and D. J. Telfer, 35-78. Clevedon: Channel View Publications, 2002.

Timothy, D. J. "Tourism and Community Development Issues." In *Tourism and Development: Concepts and Issues*, edited by R. Sharpley and D. J. Telfer, 149-64. Clevedon: Channel View Publications, 2002.

Vaugeios, N. "Tourism in Developing Countries: Refining a Useful Tool for Economic Development." Mimeo, 2003.

World Tourism Organization. *Facts and Figures.* Madrid: UNWTO, various years. http://unwto.org/en

World Travel & Tourism Council. *Tourism Impact Data & Forecast.* London: WTTC, 2002. http://www.wttc.org/eng/Tourism_Research/

PART V

Competitiveness Aspects from Selected Countries

Chapter 14
Competitiveness, Entrepreneurship, and the Business Environment in Greece: Aspects from the EU South

Aristidis Bitzenis, John Marangos, Vasileios A. Vlachos, Nikos Astroulakis, Giorgos Meramveliotakis & Antonis Tsitouras

ABSTRACT

The purpose of this chapter is to determine the competitiveness, exercise of entrepreneurship and quality of the business environment in Greece, based on the analysis of the motives and barriers of inward foreign direct investment (FDI) for the period 1995-2003. The analysis was based on research that was carried out using a questionnaire, which was sent to 150 multinational enterprises (MNEs) that had invested in Greece in the aforementioned period. The sample size consisted of fifty-two MNEs and the response rate was 34.6 percent. According to the questionnaire results, the main motives for FDI in Greece, which is considered as a proxy for the level of entrepreneurship in Greece, were: the prospects for market growth, political stability, economic stability, the size of Greek market, social stability, and the 2004 Olympic Games. The primary barriers to entrepreneurship in the Greek market mentioned by MNEs were bureaucracy, followed by the taxation system, corruption, and the labor market. Government officials and policy makers in Greece, students of economics, in particular, of inter-national development and international business/management, would benefit from this novel approach in determining motives and barriers of FDI in Greece as a proxy for the level of entrepreneurship and, consequently, developing the appropriate policy response with the goal of further stimulating FDI in Greece.

INTRODUCTION

The level of entrepreneurship and the business environment in Greece undoubtedly has been questioned by both domestic and international investors. This is a major concern as the level of entrepreneurship and the business environment in Greece directly influences the level of both foreign and local investments, and thus production, economic growth, unemployment, and living standards. The purpose of this chapter is to determine the level of competitiveness, entrepreneurship, and the business environment in Greece by examining the motives and the barriers that resulted in limited inward foreign direct investment (FDI) in Greece during the period 1995-2003. Our critical analysis is based on research by Bitzenis and Tsitouras (2007a; 2007b) and Bitzenis et al. (2009a; 2009b) that used a questionnaire survey with the participation of fifty-two multinational enterprises (MNEs) that had invested in Greece. Moreover, the project sought to determine whether there is any correlation between the sector within which the MNE operates with the consideration of specific FDI motives and barriers that the foreign firms encountered before or during their investment project in Greece.

The motives and barriers that determine the participation of MNEs in Greece reported in this survey are uncritical indications of entrepreneurship and the level of business environment in Greece. According to our knowledge, on the one hand, while the FDI's contribution to social and economic development in Greece has been analyzed extensively, on the other hand, determining the motives and barriers to entry by MNEs in the Greek market through a questionnaire survey has not been explored. Government officials and policy makers in Greece, students of economics, in particular, of international development and international business/management, would benefit from this novel approach in determining motives and barriers of FDI in Greece as a proxy for the level of entrepreneurship and, consequently, developing the appropriate policy response with the goal of further stimulating FDI in Greece. The chapter wishes to contribute empirically to the economics literature, especially within the context of the international business and entrepreneurship literature, by demonstrating the relevance of theoretical propositions by using Greece as a case study. Greece was chosen as a case study because Athens in Greece was selected as the host city of the 2004 Olympic Games and, within this context, the investment motives and barriers to entry by MNEs using a questionnaire survey have not been investigated in the literature.

The chapter is organized as follows. Section one presents the theoretical issues of the theme. Section two develops the research methodology and design. Section three provides the research findings by tabulating the most important motives and barriers, and further analyzes each motive and barrier in detail. Finally, section four supports the concluding remarks and policy implications.

THEORETICAL ISSUES

Competitiveness as a catchall phrase in the twentieth century has been at the core of the economic analysis. The term, as a comparative concept, can equally refer to microeconomic as well as to macroeconomic analysis. At a microeconomic level the concept deals with the performance of a firm's productivity, while at a macroeconomic level it is concerned with the effectiveness of national productivity. According to Porter (1990: 73), "a nation's competitiveness depends on the capacity of its industry to innovate and upgrade." Particularly, national competitiveness should be analyzed as a function of the business environment, the level of FDI, and the quality of entrepreneurial activity. To our view, the enhancement of competitiveness is strongly correlated with a positive business environment and with a flourishing entrepreneurship. For that reason, the subsequent analysis begins with the inquiry of the entrepreneurship concept.

The origination of the term entrepreneurship traces back to Schumpeter's economic thought. In Schumpeter's view (1934), the entrepreneur is the person who takes the risk to: establish a new organization; introduce a new good or service; create a novel method of production; enter in a new market; and acquire new raw materials to establish a supply chain. Thus, as it has been argued by Bitzenis and Nito (2005), and Howorth et al. (2005), an entrepreneur can be an innovator, a risk taker, a person who operates resources, recognizes opportunities, and establishes one or more businesses. An entrepreneur also develops, builds and sustains a business based on new ideas, maximizes benefits and profits, and meets personal objectives (Hayek 1937; Schumpeter 1950; von Mises 1963; Knight 1971; Kirzner 1973; Ritchie and Brindley 2005).

In the last twenty years, the idea of entrepreneurship has become the fundamental bedrock in understanding the evolution of economic development. Indeed, current economic scholars, such as Gartner (1988), Jarilo (1989) and Wiklund and Shepherd (2005), regard entrepreneurship as one of the driving forces of economic growth. It is, therefore, important to stimulate competitiveness through entrepreneurship and a positive business environment via the formation and expansion of commercial businesses and enterprises, which can play a key role in employing underused resources for the creation of wealth.

In this vein, the Greek case is coming to the forefront. The purpose of this section is to display a picture of the literature concerning the state of competitiveness and entrepreneurship in Greece which influences the Greek business environment. The following surveys approach the notion of entrepreneurship in terms of market structure, organizational form of firms, and behavioral pattern of the entrepreneur, and apply a number of factors that affect competitiveness, the exercise of entrepreneurship, and the development of an optimistic business environment. The methodology that is adopted encompasses the common methods of statistical analysis, questionnaires and interviews. More or less, all the surveys discover that the socioeconomic environment in Greece does not encourage advance of entrepreneurial activities, negatively influencing competitiveness and the business environment and thus numerous economic and policy implications are derived.

To embark on our analysis, a historical retrospection of Greek industrial development aspects of competitiveness is required. According to Giannitsis (1988: 17-38), there were three crucial factors that determined the degree of Greek industrial development from the end of World War II to the early 1980s: firstly, the way that accumulation of capital took place; secondly, the integration of the Greek market into international markets; and thirdly, governmental functions and policies. Regarding the first, the accumulation of capital in the manufacturing field was relatively low. Indicatively, during the period of 1960-76, investments at the manufacturing field represent the lowest proportion in terms of GDP among OECD countries. Additionally, domestic entrepreneurs were focusing on more speculative investments instead of developing a sustainable productive industrial model. What is striking is that the rate of industrial development during this period was based mainly on FDI and foreign technology rather than on endogenous (domestic) productive forces. Moreover, the association of the inward-looking character of FDI (not export oriented) and the parallel rise of a westernized consumption model created large deficits to the balance of payments. At the same time, the substitution of market functions continually by government intervention established an unproductive and costly bureaucracy which had significant negative effects on Greek competitiveness.

For the subsequent decades, 1980s-2000s, the entrance of Greece to the European Union (EU) and to EU's Economic and Monetary Union (EMU), as well as the introduction of the single currency Euro was considered a historical opportunity for the Greek economy to overcome structural weaknesses and to be adjusted to the contemporary needs of international competition and globalization. However, the course of events did not confirm the above expectations. Regarding the business environment, a twofold effect has been in progress. On the one hand, the Greek business environment has become more stable and secure via the monitoring of EU institutions and organizations (EU Central Bank, Euro, European directives). On the other, through the openness and internationalization of the Greek market, as a part of the European market, the business environment has been exposed to more risky and hazardous conditions of globalized exchanges.

As the public sector has always been the major employer in Greece, the primary concern is whether the restrictions on public spending imposed by the Stability and Growth Pact (SGP) are able to affect growth. The cessation of any negative effects of public investment spending on private investment as an indirect effect of the SGP, the constant effort for privatization and deregulation, and the aid of structural funds, were and are still expected to substitute public investment with private, domestic and foreign, direct investment (Apergis 2000; Mamatzakis 2007). This change of direction in the organization of the Greek economy is the result of the assumption that EMU membership implies greater FDI inflows. Studies indicate that after the introduction of the Euro, the FDI that reached the Euro area was largely a manifestation of the end-of-century takeover boom, a global phenomenon of which the Euro was only a subsidiary cause. Even though the intra-Euro area FDI turned out to be weak, both in relation to previous trends and as a share of major economies' global FDI flows, the Euro appears to have given a modest stimulus to inflows from major investing economies outside the Euro area (Petroulas 2007; Taylor 2008).

The scope of EMU is economic competitiveness and flexibility to be accompanied by greater opportunities and stronger social cohesion. Greece, Ireland, Italy, Portugal, the Netherlands, and Spain experienced a significant decline in their competitiveness position *vis-a-vis* the rest of the Euro area. With the exception of the Netherlands, all countries in this group were still on an appreciation trajectory at the end of 2007, regarding the improvement of their competitiveness position (European Commission 2008).

The implementation of a number of structural policies are required in order to improve Greece's long-term economic performance and help speed economic and social convergence with average EU member countries: more flexible and effective labor market policies; competition policy reform; the liberalization of product markets, in particular the energy, telecommunication, and transport sectors; policies to foster entrepreneurship; and financial market reform, including the implementation of a better corporate governance regime. These areas are particularly important for rapid growth as they offer substantial scope for catching up with international levels of competitiveness (Koutsogeorgopoulou and Ziegelschmidt 2005).

Export market share losses appear associated with rigidities in resource allocation (sectoral, geographical, technological) relative to peers and lower productivity gains in high value-added sectors. Increased import penetration, offshoring and FDI could improve productivity and export performance (Bennett et al. 2008). Changes in manufacturing shares have a positive and significant impact on competitiveness measured by per capita income, confirming that manufacturing matters (Pitelis and Antonakis 2003).

Significant empirical research has also been carried out in three Greek national reports, Ioannidis (2004), Ioannidis, Politis and Tsakanikas (2005), and Ioannidis and Tsakanikas (2006)—all supported by the Foundation for Economic and Industrial Research (IOBE), published by the Global Entrepreneurship Monitor (GEM). These reports use a number of methodological tools for the monitoring and evaluation of policies and actions toward the promotion of competitiveness, entrepreneurship, and a positive business environment. The research output is derived from adult population surveys, questionnaires, face to face interviews, and macroeconomic data. Specifically, the data is collected from a population telephone survey (approximately 2,000 people), and also from thirty-six interviews with the country's experts and with the help of statistical data received from the World Bank, the IMF, Eurostat, the United Nations (UN), and the Organization of Economic Co-operation and Development (OECD) (Ioannidis 2004: 4; Ioannidis, Politis and Tsakanikas 2005: 110; Ioannidis and Tsakanikas 2006: 136).

With the aforementioned methodological approaches, the reports attempt to describe the entrepreneurial landscape of Greece and, thus, the prevailing business environment. Therefore, these studies capture a holistic approach to the study of competitiveness, entrepreneurship, and provide a variety of factors determining the level of entrepreneurial activity and the business environment. As a result, a framework of nine conditions was employed in order to analyze the structure of the Greek entrepreneurial environment. These were: the financial support (the ability to finance a new venture or to extend an already existing entrepreneurial activity), government policies (the extent to which the specific policies encourage or discourage new and growing firms), government programs (specialized programs for the enhancement of national, regional, and municipal entrepreneurship), education and training (how the educational level is associated with more intense entrepreneurial activity), research and development (R&D) transfers (whether or not R&D leads to new commercial opportunities), commercial and professional infrastructure (the legal and institutional framework for the promotion of entrepreneurship), market openness-barriers to entry (the degree of liberalization of the market), access to physical infrastructure (the facility to obtain physical resources, utilities, transportation, land, etc. for operating a new venture) and cultural and social norms (the extent to which the overall informal institutional structure of the society advances individual initiatives of conducting business) (Ioannidis 2004: 6-8; Ioannidis, Politis and Tsakanikas 2005: 106-9; Ioannidis and Tsakanikas 2006: 133-35).

The key conclusions of the three Greek national reports and the proposals concerning the development of competitiveness, entrepreneurship, and a positive business environment in Greece can be summarized as follows. The Europeanization and globalization of the Greek economy and particularly the entry to the EMU constitute the contemporary economic environment where entrepreneurs are activated. However, the structure of Greek entrepreneurship in terms of sectoral distribution appears to be vastly different from the counter-structure of entrepreneurship in many other European countries. As Ioannidis and Tsakanikas (2006: 39-42) remark, Greek entrepreneurs continue to be overwhelmingly focused on consumer-oriented endeavors. These activities represent 61.4 percent of the whole entrepreneurial actions in Greece, in contrast to 34.2 percent of Europe's average. The inference is of a "shallow entrepreneurship" since businesses based mostly on the consumer sector (contrary to the extractive sector, industrial sector, or business services) are anticipated to have limited effect in terms of economic growth, employment, exports, etc. This is because an entrepreneurial activity centered mostly on the consumer sector is related with the last link of the "value chain" that is the final consumer and thus has rather limited growth potential.

Furthermore, competitiveness and entrepreneurship in Greece present inherent structural weaknesses attributed to specific behavioral traits and to prevailing socio-political conditions creating a negative business environment. Related to the former, Ioannidis, Politis and Tsakanikas (2005: 80) stress as the determinant behavioral trait the "fear of failure factor" that discourages individuals to start up an entrepreneurial activity. As a result, less innovative and less risky ventures actually take place in the economy, thus negatively affecting the business environment. In addition, Ioannidis, Politis and Tsakanikas (2005: 81) and Ioannidis and Tsakanikas (2006: x-xi), also record the ambiguous attitude of Greek society toward the notion of entrepreneurship. Although individuals consider entrepreneurship as a desirable career choice (i.e., high level of status and respect for entrepreneurs), on the other hand, due to the fact that the notion of entrepreneurship is considered as a means of wealth creation rather than as a means of redistribution (i.e., individuals detest disparities in income levels preferring that everyone had a similar standard of living), there is the belief that entrepreneurship is valueless in terms of social justice creating in this way a negative business environment. Regarding the prevailing socio-political conditions, Ioannidis and Tsakanikas highlight bureaucracy (2006: 112-13) and the educational system (2006: x) as the most severe barriers in the promotion of entrepreneurial activities. Specifically, in Greece, the "monster" of bureaucracy generates considerable rigidities for starting up a new business. As well, the educational system does not provide sufficient practical skills to graduates required to start-up a business.

In the end, the three national reports recommend the necessary policy implications for the enhancement of competitiveness, entrepreneurial activity, and creating a positive business environment. What is proposed is in line with the aforementioned problems. Thus, some of the suggestions are to diminish the barriers that prevent the establishment of businesses and to implement uncomplicated procedures for starting up a venture. Aiming to encourage individuals to take the risk by initiating a new business, bankruptcy laws should be modified in the direction of allowing the entrepreneur a second chance, consequently enhancing the business environment. Moreover, Greece has to "update" the educational system to encourage universities to develop an entrepreneurial culture, thus stimulating a positive business environment. Eventually, an ultimate suggestion for embedding the idea of entrepreneurship in Greek society is to promote its positive effects (Ioannidis 2004: iv-vi; Ioannidis, Politis and Tsakanikas 2005: 100; Ioannidis and Tsakanikas 2006: 112-25). As is evident, the above national reports adopt a wide approach, exhibiting a panorama of the current entrepreneurial activities in Greece. Meanwhile, the following surveys deal with competitiveness, the concept of entrepreneurship, and the business environment by focusing on more specific aspects.

Souitaris (2002) espoused a Schumpeterian view by emphasizing the role of innovation. The author was concerned about identifying the determinant factors that influenced the intensity of the innovation process in Greece. Especially, Souitaris (2002) attempted to estimate the correlation between seventeen firm-specific competency factors with the technological innovation in the Greek industry and attempted to elucidate the results by providing the particular socio-economic context of Greece. For that reason, he developed a four-dimensional framework associating market, human resources, and technical and organizational competencies of the firm with innovation activity (Souitaris 2002: 63-66). The author identified seventeen innovation-determining factors (which range from intensity of R&D and the strength in marketing, to interdepartmental teamwork, and the thinking time of engineers and managers) and ranked them into "major importance," "moderate importance," and "unimportant" categories by using a regression analysis. The "most important" were identified as the intensity of R&D, the proportion of the highly educated employees, the strength in marketing, the high proportion of staff with managerial responsibilities and previous experience, and the ability of the firm to give incentives to the employees to contribute to innovation (Souitaris 2002: 68-70). His aim was to test the "awareness" of Greek managers with the aforementioned "objective" results. In other words, Souitaris (2002) investigated whether Greek managers are generally aware of the important firm-specific competencies advancing technological innovation. Using a questionnaire (having a 100 percent response rate of 105 firms), he concluded that with a few exceptions, Greek managers were very well aware of the critical factors that determined the level of a firm's innovation (Souitaris 2002: 71-72).

Given these findings, Souitaris purported to determine the extent to which the business environment accelerated the intensity of innovation and thus enhanced the business environment. He revealed that the most critical determinants of technological innovation were generally scarce in the Greek case. Greek SMEs, with low financial resources, were weak in the promotion of their products. The educational system was characterized as "outdated" and the result was that firms were staffed with low quality graduates. Additionally, low labor mobility in Greece implied a low proportion of managers and employees with previous work experience. Besides, Greek entrepreneurs were usually reluctant to allocate responsibilities when their businesses grew and, as a consequence, there was a low proportion of staff with managerial responsibilities. As well, Greek firms did not give incentives to the lower level employees to contribute to the innovation process (Souitaris 2002: 72). The conclusion was that these inherent rigidities and obstacles did not stimulate the innovation process and thus did not promote entrepreneurial initiatives and/or a positive business environment.

Drawing upon the experience of the function of Greek firms, Makridakis et al. (1997) offered a different perspective in the study of entrepreneurship. They attempted to appraise the level of entrepreneurship under the view of what the authors labeled as the "dualism" of firms: the spectrum possessing in one pole the family-owned enterprises and, to other extreme, the multinational subsidiaries (Makridakis et al. 1997: 385-88). Using the ordinary methods of questionnaires and interviews (300 out of 2,027 firms responded), they investigated if there was any difference in the performance between the family-owned firms and multinational subsidiaries. Family-owned enterprises are administrated by Chief Executive Officers (CEOs), who are usually the owners, founders, or descendants, contrasting to the CEOs in multinational subsidiaries, who are professional managers with international experience. The upshot is that the productivity and overall performance of the former lags considerably behind the latter. Given the above and taking into consideration that family-owned enterprises mainly typify the majority of firms in Greece, a deficit in the level of entrepreneurship in Greece is demonstrated (Makridakis et al. 1997: 399). Accordingly, the conclusion is straightforward as authors mainly assign the weakness of Greek entrepreneurship and the negative business environment to the managerial skills of the person who manages the family-owned company, who is uneducated, autocratic, and paternalist contrary to well-educated and cosmopolitan professional CEOs of multinational subsidiaries.

In contrast, Naumes and Naumes (1994) argued that the profile of professional Greek CEOs was not too different from that of American CEOs. Looking at similarities and differences in the behavioral patterns of Greek and American entrepreneurs, the authors discerned a more or less similar mode of decision-making. Particularly, the results, obtained from 398 questionnaires (including 381 responses from U.S. entrepreneurs and 17 replies from Greek CEOs), indicate that the risk propensity is similar between the two groups. In addition, it is asserted that the Greek and U.S. entrepreneurs' economic and political values are also consistent. The outcome is that both groups share in a same manner of decision-making, achieving their objectives in a rational and self-interested fashion. What is interesting is that Naumes and Naumes (1994: 10-11) argued that the above similarities tend to moderate the effects drawing from their cultural disparities. On the other hand, Kalantaridis' (1997) endeavor was toward the opposite direction. He attempted to demonstrate how cultural homogeneity and local social factors prompt entrepreneurial activities and quality of the business environment. Using a historical and social analysis, he pointed out that the embeddedness of entrepreneurship in small communities was not only determined by strictly market conditions and profit opportunities, but was also influenced by the presence of local social values. Based upon the experience of the Polikastro-Peonia's garment producing district of Northern Greece, he argued that the establishment and advancement of entrepreneurial activities and a positive business environment in this area can be traced also to the close relationships of kin and friendship that have been primarily attributed to locality.

In preparation for our analysis, we have attempted in this section to outline the main literature concerning the state of Greek competitiveness, entrepreneurship, and business environment. From a methodological and analytical viewpoint, it could be argued that the majority of the aforementioned literature shares a common perspective: the analysis of competitiveness, entrepreneurship, and the business environment from an "inside" perspective. This approach deals with competitiveness, entrepreneurship, and the business environment based on internal market conditions by domestic players. This means that only domestic players and factors are taken into examination, constituting a "narrow" point of view. However, the intensity of the globalization process imposes the embodiment of "foreign" factors and thereby the adopting of an "outside" approach for the study of competitiveness, entrepreneurship, and the business environment. In other words, what follows is an attempt to enrich and incorporate factors of global competition in the appreciation of Greek entrepreneurship and the business environment concomitantly. The aforementioned reports describe the influence of the local environment on domestic entrepreneurship. These reports and their results may not be directly applicable to MNEs, as MNEs differ in the way that the investment decision-making is influenced by the local business environment.

For the aforementioned reasons, inward FDI as an additional factor determining competitiveness, entrepreneurial activity, and the business environment is introduced. The aim of the current research is to determine the level of competitiveness, entrepreneurship, and the business environment in Greece by examining the motives and the barriers that resulted in limited inward FDI during the period 1995-2003. Previous studies concerning FDI inflows in Greece focused on FDI attractiveness and highlighted inefficient public governance, high taxation, inefficient infrastructure, and general macroeconomic conditions as the decisive factors of foreign investors' averseness (Apergis and Katrakylidis 1998; Filippaios and Kottaridi 2004; Pantelidis and Nikolopoulos 2008). No more than two references exist on the determination of motives for inward FDI in Greece. The work of Georgopoulos and Preusse (2006) indicates Greece's inability to attract considerable market-seeking, export-oriented, and efficiency-seeking FDI due to location weaknesses. Pantelidis and Nikolopoulos (2008) imply in their study that the primary FDI inflows to the Greek economy are market and efficiency-seeking motives for FDI.

RESEARCH METHODOLOGY AND DESIGN

Bitzenis and Tsitouras (2007a; 2007b) and Bitzenis et al. (2009a; 2009b) designed a questionnaire to extract valuable information regarding the determinants of FDI, that is, the motivations and entry barriers for inward FDI in Greece that resulted in limited inward FDI during the period 1995-2003, as demonstrated in Table 14.1.

TABLE 14.1
FDI Inflows in Greece, 1970-2003 (in millions of US$)

Year	FDI Inflow ($ millions)	% Change of Previous Period	Year	FDI Inflow ($ millions)	% Change of Previous Period
1970	7		1987	39	2
1971	8		1988	59	5
1972	9		1989	63	
1973	14	6	1990	90	4
1974	18	3	1991	1,13	2

1975	19		1992	1,14	
1976	22	1	1993	97	-1
1977	27	2	1994	98	
1978	32	1	1995	105	
1979	36	1	1996	1,05	
1980	50	3	1997	98	-
1981	40	-1	1998	8	-9
1982	30	-2	1999	57	57
1983	31		2000	1,08	9
1984	24	-2	2001	1,58	4
1985	28	1	2002	5	-9
1986	30		2003	4	-

Source: Bank of Greece, various years; UNCTAD 2003, 2004.

The importance of FDI, reflecting the level of competitiveness, entrepreneurship, and the business environment in the European Union (EU), has increased significantly over the years as indicated by the ratio of FDI inward stock to GDP, which has risen from 10.6 percent in 1990 to 31 percent in 2001. Also, an increasing share of FDI flows worldwide has been absorbed by the EU, which, to a great extent, coincides with the Single Market Program (SMP). Greece, however, has not followed similar patterns in terms of FDI inflows reflecting the level of competitiveness and entrepreneurship and the negative, to some extent, business environment. In general, the share of Greece in total FDI inflows to the EU has not exceeded 1.0%, which is the lowest among the member states (UNCTAD 2003). At the end of 2002, according to UNCTAD (2004), 701 foreign MNEs operated in Greece with a number of 87,558 employees (2 percent approximately, of the total employees of Greece) and sales of $20,489 billion. Worse still is the fact that the share of Greece in total FDI in the EU has continued to fall since the 1990s, because of Greece's poor location, negative business climate, and weak skills base (EIU 2004). Athens was chosen as the host city of the Olympic Games of 2004 during the 106th IOC Session held in Lausanne on September 5, 1997. Academic/scientific literature suggests that hosting major sporting events has a positive contribution to the host area economy, expecting a boost in infrastructure, financial flows, and economic development (Berman et al. 2000; Veraros et al. 2004). This announcement can be considered as one of the most decisive factors responsible for the FDI boom that took place in Greece in the time period after the announcement and before the conduct of the Olympic Games of 2004. Thus, in the time period 1999-2001 Greece received more than US$3 billion.

The application of a logit or probit model would be appropriate for the examination of such data (Salavrakos and Petrochilos 2003). If this was the case, the dependent variable in this study would represent only foreign enterprises investing directly in Greece, leading to a biased outcome. Instead, descriptive statistics are employed, keeping in mind that Holland et al. (2000) concluded that econometric evidence supports the findings of survey studies.

The questionnaires of the survey reported in this chapter were collected between June and September of 2004. The construction of the three-part questionnaire was mainly based on Dunning's (1988; 1993) theory, the eclectic theory (OLI—eclectic paradigm of international production), although the Universal model was also used (Bitzenis 2003). The questionnaire used in the research study consisted of three parts. In the first part, the questions provided the necessary background information on certain issues that were considered important in characterizing the sample population. In the second part, one question included seven groups of sub-questions with related factors that were considered to be of major importance and allowed the managers of the enterprises to select the most appropriate answer for their case. These groups of sub-questions were initially selected based on Dunning's OLI theory, but necessary amendments were made using the Universal model (Bitzenis 2003).

Therefore, in the second part of the questionnaire, seven groups of hunters (seekers) have been created: locational hunters (historical links, cultural closeness or distance, geographical proximity, stability, climate etc.), factor hunters or natural resource hunters (access to low cost of acquiring natural resources and raw materials [Dunning 1988: 13]), market hunters (size of the market, prospects for market growth, increasing market share), strategic market hunters (follow the competition, follow the clients, a way to survive, acquiring of assets, international pressures, globalization etc.), efficiency hunters (economies of scale, of scope, risk diversification), exploiting the ownership advantages hunters (brand name, know-how, past experience, existing business links etc.), and hunters of financial aspects (favorable investment law framework, subsidies, tax exemptions).

In the third part, there are twenty entry barriers (instability, bureaucracy, corruption, unstable legal system, etc.). In accordance with Dunning (1998; 1993), we have included in our survey: the Locational (L) (natural resources availability and cost, investment incentives, characteristics of the country—language, culture...), Internalization (I) (avoid costs, control supplies, avoid or exploit government intervention), and Ownership advantages (O) (intangible asset advantages, product innovations, know-how, multinationality). Dunning (1993; 1988) also defines natural resource seeking (vertical integration, availability, cost), market seeking (market size and characteristics, investment incentives [Dunning 1993: 82]), efficiency seeking (economies of scale and scope, risk reduction through product diversification [Dunning 1988: 13]) and strategic asset seeking (gain new product lines or markets, economies of synergy, economies of common governance, improved competitive or strategic advantage, reduce or spread risks [Dunning 1993: 82]).

A descriptive/analytical type of research was undertaken, as it was best suited for the research objectives examined. The sample was determined on a quota basis (non random selection) involving the selection of subjects based on the identification of specific characteristics to increase representativeness. In quota sampling, the target population is divided into subgroups on the basis of different characteristics. In the case of this survey, the subgroups were: the companies from different types of industries, the volume of investments, and the number of employees, then a quota was determined for each subgroup. Thus, based on the criterion of the largest investment deals in Greece, a quota was made with the help of a few official documents whichwere retrieved from the Hellenic Center for Investment (ELKE) consisting of 101 foreign companies. Another forty-nine companies were added from the authors' research from directories of various Chambers of Commerce and Industry as well as embassies. As a result, a final list of 150 foreign companies was developed. The aim of this chapter is to analyze and to draw conclusions regarding the motives and barriers of FDI during the period 1995-2003 as indicators of entrepreneurship and the business environment in Greece.

To determine the most appropriate sample and sampling technique, the authors took into consideration the aim of the current study, which was to identify the motives and barriers that foreign firms had evaluated when they decided to invest in Greece as indicators of entrepreneurship and the business environment. Bitzenis and Tsitouras (2007a; 2007b) and Bitzenis et al. (2009a; 2009b) chose to adopt the non-probability sampling method, using the technique of purposive sample. This strategy was considered the most appropriate because the questions contained within the questionnaire required the views of people who were or would have been involved in the examination of Greek business factors/conditions that was FDI motives/obstacles.

Furthermore, it was investigated whether there was any relation of the sector that each MNE belonged to in determining the specific motives and barriers that encouraged or discouraged MNEs to undertake FDI projects in Greece. Thus, it was necessary for Bitzenis and Tsitouras (2007a; 2007b) and Bitzenis et al. (2009a; 2009b) to have a proportional distribution of MNEs in the field of economic activity. Finally, the survey instrument was pre-tested by interviews with three managers of MNEs. The overall aim of this study was to identify the kind and the type of incentives and barriers that foreign firms considered in order to decide whether they should make an investment in Greece. The study went beyond the simple description of events, and sought to find answers to all reasonable queries. Subsequently, the level of FDI determined, to a great extent, the aspect of Greek economic competitiveness.

Fifty-two out of 150 MNEs responded, which equates to a response rate of 34.6 percent. Literature has shown that this response rate in the subject area is sufficient and, according to statistics, a response rate of 10 percent of the population of interest is regarded as big enough to allow secure inferences about the population of interest. The usual way of replying to questionnaires, via mail, was extremely low in this study. Only 5.78 percent of the companies replied in this way. The highest yield was the result of email or internet websites with 57.69 percent of the total response rate, followed by fax and telephone with 28.84 percent. The one to one interviews had success in 7.69 percent of the total response rate (see Figure 14.1).

The sample is representative because there is a proportional distribution of MNEs in various sectors of economic activities. The industrial sector accounted for 53.84 percent (Mining 5.77 percent + Manufacturing 40.38 percent + Construction 7.69 percent, see Figure 14.2), while the FDI inflows in Greece in the same sector and at the same period were 52.69 percent (Mining 5.04 percent + Manufacturing 44.10 percent + Construction 3.55 percent). Furthermore, the trade sector in the survey questionnaire accounted for 25 percent of respondents, while the FDI inflows in Greece in the same sector were 11.53 percent. Finally the responses from the services sector accounted for 21.16 percent (Transportation & Communication 7.69 percent + Leasing/Real Estate 5.77 percent + Hotels 3.85 percent), while the FDI inflows in Greece in the same sector and at the same period were 35.78 percent

(Transportation & Communication 21.51 percent + Leasing/Real Estate 4.19 percent + Hotels 10.08 percent) (see Figure 14.2).

The total investment amount for the fifty-two foreign companies was US$ 1,465,022,000 which is 29.90 percent of the total Greek FDI inflows (US$ 5,051,800,000) during the period 1995-2003. The majority of respondents invested between US$ 25 and US$ 50 million (41.38 percent) in Greece, followed by foreign investors that invested between US$ 50 and US$ 100 million (33.69 percent). A significant number of respondents (20.16 percent) invested between US$ 1 and US$ 25 million (see Figure 14.3).

In administering the survey, particular attention was directed toward ensuring that individual survey respondents were equipped to represent the position of the company as a whole. About one third of respondents held a top position such as Chief Executive Officer, President, Chief Financial Officer, or Chairman, and nearly all other respondents held senior management posts, and/or were involved directly in strategic planning (see Figure 14.4).

FIGURE 14.1
Method of Reply of Respondents

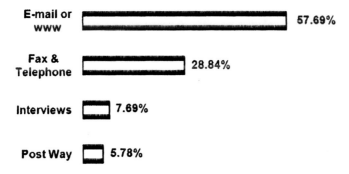

FIGURE 14.2
Respondents by Industry in Percent

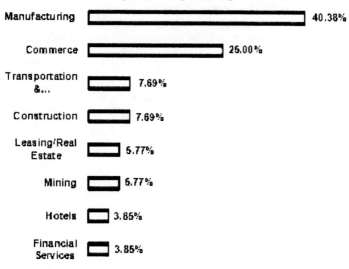

Manufacturing	40.38%
Commerce	25.00%
Transportation &...	7.69%
Construction	7.69%
Leasing/Real Estate	5.77%
Mining	5.77%
Hotels	3.85%
Financial Services	3.85%

FIGURE 14.3
Respondents by Amount of Investment in Million US$

Under 1 million US$	4.77%
1 million to 25 million US$	20.16%
25 to 50 million US$	41.38%
50 to 100 million US$	33.69%
Above 100 million US$	4.77%

FIGURE 14.4
Positions Held by Individual Respondents in Percent

RESEARCH FINDINGS: MOTIVES AND BARRIERS
OF FDI IN GREECE

The statistical literature has shown that the response rate, 34.6 percent is sufficient to allow secure inferences about the population of interest. The managers that were surveyed were asked to mention any number of motives and barriers that they considered to be the most decisive for their company in undertaking an FDI project in Greece. Therefore, the sum of the per-centages found in the Tables is not equal to 100 percent. From Table 14.2, it can be pointed out that the main motives for FDI in Greece reflecting the entrepreneurship and the business environment in the Greek market were the prospects for market growth (86 percent), political stability (78 percent), economic stability (77 percent), the size of the Greek market (61 percent), social stability (59 percent), and the Olympic Games 2004 (58 percent).

TABLE 14.2
The Most Important Motives for FDI in Greece

Motives	Percentage of Respondents	Sector Relevance
Prospects for Market Growth	86.50	No
Political Stability	78.80	No
Economic Stability	76.90	No
Size of Greek Market	61.50	Yes
Social Stability	59.60	No
Olympics Games 2004	57.70	No

Source: Authors' questionnaire results.

From Table 14.2 it is revealed that the prospects for market growth ranks first at 86.5 percent; it received 61.5 percent of the positive responses. MNEs from all sectors that considered Greece as a promising market responded positively. All multinationals belonging to the banking/services sector argued that this is an important motive, while 92.3 percent of MNEs operating in the trade and food industry and 78.6 percent in the industrial/ manufacturing sector also determined that this was an important motive. Thus, the sector within which the MNE operates does not influence this motive. Although Greece is not a big market, this high percentage in considering the prospects for market growth as a decisive motive is mainly due to the preparation of the Olympic Games. From Table 14.1, we can see that this is the case. The "Host to the Olympics 2004 in Greece" as an FDI motive was mentioned by 57.7 percent of MNEs. It is also worth pointing out that the MNEs that mentioned the FDI motive, prospects for market growth, as significant also considered "Host to the Olympics 2004 in Greece" as a motive for FDI in 90 percent of the cases. It is obvious that the tremendous infrastructure investments, which took place prior to the Athens 2004 Olympics, will provide a solid platform for future market growth. These findings are consistent with the Ioannidis and Tsakanikas (2006: 39-42) conclusion that Greek entrepreneurs focus on consumer-oriented endeavors. It appears that FDI in Greece during the period of investigation is also consumer-oriented, especially due to the hosting of the Olympics 2004, which created a positive business environment for increasing final consumption.

The existence of the combined motive "Economic and Political Stability" in the second and third place was an expected outcome since Greece has been the only member country in the EU region since 1981 and until May 2004, and a full member of the Eurozone as of January 2001. Greece has undergone extensive restructuring, enough to secure, at least, a nominal convergence with its European Union partners. Political stability as a motive to enter the Greek market received 78.8 percent positive responses. Regarding the sectors to which each MNE belongs, 75 percent from manufacturing sector, 84.6 percent from trade and food sector, and 81.8 percent from banking/services sector argued that political stability was a significant motive. Thus, the sector within which the MNE belongs does not influence the political stability motive. With regard to economic stability as a motive, it received a positive response of 77 percent; again the sector in which the MNE operates does not influence this motive: 75 percent from the industrial/ manufacturing sector, 84.6 percent from the trade/food sector, and 72.7 per-cent from the banking/services sector argued that political stability was a significant motive. Therefore, the aforementioned finding in connection with Naumes and Naumes' (1994) deduction that Greek and U.S. entrepreneurs share quite similar economic and political values, could provide a rationale for the fact that the majority of FDI in Greece is originated in the United States. Another reason may be due the fact that a lot of Greeks migrate to the United States and as a result there is a strong Greek community in the United States establishing trade relations between the United States and Greece.

Of the fifty-two multinationals that responded to the survey, thirty-two (61.5 percent) argued that the size of the Greek market is an important motive. Regarding the sectors to which each MNE belongs, 42.9 percent from the industrial/manufacturing sector, 92.3 percent from the trade/food sector, and 72.7 percent from the banking/services sector argued that it was a significant motive to enter the Greek market. Thus, it appears that the sector within which the MNE operates influences the significance of this motive. The size of the Greek market (around eleven million possible consumers) is more important mainly for the MNEs in the trade/

food sector and the services sector than for other sectors such as the industrial or the manufacturing sector due to the proximity of these sectors to consumers. Hence, in addition to Ioannidis and Tsakanikas' (2006: 39-42) inference that the Greek entrepreneurs mainly focus on consumer-oriented activities, it is also deduced that FDI in Greece is consumer-oriented. Furthermore, FDI is inward-looking and the subsequent inward technology has as the result the shortage of Greek technological innovations. This means that Greece has been a "consumer" rather than a "producer" of R&D and technology, with profound negative implications for Greek industrial development and competitiveness.

Social stability as a motive to enter the Greek market received a 59.6 percent positive response. There is no impact of the specific sector that the MNEs operate, as 53.6 percent from industrial/manufacturing sector, 61.5 percent from trade/food sector, and 72.7 percent from banking/services sector argued that social stability is an important motive. This finding is consistent with Kalantaridis (1997) that social values and hence social stability enhance entrepreneurship and stimulate an optimistic business environment.

The decision that Greece would host the 2004 Olympics was announced in 1997. This decision encouraged many multinationals to enter the Greek market prior to the 2004 Olympics. At the same time, the findings from the questionnaire reveal that 57.7 percent of MNEs considered the Olympics as an important FDI motive. Olympics 2004 created numerous opportunities for foreign companies in the field of security, transportation, construction, catering, etc. The companies from the various sectors that responded positively have seen more or less this motive in the same way. So, the sector that each multinational belongs to was indifferent in the consideration of this motive as a decisive FDI motive. 53.6 percent of multinationals from the industrial/manufacturing sector, 61.5 percent multinationals from the trade/ food sector, and 63.6 percent multinationals from the services/banking sector considered this motive as vital. This re-confirms, in addition to Ioannidis and Tsakanikas' (2006: 39-42) characterization of the Greek entrepreneurship as "shallow," the above assertion that FDI in Greece is also consumer-oriented.

The primary barriers with which investors had to deal, reflecting entrepreneurship and the business environment in the Greek market, is shown in Table 14.3. The biggest obstacle was bureaucracy (86.53 percent), followed by the taxation system (71.15 percent), corruption (65.78 percent), high corporate tax (63.46 percent), the labor market (61.53 percent), and the legal system (55.76 percent). In the following, we analyze each motive and barrier in detail and discuss the studies analyzed in the literature review under a comparative/critical perspective with the goals of the current study.

The high percentage of 86.5 percent of the surveyed companies mentioned bureaucracy as an important barrier for their FDI in Greece negatively affecting entrepreneurship and the business environment (Table 14.3), which is consistent with Ioannidis and Tsakanikas (2006: 112-13). Using the survey, we found that the sector that each MNE belongs to does not play a significant role in the consideration of bureaucracy as a barrier for FDI. In other words, 85.7 percent of MNEs of the industrial/manufacturing sector, 100 percent of the services sector, and 76.9 percent of the trade/food sector looked upon bureaucracy as a decisive FDI barrier. These are extremely high percentages. Also, the high percentage of 71 percent of the surveyed companies mentioned the Greek tax system as an important barrier for their investment in Greece negatively affecting entrepreneurship and the business environment. The sector that each MNE belongs to does not play any role whatsoever in the consideration of the Greek tax system as a barrier. In other words, 75 percent of MNEs of the industrial/manufacturing sector, 69.2 percent of MNEs of the trade/food sector, and 63.6 percent of MNEs of the services/banking sector recognized the Greek tax system as a decisive FDI barrier. These percentages are indeed very high.

TABLE 14.3
The Most Important Barriers to FDI in Greece

Barriers	Percentage of Respondents	Sector Relevance
Bureaucracy	86.53	No
Taxation System	71.15	No
Corruption	65.78	Yes
Corporate Tax	63.46	Yes
Labor Market	61.53	No
Legal System	55.76	Yes

Source: Authors' questionnaire results.

From the questionnaire responses we note that 65.78 percent of the total foreign MNEs listed corruption, bribery or other illegal actions as important obstacles for their FDI projects in Greece negatively affecting entrepreneurship and the business environment: 78.6 percent foreign MNEs from the industrial/manufacturing sector and 76.9 percent MNEs from the trade/food sector saw corruption as an important FDI barrier. However, only 18.2 percent of the services and banking companies were affected negatively by corruption. Thus, it can be argued that the sector that each MNE belongs to plays a decisive role in the consideration of corruption as an FDI barrier. It appears that banking/services sector is not affected easily by corruption as the regulatory framework is mostly determined by the European Commission, the European Central Bank (ECB) and, in general, the Economic and Monetary Union (EMU) since in 2001 Greece became an EMU member and adopted the Euro as its national currency.

A possible solution to the problems of corruption and the ambiguous attitude of Greeks toward entrepreneurship (Ioannidis, Politis and Tsakanikas 2005: 81; Ioannidis and Tsakanikas 2006: x-xi) could be to combat bureaucracy by diminishing the considerable rigidities for starting up a new business, and the modernization of the educational system concomitantly. Regarding the latter, the modernization of the educational system provides practical skills to graduates, cultivates an entrepreneurial culture and, consequently, leads to the embeddedness of entrepreneurship in the Greek society (Ioannidis 2004: iv-vi; Ioannidis, Politis and Tsakanikas 2005: 100; Ioannidis and Tsakanikas 2006: 112-25; Souitaris 2002; Makridakis et.al. 1997). Moreover, the fight against corruption could be realized via the rationalization of bureaucratic *modus operandi*. Simplifying and facilitating the procedures of starting up a business leads to lower transaction costs and therefore enhances the efficiency of the business environment. Hence, it diminishes the reasons for corruption.

Moreover, from the total MNEs that were surveyed, 63.5 percent perceived the corporate tax as a barrier, thus negatively affecting entrepreneurship and the business environment. The examination of the high corporation taxation rate as an FDI barrier based on the sector that each multinational belongs to, reveals that there is a difference in the consideration of this barrier on the basis of sectors. Regarding the sectors that each MNE belongs to, 64.3 percent from the industrial/manufacturing sector, 76.9 percent from the trade/food sector, and 45.5 percent from the banking/services sector argued that the corporate tax was a significant barrier to enter the Greek market. It appears again that the banking/services sector is not affected as much by high corporate taxes for the same reason as explained above, as the regulatory framework is mostly determined externally by the administrative bodies of the EU. Thus, the sector in which the MNEs operate is important in determining whether a high corporate tax is a barrier to entry.

A high percentage of 61.5 percent of the surveyed companies saw the labor market structure in Greece as an important barrier for their foreign direct investment projects in Greece negatively affecting entrepreneurship and the business environment. Furthermore, no significant differences among business sectors exist: 67.9 percent of MNEs of the industrial/ manufacturing sector and 61.5 percent of the trade/food sector looked upon labor market structure as a decisive FDI barrier. At the same time, 45.5 percent of the MNEs of the banking/ services sector mentioned the above as a decisive barrier. Hence, we can underpin that the sector that each MNE belongs to and the importance of the above barrier as a decisive FDI obstacle are indifferent.

A relatively high percentage (55.8 percent) of MNEs responded that the Greek legal framework was a significant FDI barrier negatively affecting entrepreneurship and the business environment. This is consistent with the suggestions to diminish the barriers that prevent the establishment of businesses and to implement uncomplicated procedures for starting up a venture, and also that bankruptcy laws should be modified in the direction of allowing the entrepreneur a second chance (Ioannidis 2004: iv-vi; Ioannidis, Politis and Tsakanikas 2005: 100; Ioannidis and Tsakanikas 2006: 112-25). MNEs of the banking/services sector with an extremely high ratio of 81.8 percent referred to the above barrier as significant. Moreover, 57.1 percent of the MNEs of the industrial/manufacturing sector also saw the Greek legal framework as a decisive FDI barrier. The percentage was lower somewhat (30.8 percent) in the food/trade sector. One can conclude that the unstable legal framework affects mostly the MNEs in the banking/services sector. It appears that the banking/services sector is mostly affected by the instability resulting from contradictions created between the Greek legal system and the regulatory environment determined by the European Commission, the ECB, and the EMU. This outcome is different from the aforementioned. The banking/services sector has not mostly been affected by corruption but rather by an unstable legal framework. Generally speaking, an unstable legal framework incorporates constant changes in laws, lack of laws, non-enforcement of laws, discrimination in the enforcement of laws, bureaucratic procedures and contradictory laws, and different domestic laws compared with laws in other Economic and Monetary Union (EMU) countries; all these inadequacies leave space for corruption.

The aforementioned barriers tend to diminish the level of Greek competitiveness. In terms of economic policy, the key factor of "competitiveness deficit" is that Greek industrial development has been based on increasing demand, while neglecting policies that would affect supply. Implemented policies have had the exclusive aim of increasing aggregate demand and, as a consequence, also raised imports to the exclusion of development of an export-oriented productive model.

CONCLUSION

In order to determine the motives and barriers of FDI inflows in Greece, Bitzenis and Tsitouras (2007a; 2007b) and Bitzenis et al. (2009a; 2009b) ran a survey for the period 1995-2003. The survey was carried out using a questionnaire, having as a target the biggest foreign investments in Greece. From the population and via a quota sampling a total number of 150 MNEs was selected as a target sample and fifty-two multinationals participated, and thus the response rate was 34.6 percent, consisting of 29.90 percent of the total Greek FDI inflows during the same period. In this chapter, we use this survey as a proxy for the level of entrepreneurship and business environment in Greece and extending the statistical analysis and the critical discussion of the results in order to conclude the main motives and barriers for FDI in Greece affecting the entrepreneurship and the business environment in the Greek market. More specifically, in the order of importance, we conclude that the prospects for market growth, political stability, economic stability, the size of Greek market, social stability, and the Olympic Games 2004 were the most decisive factors for a preferable business environment that favored sound entrepreneurship and competitiveness. The size of the Greek market is more important for the MNEs in the trade/food and services sectors than for other sectors due to the proximity of this sector to consumers. The primary barriers in the Greek market reflect an unfavorable business environment as well as a deficit in entrepreneurship and competitiveness. In the order of importance are bureaucracy, followed by the taxation system, corruption, corporate tax, the unfavorable labor market structure, and the unstable legal system. It appears that the banking/services sector is not affected by corruption as the regulatory framework is mostly determined by the European Commission, the ECB, and the EMU. However, at the same time, the framework creates inconsistencies with the Greek legal system producing an unstable legal environment negatively affecting the sector.

The chapter contributes to the body of knowledge regarding the level of competitiveness, entrepreneurship, and the business environment in Greece by determining the motives and barriers to entry by MNEs in the Greek market through a questionnaire survey. Prior studies on entrepreneurship in Greece have concentrated only on domestic players and factors. However, the globalization process imposes the embodiment of international players and conditions to derive a more accurate study of entrepreneurship and the business environment. In other words, this chapter is an attempt to enrich and incorporate factors of global competition in the appreciation of Greek entrepreneurship and the business environment in tandem. For that reason, inward FDI as an additional factor for determining entrepreneurial activity and the business environment was introduced. In addition, our study investigated the relevance of the sector in which the MNE is initiating the investment in determining the motives and barriers to entry by MNEs. Our findings of the questionnaire survey of fifty-two MNEs that had invested in Greece, with respondents holding a top position such as Chief Executive Officer, President, Chief Financial Officer, Chairman, senior management and/or involved directly in strategic planning, do not reveal a contradiction with the previous literature, but rather provide a more holistic picture. As with Greek entrepreneurship, it appears that FDI in Greece during the period of investigation is also consumer-oriented, and economic, political, and social stability is valued highly. Meanwhile, as with Greek entrepreneurship, bureaucracy, corruption, and the legal framework negatively affect FDI. In extending previous research, our study also revealed that hosting the Olympics 2004 created a positive business environment for FDI, while the size of the market depends on the sector initiating the investment. Regarding the barriers to entry by MNEs, the taxation system, corporate taxes, and the labor market affected negatively the decision to enter, which was not mentioned in previous research. Meanwhile, the sector initiating the FDI plays an important role in determining whether corruption, corporate taxes, and the legal system are significant barriers to entry.

Issues of concern and limitations with our study is that the investigation of the motives and barriers of MNEs when investing in Greece has been done by using questionnaires and interviews of the local managers of the MNEs' subsidiaries. The underlying assumption made is that the views of the local managers will reflect the views of the mother company when deciding to invest. This assumption is not necessarily true. A local subsidiary's manager can have a different perception of the domestic environment than the headquarters' managers. Also, we discuss the motivations in 2004 when the research took place whilst an investment might have been made between 1995 and 2004. Given that there is a time difference, the current evaluation of the local environment from the domestic managers of MNEs does not necessarily reflect the motivations of the MNE in the past when they entered the Greek market, at the time when they actually made the decision to invest in Greece. Our questions were directed at the time that the investment took place, but the influence of current conditions cannot be avoided. Meanwhile, as a goal for future research, a full sample should include those MNEs that considered Greece as an option but at the end opted out in pursuing the investment; in the case that we investigated the motives proved stronger than the obstacles. Thus, it can be argued that the sample may be biased. Independent of the issues just outlined, we still strongly believe that there is a contribution to the literature from this novel approach in determining motives and barriers of FDI in Greece.

Directions for further research, in addition to overcoming the aforementioned weaknesses of our study, should target the impact of the Olympics 2004 on the level of entrepreneurship and the business environment by identifying whether the momentum associated with the positive outcomes due to the Olympics was further exploited and changed the business landscape in Greece on a permanent basis. Therefore, it can be concluded that it is crucial for Greece to enhance the motives and reduce the barriers to FDI so as to stimulate entrepreneurship and create a positive business environment in order to receive significant FDI inflows. The research reveals that while the Olympic Games cannot be a motive anymore for FDI, policy makers have to enhance and maintain the momentum after the Olympic Games by translating the Olympic Games motive into market growth, and maintaining political, economic, and social stability. Modernizing the education system is imperative for the development of skills and fighting corruption. At the same time, the rationalization of the bureaucratic *modus operandi* will diminish the reasons for corruption. With regard to the barriers to FDI of bureaucracy, taxation system, corruption, and the labor market, there is a need for Greece to adopt a regulatory framework that would reduce these impediments. In particular, the research reveals that care should be taken with the banking/services sector. In sum, there is a need for Greece to modernize and to upgrade state administration by adopting more effective organizational and governmental policies, to reduce the barriers to entry and, at the same time, to enhance the motives for entry. Greece needs to adopt regulatory reforms to foster entrepreneurship, competitiveness, and create a positive business environment by enhancing and maintaining the momentum after the Olympic Games.

REFERENCES

Apergis, N. "Public and Private Investments in Greece: Complementary or Substitute 'Goods'?" *Bulletin of Economic Research* 52, no. 3 (2000): 225-34.

Apergis, N. and C. Katrakylidis. "Does Inflation Uncertainty Matter in Foreign Direct Investment Decisions? An Empirical Investigation for Greece, Spain and Portugal." *Rivista Internazionale di Scienze Economiche e Commerciali (International Review of Economics and Business)* 45, no. 4 (1998): 729-44.

Bank of Greece. *Governor's Annual Reports*, Various Issues. Athens, 1998-2003.

Bennett, H., Escolano, J., Fabrizio, S., Gutierrez, E., Ivaschenko, I., Lissovolik, B., Moreno-Badia, M., Schule, W., Tokarick, S., Xiao, Y. and Z. Zarnic. "Competitiveness in the Southern Euro Area: France, Greece, Italy, Portugal and Spain." *IMF Working Paper No. 08/112*, International Monetary Fund, 2008.

Berman, G., Brooks, R. and S. Davidson. "The Sydney Olympic Games Announcement and Australian Stock Market Reaction." *Applied Economics Letters* 7, no. 12 (2000): 781-84.

Bitzenis, A. and E. Nito. "Obstacles to Entrepreneurship in a Transition Business Environment: The Case of Albania." *Journal of Small Business and Enterprise Development* 12, no. 4 (2005): 564-78.

Bitzenis, A. "Universal Model of Theories Determining FDI: Is There Any Dominant Theory? Are the FDI Inflows in CEE Countries and Especially in Bulgaria a Myth?" *European Business Review* 15, no. 2 (2003): 94-104.

――― . "Decisive Barriers that Affect Multinational Business in a Transition Country." *Global Business and Economics Review: Special Issue - The Political Economy of Transition* 8, nos. 1-2 (2006a): 87-118.

――― . "Determinants of Greek FDI Outflows in the Balkan Region: The Case of Greek Entrepreneurs in Bulgaria." *Eastern European Economics* 44, no. 3 (2006b): 79-96.

――― . "Determinants of Foreign Direct Investment: Evidence from Multinationals in the Post-crisis Era of Bulgaria in the Late 1990s." *Southeast European and Black Sea Studies* 7, no. 1 (2007): 83-111.

Bitzenis, A. and A. Tsitouras. "Motives of Foreign Direct Investment in an EMU Country: The Case of Greece." Working Paper, 2007a.

――― . "Decisive FDI Obstacles as an Explanatory Reason for Limited FDI Inflows in an EMU Country: The Case of Greece." Working Paper, 2007b.

Bitzenis, A., Tsitouras, A. and V. A. Vlachos. "Motives of Foreign Direct Investment in a Small EMU Member State: The Case of Greece." *East-West Journal of Economic and Business*, forthcoming, 2009a.

————. "Decisive FDI Obstacles as an Explanatory Reason for Limited FDI Inflows in an EMU Member State: The Case of Greece." *Journal of Socio-Economics* 38, no. 4 (2009b): 691-704.

Dunning, H. J. "The Eclectic Paradigm of International Production: A Restatement and Some Possible Extensions." *Journal of International Business Studies* 19, no. 1 (1988): 1-32.

————. *Multinational Enterprises and the Global Economy.* Wokingham: Addison-Wesley, 1993.

————. "The Eclectic Paradigm of International Production: A Personal Perspective." In *The Nature of the Transnational Firm,* edited by C. Pitelis and R. Sugden. London: Routledge, 2000.

ELKE 2004. http://www.elke.gr/default.asp?V_DOC_ID=1 (accessed September 14, 2004).

Economist Intelligence Unit. EIU, 2004. http://www.eiu.com/html.com (accessed September 12, 2004).

European Commission. "EMU @ 10: Successes and Challenges after 10 Years of Economic and Monetary Union." *European Economy Special Report 2.* Brussels: European Commission - Directorate General for Economic and Financial Affairs, 2008.

Filippaios, F. and C. Kottaridi. "Investment Patterns and the Competitiveness of Greek Regions." *Review of Urban and Regional Development Studies* 16, no. 2 (2004): 93-112.

Gartner, W. B. "Who is an Entrepreneur? Is This the Wrong Question?" *American Journal of Small Business* 12, no. 4 (Spring 1998): 11-32.

Georgopoulos, A. and H. G. Preusse. "European Integration and the Dynamic Process of Investments and Divestments of Foreign TNCs in Greece." *European Business Review* 18, no. 1 (2006): 50-59.

Giannitsis, T. *Greek Industry: Development and Crisis.* Athens: Gutenberg, 1988 (in Greek).

Hayek, F. A. "Economics and Knowledge." *Economica* 4, no. 13 (February 1937): 33-54.

Holland, D., Sass, M., Benacek, V. and M. Gronicki. "The Determinants and Impact of FDI in Central and Eastern Europe: A Comparison of Survey and Econometric Evidence." *Transnational Corporations* 9, no. 3 (2000): 163-212.

Howorth, C., Tempest, S. and C. Coupland. "Rethinking Entrepreneurship Methodology and Definitions of the Entrepreneur." *Journal of Small Business and Enterprise Development* 12, no. 1 (2005): 24-40.

Ioannidis, S. "Entrepreneurship in Greece." *Foundation for Economic and Industrial Research (IOBE),* Global Entrepreneurship Monitor 2003. Athens, October 2004 (in Greek).

Ioannidis, S. and P. Tsakanikas. "Entrepreneurship in Greece 2005-2006." *Foundation for Economic and Industrial Research (IOBE),* Global Entrepreneurship Monitor 2006. Athens, November 2006 (in Greek).

Ioannidis, S., Politis, T. and P. Tsakanikas. "Entrepreneurship in Greece 2004-2005." *Foundation for Economic and Industrial Research (IOBE),* Global Entrepreneurship Monitor 2006. Athens, October 2005 (in Greek).

Jarilo, C. "Entrepreneurship and Growth: The Strategic Use of External Resources." *Journal of Business Venturing* 4 (1989): 133-47.

Kalantaridis, C. "Between the Community and the World Market: Garment Entrepreneurs in Rural Greece." *Entrepreneurship and Regional Development* 9, no. 1 (1997): 25-44.

Kirzner, I. M. *Competition and Entrepreneurship.* Chicago: University of Chicago Press, 1973.

Knight, F. H. *Risk, Uncertainty and Profit.* Chicago: University of Chicago Press, 1971.

Koutsogeorgopoulou, V. and H. Ziegelschmidt. "Raising Greece's Potential Output Growth." *OECD Economics Department Working Papers No. 452,* OECD Publishing, 2005.

Makridakis, S., Caloghirou, Y., Papagiannakis, L. and P. Trivellas. "The Dualism of Greek Firms and Management: Present State and Future Implications." *European Management Journal* 15, no. 4 (1997): 381-402.

Mamatzakis, E. C. "EU Infrastructure Investment and Productivity in Greek Manufacturing." *Journal of Policy Modeling* 29, no. 2 (2007): 335-44.

Naumes, W. and M. J. Naumes. "A Comparison of Values and Attitudes toward Risk of Greek and American Entrepreneurs." *International Journal of Value-Based Management* 7, no. 1 (1994): 3-12.

Pantelidis, P. and E. Nikolopoulos. "FDI Attractiveness in Greece." *International Advances in Economic Research* 14, no. 1 (2008): 90-100.

Petroulas, P. "The Effect of the Euro on Foreign Direct Investment." *European Economic Review* 51, no. 6 (2007): 1468-91.

Pitelis, C. and N. Antonakis. "Manufacturing and Competitiveness: The Case of Greece." *Journal of Economic Studies* 30, no. 5 (2003): 535-47.

Porter, M. "The Competitive Advantage of Nations." *Harvard Business Review* (March-April 1990): 73-91.

Ritchie, B. and C. Brindley. "Cultural Determinants of Competitiveness within SMEs." *Journal of Small Business and Enterprise Development* 12, no. 1 (2005): 104-19.

Salavrakos, I. D. and G. A. Petrochilos. "An Assessment of the Greek Entrepreneurial Activity in the Black Sea Area 1989-2000: Cases and Prospects." *Journal of Socio-Economics* 32, no. 3 (2003): 331-49.

Schumpeter, J. *Capitalism, Socialism and Democracy*, 3rd edition. New York: Harper & Row, 1950.

——— . *The Theory of Economic Development*. Cambridge, MA: Harvard University Press, 1934. (New York: Oxford University Press, 1961.)

Souitaris, V. "Firm-specific Competencies Determining Technological Innovation: A Survey in Greece." *R&D Management* 32, no. 1 (2002): 61-77.

Taylor, C. "Foreign Direct Investment and the Euro: The First Five Years." *Cambridge Journal of Economics* 32, no. 1 (2008): 1-28.

UNCTAD. *World Investment Report*. New York & Geneva: United Nations, 2003.

——— . *World Investment Report*. New York & Geneva: United Nations, 2004.

Wiklund, J. and D. Shepherd. "Entrepreneurial Orientation and Small Business Performance: A Configurational Approach." *Journal of Business Venturing* 20 (2005): 71-91.

Veraros, N., Kasimati, E. and P. Dawson. "The 2004 Olympic Games Announcement and its Effect on the Athens and Milan Stock Exchanges." *Applied Economics Letters* 11, no. 12 (2004): 749-53.

von Mises, L. *Human Action: A Treatise on Economics*, 3rd edition. Washington, DC: Henry Regnery, 1963.

Chapter 15
Macro Competitiveness of the Vietnamese Economy[1]

Swapan Sen

ABSTRACT

While assessing Vietnam's competitiveness, Porter (2008) included macro policies among key determinants of competitiveness. Separately, Pincus (2009) suggests that Vietnam has run out of macro policy options such as fiscal stimulus
(because budget deficit is too large) and monetary policy (because inflation is
too high), thus leaving reduction of the effective exchange rate as only viable
policy alternative to enhance Vietnamese economic performance. We argue that
both commentaries have missed key aspects of Vietnam's competitiveness
whose recent erosion is due to the political economic malaise of Vietnamese
capitalist development that is crony, state run, and debt financed. Human resource development appears thwarted by old socio-political feuds. Further, Vietnam's FDI inflows and worker's remittances are large enough to make the
policy recommendation of currency depreciation costly and ineffective.

INTRODUCTION

The Vietnamese economy exhibited extraordinary growth and development in
recent years. GDP growth during 2001-2007 was over 6 percent per year which
was second to the Chinese only. GDP stood over $65 billion at the end of 2008.
Foreign direct investment increased to US$20 billion by 2007. Thus, policies of
liberalization and privatization had immediate impact on economic growth.
However, most of the growth occurred in the property and real estate markets
and the financial sector, and the expansion of trade was restricted mainly to
mining and agricultural products. Money supply increase was fast and credit

expansion was even faster, resulting in inflation rates as high as 20-25 percent per year. State enterprises accounted for most of the new investments, the bulk of which went to seaport development. As the government budget deficit kept rising past 5 percent of GDP, credit expansion needed to be reined in, and a collapse occurred in the Vietnamese economy shortly before the global financial crisis hit the region in late 2008. Thus, just when Vietnam was becoming an attractive destination of foreign investment and its economic competitiveness was improving, it faced an economic downturn which was accentuated by a global crisis and an erosion of its competitiveness.

An industry's competitiveness, according to Porter (1980), depends on several forces: the intensity of rivalry among competitors; the threat of new entry; the threat of substitute products; the bargaining power of buyers; and the bargaining power of suppliers and consumers. The key to these factors is productivity. A nation's competitiveness depends on the productivity of its local firms (both domestic and foreign), as well as its export industries. In addition, it can enhance its competitiveness by coordinating economic policy among neighboring countries. Regional cooperation through free trade zones is often used to improve a country's competitiveness strength.

Traditional international trade theory adopts a narrow measure of price competitiveness which emanates from cost effectiveness—whoever produces the traded good at lower cost is more competitive. This concept works well when competing firms supply homogenous products in geographically proximate markets. Such propositions are empirically verifiable: compare export unit values, unit labor costs, consumer prices, and the effective exchange rate.

Most emerging economies however aspire to export new goods. As the nation's economy continues growing, and its industrial structure diversifies, the nation aspires to develop new products for export. Developing new product capabilities include development of resources, technology, and markets. This is consistent with dynamic comparative advantage. Companies or countries pursue their comparative advantage in an existing product but keep seeking to develop comparative advantage in higher value items. This involves a higher level of processing and manufacturing development. Typically, countries known for mining and agricultural exports seek to develop comparative advantage in manufacturing industries and services.

In addition to sophistication of company operations and productivity growth as key to competitiveness, Porter (2009) points to quality of national business environment, social infrastructure, political institutions, and macro policy as determinants of competitiveness. In this chapter, we analyze the institutional and macro determinants of Vietnam's competitiveness. First, we present the current status of Vietnamese competitiveness as reflected in the global competitiveness report. Next, we present exclusionary higher education as one institutional factor that is adversely influencing Vietnamese economic competitiveness. Macro policy options are discussed next, and conclusions are summarized at the end. Whereas western policy advisors recommend more economic reform, the emphasis may just well be on socio-political reforms.

THE GLOBAL COMPETITIVENESS REPORT 2008-2009

The World Economic Forum publishes rankings of competitiveness among the countries. These rankings are calculated from both publicly available data and the Forum's own Executive Opinion Survey. Rankings are published overall and in subcategories of travel and tourism (TT), information technology (IT), enabling trade (ET), financial development (Finance), and Gender Gap (GG). Vietnam's rank is shown in addition to some significant nations.

TABLE 15.1
Competitiveness Ranking by World Economic Forum, 2008

Country	Rank	TT	IT	ET	Finance	GG
USA	1	8	3	14	1	27
Singapore	5	10	4	2	10	84
Japan	9	25	17	13	4	98
Hong Kong	11	12	12	1	8	NA
South Korea	13	31	11	24	19	108
Malaysia	21	32	28	29	20	96
China	30	47	46	48	24	57
Thailand	34	39	47	52	29	52
India	50	62	54	71	31	113
Vietnam	70	89	70	91	49	68

Note: For GG (Gender Gap), sub-indices here include "economic participation and opportunity," "educational attainment," "health survival," and "political empowerment."

Table 15.1 above shows that the international competitiveness of Vietnam is not very high. It is however improving. At the turn of the century, the Vietnamese economy possessed unique advantages in natural resources and a workforce that was young, abundant, and well educated. Yet, labor costs were low. Since the introduction of economic liberalization (*Doi Moi*) in the late 1980s, Vietnam's overall foreign trade expanded and the structural composition of Vietnam's external trade started changing from agriculture and mining to traditional manufacturing such as textiles. The U.S. International Trade Committee noted that Vietnam and Indonesia are competing with China in exports to the American market in terms of labor power, price setting, and product quality. Vietnam's exports of textiles and apparel to the U.S. market alone constitute 55 percent of the country's total exports.[2]

In the immediate aftermath of the Asian crisis of 1997, Vietnam's exports suffered because of loss of demand from other economies in the region and relative appreciation of the Dong. The Asian crisis reversed initial export promotion policy to import substitution and also increased the scope of public sector enterprises. In spite of such setbacks, significant economic development was achieved in the early years of the current century.

THWARTED CAPITALIST DEVELOPMENT

Vietnam's transition to market economy began in the 1990s within its socialist political regime. The Chinese served as a role model that Vietnam had neither the political will nor the economic ability to emulate. The Vietnamese effort resulted in capitalist development that was speculative (real estate and stock market bubble), crony (political protection to select companies), state driven (state enterprises accounting for a majority of investment and employment), and debt financed (debt accounting for two-thirds of total assets). These results are summarized in Table 15.2 below.

TABLE 15.2
Vietnamese Enterprises 2001-2007

	State (%)	Private Domestic	Private Foreign
Investment 2001-2004	54	14	32
Investment 2007	46	36	19
Employment growth 2007	-7	15	19
Debt Ratio	76	61	57

Source: Pincus 2009.

Note that the decline of the relative share of the state enterprises in investment and employment did not change its commanding role in the economy. Majority investment occurred in regional seaport development. An average investment of $100 million was made in twenty regional ports. Whereas some consider this investment misplaced and wasteful, Vietnam's private investment, which was mostly directed toward speculative pursuits in real estate and the stock market, did not fare much better. Vietnam's stock index which stood at 300 in 2004, climbed to 1,100 in 2007 before declining to 310 in March of 2008, months before the global financial crisis hit. The nature of the real estate bubble would be evident from Table 15.3.

TABLE 15.3
Real Estate Price Increases in 12 Months, Dec 2007-Dec 2008

Area	Price/sq. meter (mn VND)	Rate of Increase in 12 months (%)
District 7 (Phu My)	27	145
Nha. Binh District (Tai Son)	16	191
Nam Nam Saigon	13	202
Gia Hoa	14	155

Source: CB Richard Ellis Co. (Vietnam) Ltd., 2008 Annual Report.

HUMAN RESOURCES DEVELOPMENT

Vietnam's population is 70 percent young (thirty years or under). Vietnam has an education system that is producing a skilled labor force which can be improved both in quantity and quality. With privatization of higher education, quality control has become a concern. Foreign educated instructors shuttle from private college to private college offering modern management education in quick modules in evening and weekend programs. The interaction between students and faculty is extremely limited. The labor force participation rate, although increasing, is still below 55 percent.

The youthful population generates pressure on politicians to create employment. The North-South divide is kept alive. Whereas American trained accountants, managers, real estate, and IT personnel are working in large numbers in Vietnam, those born in families that collaborated with the Americans during the war—that ended long ago—still do not have access to college and therefore employment. As long as party affiliation and loyalty are among the qualifications for jobs, human resource development is likely to remain a constraint on Vietnamese economic competitiveness.

MACRO POLICY OPTIONS FOR IMPROVING COMPETITIVENESS

Macro policy options are vital for regional and international competitiveness of a nation. For example, during the 1997 Asian crisis, when neighboring nations' currencies depreciated, Vietnamese exports lost competitiveness. It was necessary to depreciate the Dong to sterilize the unintended foreign exchange appreciation. In fact, we will see shortly that the entire gamut of macroeconomic policy is relevant for the country's competitiveness.

In recent years, real estate and stock market speculation attracted hot money from abroad and steamed up Vietnam's credit (45 percent in 2007) and inflation (25 percent in 2007) to rates much higher than what prevailed in neighboring countries in the region. As the Vietnamese government absorbed the cost of sterilization and subsidies in food and transportation, the government budget deficit rose sharply and exceeded 5 percent of GDP. This led some economists to think that Vietnam has run out of policy options in both monetary and fiscal fronts, leaving foreign exchange depreciation as the only viable policy option. For example, Pincus (2009) suggests that Vietnam cannot afford further fiscal stimulus (because the budget deficit is already too large) and monetary policy stimulus (because inflation is already too high), thus leaving reduction of the effective exchange rate as the only viable policy alternative to enhance Vietnamese economic performance.

Standard economic theory suggests that large foreign exchange inflows provide a cushion against domestic currency depreciation. For the size of the Vietnamese economy (2007 GDP of $65 billion), the annual FDI flow of $20 billion is rather large (the amount actually committed is $16 billion). Inward remittances of $6+ billion add to foreign exchange inflows on top of that. Such inflows are likely to create pressure for the Vietnamese Dong to appreciate. To sterilize[3] the effect of such inflows on the domestic currency, the Vietnamese state will require massive foreign currency purchase that can be costly and wasteful. In fact, sterilization induces further inflow of foreign capital. As long as such inflows remain substantial, depreciation of the Dong is unlikely to be a successful strategy for improving Vietnam's competitiveness.

SUMMARY AND CONCLUSIONS

In this chapter we presented an analysis of the institutional and macro factors impacting the competitiveness of the Vietnamese economy. We find that state enterprises account for the lion's share of investment that is excessively debt financed. It appears that cronyism of the state is thwarting capitalist development of Vietnam. In addition, exclusionary political feuds seem to hinder human resource development. Thus, the status of Vietnam's competitiveness may depend more on socio-political reforms than on economic incentives.

NOTES

1. This paper is the result of Swapan Sen's participation in a Faculty Development Seminar in Vietnam organized by the University of Wisconsin-Madison/CIBER in 2009. The opinions expressed are the author's personal.
2. Asian Textile Business, May 2005.
3. Sterilization is a monetary action by the central bank of a country to counteract the effect of a changing monetary base. For example, to weaken the Dong, the Vietnamese Central Bank would have to buy foreign currency. The increased supply of the Dong to buy foreign exchange would weaken the Dong. Such costs are not negligible. Goldman Sachs reports that China is losing $4 billion a month in sterilization costs against the dollar (Goldman Sachs, Feb 1, 2008).

REFERENCES

Pincus, J. "Ho Chi Minh City." Harvard Kennedy School (Resident Academic Advisor, Vietnam Program), January 5, 2009.
Porter, M. *Competitive Strategy: Techniques for Analyzing Industries and Competitors.* New York: The Free Press, 1980.
———— . "Vietnam's Competitiveness: Ho Chi Minh City." Institute for Strategy and Competitiveness, Harvard Business School, December 1, 2008. http://www.isc.hbs.edu/pdf/20081201_Vietnam.pdf
Sachs, Goldman. "China, Mounting Losses from Currency Sterilization," 2008.

Chapter 16
Foreign Direct Investment in the Banking Sector: Case Study of the Czech Republic and The Bahamas

Gordana Pesakovic & Olivia C. Saunders

ABSTRACT

In our exploratory study, we compare two countries: one small transition economy and one small-island emerging country. We investigate foreign direct investment (FDI) in the banking industry, and the outcomes on the domestic economy. Although the foreign ownership in the banking sector is dominant in the case of The Bahamas and the Czech Republic, it is evident that there are differences in the outcomes of FDI. Contribution of our study is in the area of comparative studies, where very rarely comparative analysis of these groups of countries is performed. We also suggest more research in this area to be conducted.

INTRODUCTION

While in the 1990s financial institutions were praised for their positive role in the global economy, the South East Asian crises of 1997 suggested that this "perfect picture" was still just a "work in progress." The recent financial crisis of 2008-09 is simply another reminder of the latter. How did transition economies perform during these times? What about the small island countries, "safe money havens": were they affected? Are there any similarities between these two distinct types of countries? What are the differences? What are the lessons learned? How applicable are these lessons for other countries?

While observing behavior of the countries during the recent crises and the effects on them, two countries got the authors' attention: the Czech Republic and The Bahamas. These two countries could not be more different geographically, historically, and culturally, to mention but a few striking differences. However, these two countries have one remarkable similarity: both countries have dominant foreign ownership in the financial sector. Barta and Singer (2005) state that in the Czech Republic the banking sector is "almost exclusively controlled by foreign banking groups." In 2009, 80 percent of banks and trust companies authorized to operate locally in The Bahamas were foreign owned (The Central Bank of The Bahamas, 2009). Both countries keenly encourage foreign investments in general and financial institutions in particular. The Bahamas is renowned as a leading offshore financial center in the Caribbean region.

The literature at first looked favorably at the role of FDI in economic development. Most of these studies were done by international institutions, academicians, and experts from developed countries. However, in the twenty-first century, differing viewpoints are coming from the growing number of scholars out of developing and emerging countries. The decades of promoting FDI as a way of enhancing economic development now permit assessments of experiences and long-lasting effects of the FDI to the economic development, the structure of the society, and environmental consequences. The evaluation of these investments is mixed.

The purpose of our exploratory study is to conduct a comparative examination of the role of FDI in the banking sector in the Czech Republic and The Bahamas.

LITERATURE REVIEW

Developing and transition economies recognized the positive effects that FDI can have for their countries' future development. To this end, polices were crafted to attract foreign investors. Usually, incentives were provided such as tax holidays, lower prices for acquired companies or land, and reduction or forgiveness of non-performing debt in the case of financial institutions (and other companies) offered for sale. When more in-depth analysis was performed, some shortcomings were revealed. Razmi (2009) suggested that these enticing policies may have negative impacts on the host country's balance of payments. Kay (2007) proposed mixed effects of FDI: wage gaps between employees working for foreign companies and domestic ones can develop; regional disparities (regions receiving FDI versus others that are not receiving them); and social cost derived from companies or regions under pressure from foreign competitors. Girma et al. (2008) focused on positive impacts which FDI has on innovation in China, while Inzelt (2008) discovered the favorable impact that FDI can have on the transfer of knowledge. Mengisty and Adams (2007) show positive and significant correlation between FDI and economic growth even though "FDI has had a net crowding-out effect on domestic investment, which suggests that FDI promotes growth through its efficiency-inducing effects rather than its augmentation of domestic investment" (Mengisty and Adams 2007: 223). Levchenko and Mauro (2007) performed a comprehensive analysis of developed and developing countries, from 1970 to 2003. Among different forms of foreign investment, they concluded that FDI has the least volatile performance during the times of crises.

Kersan-Skabic and Orlic (2007) compared FDI in Central and East European (CEE) countries and the Western Balkans. The results of their study suggest that the following factors were influencing FDI: GDP, level of corruption, sufficient infrastructure, wages, and negotiations with the EU (which were important in the case of CEE). However, for the countries of the Western Balkans, wages, level of corruption, an agreement with the EU, and privatization were significant.

Jiatao and Guisinger (1992) analyzed FDI of service MNCs and concluded that FDI is "negatively related to the cultural distance between the home and host countries" in the case where the target of this FDI is local customers: when the target market is the home country's clients in the host country, then cultural factors are not important. On the other side, market size of the host country, the openness of the host country, the international competitiveness of the service industry of the foreign investor, the growth in firm size, and the global oligopolistic reaction are positively related to FDI.

Welfens (2008) pointed out the importance of FDI in the banking industry since 1985 when it "became one of the leading sectors in not only OECD countries but worldwide." Tanna (2009) conducted a study on 566 publicly traded commercial banks operating in seventy-five countries (2000-2004). The focus of this study was "the impact of FDI on total factor productivity growth." The findings suggest that time plays an important role. In the short run, "inward FDI has a negative effect" on the factor productivity of banks. However, in the long run, the impact is positive.

During the transition period, the Czech Republic was the recipient of a significant amount of FDI. The country's geographical position combined with the well educated and skillful workforce and capitalistic experience (Czechoslovakia was the second most industrialized European country before World War II) provided strong attractions for the inflow of FDI. In the first phase (1993-2002), FDI was coming from other countries. Since then, the major source of FDI is coming from inside the country through reinvested profits from foreign-owned companies (Hlavacek 2009). Financial services were the largest recipient of FDI in the Czech Republic.

In addressing the effects of FDI on the Czech Republic and Latvia, Javorcik (2008) correctly concluded that spillover effects of FDI depend on the specific host country conditions and the form of FDI. Therefore, Javorcik suggested that "the focus of the debate should shift from attempting to generalize about whether or not FDI leads to productivity spillovers to determining under *what* conditions it can do so" (Javorcik 2008: 139).

In a comparative analysis of the Czech Republic, Poland and Hungary in relationship to "substitution between domestic and foreign currency loans in

Central Europe" from 1997 until 2007, Brzoza-Brzezina et al. (2008) found that despite the fact that all three countries shared somewhat similar economic history for almost fifty years, their attitudes toward domestic and foreign currency loans differ. While substitution was significant in the cases of Poland and Hungary, it was "considered negligible" in the case of the Czech Republic. We suggest that most likely the following facts influenced the approach of Czechs: for much of the time Czech currency was appreciated; low inflation rate were registered, and interest rates were low. As well, we suggest that culture differences should also be taken into consideration. Czech people may be more risk averse than the other two nations.

A comprehensive study (Barta and Singer 2005) revealed ups and downs of the transition process of the banking industry in the Czech Republic since the beginning of the 1990s. Fifteen years of transition were characterized by a shift from the "largely state-owned, undercapitalized and poorly managed banks ... into a foreign-owned, reasonably sound and competitive banking sector" (Barta and Singer 2005: 212). Podpiera and Weill's (2007) study identified bad management as the major cause for banking failures. Their sample includes forty-three banks in the Czech Republic from 1995 to 2005. Their findings support cost efficiency as an important factor for the bank's well being. Since foreign ownership has a positive influence on cost efficiency, they propose that "supervisory authorities in emerging markets should strongly favor foreign ownership in the banking industry" (Podpiera and Weill 2007: 14).

Academic literature on the economy of The Bahamas is sparse, more so with respect to FDI. Hammond et al. (2008) focused their study on the role of FDI in the construction sector. Although these investments were significant, their impact on the local economy was mixed. Instead of increasing demand for local workforce, "unprecedented numbers of guest workers and professionals" were employed. On the other hand, "the level of tax concessions outstripped the anticipated central government tax receipts." Pesakovic and Saunders (2009) in studying eight Heads of Agreements for FDI in The Bahamas found that FDI limited local ownership in tourism and financial sector, the two leading sectors in the economy. Since 2000, foreign investment in the financial services industry in The Bahamas has been restrained by international pressures (Vlcek 2008). The number of banks and trust companies granted public licenses peaked at 303 in 1995 and fell to 128 in 2009 (Central Bank of The Bahamas 2010).

Demeritte (2000) referenced Goldsmith (1969) along with Shaw (1973) and McKinnon (1973) in supporting the view that liberalization of the commercial banking system leads to higher savings, improved resource allocation, and economic growth. Demeritte describes the financial sector in The Bahamas as bank dominated. "By and large, the big foreign-owned branches have traditionally provided financing to selected enterprises through lines of credit and overdrafts, often participating in management as well as monitoring the client activities, acting as lenders, as well as supervisors in close cooperation with the government regulators" (Demeritte 2000: 5).

For all emerging and developing economies, there is a drive for development. FDI should be a key aspect of the development process.

RESEARCH QUESTIONS

In this chapter, we explore the characteristics and effects that dominant foreign ownership in the banking industry has in/on these two countries. The rationale for selecting these two countries is:

1. Czech Republic is a high-income economy moving through the transition from a centrally planned economy to a market-oriented economy; from a larger country (Czechoslovakia) to a smaller country (Czech Republic). The country's political alliance has switched from the Council for Mutual Economic Assistance, economic integration of the Eastern Bloc with the Soviet Union on the top, to the European Union (EU); from the Warsaw pact to NATO pact. It is a country of 10.5 million people.

2. The Bahamas is a high-income economy located in the Atlantic Ocean and bordered by the United States, Cuba, and Hispaniola. It was once a colony of the United Kingdom, gaining its Independence in 1973. The country has switched its main economic partner, from the U.K. to the United States. Since independence, it has formed closer ties with its neighbors by joining the Caribbean Community (CARICOM) and is a member of other western hemispheric organizations, i.e., the Inter-American Development Bank (IDB) and the Organization of American States (OAS). The population of the country is around 330,000.

3. Despite historical, geographical, cultural, size, economic, and political differences between these two countries, it is interesting to find out that they have something in common. They both have significant (dominant) foreign ownership in the banking industry.

Therefore, the scope of our exploratory analysis will focus on the following research questions:

1. What role does FDI play in the banking industry of the Czech Republic and The Bahamas?

2. What are the major characteristics of the banking industry in the Czech Republic and The Bahamas?

The variables examined are employment, assets to GDP, interest margin, credit, and operational practices. We cover the period from 1995-2008. The main reason for this time frame is related to the developments in the Czech Republic, and the transition and privatization process in banking industry (some data for the Czech Republic are available only until 2002). We use secondary data from the financial institutions in both countries, together with data from other international institutions.

We suggest that the findings of this study will contribute to the body of knowledge of the comparative studies and development studies in general, and studies addressing the role of FDI and banking industry, in particular.

FINDINGS AND ANALYSIS

Restricted by the availability and consistency of data for the two countries under study, we have examined the following data: employment, assets to GDP, interest margin, credit, and operational practices, and looked at how foreign banks have impacted the economies of the Czech Republic and The Bahamas.[1]

Case Study of The Bahamas

In 2007, sixteen of the twenty-one domestically operating banks were foreign owned. Using assets of domestic banks as a percentage of total bank assets, we estimate that foreign banks control some 75 percent of the local banking sector.[2]

Growth in the sector
The Bahamas is known worldwide as a tax haven and offshore financial center. The number of banks (which also includes trust companies) peaked in 1995 and reported steady decline since, as shown in Figure 16.1. The majority of them operate outside the domestic market. For example, in addition to the 131 banks with public licenses in 2008, there were 130 operating under a restricted license and ten classified as non-active. Of the 131 banks, only twenty are licensed to operate locally, twenty-six are Euro-currency branches of foreign banks, and eighty-five are merely Bahamian-based or subsidiaries of foreign banks. Eight are commercial banks.

FIGURE 16.1
Number of Banks and Trust Companies (Public Licenses)

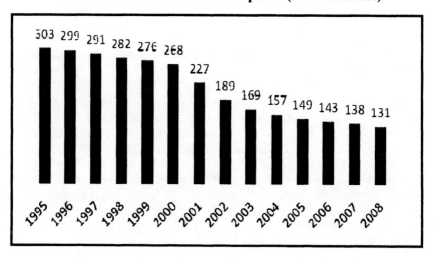

Employment

One of the key benefits of FDI is the employment it generates particularly for the local labor force. There has been an upward trend in employment in the industry (see Figure 16.2). Between 2000 and 2008, employment of Bahamians in banks averaged 94 percent. Employment in the industry for the years 1994 through 2004 averaged 2.4 percent of the country's labor force.[3]

FIGURE 16.2
Total Employment in Banks and Trust Companies

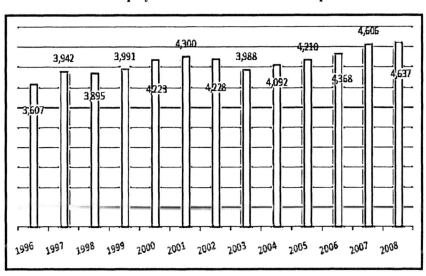

In a special study conducted by the Department of Statistics in 2003/04[4] for the two main islands, New Providence and Grand Bahama, the average annual wages in the financial intermediation industry was $38,886. This is below the mean household income in New Providence, $41,119, and above that in Grand Bahama, $37,160.[5] For the years 2002 to 2004, wages paid to employees represented less than 6 percent of household income, 5.7 percent in 2002, 5.5 percent in 2003, and 5.4 percent in 2004. Remuneration (wages and bonuses) grew from $33,623.9 in 1996 to $57,832.1 in 2008 representing an average growth rate of 4.7 percent. This growth has been somewhat erratic as shown in Table 16.1.

Staff training

The average yearly expenditure on staff training between 1996 and 2008 is $2.6 million. This represents an average annual expenditure of $579 per employee. Expenditure on training has averaged a 6.9 percent growth rate for the same period but has been inconsistent with large swings, as shown in Table 16.2. Staff training represents 0.7 percent of total expenditure of banks in the country.

Pesakovic & Saunders

Table 16.1

Growth of Wages	
Year	Growth Rate (%)
1997	0.7
1998	6.8
1999	6.4
2000	6.6
2001	2.8
2002	6.7
2003	2.4
2004	4.0
2005	-0.9
2006	1.1
2007	14.6
2008	5.3

Table 16.2

Staff Training	
Year	Growth Rate (%)
1997	25.0
1998	25.0
1999	8.0
2000	14.8
2001	-29.0
2002	31.8
2003	-20.7
2004	4.3
2005	12.5
2006	3.7
2007	10.7
2008	-3.2

There has been an upward trend in overall salaries nonetheless, as Figure 16.3 shows.

FIGURE 16.3
Salaries ($ million)

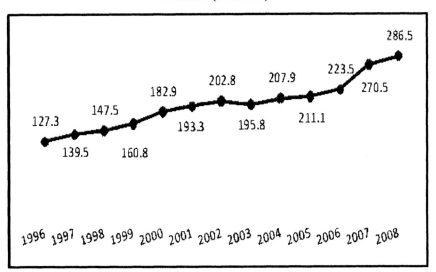

Capital expenditure

Capital expenditure represents re-investment by the banks in the country and has not been consistent in The Bahamas. Capital expenditure reached a high in 2001 at $48.7 million and a low of $15.4 million in 2003. Over the years 1996 through 2008, the average capital expenditure was $27.8 million with an average growth rate of 8.1 percent annually (Figure 16.4).

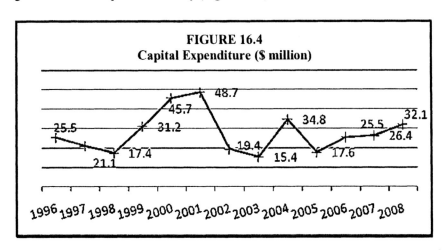

FIGURE 16.4
Capital Expenditure ($ million)

Pesakovic & Saunders

Revenues to the government

Given the incentives and encouragement to operate in The Bahamas along with the fact that there are no taxes on profits or earnings, the fees/taxes that the government collects is an important consideration when assessing the benefits of FDI to the country. Six of the years 1997 to 2008 show declines in the growth rate of fees to the government by banks. Even though the number of banks declined in 2007 and 2008, there were positive growth rates in fees paid. Bank fees (paid as a percentage of total revenues of government from business and professional fees) declined, indicating perhaps the reduced importance of banks to overall government revenues. In 1996, fees from banks represented more than 50 percent of overall government revenues from business and professional fees (see Table 16.3).

TABLE 16.3
Fees to Government (S million and Percentages)

Year	Total Fees to Government ($ millions)	Growth Rate of Fees to Government (%)	Percentage of Fees Paid by Banks to Total Government Revenues from Business and Professional Fees
1996	16.6	---	50.5
1997	15.3	-7.8	45.4
1998	10.8	-29.4	18.5
1999	14.4	33.3	26.1
2000	17.5	21.2	31.9
2001	16.5	-5.4	29.6
2002	15.6	-5.5	29.0
2003	16.4	5.1	29.1
2004	18.9	15.2	31.2
2005	18.1	-4.2	24.4
2006	18.1	0.0	23.1
2007	18.6	2.8	21.0
2008	19.5	4.8	17.4

Total bank expenditure to GDP

One measure of the contributions of a sector to the overall output (GDP) in the economy is the ratio of expenditure to the GDP. Using this measure, banks have contributed less than 9 percent to GDP for the years from 1996 to 2007. This contribution has averaged 7.3 percent between 1996 and 2007. The contribution peaked in 2000 and 2001 at 8.2 percent and 8.4 percent respectively. This is a surprising result as banking and financial services is the second most important sector in the country after tourism.

Another way to ascertain the level size of a sector in an economy is by finding the relationship of domestic assets to the GDP. For The Bahamas, the ratio of domestic assets to GDP went over 100 percent in 2002 growing, except in 2003, to 116 percent in 2007 (see Table 16.4). In terms of credit, it is clear from Table 16.5 that credit has been a major factor driving the economy as the ratio of private bank credit to GDP soared over 400 percent in 2004 and 2007.

Table 16.4

Domestic Assets (Percentage of GDP)	
Year	Percentage (%)
1998	89.9
1999	92.6
2000	94.0
2001	99.0
2002	103.6
2003	99.3
2004	104.3
2005	106.3
2006	112.8
2007	116.8

Table 16.5

Private Credit by Commercial Banks (Percentage of GDP)	
Year	Percentage (%)
1998	22.6
1999	122.8
2000	144.9
2001	177.0
2002	189.1
2003	344.0
2004	244.9
2005	434.2
2006	315.0
2007	409.3

Interest margin
Consistently hovering around and above 5 percent, the interest rate margins over the years suggest high profits and high cost of credit relative to interest on savings instruments (see Table 16.6).

Table 16.6

Interest Rate Margins	
Year	Interest Rate (%)
1999	5.18
2000	6.08
2001	6.06
2002	4.99
2003	4.70
2004	4.92
2005	5.40
2006	5.63
2007	5.50
2008	5.39

Case Study of the Czech Republic

The Czech Republic went through a period of significant transition changes in the banking sector since 1995. The number of foreign and domestic banks for the period 1995 to 2002 is shown in Table 16.7. A supremacy of foreign banks in the Czech economy is evident, especially since 1997.[6] This dominance is further demonstrated by the relationship between domestic bank assets and the GDP as shown in Table 16.8. This ratio declined by 10 percent from 1995 to 2002.

Moreover, credit does not play as much a part in the Czech economy as in The Bahamas. Private credit by commercial banks as a percentage of GDP moved from a high of 58.6 percent in 1995 to a low of 32.9 percent in 2002 (see Table 16.9). Decline of private credit by commercial banks can partly explain the lower rate of non-performing loans in the country since 1999. Gersl (2007) reports a significant drop in non-performing loans to total loans: from 43.4 percent in 1999 to only 4 percent in 2005. This can influence overall lower exposure of the Czech banking system to the financial crisis of 2008-09. Besides, net interest margins of foreign and domestic banks are reported in Table 16.10. The margin is consistently higher for domestic banks during the period 1995-2000. However, since 2001, when almost the whole banking sector moved to foreign owners, this has changed. Nonetheless, the rates are lower than in The Bahamas.

Table 16.7

Number of Banks		
Year	Foreign	Domestic
1995	23	31
1996	23	24
1997	24	21
1998	25	19
1999	27	14
2000	26	12
2001	26	11
2002	26	11

Table 16.8

Domestic Bank Assets (Percentage of GDP)	
Year	Percentage (%)
1995	120.0
1996	113.1
1997	119.0
1998	113.0
1999	111.0
2000	113.6
2001	114.9
2002	110.0

Table 16.9

Private Credit by Commercial Banks (Percentage of GDP)	
Year	Percentage (%)
1995	58.6
1996	54.3
1997	56.7
1998	52.3
1999	46.1
2000	41.0
2001	36.4
2002	32.9

Table 16.10

Net Interest Margin (%)		
Year	Foreign	Domestic
1995	2.03	3.02
1996	1.61	2.27
1997	0.99	2.56
1998	2.20	3.92
1999	2.08	3.33
2000	2.33	3.05
2001	2.71	1.94
2002	2.60	1.65

CONCLUSION

In our exploratory study, we compared two countries: one small transition economy and one small-island emerging country. We investigate FDI in the banking industry, and the outcomes on the local economy. Although the foreign ownership in the banking sector is dominant in the case of The Bahamas and the Czech Republic, it is evident that there are differences in the outcomes of FDI. For The Bahamas, large swings in some of the variables examined suggest a level of inconsistency and perhaps volatility in the contributions of banks in the country. In the case of the Czech Republic, two distinct periods are identified:

up to and including 2000, and after 2000, based on the changing position of the foreign ownership. The interesting findings are related to the volume of private lendings of the commercial banks. This fact is most likely responsible for a smaller number of non-performing loans of the Czech banks in general, and smaller exposure to the 2008/09 financial crisis.

The primary contribution of this study is in the area of the comparative studies, where very rarely comparative analysis of these groups of countries has been performed. We suggest more research in this area to be conducted. The comparative research can benefit the academia, and policy makers can acquire important lessons. Therefore, based on the findings from this study, we suggest the following research questions to be examined in future studies:

1.   What impact does FDI in the banking industry have on the workforce employed in this sector? What are the HR policies in relationship to employing the local qualified workforce in top management positions?
2.   Does national culture influence banking practices in these countries?
3.   Is there any difference in non-performing loans in the local market and in the headquarters' market? If there is a difference, what is the role of national culture versus corporate culture?

NOTES

1. Note that these data and calculations are preliminary.

2. The sources of the data in this section are taken from or calculated from the Central Bank of The Bahamas data or the Department of Statistics data unless otherwise indicated.

3. 2004 is the latest published data.

4. *Occupational Wage Survey 2003/2004.*

5. Department of Statistics, *Labour Force and Household Income Report*, Nassau, Bahamas, 2005.

6. Data for this section is from Katalin Mérő and Marianna Endrész Valentinyi, "The Role of Foreign Banks in Five Central and Eastern European Countries," Magyar Nemzeti Bank (Banking Department), November 2003.

REFERENCES

Barta, V. and M. Singer. "The Banking Sector after 15 Years of Restructuring: Czech Experience and Lessons." *Bank for International Settlements Papers No. 28: 2-3-212*, BIS, 2005.

Brzoza-Brzezina, M., Chimielewski, M. and J. Niedzwiedzinska. "Substitution between Domestic and Foreign Currency Loans in Central Europe. Do Central Banks Matter?" *Munich Personal RePEc Archive Paper 6879* (online publication), January 25, 2008. www.mpra.ub.uni-muenchen.de/6879

Degryse, H. et al. "Foreign Banks Entry and Credit Allocation in Emerging Markets." *IMF Working Papers 270*, IMF, 2009.

Demeritte, K. "Capital Market Developments and the Banking System." *Central Bank of The Bahamas Working Papers*, 2000.

Gersl, A. "Foreign Banks, Foreign Lending and Cross-border Contagion: Evidence from the BIS Data." *Czech Journal of Economics and Finance* 57, nos. 1-2 (2007): 27-40.

Girma, S. "Foreign Direct Investment, Access to Finance, and Innovation Activity in Chinese Enterprises." *The World Bank Economic Review* 22, no. 2 (2008): 367-82.

Higgins, J. K. *The Bahamian Economy: An Analysis*. Nassau, Bahamas: The Counsellors Ltd., 1994.

Hlavacek, P. "The Foreign Direct Investments in the Usti Region: Theory, Actors and Space Differentiation." *E+M Economie a Management* 4 (2009): 27-39.

Inzelt, A. "The Inflow of Highly-skilled Workers into Hungary: A By-product of FDI." *Journal of Technology Transfer* 33, no. 4 (2008): 422-38.

Javorcik, B. S. "Can Survey Evidence Shed Light on Spillovers from Foreign Direct Investment?" *The World Bank Research Observer* 23, no. 2 (2008): 139-59.

Jiatao, L. and S. Guisinger. "The Globalization of Service Multinationals in the 'Triad.'" *Journal of International Business Studies* 23, no. 4 (1992): 675-91.

Kay, N. "Foreign Direct Investment in the Czech Republic: A Challenge for Domestic Firms." *ECFIN Country Focus* 4, no. 2 (2007): 1-6.

Kersan-Skabic, I. and E. Orlic. "Determinants of FDI Inflows in CEE1 and Western Balkan Countries. (Is Accession to the EU Important for Attracting FDI?)" *Economic and Business Review for Central and South Eastern Europe* 9, no. 4 (2007): 333-52.

Levchenko, A. A. and P. Mauro. "Do Some Forms of Financial Flows Help Protect against 'sudden stops'?" *The World Bank Economic Review* 21, no. 3 (2007): 389-411.

Lucas, R. E. "On the Mechanics of Economic Development." *Journal of Monetary Economics* 22 (1988): 3-42. Also in *Development Economics*, edited by D. Ray. Princeton, NJ: Princeton University Press, 1998.

Mengisty, B. and S. Adams. "Foreign Direct Investment, Governance and Economic Development in Developing Countries." *The Journal of Social, Political and Economic Studies* 32, no. 2 (2007): 223-49.

Pesakovic, G. and O. C. Saunders. "Negotiated Foreign Direct Investment: Case Study of The Bahamas." Paper presented at the 6th International Critical Management Studies Conference, Warwick Business School, University of Warwick, July 13-15, 2009.

Podpiera, J. and L. Weill. "Bad Luck or Bad Management? Emerging Banking Market Experience." *Working Paper Series 5*, Czech National Bank, 2007.

Pruski, J. and D. Zochowski. "Changes in the Financing Structure of the Real Economy in Poland: Challenges for the Banking Sector." *Bank for International Settlements Papers No. 28: 313-325*, BIS, 2005.

Pruteanu-Podpieara, A. and J. Podpiera. "The Czech Transition Banking Sector Instability: The Role of Operational Cost Management." *Econ Change Restructuring* 41 (2008): 209-19.

Streeten, P. P. "Human Development: Means and Ends." *American Economic Review* 84 (1994): 232-37.

The Central Bank of The Bahamas. *Quarterly Statistical Digest*. Nassau, various years.

United Nations. www.hdr.undp.org/en/humandev/

Vlcek, C. "Competitive or Coercive? The Experience of Caribbean Offshore Financial Centers with Global Governance." *The Round Table* 97, no. 396 (June 2008): 439-52.

Index

About the Contributors

Alleyne, Dillon: Dr. Alleyne obtained his Ph.D. in Economics from the University of the West Indies, Mona, Jamaica. He is currently an Economic Affairs Officer, and coordinator of the Economic Development Unit at the UN-ECLAC, Sub-Regional Headquarters for the Caribbean, Port-of-Spain, Trinidad and Tobago. Dr. Alleyne was a Senior Lecturer in the Department of Economics at the University of the West Indies, Jamaica. His work covers a range of issues including labor market behavior, tourism analysis, public finance, and econometric analysis in the Caribbean.

Astroulakis, Nikos: Mr. Astroulakis is a Ph.D. candidate in the Department of Economics at the University of Crete, Greece, with a specialization in Political Economy and Development Ethics. His publications include a book chapter and two papers in the *Journal of Economic Issues*. He has studied Economics, Sociology, and Business at the University of Crete, University of East Anglia, University of Kent, and Technological Institute of Patras.

Bailey, Jessica M.: Dr. Bailey received her doctorate in Marketing from the University of Missouri-Columbia in 1983. She is presently the Dean of the School of Business and Economics at Winston-Salem State University in North Carolina. Dr. Bailey serves in leadership roles with various organizations devoted to economic development and change in the Piedmont region of the state of North Carolina. During the last twenty-five years, she has held senior/ executive positions with various universities in the United States. Dr. Bailey is the author of many scholarly works in the fields of marketing and international business. Her research interests include international business and educational administration.

Bitzenis, Aristidis: Dr. Bitzenis is an Assistant Professor at the University of Macedonia in Thessaloniki, Greece, at the Department of International and European Studies. His main research interests include foreign direct investment, privatization, globalization, European business environment, and corporate restructuring in South East Europe. He has published extensively and participated

301

in various conferences in his research field. His publications or those in process of publication include five books, seven book chapters, fourteen entries in encyclopedias, and thirty-seven refereed journal articles.

Cavico, Frank J.: Dr. Cavico is a Professor of Business Law and Ethics at the H. Wayne Huizenga School of Business and Entrepreneurship of Nova Southeastern University in Ft Lauderdale, Florida. He has been involved in an array of teaching responsibilities, at the undergraduate, master's and doctoral levels, encompassing such subject matter areas as business law, government regulation of business, constitutional law, administrative law and ethics, labor law and labor relations, health care law, and business ethics. His most recent law review publications examined trade secret law, the law of intentional interference with contract, a comparative legal and ethical analysis of "whistleblowing" in the private sector, the tort of intentional infliction of emotional distress in the private employment sector, and the covenant of good faith and fair dealing in the franchise business relationship.

Chin-Loy, Claudette: Dr. Chin-Loy completed her doctoral degree in Business Administration at Nova Southeastern University, Huizenga School of Business, with a specialization in human resources management. She has been teaching business and management courses for the past ten years with a number of universities and currently works at the H. Wayne Huizenga School of Business. She has collaborated on research and has been consulting widely in the United States and the Caribbean in Human Resources Management and Diversity Management. Her research interests include organizational culture/climate and organizational learning.

Clayton, Anthony: Dr. Clayton is the Alcan Professor of Caribbean Sustainable Development at the University of the West Indies; Visiting Professor at the Center for Environmental Strategy in the School of Engineering at the University of Surrey; Visiting Professor at the Institute for Studies of Science, Technology and Innovation in the School of Social and Political Studies at the University of Edinburgh; Adjunct Distinguished Professor of Sustainable Development in the Faculty of Business and Management, University of Technology, Mona, Jamaica; and Fellow of the Caribbean Academy of Science. Dr. Clayton has published a very wide range of books, journal articles, and papers on all aspects of policy analysis, strategic planning, and development issues. He has undertaken policy studies for many governments and intergovernmental agencies, including UNEP, UNIDO, the Commonwealth Secretariat, and the Organization of American States.

Dengler, Robert A.: Dr. Dengler completed his Ph.D. in Organization Development at Benedictine University, following both a MS-MIS and an MBA degree. He teaches graduate courses in organization effectiveness and the MBA capstone Strategic Management course at Roosevelt University in Chicago. Dr. Dengler has held consultant and executive positions in industries as varied as international association management, energy, and healthcare. His interest in academic personal productivity led to founding ActiveScholar.com to develop software to assist academics in the area of research writing and career management.

Freckleton, Marie: Dr. Freckleton holds a Ph.D. from the University of Bradford, United Kingdom. She is currently Senior lecturer in the Department of Economics, University of the West Indies, Mona campus, Jamaica. She has published in the areas of economic development and international trade policy. Her main research interests are economic integration, international competitiveness, and economic development of small island states.

Gibbs, David: Mr. Gibbs obtained his B.Sc. in Political Science and Sociology in 1999, and Post Graduate Diploma in International Relations in 2009, both from the University of the West Indies. He is a Foreign Service Officer, in the Ministry of Foreign Affairs, Barbados.

Herring, Robert A. III: Dr. Herring obtained his Ph.D. in Management from Florida State University. He is currently Professor of Management, School of Business and Economics, Winston-Salem State University, North Carolina. His current research interests, on which he has written papers and publications, include behavioral antecedents of faculty productivity, quality management, employee assistance programs (EAPs), and management education. Dr. Herring has extensive leadership and administrative experience as an officer in the U.S. Navy/Naval Reserve and in academic administration.

Higgins, M. Eileen : Dr. Higgins has been teaching at Frostburg State University, Frostburg, Maryland, for the past twenty-one years. She teaches MBA classes in Organizational Behavior, Strategic Human Resource Management, The Leadership Process, Business Ethics and Social Responsibility, and Strategic Change Management, and undergraduate classes in International Management, Leadership and Human Behavior, Business, Government and Society, Human Resources Management, Management of Organizations, and Professional Development. Her research interests and publications are in the area of spirituality at work and moral leadership. Dr. Higgins has presented papers at numerous conferences and has had papers published in various scholarly journals. Recently, she was an invited member of the Oxford Round Table on "Ethics: A Convolution of Contemporary Values" and presented a paper at this conference.

Karagiannis, Nikolaos: Dr. Karagiannis obtained his Ph.D. from the University of Leeds, England, in 1996. He is currently teaching Economics at Winston-Salem State University, North Carolina. Dr. Karagiannis is the deputy Director of the Center for Economic Analysis at Winston-Salem State University, and the Managing Editor of the journal *American Review of Political Economy* (ARPE).

He has authored, co-authored, and co-edited twelve books, and has published widely in scholarly journals and edited books in the areas of economic development, public sector economics, and macroeconomic policy analysis. He has engaged in extensive research in the Caribbean region, specifically in Jamaica and The Bahamas. He is particularly interested in Developmental State theory and policy.

Katsivela, Marel: Dr. Katsivela is an Assistant Professor with the University of Ottawa Faculty of Law, Common Law section. She has studied Law in France, the United States, and Canada, and obtained her Ph.D. from the University of Montreal in 2004. She is admitted to the bars of New York and Greece. Her areas of research are maritime law and comparative law. Dr. Katsivela has also published widely in these areas in edited volumes and scholarly journals. She was an Assistant Professor of Law at the College of The Bahamas where she taught at the LL.B program for four years in the areas of Contracts, International Trade Law, and Private International Law.

Madjd-Sadjadi, Zagros: Dr. Madjd-Sadjadi obtained his Ph.D. in Political Economy and Public Policy from the University of Southern California in 1996. He is Associate Professor of Economics and Chair, Department of Economics and Finance, Winston-Salem State University, North Carolina, and the editor-in-chief of the *American Review of Political Economy*. Dr. Madjd-Sadjadi is the former Director of the Center for Economic Analysis at Winston-Salem State University, and the former Chief Economist of the City and County of San Francisco. He has published widely in leading economics and political science journals. His research interests include the history of economic thought, institutional economics, the economics of crime, regional economics, and the economics of undocumented immigration.

Marangos, John: Dr. Marangos is Associate Professor of Political Economy at the Department of Economics, University of Crete, Greece. Focal points for his research include transition economics, international development, and innovative methodologies for teaching economics. His publications or those in process of publication include five books, eight book chapters, thirteen entries in encyclopedias, and sixty refereed journal articles. Dr. Marangos is the editor of the *Forum of Social Economics* and section editor for the *Global Business and Economic Review*.

McFarlane, Donovan A.: Dr. McFarlane is the founder of the Donovan Society LLC. Dr. McFarlane earned an MBA as well as BS in Business Administration from the H. Wayne Huizenga School of Business and Entrepreneurship, Nova Southeastern University, and MIB degree and Graduate Certificate in International Business from St Thomas University. He also earned an MBA in Human Resources Management from Frederick Taylor University, MBA from Barrington University, DBA from California Pacific University, BS, MS, Ph.D. from American Institute of Holistic Theology, Msc.D., M.Msc., B.Msc. from University of Metaphysics, MPsy.D. from the University of Sedona, and MRS from Nations University. Published in both academic peer-reviewed and professional journals, Dr. McFarlane is a member of the International Honor Society for Business Management and Administration, the National Catholic College Honor Society, and National Honor Scholars Society.

Meramveliotakis, Giorgos: Mr. Meramveliotakis is currently completing his Ph.D. thesis at the Department of Economics of the University of Crete with a specialization in political economy. He is teaching economics at the Technological Educational Institute of Crete in the Department of Marketing. He has published on aspects of political economy in journals such as *Journal of Economic Issues* and has presented widely on various subjects of political economy and history of economic thought in numerous conferences.

Mohammed, Debbie: Dr. Mohammed obtained her Ph.D. from the University of the West Indies, St Augustine, in 2005 with a specialization in International Trade. She has taught international trade and development at the Institute of International Relations, UWI, St Augustine for the last six years. She has written extensively on issues of Caribbean trade policy and competitiveness, regional economic integration, and foreign policy and development. She has served on various regional and national committees related to the CSME, CARICOM trade relations and Trinidad and Tobago's Free Trade Agreement negotiations. She has also collaborated on research and consulting projects in the area of firm and national capacity building, and with a number of regional and international organizations. Her research interests include strategies for building and enhancing firm competitiveness in small economies, and policy approaches to development involving innovation.

Mujtaba, Bahaudin G.: Dr. Mujtaba is an Associate Professor of Management and Human Resources at the H. Wayne Huizenga School of Business and Entrepreneurship of Nova Southeastern University, Ft Lauderdale, Florida. He is the author and co-author of seventeen professional and academic books dealing with diversity, ethics, and business. During the past twenty-five years, he has had the pleasure of working with human resource professionals in the United States, Brazil, Bahamas, Afghanistan, Pakistan, St Lucia, Grenada, Thailand, Malaysia, China, and Jamaica. This diverse exposure has provided him many insights in ethics, culture, and management from the perspectives of different firms, people groups, and countries.

Pagiavlas, Notis: Dr. Pagiavlas is an Associate Professor of Marketing and founding Director of the Center for Entrepreneurship at Winston-Salem State University. Dr. Pagiavlas has earned a Ph.D. in Marketing from the University of Texas, Arlington, and a Bachelor's in Economics from the University of California, San Diego. Besides his exuberance for teaching and research, he has developed numerous experiential learning opportunities for his students that combine business case challenges with academic research. His work has appeared in numerous peer reviewed journals, global conferences, and practitioner forums. Dr. Pagiavlas also contributes as marketing expert in court cases and serves on numerous boards, including community development corporations, arts, and entrepreneurship.

Pesakovic, Gordana: Dr. Pesakovic is a Professor of International Business and Economics. She holds a Ph.D. in Economics from the University of Belgrade. She has extensive teaching experience in the United States, South America, Asia, and Europe. Dr. Pesakovic has published a number of articles and chapters in books. Her research areas of interest include emerging economies, sustainable development, and cross-cultural studies.

Richardson, Craig: Dr. Richardson is Associate Professor of Economics at Winston-Salem State University, in Winston-Salem, North Carolina. His research interests include property rights and their importance for economic growth, as well as health policy. He is the author of *The Collapse of Zimbabwe in the Wake of the 2000-2003 Land Reforms* (2003), and regularly consults The Institute for Liberty and Democracy, based in Lima, Peru. Dr. Richardson has also served as a Visiting Research Fellow at the American Institute for Economic Research for the past six years.

Sadri, Morteza: Dr. Sadri received his doctorate in Urban Planning from the University of Washington in 1985. He is the president and founder of Liaison International, Inc., an international trade and business consulting firm specializing in market research and international market development, with representation in the United States and abroad. Dr. Sadri has taught a wide variety of courses in Marketing, Management, and International Business in the United States and overseas.

Saunders, Olivia C.: Dr. Saunders is an Associate Professor at the College of The Bahamas where she has worked for more than twenty years teaching primarily in the area of Economics. She holds a Doctor of Business Administration degree with an International Business concentration from the University of Sarasota. Her academic interest is focused on so-called developing states and their advancement. Attendant to this is an interest in the world economic system that perpetuates marginalization.

Sen, Swapan: Dr. Sen is Professor of Finance and MBA Coordinator at the School of Business and Economics, Winston-Salem State University. Professor Sen has published widely in academic journals including *Economic Systems, The American Economist, International Journal of Finance, Journal of Emerging Markets, Journal of Economics & Finance, Finance India*, and *Applied Finance Journal*.

Stewart, David: Dr. Stewart obtained his Ph.D. in Business Administration with a concentration in Finance from the University of Tennessee in 1997. He is Associate Professor of Finance and the former Chair, Department of Economics and Finance, Winston-Salem State University, North Carolina. His research interests include financial planning, market efficiency, and international finance. Dr. Stewart has also led Winston-Salem State University to becoming the first HBCU to feature a finance degree program registered with the Certified Financial Planner Board of Standards.

Stitts, Doria (Kathy): Dr. Kathy Stitts is Associate Provost for Lifelong Learning at Winston-Salem State University (WSSU) focusing on adult learning, distance education, continuing education, and summer school. Prior to her current appointment, Dr. Stitts served as Associate Dean and Associate Professor of Marketing of the School of Business and Economics at WSSU. Prior to her tenure at WSSU, Dr. Stitts served as Associate Professor and Chairperson of the Department of Management and Marketing at Virginia State University. She serves in leadership roles with various organizations and has received a number of awards. Dr. Stitts' research interests include relationship marketing, professionalism, etiquette, assessment, and ethics. She has given presentations and motivational speeches to various audiences.

Testas, Abdelaziz: Dr. Testas obtained his Ph.D. from the University of Leeds, England, in 1997. He is currently working for Nielsen (Sunnyvale, Northern California, United States) as a Researcher in the Measurement Science Department. He has published widely in scholarly journals in the areas of North African economic development, trade and integration.

Tsitouras, Antonis: Mr. Tsitouras obtained his Master's degree in the area of Management and Finance from the University of Glamorgan, Wales, in 2004. He is currently working as a project manager in a Greek construction company which is situated at the Northwest of Greece (TE.NA S.A.). He has participated in, and undertaken many construction projects in the area of Greece and the Balkans. He has co-authored two papers in refereed journals in the areas of economic development and public sector economics. He is particularly interested in Developmental State theory and policy.

Vlachos, Vasileios A.: Mr. Vlachos is a Ph.D. candidate at the Department of International and European Studies of the University of Macedonia in Thessaloniki, Greece. His current research interests are focused on the association between foreign direct investment, international transactions and economic development.